Robert Mapplethorpe: Portraits

This catalogue has been published in conjunction with the exhibition Robert Mapplethorpe: Portraits, organized by the Palm Springs Art Museum.

This exhibition is organized by the Palm Springs Art Museum and sponsored in part by the Helene & Lou Galen Exhibition Fund and the Faye & Herman Sarkowsky Exhibition Fund.

Palm Springs Art Museum
Palm Springs, California
January 17–April 19, 2009

The Center for Creative Photography
Tucson, Arizona
June 27–September 27, 2009

San Jose Museum of Art
San Jose, California
Fall 2010

Front cover. Robert Mapplethorpe, Kathy Acker, 1983. Plate 54

Library of Congress Control Number: 2008930223
ISBN 978-0-9816743-1-5

Director
Steven Nash

Deputy Director for Art/ Senior Curator
Daniell Cornell

Guest Curator
Gordon Baldwin

Editor
Frances Bowles

Proofreader
Kathy Kaiser

Design by
Yoonjai Choi
Georgianna Stout
2x4, New York

Printed by
Die Keure, Belgium

Robert Mapplethorpe: Portraits

Gordon Baldwin
with an essay by Daniell Cornell

Palm Springs Art Museum

Contents

Director's Foreword

Steven Nash,
Executive Director

We now have enough perspective on the life and art of Robert Mapplethorpe to analyze dispassionately the meaning of his legacy, without the undue emphasis on the more notorious aspects of his work that has, in the past, dominated critical discourse. As this legacy comes into sharper focus, the significance of Mapplethorpe's work in portraiture takes on a wider dimension. By far the largest portion of his considerable photographic output, portraiture is, arguably, the genre in which he made his most important contributions to the history of photography. His list of sitters includes the names of many of the leaders in the artistic and literary milieu of his era, people often captured in images now ingrained in our collective cultural memory.

It is, however, a body of work that remains inadequately studied. Mapplethorpe's studio practices have been insufficiently researched. Many of his portraits, including some of his best work, are unpublished. There remains a lot to be learned about his relationships with individual sitters and about their interactions during the portrait sessions. And, most significantly, we have not seen an adequate assessment of Mapplethorpe's gifts as a portraitist and how he changed the evolution of the genre. Our exhibition and its accompanying catalogue are intended to help correct this situation.

The exhibition includes 104 photographs, most selected from the archives of the Robert Mapplethorpe Foundation in New York. These works concentrate on figures prominent in the world of art and culture in and around New York in the late 1970s and during the 1980s. On Mapplethorpe's roster of clients can be found a pantheon of many of the most significant artists, art dealers, writers, musicians, designers, dancers, and actors of the period, as well as a host of ancillary figures. The show therefore offers an overview of Mapplethorpe's career in portraiture and, by implication, the environment in which it flourished. Many of the sitters were Mapplethorpe's friends or people he knew and respected within this cultural milieu. These relationships helped to inspire a special rapport between photographer and sitter that becomes obvious in the open and trusting spirit of engagement evident in the photographs. Many images in the exhibition have already attained an iconic status, but there is also a significant number of fascinating, lesser-known works, some of them previously unpublished, that help expand the Mapplethorpe canon.

The lion's share of the work behind the exhibition and catalogue has been provided by our guest curator, Gordon Baldwin, formerly a member of the Department of Photographs at the J. Paul Getty Museum in Los Angeles and now a freelance curator and photography historian. Gordon selected the images and wrote one of our introductory essays and the lengthy and illuminating commentaries found in each of the catalogue entries. These contributions benefit especially from his interviews of numerous sitters for the portraits and of assistants who worked with Mapplethorpe in his studio and from his research in the archives of the Robert Mapplethorpe Foundation and the archive at the Getty Research Institute, which holds a part of the papers of Sam Wagstaff, Mapplethorpe's patron and partner. Another introductory essay is written by Dr. Daniell Cornell, Deputy Director for Art and Senior Curator at the Palm Springs Art Museum. In the past, Daniell has written on Mapplethorpe in the context of gender issues in twentieth-century photography, and here he provides a critical framework for the exhibition, addressing formal and expressive agendas in Mapplethorpe's portraits and discussing their influence on our conception of this genre.

We hope that the exhibition and catalogue will be regarded as an important contribution to Mapplethorpe studies. We hope even more that the exhibition provides a powerful aesthetic and emotional experience for those who see it. These works are remarkable, both for their formal intensity and for Mapplethorpe's uncanny ability to expose fundamentals of identity and character. As visual constructions, they are endlessly inventive and, as narratives about human nature and what it takes to encapsulate it in good portraits, they are rich with insight. He was a photographer who truly expanded the meaning and scope of modern portraiture.

Acknowledgments

Among the principal pleasures of working on the subject of Mapplethorpe's portraiture have been the lively conversations that were engendered as a variety of people enthusiastically responded to inquiries about the artist, his life, and his work. Many people have been generous in sharing reminiscences, suggesting places where research might profitably be pursued, and providing real information about the photographer at various stages of his career. For their stimulating engagement with the topic, I am grateful to Bill Berkson, Irene Borger, Sonia Braga, Frish Brandt, Paul Bridgewater, Marisa Cardinale, Dagny Corcoran, Charlie Cowles, James Crump, James Danziger, Laura Donnelley, Fay Gold, Mark Haworth-Booth, Bill Hunt, Deborah Irmas, Harold Jones, Judith Keller, Klaus Kertess, Hans Kraus, Marcus Leatherdale, Carol Leflufy, Kim Light, Gerard Malanga, Michael Maloney, Richard Marshall, Sylvia Martins, Mary and Weston Naef, Roberta Neiman, Simon Norfolk, William O'Connor, Irene Oppenheim, Eiko Otake, Sandra Phillips, Michael Rand, Danniel Rangel, Amy Rule, Janet Sirmon, Roger Taylor, Anne Tucker, Anne Waldman, Sylvia Wolf, and Philip Yenawine. Lynn Davis, Dimitri Levas, Brian English, Jack Fritscher, and Edmund White have been particularly informative about a man each of them knew well, and Brian's technical expertise has been invaluable.

This exhibition and catalogue would have been wholly impossible without the Mapplethorpe Foundation. Its president Michael Ward Stout, Joree Adilman, whose patience, I fear, has been sorely tried, and Tess Carota, Jennifer Fiore, Eric Johnson, and Adam K. Rosenthal have been essential.

At the Palm Springs Art Museum, the director Steven Nash, in myriad ways has been steadfastly, energetically, and amiably supportive of this exhibition. Janice Lyle and Katherine Plake Hough were important in initially developing the show. Daniell Cornell has written a provocative essay placing Mapplethorpe in a cultural context and has been essential in assembling the pictures. Kathy Carr has gracefully facilitated too many aspects of the exhibition to enumerate. Greg Murphy has provided additional support and Marilyn Pearl Loesberg supplied enthusiasm.

People at other commercial and cultural organizations who have been genially cooperative include María del Carmen Carrión, Jay Gam, Vicki Gambill, Denis Gardarin, Julia Gruen, Peter Hale, Joanne Heyler, Chuck Mobley, Tracey Norman, Erin O'Toole, and Marisa Weintraub. Britt Salvesen at the Center for Creative Photography, the University of Arizona, Tucson, had the happy idea for a symposium on photographic portraiture.

Perspicaciously, and with palpable appreciation for nuance, Frances Bowles has edited this catalogue. Yoonjai Choi at 2x4 Inc., New York, is responsible for its contemporary elegance, and Georgianna Stout has expertly piloted it through production.

I would particularly like to thank David Knaus for his wise counsel, patience, balance, and good humor.

Gordon Baldwin

On behalf of the Palm Springs Art Museum, I would like to add to Gordon Baldwin's gracious acknowledgments my own expression of gratitude to the following individuals. Most importantly, I cannot thank Gordon enough for the marvelous job he has done as Guest Curator for this exhibition. The project turned out to be more expansive and laborious than any of us originally imagined it could be, and Gordon has tackled all aspects of the preparation and development, from selecting the images and thoroughly researching each work to preparing catalogue texts and working assiduously on book design and exhibition installation, with unfailing dedication, professionalism, and good spirit. It has been a pleasure to work with him.

Daniell Cornell, our Deputy Director for Art and Senior Curator, has also contributed importantly to the project, both as the author of an insightful catalogue essay and the facilitator for many administrative, publication, and installation logistics. He joined our staff well after the exhibition planning had been launched but immediately assumed a central role. He and I also want to reiterate Gordon's appreciative acknowledgment of the Robert Mapplethorpe Foundation and its very capable staff, for all they have done to make this exhibition possible.

Internally, a great many individuals on the staff of the Palm Springs Art Museum have contributed to the organization and presentation of the exhibition. Kathy Clewell, Director of Registration and Collections Management, and Sandy Davis, Registrar, handled all logistics of shipping, insurance, and framing. Working closely with Gordon Baldwin and Daniell Cornell, our Exhibition Services Manager, Tom Johnson, managed the design and production of exhibition graphics and the installation plan. He was ably assisted by our installation team under the supervision of Steve Hubbard, Deputy Director of Operations. Robert Brasier, Deputy

Director of Education and Public Programs, worked with his education staff to produce an exciting series of educational components. Public relations for the exhibition were handled by Bob Bogard, Director of Marketing Communications. And help with a diverse array of administrative matters was provided by Kathy Carr, Executive Administrator.

For the organization of the tour of the exhibition and various educational programs, most notably our jointly organized symposium, we have benefited from the advice and extremely helpful assistance of Britt Salvesen, Director of the Center for Creative Photography at the University of Arizona in Tucson. Of course, the various lenders to the exhibition made it all possible by generously sharing their cherished artworks for a lengthy period of time. The all-important aspect of funding for the exhibition came from our museum's Sarkowsky Art Exhibition Fund.

Steven Nash, Executive Director

In the Studio

Gordon Baldwin

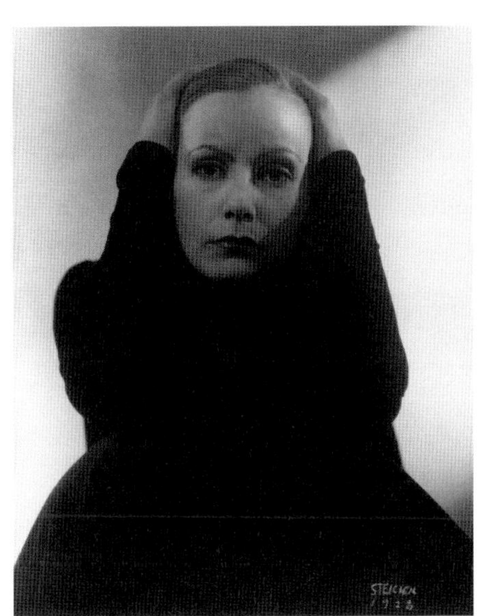

(fig.1)
Edward Steichen, Greta Garbo, 1928; gelatin silver print. J. Paul Getty Museum

Portraits were paramount as subject matter from the very beginning of the history of photography, just as they were from the onset of Robert Mapplethorpe's photographic career. His earliest were Polaroids, made with a borrowed camera in 1970, a year after he stopped attending Pratt Institute, where he had studied art but not photography. He was living with the poet and singer Patti Smith, first in the Chelsea Hotel and then in a nearby loft. Naturally, as she was then his muse as well as girlfriend, she was his first subject, but concomitantly he made self-portraits, which were often autoerotic. Soon there were other sitters and other kinds of subjects, such as his friend, David Croland, other men with whom he had started going to bed, and the occasional still life. He acquired his own Polaroid camera in 1971, a gift from John McKendry, a curator at the Metropolitan Museum of Art, who also introduced him to portraits in the museum's collection by Julia Margaret Cameron, Alfred Stieglitz, Paul Strand, and Edward Steichen (fig.1). Prints from the Polaroid were gratifyingly instantaneous, could be made without assistance, and could be held in the hand. Save for their usually simple compositions, these earliest works show few clues about what his later work would look like. In mid-November 1972, at the Gotham Book Mart in New York, he had his first exhibition.«1»

By 1973 he had graduated to a large-format Polaroid camera and had met Sam Wagstaff, who became his lover and great patron, first buying Mapplethorpe a loft on Bond Street in which to live and work and then, in 1976, a Hasselblad camera.«2» Most of his portraits from that year and the following were made on his own initiative rather than on commission. He used the light from the studio's south-facing windows for some, but more were set elsewhere: in his sitters' houses in New York or in London or on the beach on the island of Mustique. Some of the abiding hallmarks of his mature style began to emerge, such as his placing his sitters off center rather than in the middle of the picture.

Portraiture on a larger scale had become feasible, and he began to receive private commissions as well as work for publication, although in 1978, many of his sitters were still simply people he selected to portray. Those that came from the S&M milieu he frequented were often photographed late at night or very early in the morning and with crude lighting, as were the black males, to whom he was increasingly attracted. These latter pictures should be classed as nude studies rather than portraits, as he seems to have been so much more interested in the bodies than in the faces. Together with Sam Wagstaff, who by now had become a benevolent friend rather than a lover, he looked at photography from earlier periods, and each of them began to form a collection of photographs, although the boundaries between their hoards remained porous. To Mapplethorpe's credit and even more to Wagstaff's, they acquired work well beyond the orthodox limitations of other collectors. Their taste, together and separately, was that of photographic omnivores. Work that they particularly admired included that of two great nineteenth-century portraitists, the Parisian paragon of energy Gaspard-Félix Tournachon (1820–1910), known as Nadar, who assembled a veritable photographic pantheon of the artistic world, and the illustrious, indomitable Englishwoman Julia Margaret Cameron (1815–1879), who made a similar collection of British artists and writers. Nadar, who was first a caricaturist and then later a photographer, specifically called his first assembly of the artistic gods of Paris a pantheon: Le Panthéon Nadar was a lithograph of a serpentine parade of caricatures of countless worthies. He later used the term panthéon to advertise his photographic constellations of individual portraits of the same sitters and many more.«3» Both Nadar and Cameron had dynamic, compelling personalities that made it possible

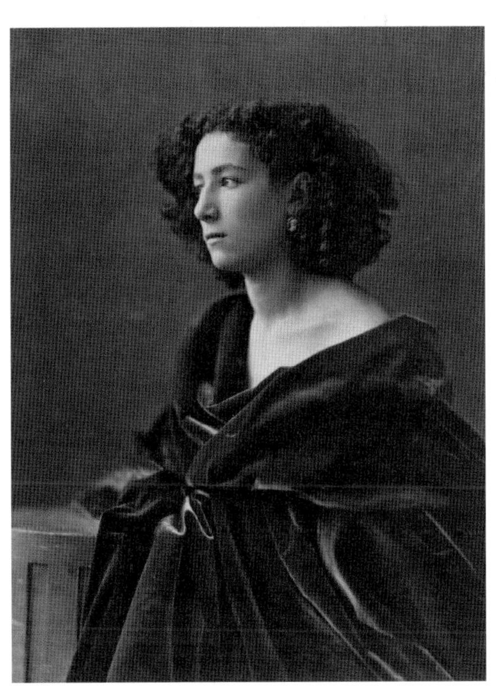

(fig.2)
Nadar, Sarah Bernhardt, negative c. 1864/print by Paul Nadar c. 1924; gelatin silver print.
J. Paul Getty Museum

for them to establish warm relationships with, and to thoroughly engage, their sitters. In its use of wholly neutral backgrounds, Mapplethorpe's work came to resemble Nadar's(fig.2); it resembled Cameron's only on the rare occasions when he moved in so close to his subjects that their heads filled the whole of the frame(fig.3). He, however, always remained more detached from his sitters than either of these earlier portraitists did.

At about this point in the late 1970s, Mapplethorpe began to employ studio assistants, the first notable one being Marcus Leatherdale (who was later to become a photographer in his own right). As Mapplethorpe believed that the selection from the contact sheet of the right image to print was of equal importance with the sitting, he always made the choice himself without input from the sitter, who had no access to the contact sheets.«4» Normally, he supplied the sitter with two variant images. He insisted that his finished prints be of superlative quality but never printed his own negatives. In 1979 he found Tom Baril, also a photographer, who was a highly skilled printer. For the next ten years, until the end of the portraitist's life, Baril printed the negatives to Mapplethorpe's (and his own) exacting standards. He also spotted the prints (retouching them to cover white spots caused by specks of dust on the negative) and, on occasion, at Mapplethorpe's request, cropped the negatives.«5» By the time Baril arrived, Mapplethorpe—because of Sam Wagstaff's sponsorship and his own assiduous efforts to promote his work—was being exhibited frequently in galleries, which necessitated the production of multiple prints. From nearly the beginning, he had made editions of his prints, even when they were private commissions, if he thought the sitter noteworthy or the result particularly good. At first, these editions were as small as three in number, but more often five, briefly grew to fifteen, and then shrunk to ten, which thereafter was the standard. He established a uniform sixteen-by-twenty-inch sheet size for the gelatin silver prints he released from the studio; the images printed on the sheets were nearly square, although usually slightly higher than wide.«6»

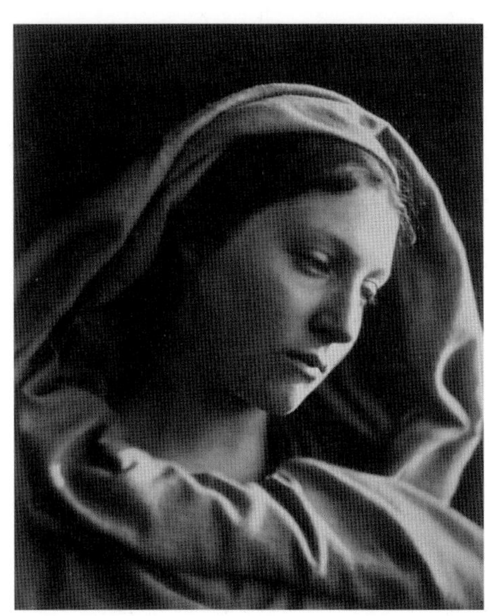

(fig.3)
Julia Margaret Cameron, Mary Mother, 1867; albumen print. George Eastman House

As private commissions for portraits multiplied along with commercial and editorial work, he needed help with scheduling, and in 1981 he hired his first studio manager, Betsy Evans, who stayed till 1983, to be succeeded by Tina Summerlin, from 1983 to 1986,«7» Dina Rukeyser, for about a year, and, finally, Suzanne Donaldson. To separate his living quarters from his workspace, at least nominally, he rented an apartment on Bleecker Street in 1981. A little before then, his much younger brother Edward became his studio assistant.«8» Mapplethorpe had by then installed three rolls of pull-down, twelve-feet-wide seamless paper, one white, one gray, one black, to be used as backgrounds in the studio, and having had formal training as a photographer, Edward brought with him knowledge about lighting, cropping, and spotting. The simplicity of the Polaroid era was past.

In order, Mapplethorpe once said, to finance the acquisition of more sophisticated studio lighting equipment, he sold his first collection of historic photographs in May of 1982 at Sotheby's in New York.«9» (However, as someone who seems to have been nearly inherently acquisitive about physical possessions, perhaps in reaction to his slightly impoverished childhood surroundings in Queens, he did not stop collecting, either photographs or other kinds of art or art glass or Stickley furniture.) The equipment he bought included soft boxes, which are fabric-covered enclosures used to soften the light of the strobes that flashed at the moment of exposure; later there were hair lights and other subsidiary lighting devices.

To facilitate the operation of his increasingly complicated career and life, he hired the designer and props stylist Dimitri Levas, who became his factotum, handling all kinds of matters but particularly indispensable in the production of the flower studies, for which Levas would choose, purchase, and arrange the blooms. To provide a minimalist geometry for the background of some of the portraits and figure studies that Mapplethorpe was making in 1984, Levas cut out a black paper circle that was then attached to either the white or gray pull-down seamless paper. There was also a white circle for use with a black background. For a fashion shoot, Levas built a free-standing cube, about ten feet square, with a circular cut out, roughly five feet in diameter, through which subjects could be framed or, in one instance, step.«10» This set was later used for portraits and figure studies. By this time, Mapplethorpe's portraits were nearly invariably made in the studio, where his control of light was close to absolute. He still used natural light but usually only as an adjunct to artificial illumination.

It was probably from the occasional fashion shoots he did that Mapplethorpe became accustomed to the idea of hiring make-up artists and hairstylists for his portraits of women. He may have known that Andy Warhol used such personnel for the Polaroids that were a preparatory step in the production of his silk-screen portraits of women. The stylists that Mapplethorpe employed were left to their own devices, only occasionally receiving specific instructions about how the subjects should look. Not surprisingly, a flattering, well-groomed look prevailed. When the cosmetician or hairdresser—sometimes the same person—had finished, the photographer would appraise the results, only rarely suggesting any but the most minor changes.«11» The use of an overall facial makeup for women had a tendency to make them resemble one another and to slightly flatten their faces, but had a welcome side effect in helping to establish the

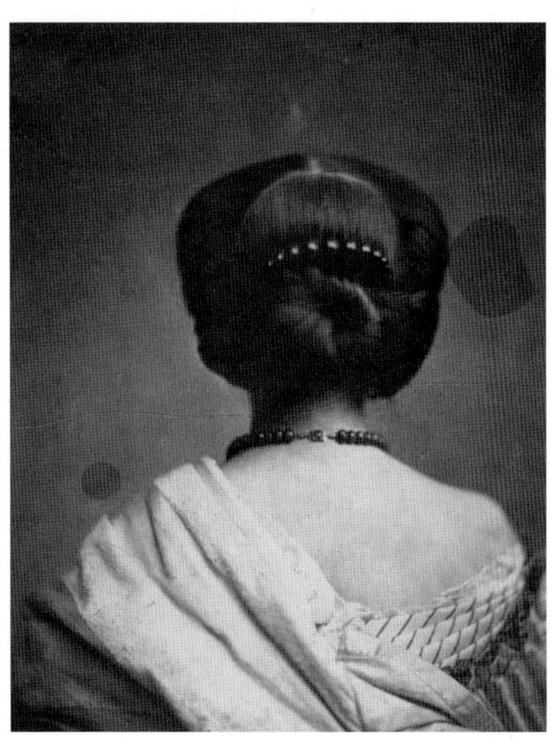

(fig.4)
Onésipe Aguado, Woman Seen from the Back, c. 1862; salted paper print. Metropolitan Museum of Art

highly polished, finished style for which Mapplethorpe's portraits were known and valued. His studio manager scheduled these portrait sittings, frequently in response to requests from the galleries that handled his work. After about 1983, more commercial assignments—and there were many—were often the results of efforts by Anne Kennedy and Carol Leflufy at Art + Commerce, an agency that specialized in obtaining editorial and advertising work for photographers.«12»

Within the crisp stylistic boundaries of his mature work, he occasionally challenged the conventional boundaries of portraiture, for which there are nineteenth-century precendents(fig.4). He would, for instance, show the backs of his sitters' heads rather than their faces. The earliest example of this is the portrait he made of Phyllis Tweel in 1979 (plate 18), but there are others: a self-portrait in 1981, four images of his friend Jack Walls made in 1982 and 1983, two of a model named Stedman in 1982 and 1983, and one of Fredericka Hunter in 1987. Mapplethorpe also made editions of portraits of sitters wearing dark glasses, among them, one of Jack Walls (plate 48) and another of himself with Lisa Lyon, the two of them sporting sunglasses. He also chose to show at least three sitters with their eyes shut: Alice Neel, Doris Saatchi (plates 73 and 57), and Princess Gloria von Thurn und Taxis. An analogous case is the portrait of Kathy Acker covering her face with her hands (plate 54). All these are examples of Mapplethorpe's strong interest in what his former studio assistant Marcus Leatherdale, referring to a series of portraits he himself had made between 1982 and 1990 and that ran as a feature called "Hidden Identities" in Details magazine, called "covert portraiture." The question, of course, is, if the eyes are mirrors of the soul, is a portrait that does not show

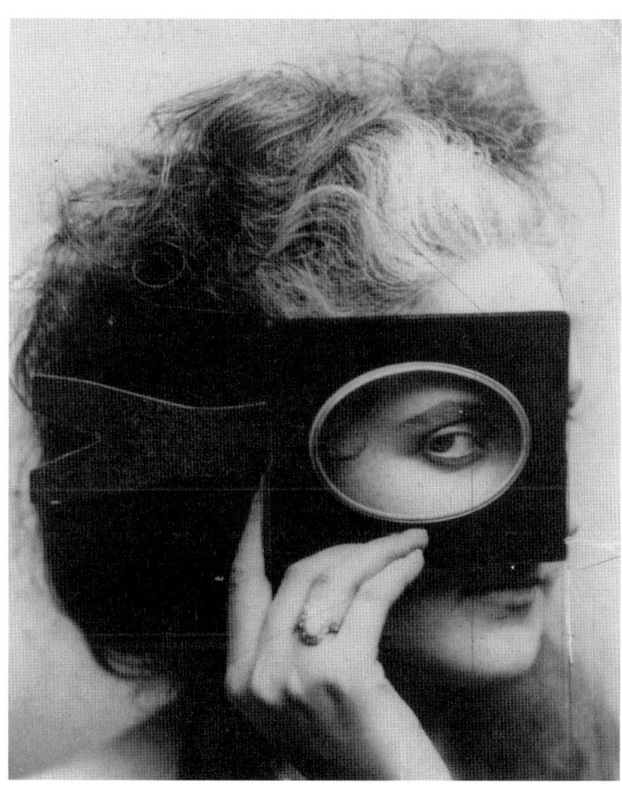

(fig.5)
Pierre-Louis Pierson, Scherzo di Follia: Game of Madness (Countess di Castiglione Holding Vignette Frame up to Her Eye), negative 1861-1867/print c. 1930: gelatin silver print. Metropolitan Museum of Art

them still a portrait? Mapplethorpe would certainly have said it is. An analogous question would be: is it still a portrait if one eye is highlighted but the rest of the face obscured, as in figure 5?

As the 1980s progressed, his roster of sitters became increasingly respectable although he never abandoned making tangible souvenirs of his nocturnal sessions with black men and, in fact, highly valued the photographic results. Major accretions to his legacy of important portraits occurred with the publication of Robert Mapplethorpe: Certain People, a Book of Portraits in 1985 and 50 New York Artists in 1986.«13» The distinguished cultural critic Susan Sontag wrote the introduction to the former, and Richard Marshall, a curator at the Whitney Museum of American Art, organized and wrote the latter, thus bolstering Mapplethorpe's artistic credibility. Averaging eight or nine one-man shows a year in major American and European cities, Mapplethorpe was also included in countless group exhibitions. He had reached the enviable position of beginning to rival the accomplishments of his nineteenth-century predecessors Cameron and Nadar, although his list of sitters was not as distinguished as was either of theirs. He was highly sought after as a portraitist, even if he was less famous than his older, more established contemporaries, Richard Avedon, Irving Penn, and the fashion and celebrity photographer Francesco Scavullo. Along with Scavullo, younger rivals who photographed Mapplethorpe included Neil Winokur, Gerard Malanga, Cynthia MacAdams, and his friend Lynn Davis (for whom, see plate 13). Peter Hujar did not.

The move, in 1985, to a much larger loft, on the fourth floor of a better building—on Twenty-third Street, which

Sam Wagstaff had bought for him with part of the proceeds of the sale of Wagstaff's collection of photographs to the Getty Museum, was a major change. It, too, had south-facing windows—which lighted the studio space behind it. Farther away from the street was a living area, on the east side of which was the front door that led to the elevator hall. Up two steps beyond the living room, on the west wall, was an area with an enclosed toilet, a light table, and a place for sitters to be made up. Just beyond these were a kitchen and a dining space. At the back of the loft on the east wall was a bedroom with an adjoining bath and, on the west, a sitting room lit by windows to the north.

He gave up the Bleecker Street apartment and lived and worked on Twenty-third Street for the rest of his life, although he retained the Bond Street studio, where the darkroom remained and which he used as a sort of command center and, occasionally, to house studio assistants. The amiable and intrepid Brian English, who started working for Mapplethorpe in 1986 and remained with him for the rest of his life, lived there for a while, as did, later, Mapplethorpe's brother Edward, when he returned from California in 1987. The high-ceilinged Twenty-third Street space, with its shiny, newly refinished wood floors, was generous enough so that he could gradually and artfully arrange much of his furniture and collections in it without encroaching on the studio area.«14»

By this time a highly effective system for making portraits was in place, and one observer described it as calm and free from drama.«15» There was always music playing. Although his clothing was casual, Mapplethorpe seems habitually and perhaps oddly formally, given his notoriety, to have worn a loosely knotted necktie when working. After initial, introductory conversations with his sitters, shooting began. In the photographer's search for perfect lighting, his assistant would be directed to make infinitesimal adjustments to the positions of reflectors, umbrellas, screens, and other studio equipment. Polaroid photographs were employed only for testing the light, no longer for creating works in their own right. After the initial setup was completed, Mapplethorpe had the Polaroid back, which was mounted on the Hasselblad, replaced by a holder for roll film. He often communicated with his sitter by gesture, waving his hands in the direction he wished the subject to move, or asking in his soft speaking voice for subtler postural shifts. There were, of course, frequent asides to his assistant(s) during a sitting, which sometimes lasted only as long as the fifteen minutes it took to shoot a roll of film. With other sitters, many more exposures were necessary in order to provide an adequate variety of images on the contact sheets from which he could choose to have Tom Baril make final prints.

His productivity in 1987 was as remarkable as the hyperactivity of his social life, despite the death of Sam Wagstaff in January. Noticeably more portraits and figure studies were made against dark backgrounds. The lighting was more polished than ever and frequently involved the use of filters and diffusion during the printing stage to make the results more flattering. Only the flower images were habitually made with natural light. He began to have Baril print some of his new negatives on twenty-by-twenty-four-inch sheets to increase their wall power and importance. He had one-man shows that year in Berlin, Cologne, New York, San Francisco, Geneva, Milan, and London and participated in several group exhibitions. In 1988, there were two major exhibitions of his work: a show at the National Portrait Gallery in London and a retrospective at the Whitney Museum that opened in July. Despite his now very evident ill health, he attended its opening. In some vain and valiant hope of staving off death from the complications of AIDS, with which he had been diagnosed in late 1986, he continued to make portraits throughout most of the year, including three of himself (for one, see plate 101). There were none in 1989, the year he died.

By the time of his death, Mapplethorpe had achieved a celebrity approaching that which Nadar, the nineteenth-century master portraitist whose work he most admired, had fashioned for himself. The following year, because of controversy surrounding the exhibition of his erotic images, he became, at least temporarily, notorious. All celebrity is fleeting, as is its nether corollary, infamy, but it is unfortunate that he became most known for the wrong reasons because his other achievements are considerable. His nude figure studies are important additions to the canon, his flowers perennially attractive depictions of transitory glory, but he should be remembered best for his portraiture. The depictions in this exhibition of almost one hundred sitters are much more recent than Nadar's, but they, too, are now period pieces, the names of the subjects and their maker dimming with time.«16» It has always been the distinguishing mark of a great portrait photographer that the style of the pictures is unmistakable; this is surely the case with Mapplethorpe's. The portraits are usually thought to be cool and formal, although their maker believed them simply to be formal. They are certainly no cooler than those of Steichen, another great American twentieth-century portraitist, and they are certainly kinder than those of Avedon. As for warmth, is it not somewhat naïve to believe that a photographer can establish and display manifestly cordial relations with such a great variety of types and personalities? The images are, of course, flattering to their sitters—that is why people go to have their portraits made. The highly polished quality of Mapplethorpe's finished prints has always been admired, as has been their composition, even if some viewers have found the formal properties overly stringent. They are of their time the—late 1970s, the 1980s—an era when one kind of stylish, glossy New York life, particularly gay New York life, reached its apogee. They are a high-water mark and to be noted and esteemed, as this exhibition seeks to do.

«1»
An exhibition at the Light Gallery in New York in January 1973 has usually been considered his first show, to be followed shortly thereafter by another, a three-person show, at the Gotham Book Mart, New York. However, Amy Rule has discovered that the files of the Center for Creative Photography in Tucson hold a postcard invitation to the Gotham show that is clearly postmarked November 8, 1972, and states that the show runs until December 2. In addition, in a review of the Light Gallery show, published in the New York Times on January 28, 1973, there is a reference to "his earlier show."

«2»
The Bond Street loft was on the fifth floor. A self-service factory elevator gave onto a space that held files and, later, the studio manager's desk. On the left was the studio, with a bank of windows facing the street. To the right were a sitting room and a bedroom. Farther back were a small kitchen, which was seldom used, and a very small bathroom.

«3»
For a discussion of pantheons of artists at various periods in various media, see Richard Brilliant's introduction "Images to Light the Candle of Fame" in Gordon Baldwin and Judith Keller, Nadar/Warhol: Paris/New York: Photography and Fame (Los Angeles: J. Paul Getty Museum, 1999), 15-27.

«4»
In an interview given in 1977, Mapplethorpe discussed the process of selection, which he said generally took a week; see Victor Bockris, Beat Punks (Cambridge, Mass.: Da Capo Press, 2000), 297.

«5»
Instances of his printing from a small section of a much larger negative are rare, but can be found in a portrait of Larry Desmedt made in 1979, a portrait of Truman Capote made in 1981 (plate 34), and a later flower picture.

«6»
At various times later in his career, he would make other kinds of prints, including platinum prints on paper and on linen, dye-transfer prints, Cibachromes, and gravures. A summary of these other print types, which were seldom used for portraiture, can be found in Janet Kardon, Robert Mapplethorpe: The Perfect Moment, with essays by David Joselit and Kay Larson and dedication by Patti Smith, exh. cat. (Philadelphia: Institute of Contemporary Art, University of Pennsylvania, 1989), 166.

«7»
Summerlin continued on a part-time basis until 1989 and then, as director of the newly formed Mapplethorpe Foundation, until about 1991.

«8»
Edward worked for his brother until 1984, when he moved to Los Angeles. He returned to the studio in 1987 and stayed until Mapplethorpe's death in 1989. During the first part of Edward's absence, Javier Gonzalez was the principal studio assistant.

«9»
Sotheby's, Photographs from the Collection of Robert Mapplethorpe, sale catalogue, New York, May 24, 1982. One wonders whether, within the relatively closed circles of the New York art world, the sale in and of itself augmented his reputation as well as his exchequer.

«10»
Levas also constructed a similar cubic set and, at least once, chose clothes for a sitter to wear for a portrait intended for publication.

«11»
Among the many people associated with the studio were, at various times, Fern Buckner, Bob Carlson, Paul Cavaco, Juan Cueva, Barbara Dente, Lawrence Fiorentini, Jake, Didier Malige, Bonnie Miller, Mark Namias, Ken-ichi Okochi, Thom Priano, John Sahag, Victor Stone, and Bill Westmoreland. They worked on individual sittings and on book projects, such as The Agency (New York: Hardison Fine Arts Library, 1983) and Some Women (Boston: Bulfinch Press, 1989).

«12»
The list of magazines for which Mapplethorpe made work is long. It includes Actual, Elle, Fashion Moda, Fortune, Harper's Bazaar, Harper's & Queen, House and Garden, Interview, L.A. Style, the London Sunday Times, Normal Magazine, Rolling Stone, Splash, Sport, Stern, Tatler, Tempo, Time, Traveler, Us, Vanity Fair, and the British, German, and Italian editions of Vogue.

«13»
Robert Mapplethorpe: Certain People, a Book of Portraits (Pasadena, Calif.: Twelvetrees Press, 1985), n.p.; and Richard D. Marshall, 50 New York Artists: A Critical Selection of Painters and Sculptors Working in New York, with photographs by Robert Mapplethorpe (San Francisco: Chronicle Books, 1986).

«14»
For images of Mapplethorpe's staff in 1988, see Zoom magazine (Paris), no. 37 (1988), 58.

«15»
Bill Westmoreland, e-mail to author, April 17, 2008.

«16»
Mapplethorpe editioned two thousand prints, but many of the same sitters, particularly Lisa Lyon. There are many, of the other sitters, that he chose not to edition.

The Public Moment: Robert Mapplethorpe's New York Portraits

Daniell Cornell

The great social result of photography, beginning in 1839, was the availability of personal depictions for people of nearly every walk of life, initially through the daguerreotype and then through the mass dissemination of images printed from negatives. However, neither the photographic portrait nor its loftier painted cousin is meant merely to be an unmediated likeness of its sitter. It is usually assumed that the portrait reveals something more than surface appearance.

The Desired Image

The collaborative nature of the painted portrait is the genre's starting point. Indeed, one could argue that, for artists to capture a moment extending beyond that depicted and to encompass the wider field of associations that define the self, the sitter must present a consistent impression to the artist over a long time. Painters rely on this cooperation to create a visual effect that the viewer can then apprehend relatively quickly. Conveying the aggregate experience of the artist with the sitter has been the hallmark of portraiture throughout its history in painting and sculpture. The successful portrait was understood to capture the essence of the individual's psychological and social register, constructing a visual synopsis of the more complex narrative that defines the sitter's identity.

Ironically, the capacity of photography to elide the period of creative activity introduces an element of ambiguity into the genre's usual goal of distilling the subject's essence out of the physical resemblance. It may seem counterintuitive to attribute essence to long duration and to ascribe its loss to the camera's immediacy, but that is exactly why the photograph pries open the formal devices of portraiture. The history of studio portraiture is filled with the stories of artists who struggled with their sitters, who were, after all, their clients. By virtue of engaging in that struggle, artists collapse the history of the painting session into a single image that summarizes the longer arc of the work's creation. In this way, the portrait,

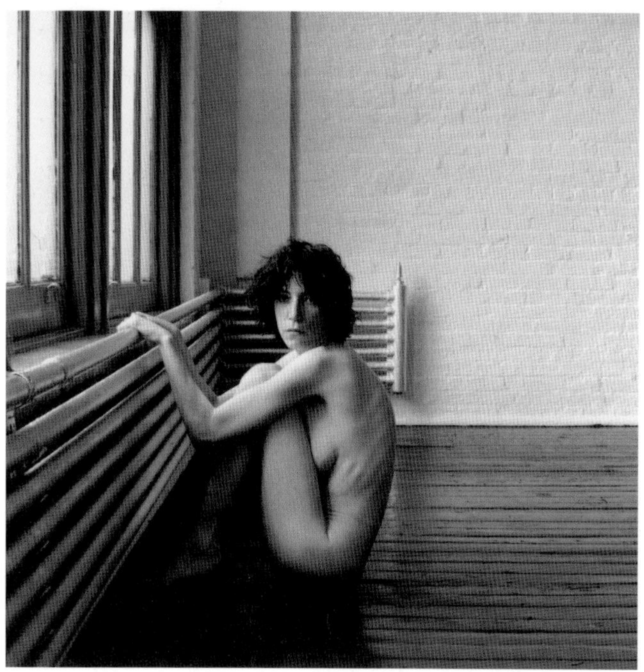

(fig.6)
Robert Mapplethorpe, Patti Smith, 1976; gelatin silver print. Robert Mapplethorpe Foundation

while claiming to be a composite image, carrying the range and nuance of characteristics that make up the individual depicted, is inflected, equally, by the artist's personality.

The photographic portrait may, in its brief interval of production, appear to resolve this dichotomy but, in fact, does not. Robert Mapplethorpe's portrait photographs engage directly with this conundrum of the image as a sign of essential traits. It is the theatrical element, which relies on the exchange between artist and subject, that gives Mapplethorpe's work its unusual power and lays bare the paradox of a still image that carries the force of the narrative in the photograph. Rather than offering a summary of the session, his portraits have the look and sensibility of a fragment, the depiction of a single moment that has been cut from a series of events.

In most of Mapplethorpe's portraits, the sitter looks out at the camera, which is to say, directly at the photographer, who has engaged his subject in a staged exchange that relies on the conventions of studio production to highlight the theatrical elements of the session (fig.6). Rarely does one experience the sitter as a passive presence even though Mapplethorpe relies on the restrained visual conventions of classicism, especially the reconciliation of opposites through "its equilibrium of volumes and forms, its control of structure and repetition."«1» Even at their most benign, the portraits are freighted with an implicit sense of confrontation. These are photographs that tell us what it feels like to be looked at, the uncomfortable experience of being appraised with which public figures constantly live. The rest of us are most likely to experience this awareness only when we are the object of another person's sexual gaze.

Mapplethorpe deploys this formality to disclose the sexuality that is usually hidden in portraits, drawing attention to details that he transforms into emblems loaded with sexual codes, as, for example, in Smutty's provocatively positioned rabbit's foot charm, Udo Kier's framed belt buckle, Gisèle Freund's mirroring portrait of Virginia Woolf, and the erupting fronds atop the palm tree beside Truman Capote (plates 37, 62, 27, and 34). By introducing the discourse of sexuality into his photographs, Mapplethorpe converts the portrait session itself into a metaphor for the dynamics of desire. These, then, are erotic portraits, even when the sitters are fully clothed. Arthur Danto has identified the power relations in these portrait sessions, whether explicit or not, as a matter of trust, which he asserts is the basic compact between sexual partners.«2»

Symmetry as Identity

One of the commonplace observations about Mapplethorpe's photography is that he relies on the classical convention of symmetry as a formal strategy to organize his compositions. His many square-format images attest to his interest in the visual articulation of symmetry. As a formal design, the square is one of the most difficult fields to use. In tending to nail down the object depicted within the confines of equally framed sides, it pushes the eye toward the center of the pictorial space. Mapplethorpe embraces the square format and the static composition to explore the potential for dynamic possibilities within symmetry; in a significant number of portraits, his subjects' direct and centered gaze is almost unnaturally symmetrical.

The face is defined by its familiar balanced structure—two eyes aligned across the center, topped by eyebrows and separated by a central nose with two nostrils, a centered mouth with two lips, the top lip, composed of two equal arcs, and two ears, one on either side. This arrangement, as psychologists have noted, is reassuring for infants, who exhibit increasing distress the more this geometry is skewed. The traditional ideal of the portrait has, therefore, a person posed frontally to capture the distinctiveness of these facial features and their expressive qualities.«3» Mapplethorpe's work is clearly aligned with this tradition.

Activating the space of the image is another formal organizing strategy that Mapplethorpe uses to reference the artifice of photographic depictions. By calling attention to the camera's interruption of time, he transforms the actions of his sitters into an analogy of the photographic session itself. Often he brings the subject's hands up into the frame, establishing, through gesture and even when they are at rest, a visual tension by implying that the centered symmetry of the image is less a fixed pose than a moment of suspended animation.

The distinctive look with which Mapplethorpe freights his sitters also implies a wary exchange. The expression is not adversarial, or even unfriendly, but it is decidedly guarded rather than relaxed. It carries the anxiety that accompanies the public persona, the resistance to being scrutinized. Mapplethorpe captures the uncanny suspension that Susan Sontag identifies as "the difference between me and the image."«4» The camera shutter fixes that difference, which drives, even dramatizes, the events of the portrait session. One notices this most acutely in the poses that indicate movement through a slight turn or tilt of the head, the pupils pulled to the corners of the eyes. The alert response indicated in this subtle movement also introduces a formal element by emphasizing the essential asymmetries that real faces exhibit on close inspection. This strategy, which Mapplethorpe would have known from Irving Penn, who often used it with his portrait sitters, is especially evident, for example, in the portraits here of Thom Gunn, Klaus Kertess, Kathleen Turner, Deborah Harry, Ed Ruscha, Susan Sontag, and Yoko Ono (plates 28, 31, 40, 49, 68, 70, and 97).

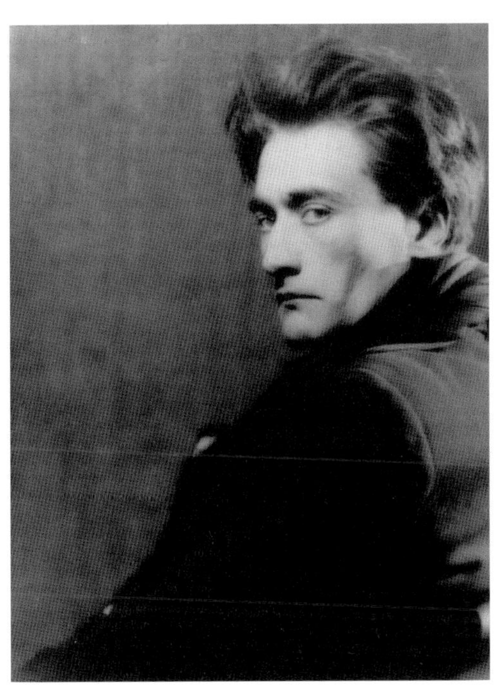

(fig.7)
Man Ray, Antonin Artaud, 1926; gelatin silver print. Museum of Modern Art, New York

In the psychoanalytic terms articulated by Jacques Lacan, the realization that others perceive one's image differently initiates a split awareness, which is responsible for the unstable and conflicting positions that an individual must negotiate in developing a sense of self, and the unbridgeable gap felt within one's self. By referencing this psychological narrative and its explanation of the trauma attending the realization that our view of ourselves is at odds with how we are seen, Mapplethorpe creates portraits that serve to elucidate the process of identity formation. In them he makes visible the personal drama, as defined in psychoanalytic discourse, that is used to structure the self. Ironically, Mapplethorpe relies on a formal use of symmetry to articulate this play of asymmetrical perceptions.

Abstract and Classic

Mapplethorpe's collective portrait of artists, performers, designers, collectors, and critics echoes the famous lithographic project, Pantheon of Famous Contemporaries, by the pioneering French photographer Nadar (Gaspard-Félix Tournachon, 1820–1910), begun in 1851. And Nadar's portrait of Parisian bohemian life offers a suggestive parallel to the New York world of avant-garde artists, performers, designers, collectors, and critics who compose the principal social circle represented in Mapplethorpe's portraits.«5» Like Nadar's, Mapplethorpe's notion of prominent personalities had more to do with his acquaintances in the network generated by a creative, intellectual elite than with considerations of social and political power. It could be said that, as an aggregate, these sitters form an intellectual portrait of Mapplethorpe in their depiction of the social arena that defined his life.«6»

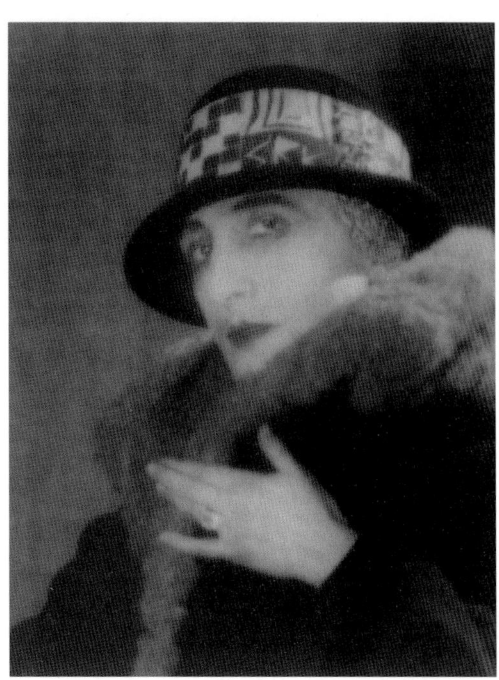

(fig.8)
Man Ray, Rrose Sélavy (Marcel Duchamp), 1923; gelatin silver print. J. Paul Getty Museum

Yet it is not only the denizens of New York City in the 1980s who are the focus of Mapplethorpe's photographs. Without resorting to the obvious distortions of surrealism, Mapplethorpe has slyly incorporated the movement's interrogation of the verisimilitude traditionally ascribed to photographic representations through the public's naïve belief that the camera truthfully depicts self-evident reality. He uses an abstract vocabulary, emphasizing formal relationships over pictorial descriptions, to reveal the constructed nature of the photographic image and the fabricated identity of his sitters in a manner that makes him heir to Man Ray and Marcel Duchamp, both of whom Mapplethorpe admired and studied while he was a student at Pratt Institute, Brooklyn, beginning in 1963.«7»

With his inventive vocabulary, Man Ray chronicled the artistic and literary personalities of avant-garde Paris in the 1920s, crossing the visual strategies of fashion and portraiture to create a hybrid image through the dramatic effects achievable in the studio (fig.7). The same effects structure Mapplethorpe's photographs and are evident, for example, in the portraits of his muse, Patti Smith (plates 3 and 91), of Carolina Herrera and Paloma Picasso, Marisa Berenson and Isabella Rossellini (plates 16, 30, 56, and 100). Duchamp's famous photographic self-portraits as his feminine alter ego, Rrose Sélavy (fig.8), are a touchstone for Mapplethorpe's performative self-portraits, including his own use of a drag persona (plate 26) and other role-playing images (plates 25 and 50). Mapplethorpe, too, creates images that are as much about the conceptual issues of representation as they are about their ostensible subject matter.

Mapplethorpe's preferred use of the studio and of a square-format Hasselblad view camera dictated that his

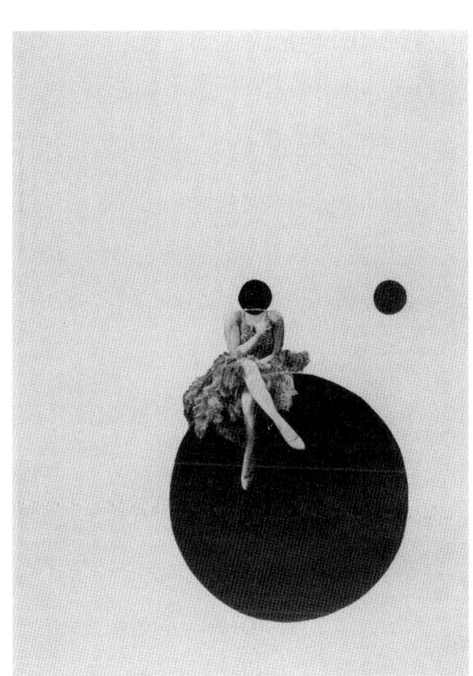

(fig.9)
László Moholy-Nagy, The Olly and Dolly Sisters, 1925; gelatin silver print, J. Paul Getty Museum

photographs would require careful consideration of formal concerns, no matter what his subject.«8» Although his influences and visual aesthetic tie his work to the avant-garde elements that inform the work of modernist artists, he also shares the interest of postmodern artists in exploring the artifice of representation by rehearsing and reinventing the visual vocabulary from a historical period. Working in the traditional genres of the artist's studio—portrait, still life, and the figure—Mapplethorpe developed a signature style that both used and called attention to principles that had been established in the 1920s and 1930s as photography embraced a modernist aesthetic defined by German new vision and surrealist artists.«9» Like his predecessors (fig.9), Mapplethorpe creates perceptual disorientation through techniques that lend an expressive quality to the images, which include the use of high- or low-angle shots, unexpected framing, close-ups, cropped edges, extreme contrasts of tone, and strong, dramatic lighting.

However, in spite of appropriating the expressionist language of modernist photography, Mapplethorpe's reinvention of its abstract compositional technique relies more on the restrained structures of classicism. His frequent blank backdrops, typically gray or black, isolate his subject, decontextualizing it in order to emphasize the formal relationships that are internal to the image. This is true whether he is working with traditional images, as in the portraits in this exhibition, or more provocative images, such as those associated with his photographs of sexual subcultures. At times, as in the portraits of Brian Ridley and Lyle Heeter, Cynthia Slater, Marcus Leatherdale, and Peter Berlin (plates 22, 29, 11, and 6), Mapplethorpe blurred the boundaries between traditional portraiture and the world of underground cultures in which he also participated.

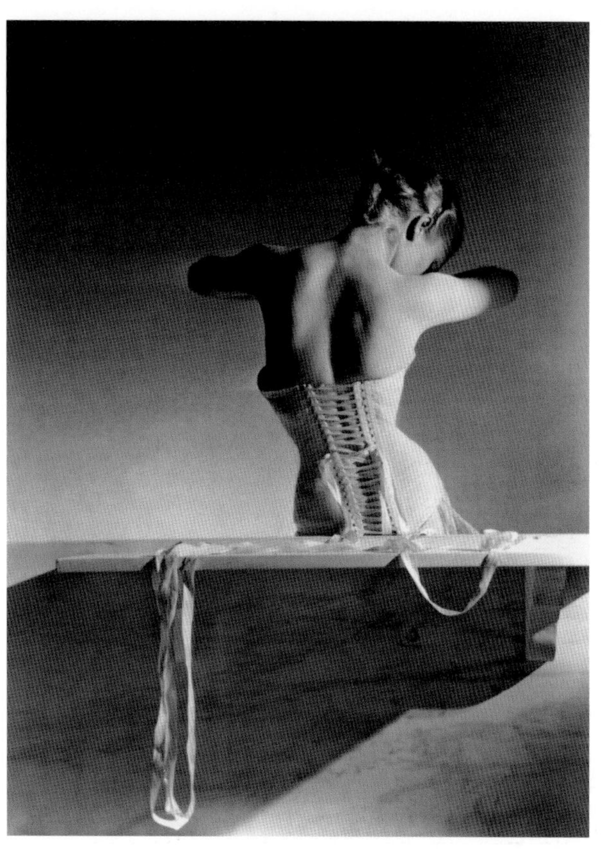

(fig.10)
Horst P. Horst, Mainbocher Corset, 1939; gelatin silver print. Art + Commerce

The erotic charge in these photographs results, not so much from the subject matter, which is domesticated by the conventions of portraiture, but from Mapplethorpe's manipulation of the composition to highlight formal relationships. He fragments and isolates figures in a spatial void with high tonal contrasts that flatten the images and align them with the optical surface of the photograph, calling attention to its production. In this way, Mapplethorpe's series of portraits provide him with an opportunity to explore the manifold possibilities of representation that the camera's visual vocabulary makes possible. The differences in his images cannot be accounted for merely by the diversity of sitters.

For example, Mapplethorpe frequently draws attention to the edge of the photograph: his subject's gaze extends beyond the frame, a visual cue that the image is cut from a wider field of view, or he introduces a linear element that creates a secondary edge within the image. This is especially effective when these internal elements are aligned with his sitters, as they are in the portraits of Fran Lebowitz, Andy Warhol, Peter Berlin, Marianne Faithfull, George Dureau, and the double portrait of Philip Glass and Robert Wilson (plates 23, 60, 6, 7, 46, and 5). Such strategies point up the camera's necessary fragmenting of reality through the selection required by the lens and its inevitable limit and edge.

Perhaps the most characteristic trope of Mapplethorpe's photography lies in the self-conscious way that he incorporates the camera's reliance on light to produce an image. Sam Wagstaff, one of Mapplethorpe's lovers as well as his longtime mentor and companion, wrote

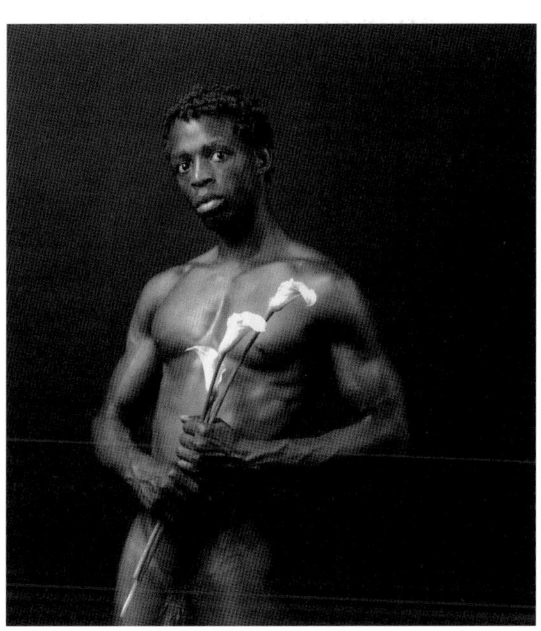

(fig.11)
Robert Mapplethorpe, Dennis Speight with Calla Lilies, 1983; Cibachrome print. Robert Mapplethorpe Foundation

that "the drama of light" was his principal strategy.«10» He deployed it similarly no matter what he photographed, reducing all his subjects to flattened planes of light and dark tonalities through the high contrasts of studio lighting developed for fashion and glamour photography by artists such as Edward Steichen, Cecil Beaton, Horst(fig.10), and George Platt Lynes.«11» Mapplethorpe exploits the play of light on skin, capturing the flesh of his sitters glowing out from a dark ground. His transformation of the body into a seductive surface mirrors the action of the photograph, which converts a piece of the world into the gelatin silver tones of its glossy, two-dimensional image.

Mapplethorpe's use of the close-up draws on the conventions of glamour photography by the film industry in creating its publicity images. His photographs elevate their subjects to larger-than-life status through the way they fill the space, at times crowding the frame. Mapplethorpe will heighten this sense of significance by pushing the heads of his sitters to the edge of his image as if they can barely be confined within the limits of the pictorial space, as in his portraits of Phillip Johnson, Lynn Davis, Cindy Sherman, Lucinda Childs, Leo Castelli, Marissa Berenson, and Annamirl van der Pluijm (plates 9, 13, 61, 63, 81, 56, and 67). At times he even crops his sitter to heighten this sensibility, evident in the photographs of Sam Wagstaff and Lisette Model (plates 17 and 32), both of whom had a significant impact on his development as a photographer.

By doubling the referential signs within his images, Mapplethorpe exploits the photograph's ability to create conceptual associations through visual relationships, presenting flowers, nude figures, and portraits as equivalent images(fig.11). His portraits are simultaneously recognizable

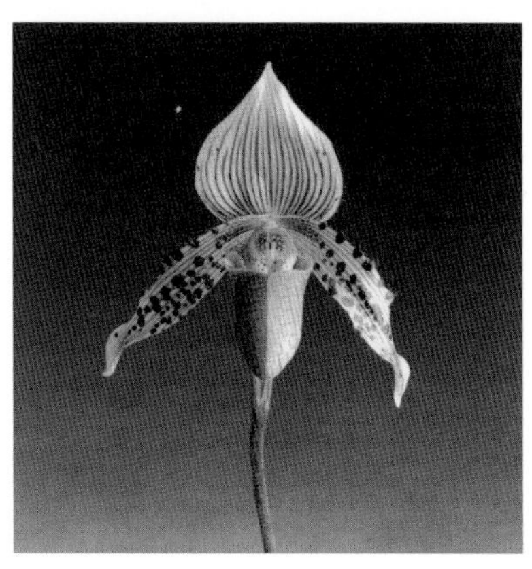

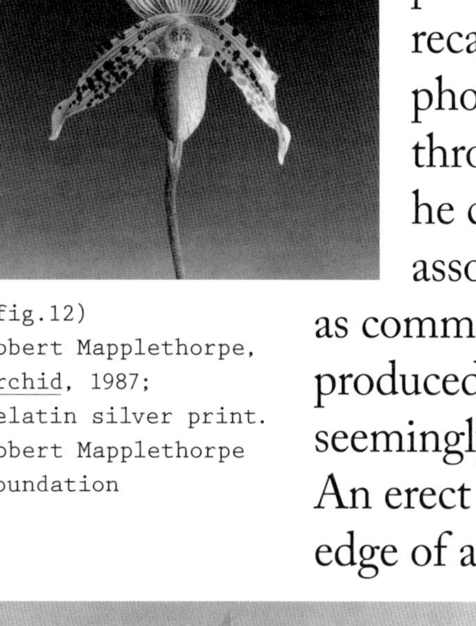

(fig.12)
Robert Mapplethorpe, Orchid, 1987; gelatin silver print. Robert Mapplethorpe Foundation

and abstract in their references; they are both sharp-focused depictions of people and complex formal patterns that simplify relationships within the image, recalling the operation of the camera and its attendant photographic processes. By suggesting equations through the use of surprising visual comparisons, he creates a referential dialectic, introducing intertextual associations that encourage viewers to read each genre as commensurate with the others. The chains of signification produced as Mapplethorpe creates associations among seemingly different subjects lead viewers to a perceptual shift. An erect orchid (fig.12) thrusting into a blank space from the edge of a photograph in close-up with high-contrast lighting takes on the personality of a portrait. In turn, this erotic display of a single flower lends a sensual appreciation to the nude figures and extends their register beyond the explicit depiction of sexual organs (fig.13).

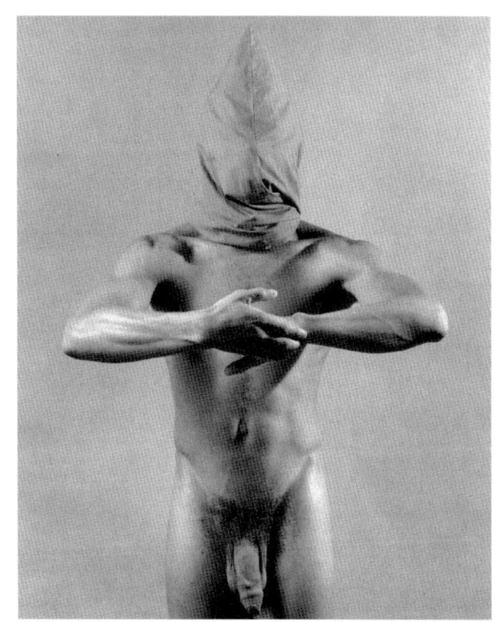

(fig.13)
Robert Mapplethorpe, Hooded Man, 1980; gelatin silver print. Robert Mapplethorpe Foundation

Deploying a consistent photographic vocabulary rooted in the conventions of 1920s and 1930s modernist abstraction and freighting it with the sexual discourses of the 1970s and 1980s, Mapplethorpe opens up the compass of desire mobilized in those earlier images through surprising visual associations. His portraits, in particular, reinvent the ways that photography functions as a public medium. Resisting the dominant tradition of documentary photography in the work of his contemporaries, Mapplethorpe created classic studio portraits that are also self-reflexive metaphors of photographic representation and the vocabulary it uses to construct the viewer's perceptions.

«1»
This, in fact, was the premise of an exhibition at Deutsche Guggenheim Berlin in 2004, the definition from Germano Celant, "Mapplethorpe as Neoclassicist," in Germano Celant and Arkadii Ippolitov, Robert Mapplethorpe and the Classical Tradition: Photographs and Mannerist Prints, exh. cat. (New York: Solomon R. Guggenheim Foundation, 2004), 38. Celant's essay is an extended consideration of Mapplethorpe's appropriation of the classicism associated with the great figures of the sixteenth and seventeenth century, such as Michelangelo, Antonio Canova, Antonio Pollaiuolo, and Leonardo da Vinci, an appropriation that positions his postmodern practice within a field wider than photography.

«2»
Arthur C. Danto, Playing with the Edge: The Photographic Achievement of Robert Mapplethorpe (Berkeley: University of California Press, 1996), 41-43.

«3»
Kimberly Lamm, "Portraiture," in The Encyclopedia of Twentieth-Century Photography, ed. Lynne Warren (New York: Routledge, 2006), 3:1288.

«4»
Susan Sontag, preface to Robert Mapplethorpe: Certain People, a Book of Portraits, (Pasadena, Calif.: Twelvetrees Press, 1985), n.p.

«5»
One of Mapplethorpe's first introductions to photography came in 1971 from John McKendry, then the curator of prints and photography at the Metropolitan Museum of Art, who showed him the museum's extensive archives. However, at that time the Met had no photographs by Nadar in its holdings, which were informed by the gift of Alfred Stieglitz's personal collection to the museum, including works by Stieglitz and the pioneering modernist photographer Paul Strand, both of whom impressed Mapplethorpe, not yet a photographer. Mapplethorpe's awareness of Nadar's Panthéon came through a newfound interest in photography, which he shared with Sam Wagstaff, whom he met in 1972 and who encouraged him to invest in photographs after showing him works by Baron von Gloeden.

«6»
It is also similar to Alvin Langdon Coburn's series Men of Mark: Pioneers of Modernism (1913), a collection of the portraits of thirty-three artists and writers living in London at that time. For a discussion of Coburn's photographs based on a recent exhibition from this series, see Nicky McHugh, "A. L. Coburn's Men of Mark," American Art Review 16, no. 2 (March-April 2004): 108-11.

«7»
Richard Marshall, ed., Robert Mapplethorpe, with essays by Ingrid Sischy and Richard Howard, exh. cat. (New York and Boston: Whitney Museum of American Art in association with Bulfinch Press, 1988), 8.

«8»
Mapplethorpe began using a Hasselblad in 1976, when he was given the camera by Sam Wagstaff.

«9»
The term new vision photography comes from László Moholy-Nagy, who published an influential collection of photographs and critical text entitled The New Vision (1928) to illustrate his belief that photography could provide an objective view that dismantles conventional ways of seeing to produce new subjective perceptions.

«10»
Sam Wagstaff, Robert Mapplethorpe: Process, exh. brochure (New York: Barbara Gladstone Gallery, 1984), n.p.

«11»
Joan Didion discusses the codes of fashion in Mapplethorpe's photographs in her introduction, "An Annotation," to Some Women: By Mapplethorpe by Robert Mapplethorpe (Boston: Bulfinch Press, 1989), n.p.

Self-Portrait, 1975

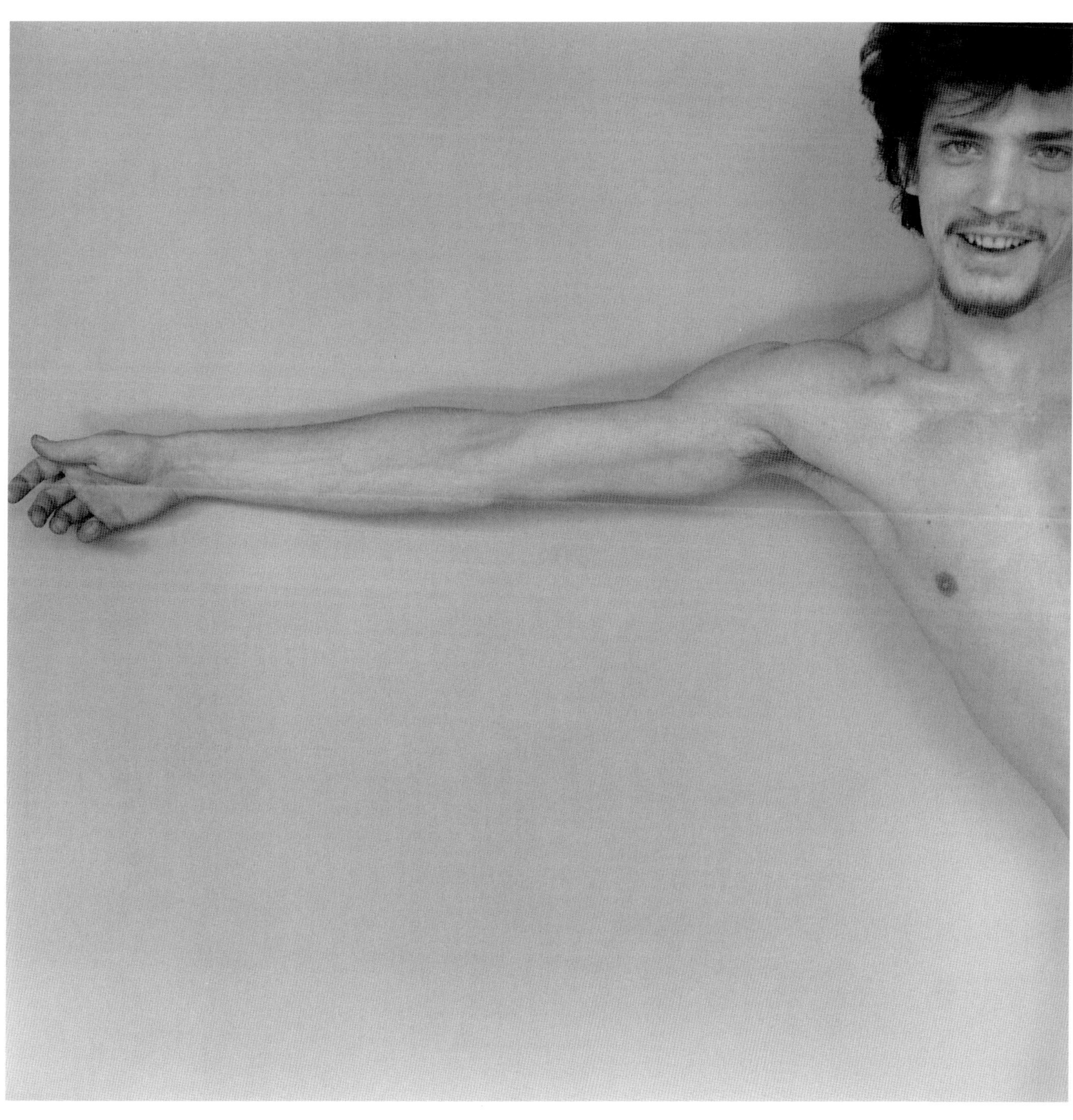

Dorothy Dean, 1974

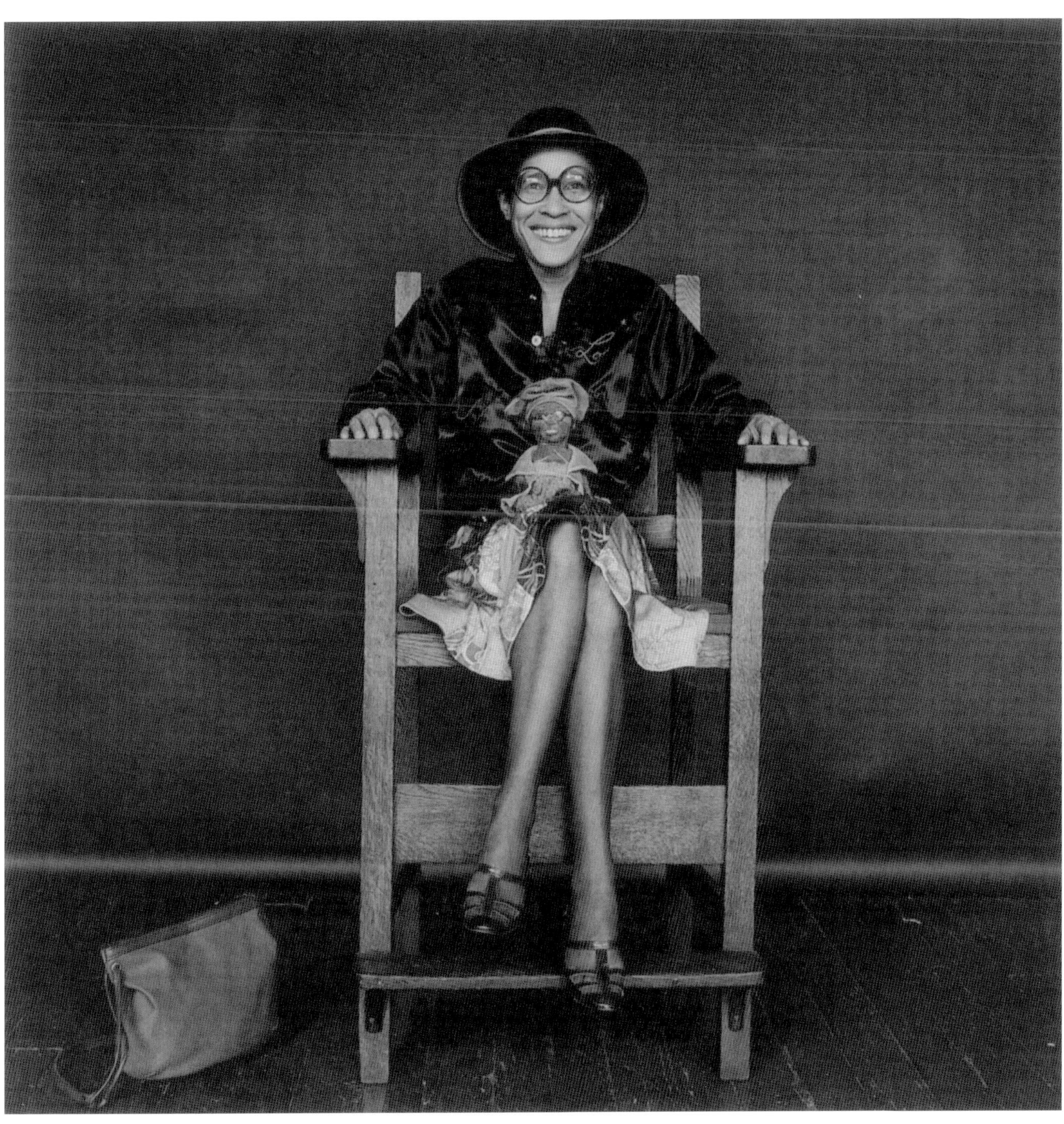

Patti Smith, 1975

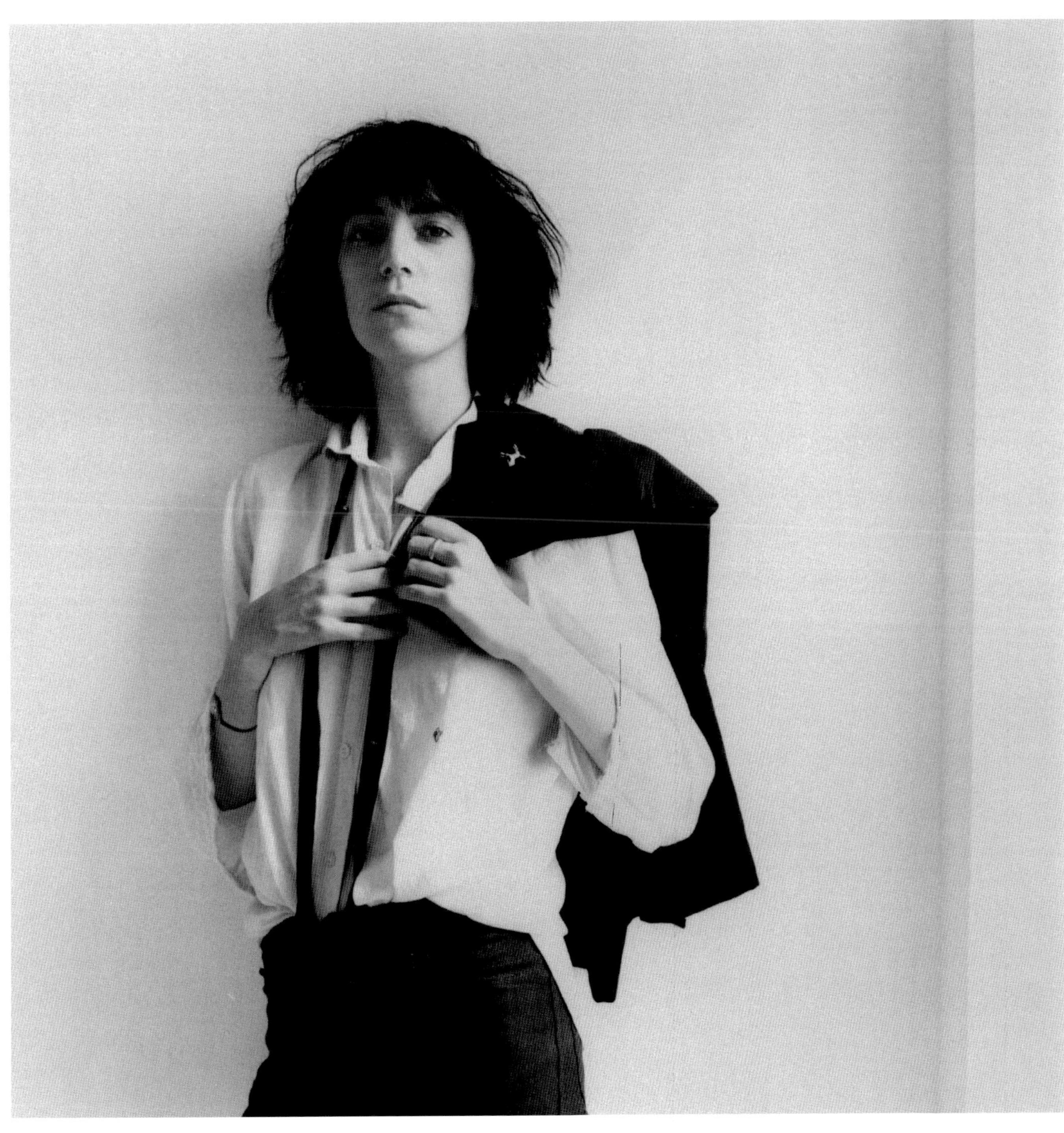

David Hockney, 1976

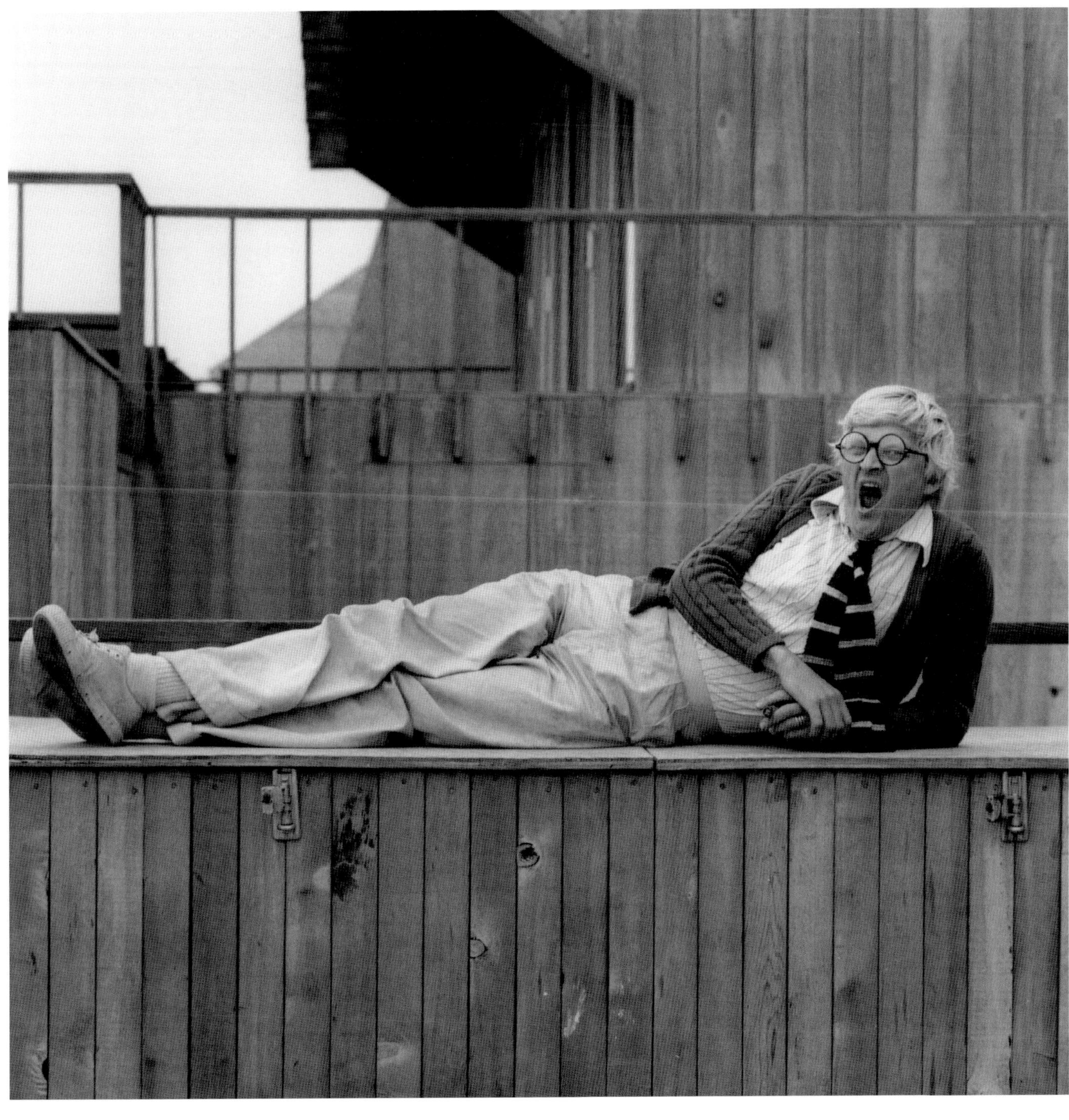

Philip Glass and Robert Wilson, 1976

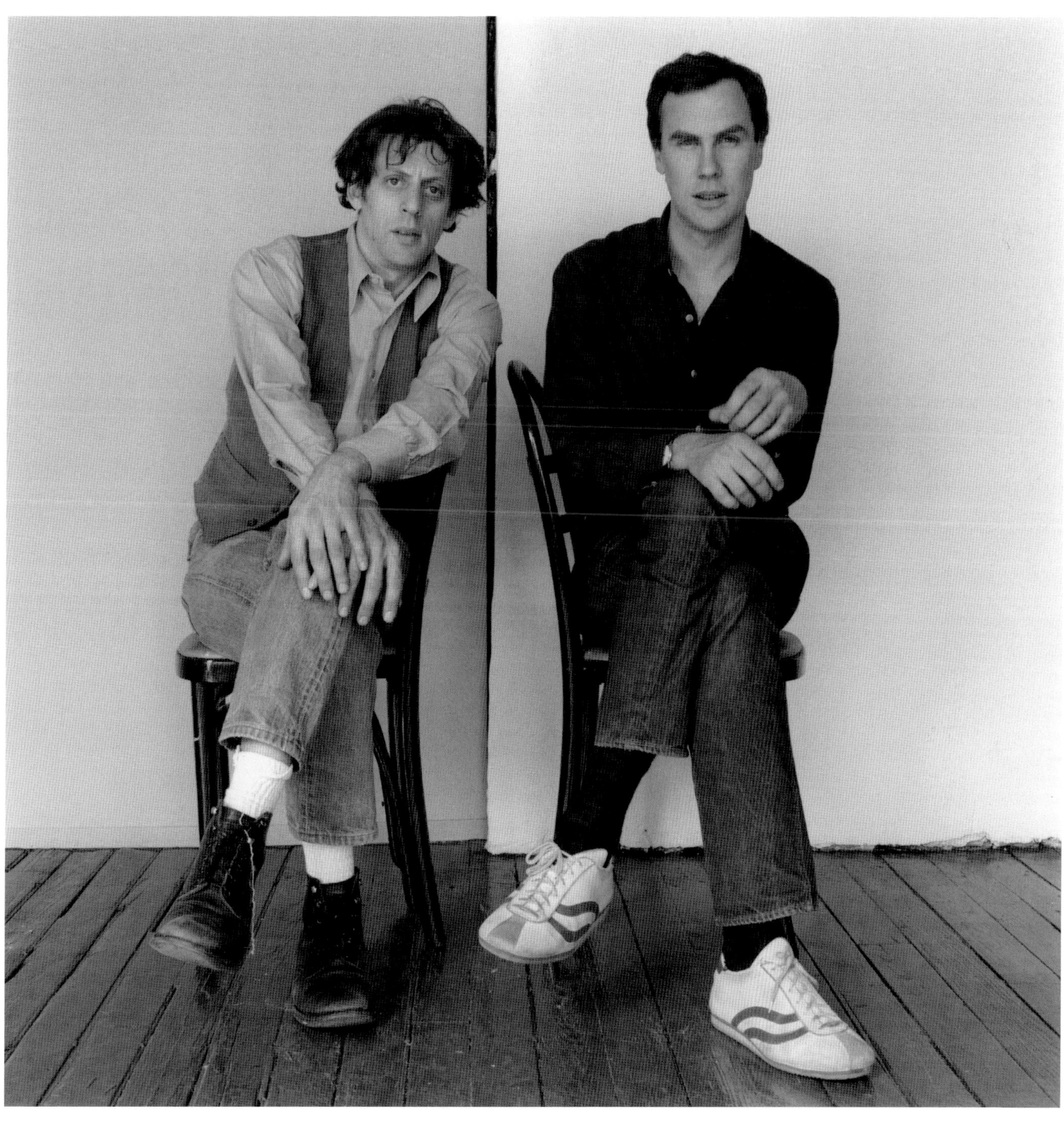

Peter Berlin, 1977

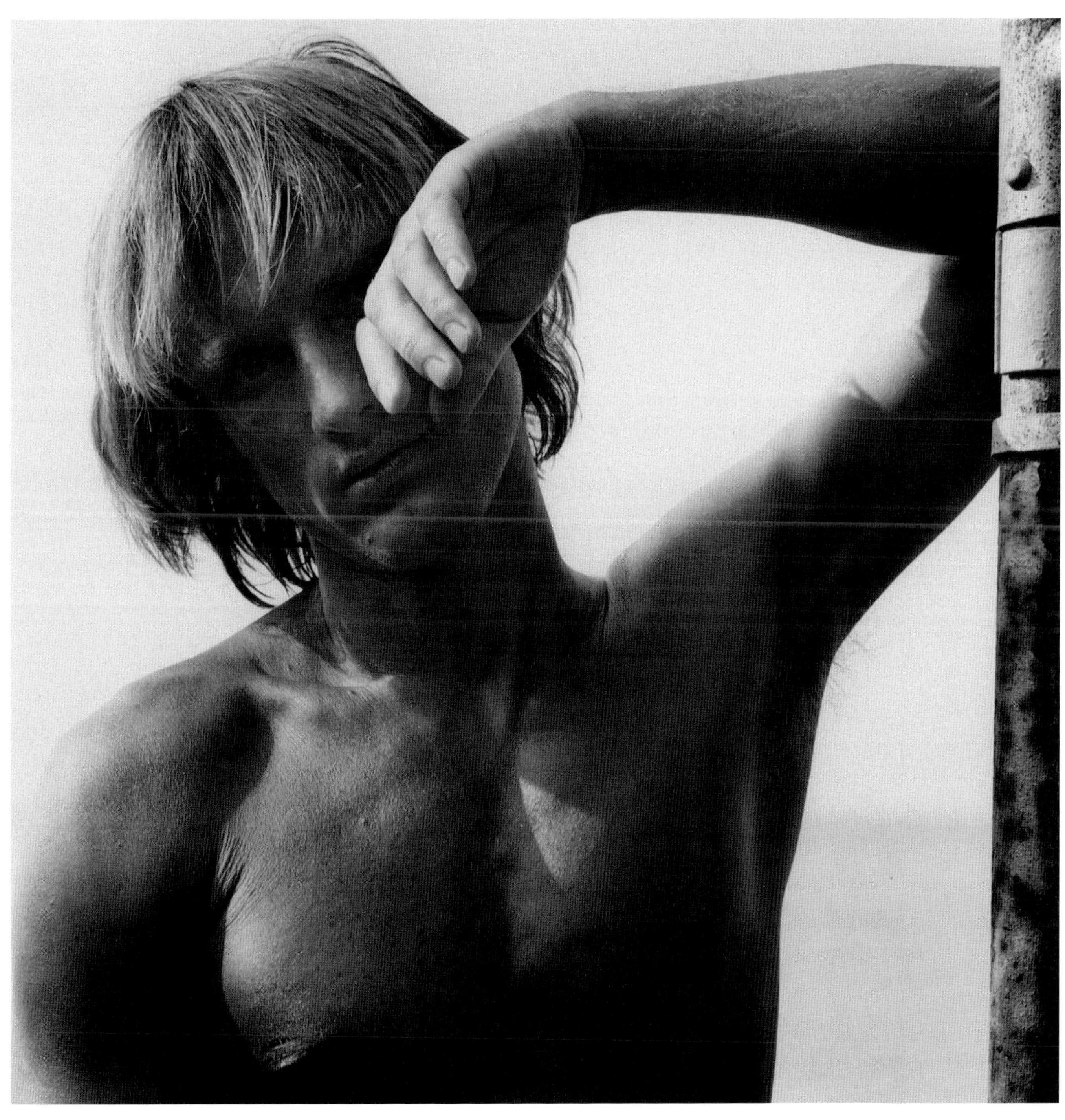

Marianne Faithfull, 1976

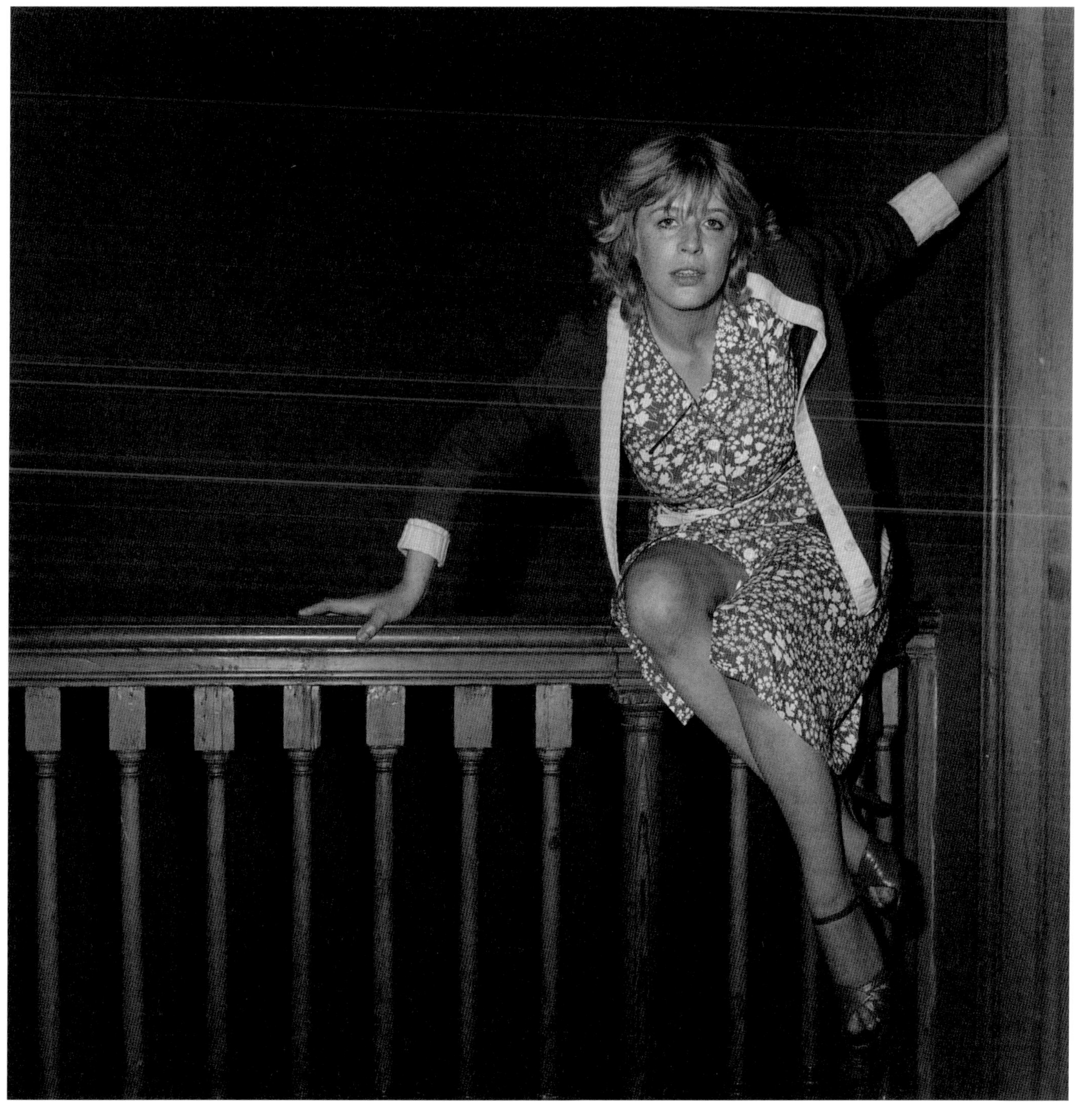

Plate 8 / Catalogue # 84

Arnold Schwarzenegger, 1976

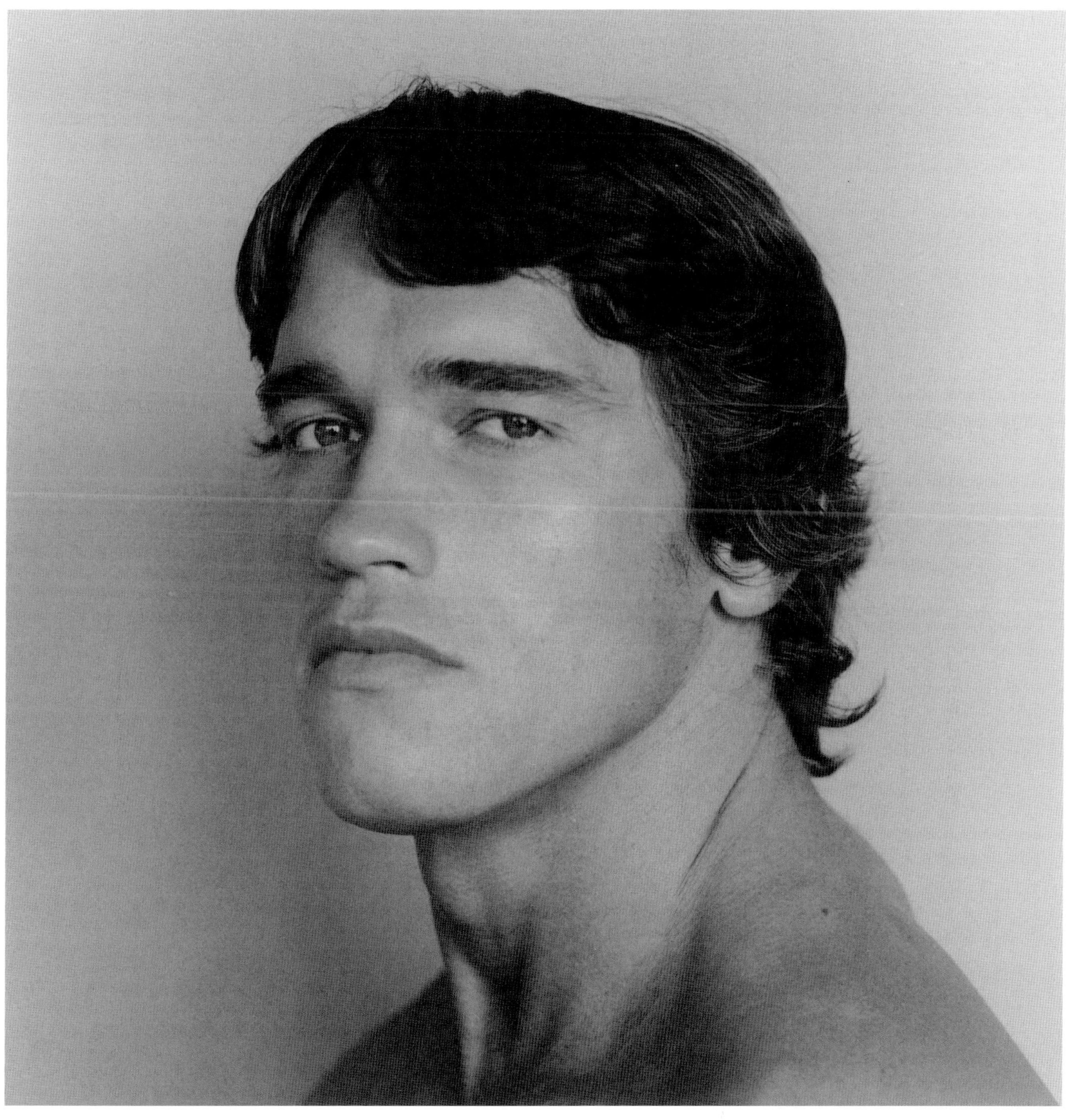

Plate 9 / Catalogue # 41

Philip Johnson, 1978

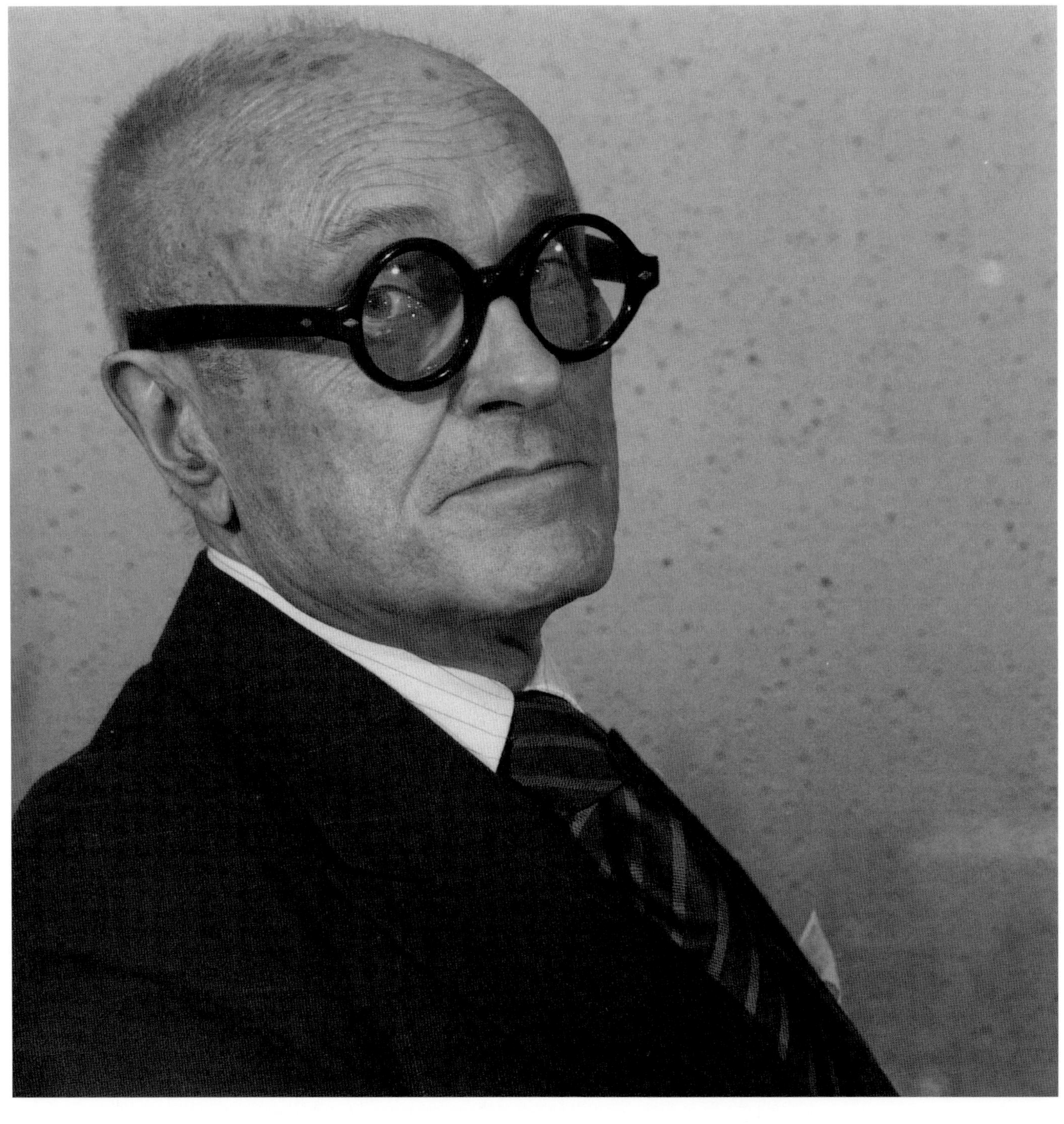

Mario Amaya, 1978

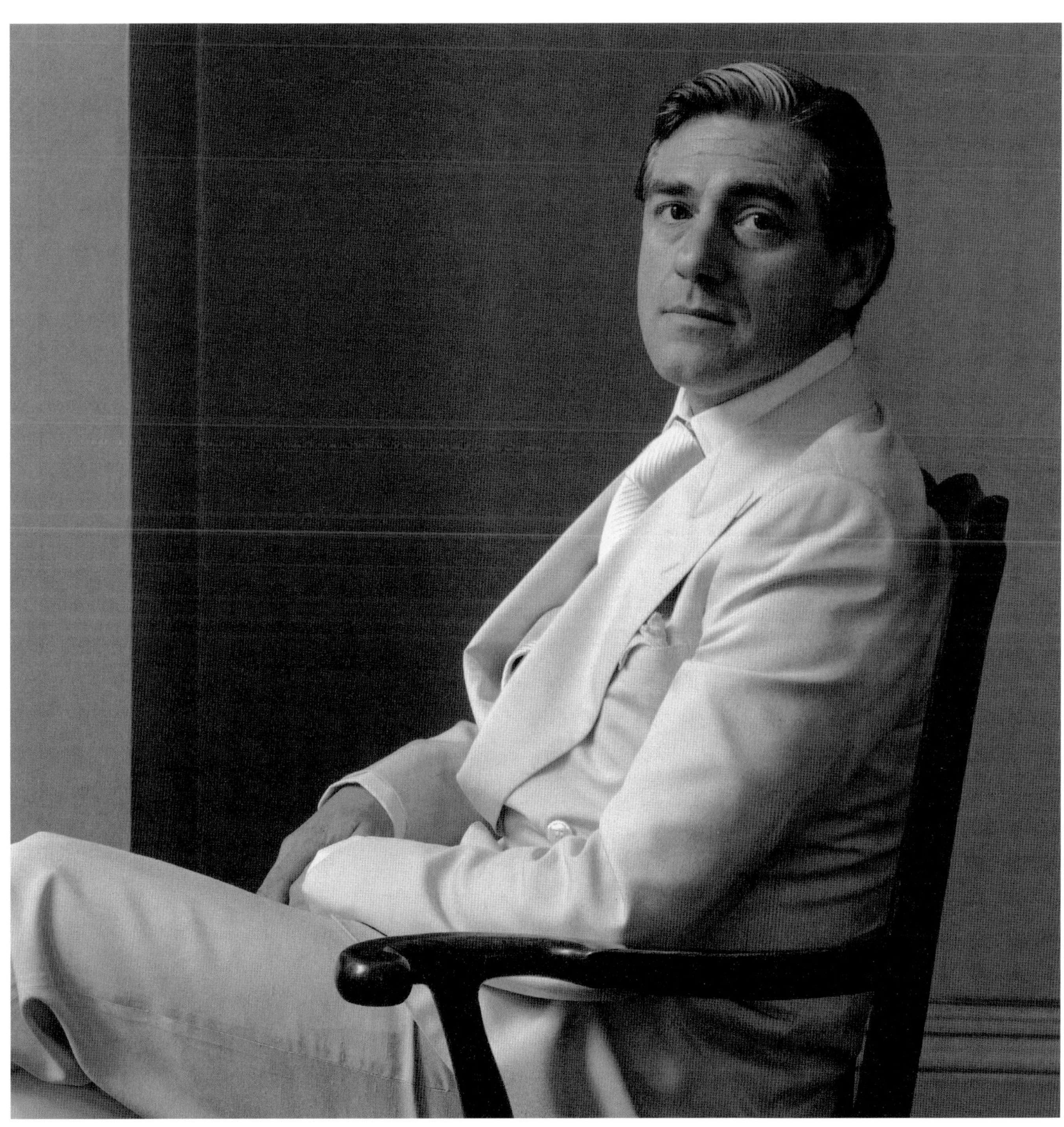

Plate 11 / Catalogue # 51 Marcus Leatherdale, 1978

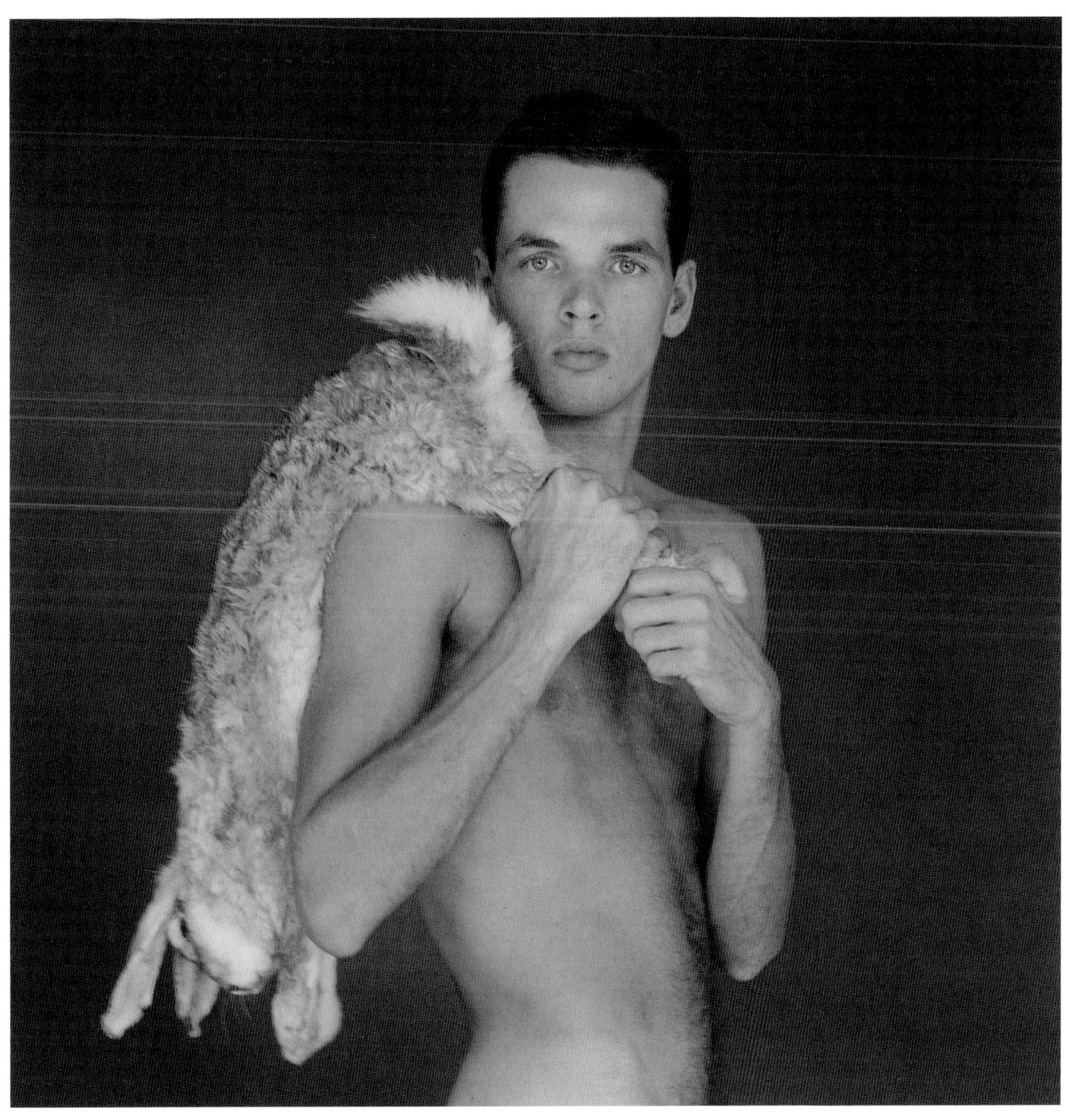

Tom of Finland, 1978

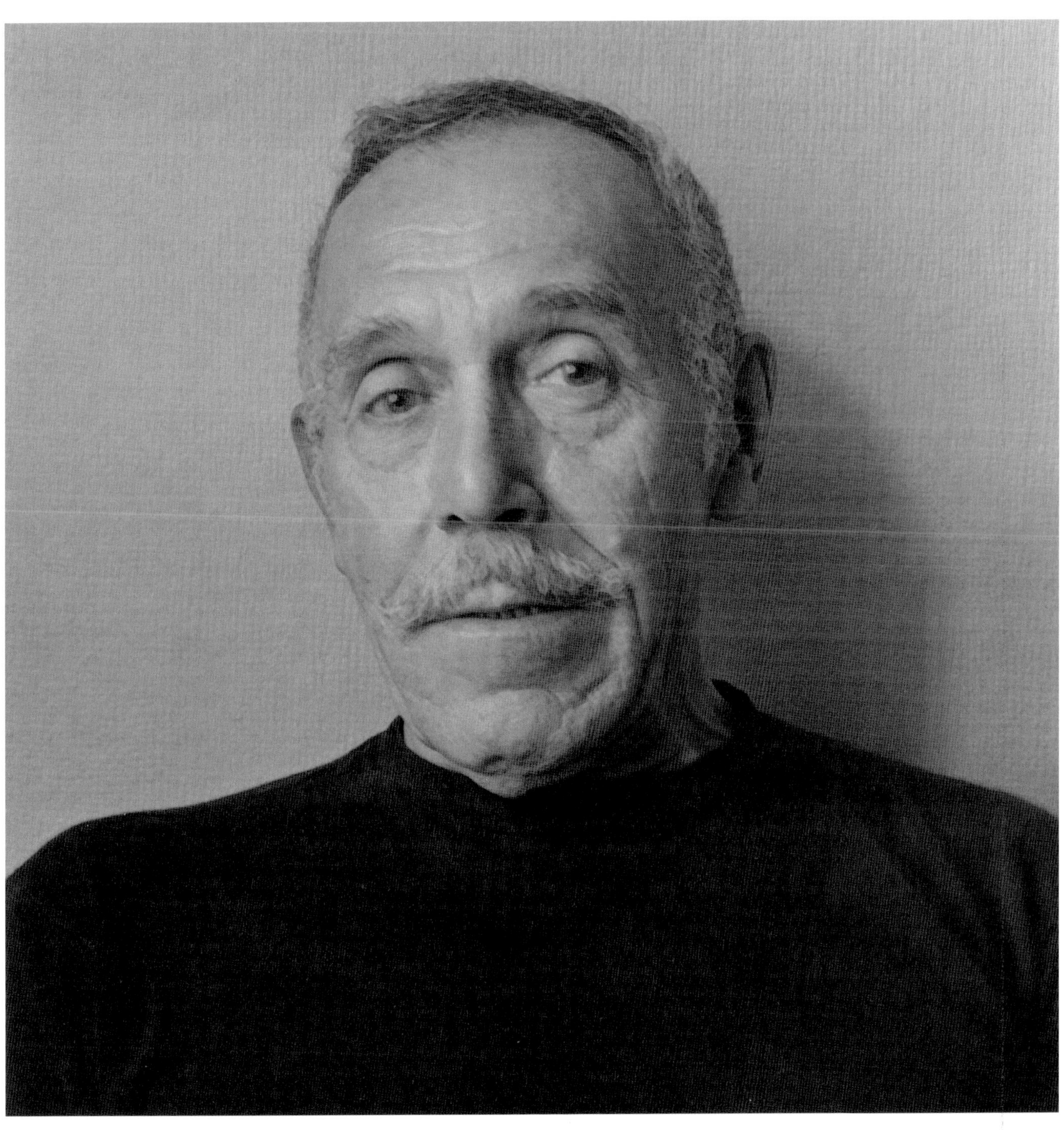

Plate 13 / Catalogue # 24

Lynn Davis, 1979

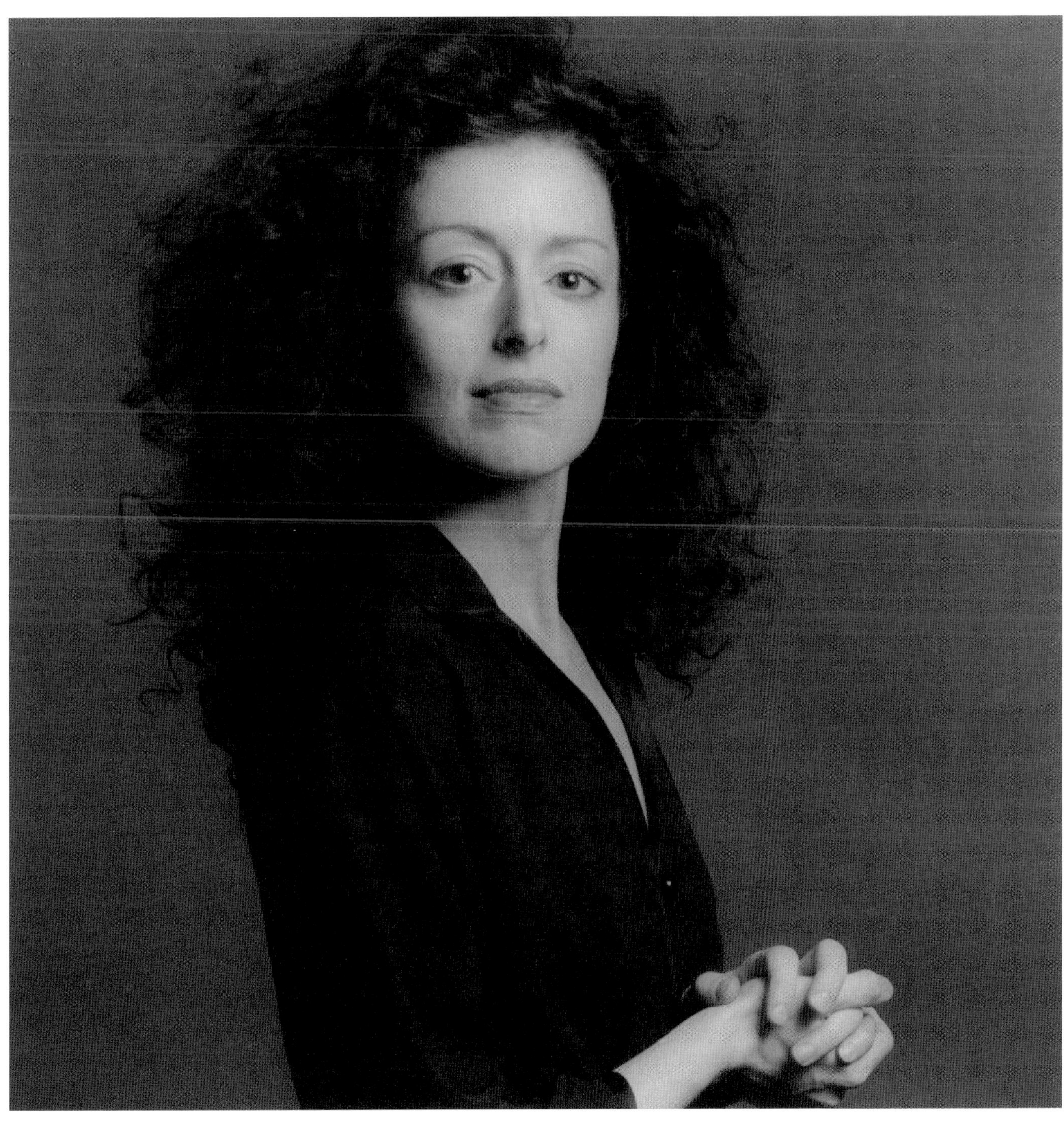

Marisol, 1979

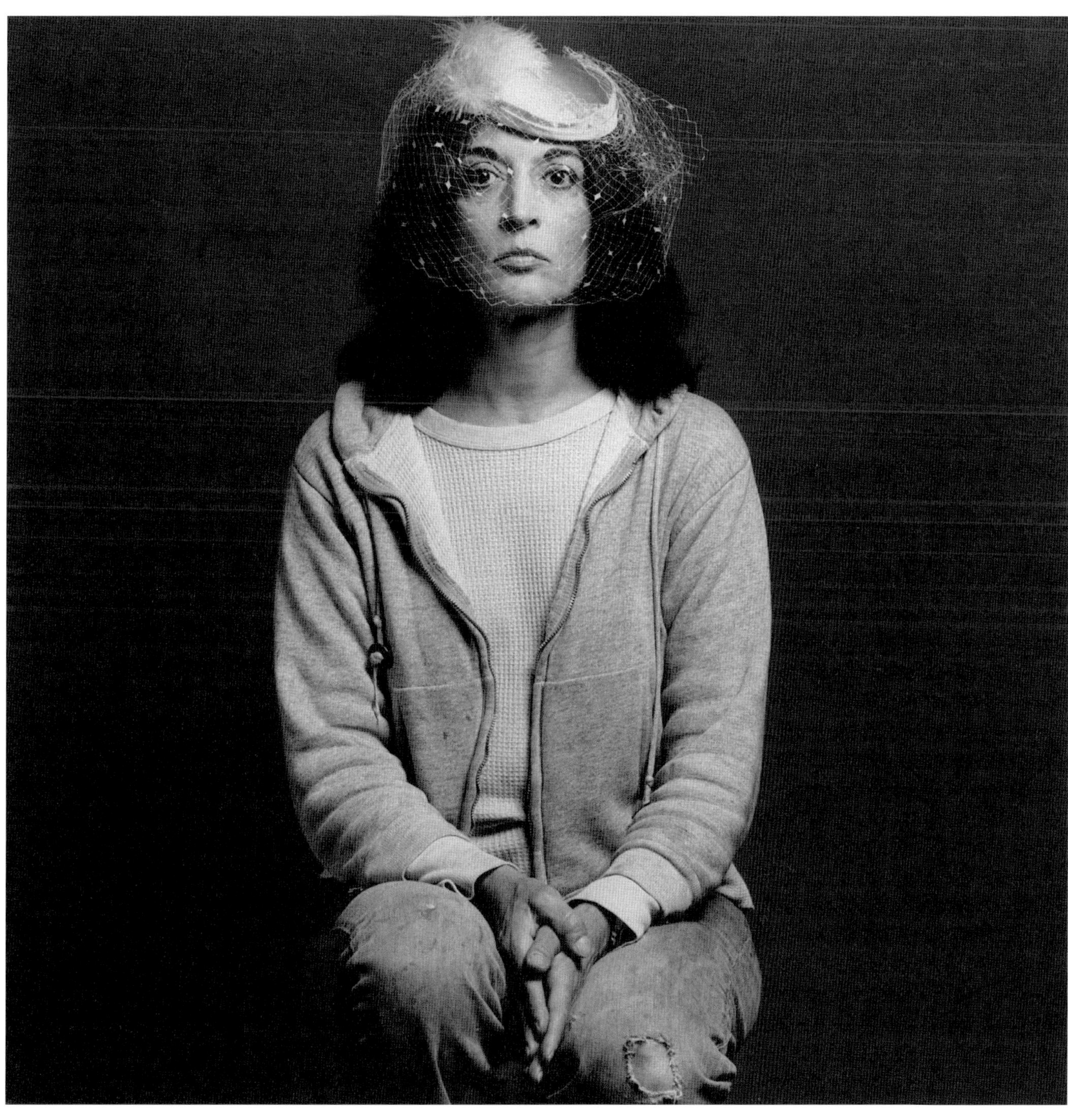

Bruce Chatwin, 1979

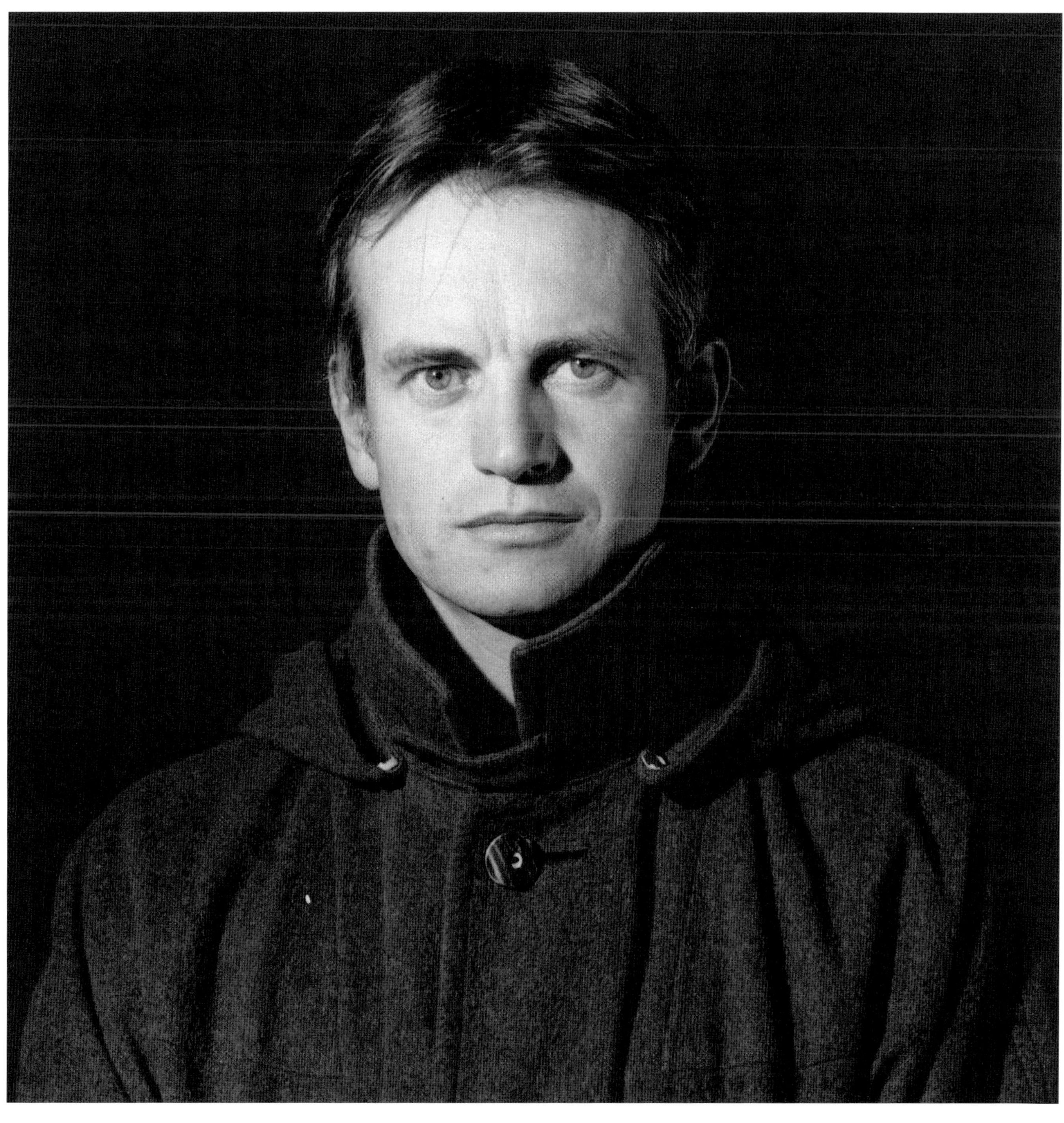

Carolina Herrera, 1979

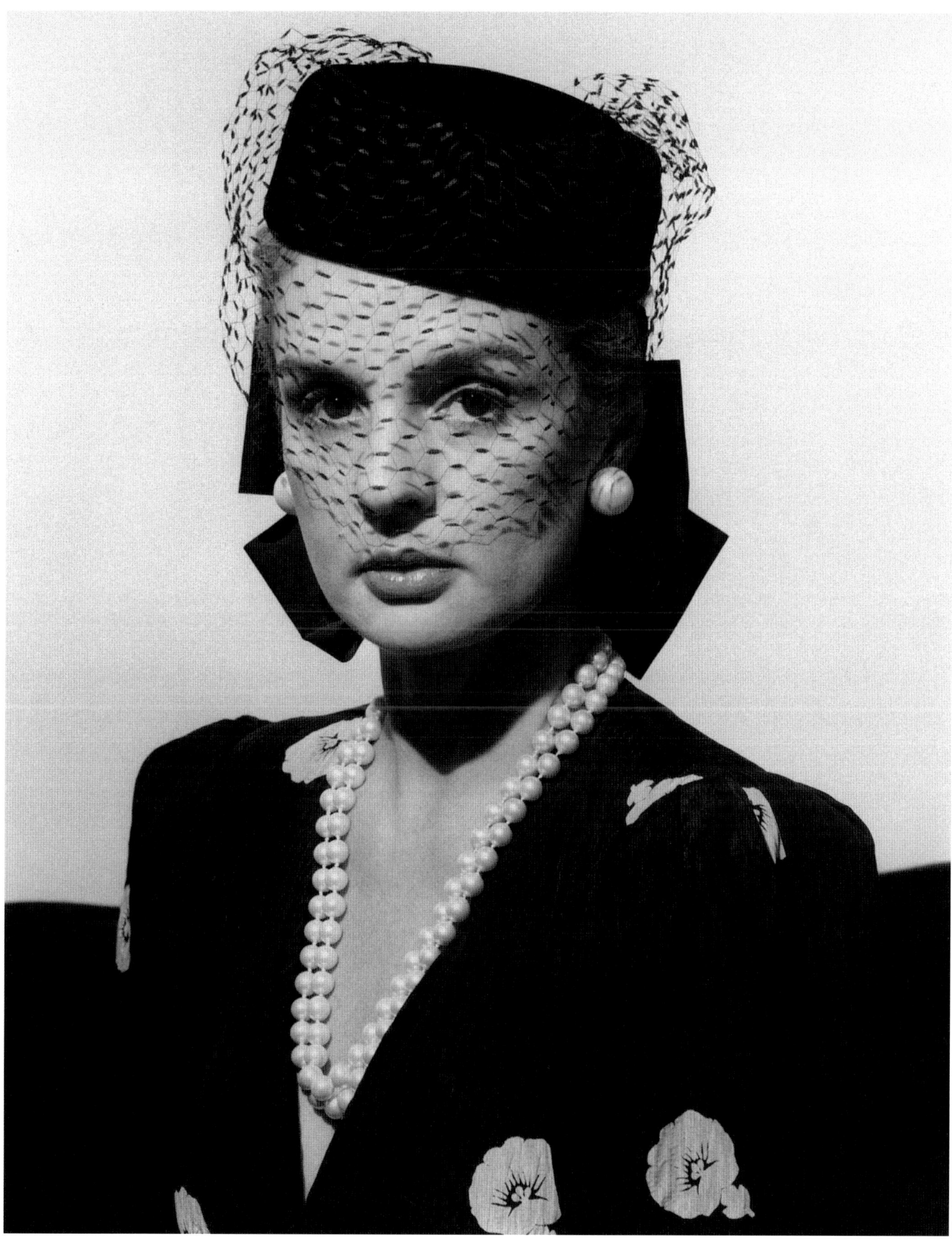

Sam Wagstaff, 1979

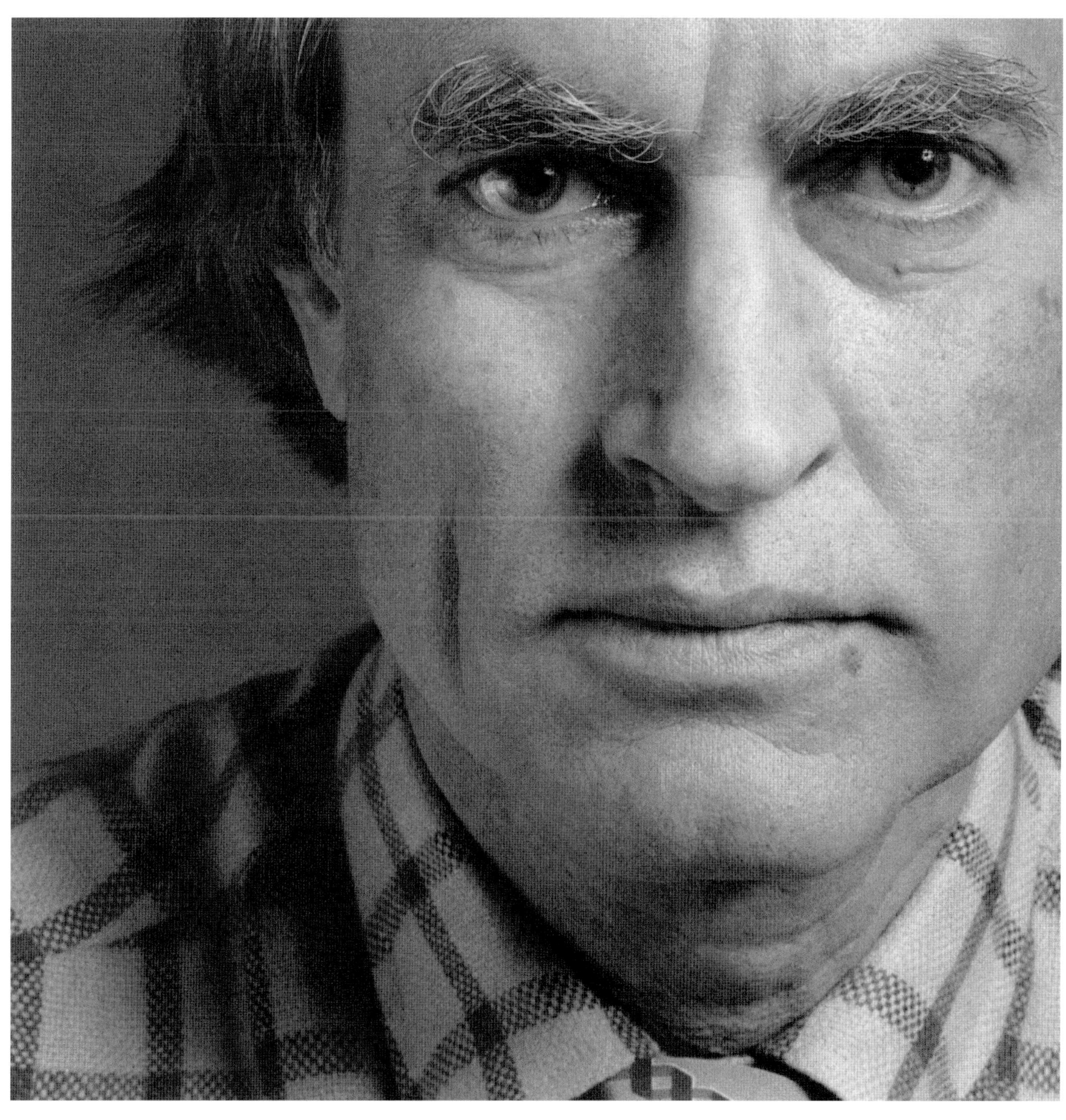

Phyllis Tweel, 1979

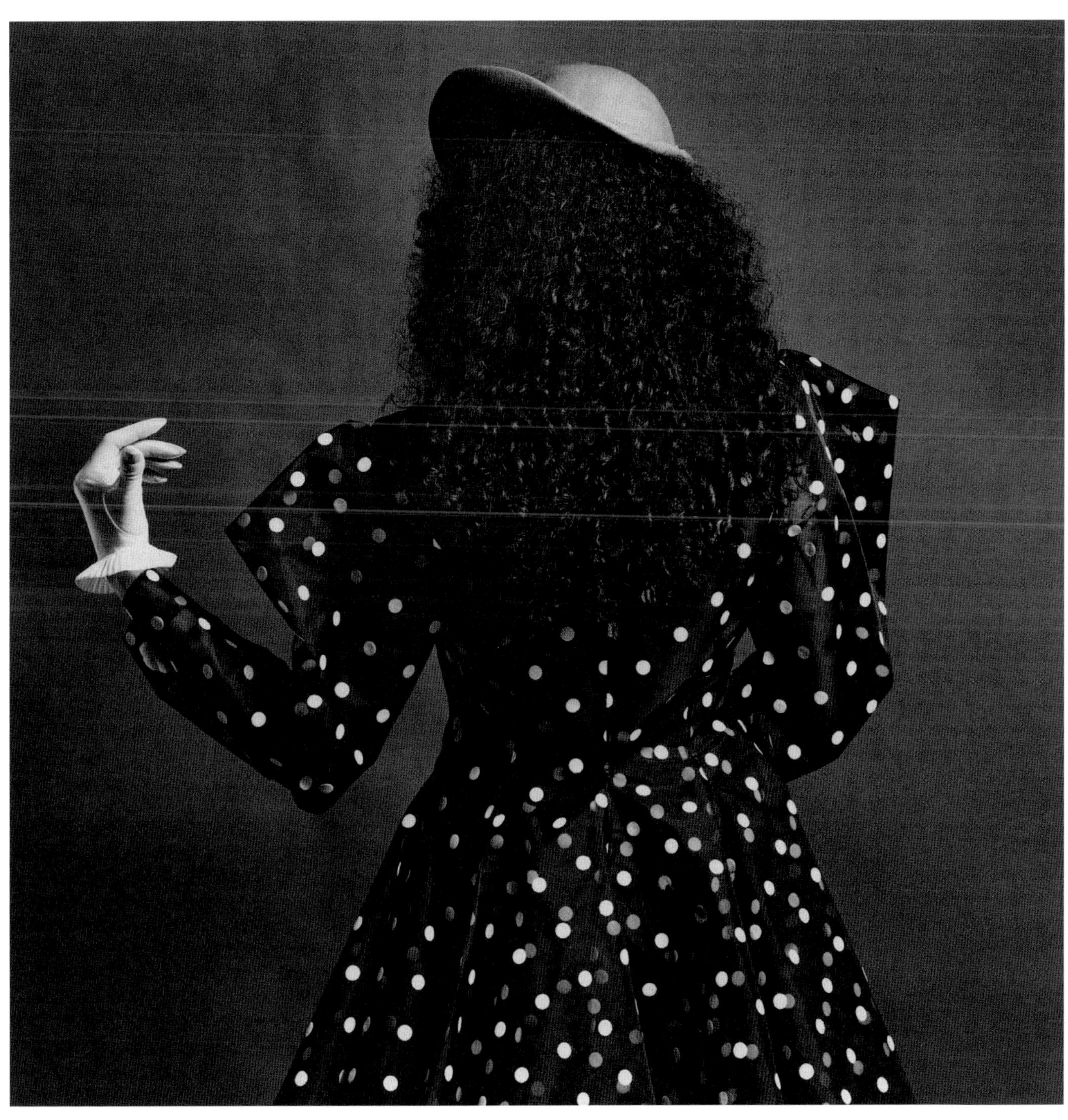

Henry Geldzahler, 1979

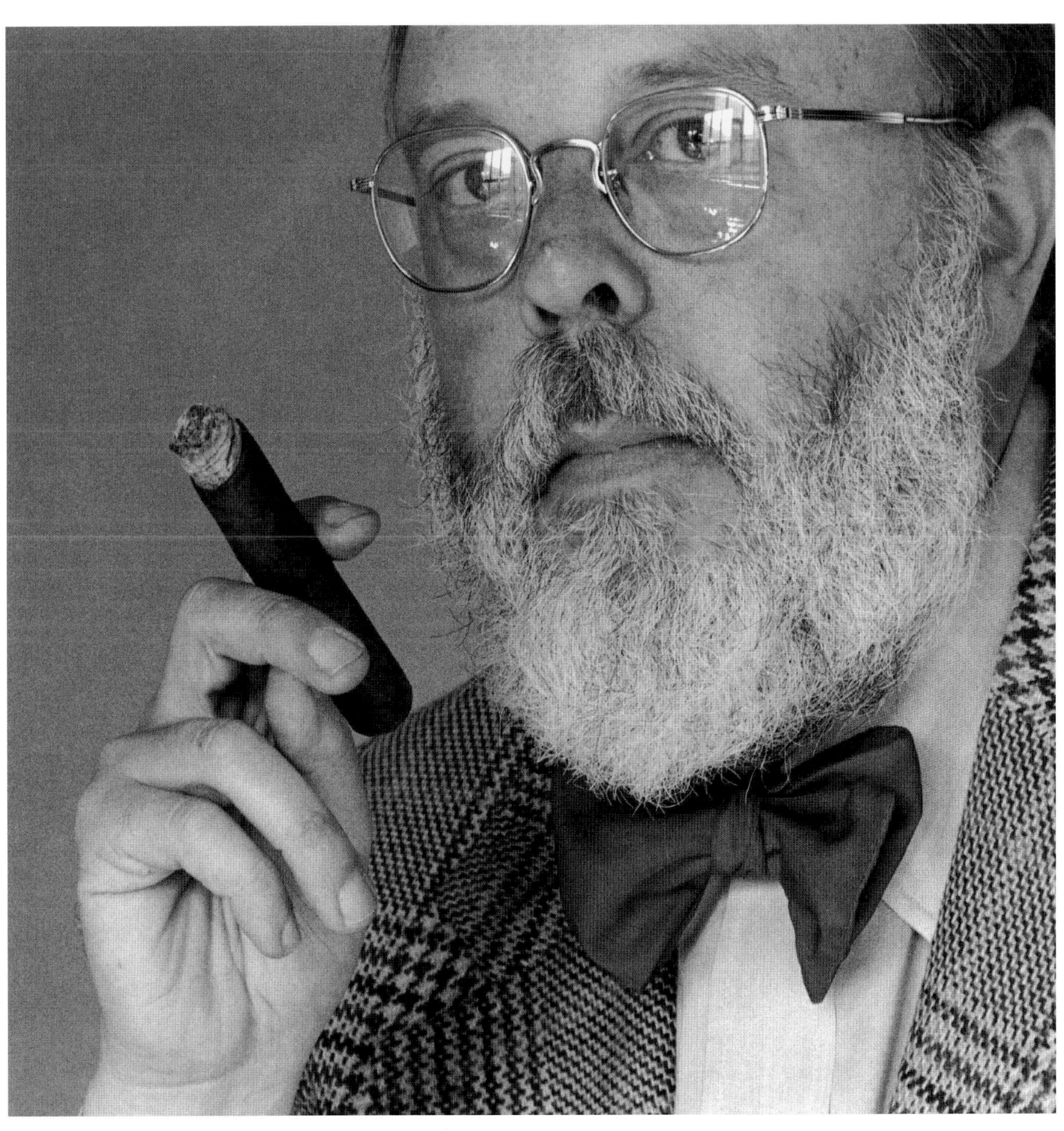

William Burroughs, 1979

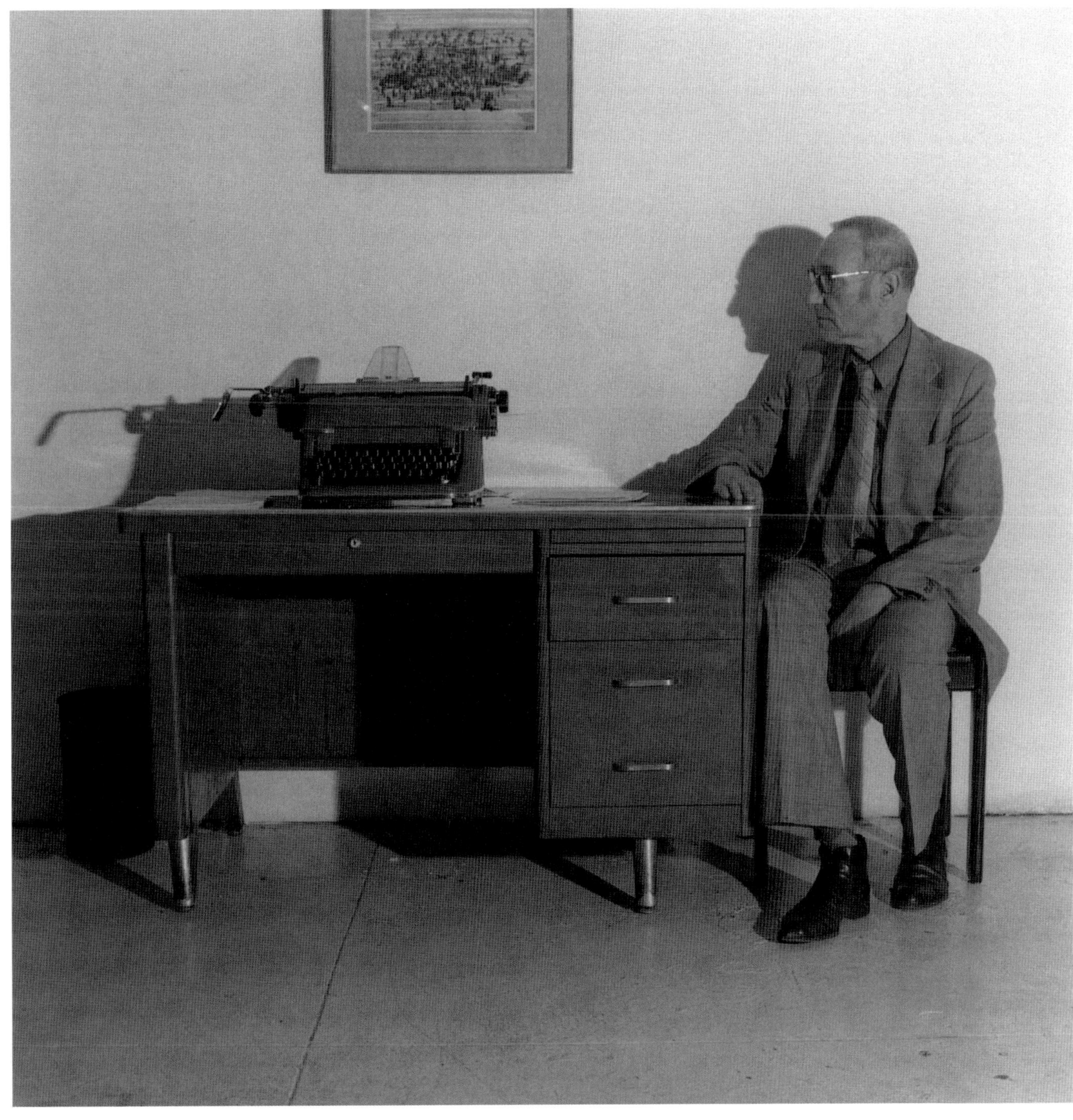

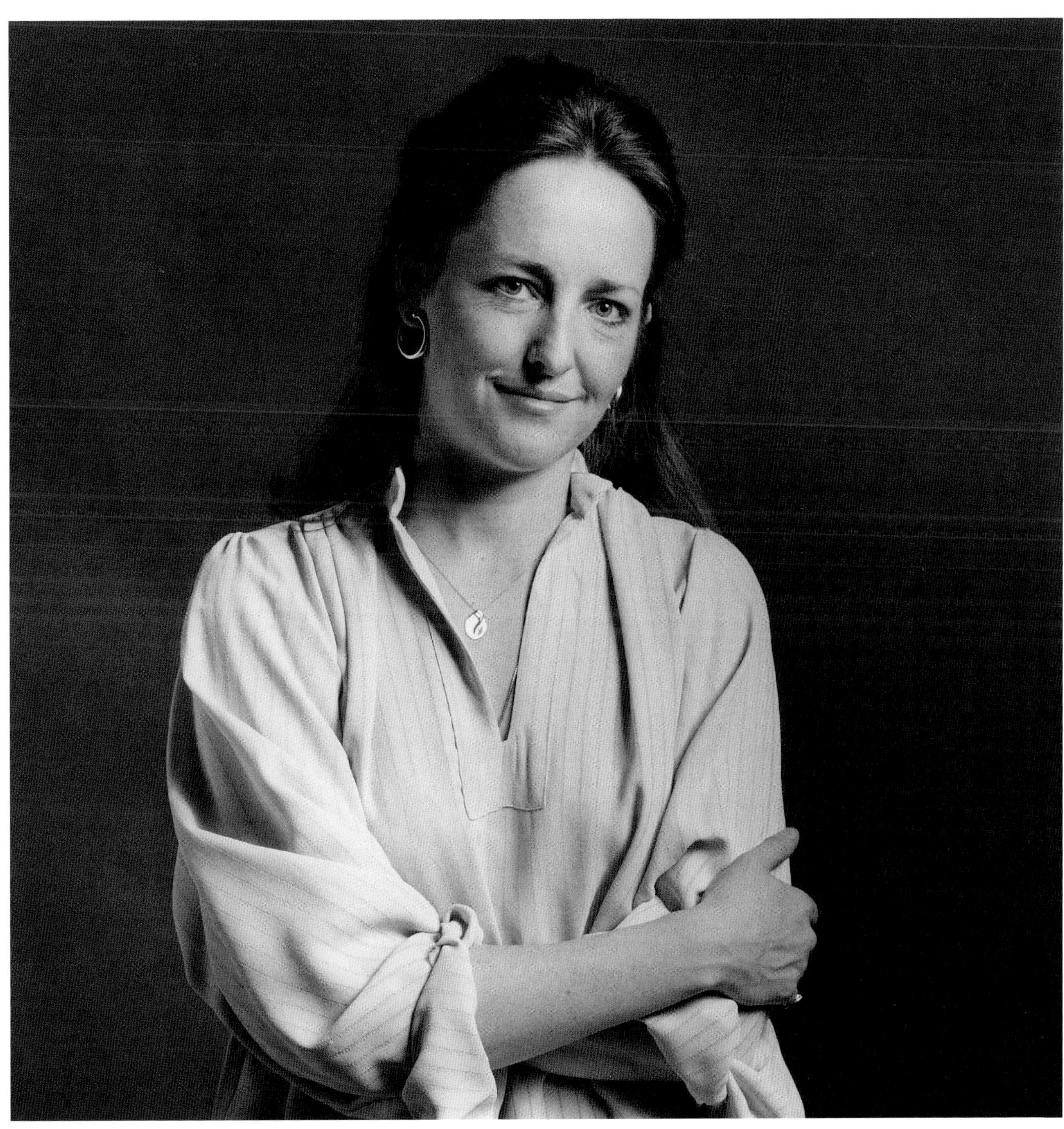

Brian Ridley and Lyle Heeter, 1979

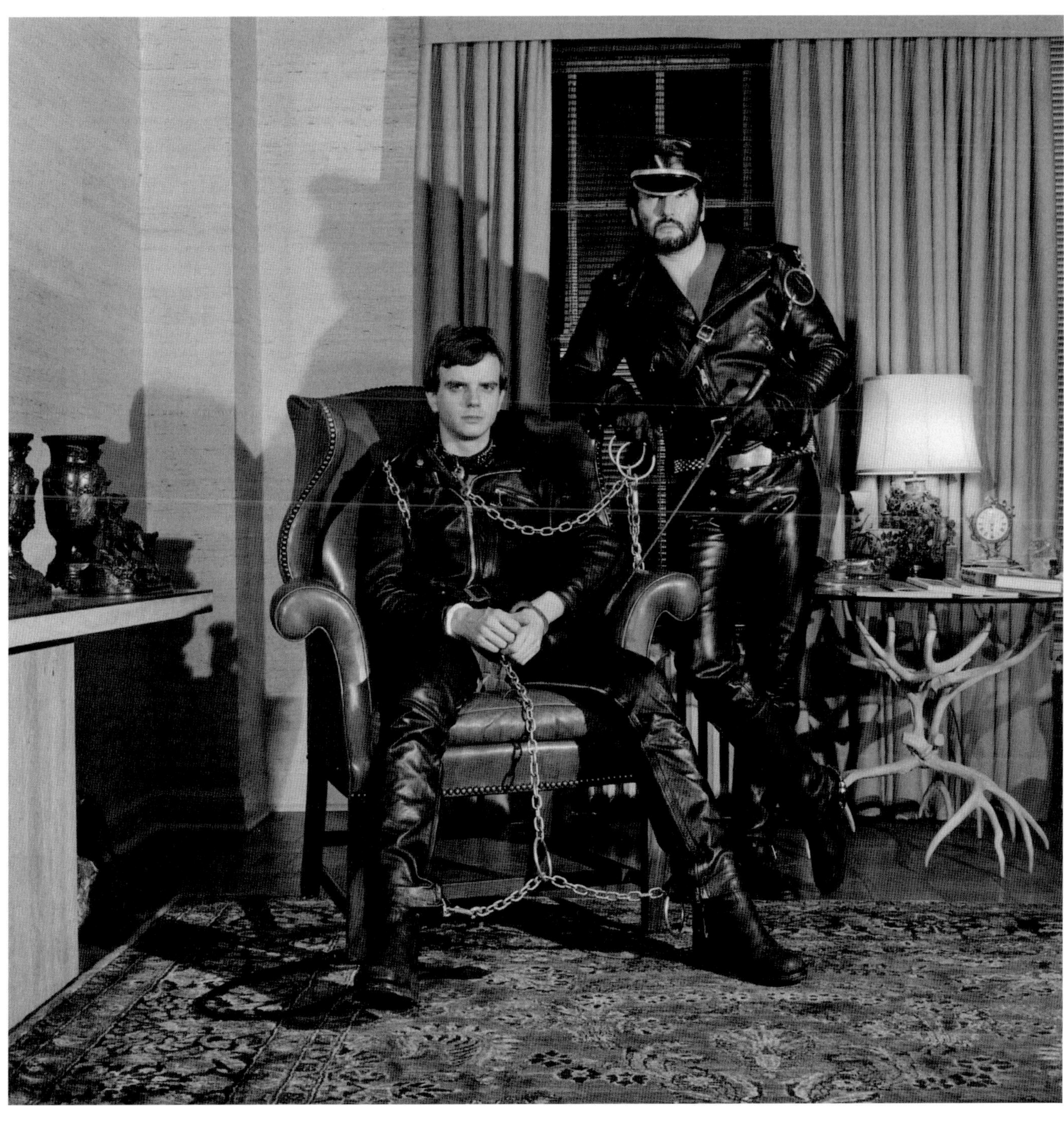

Fran Lebowitz, 1980

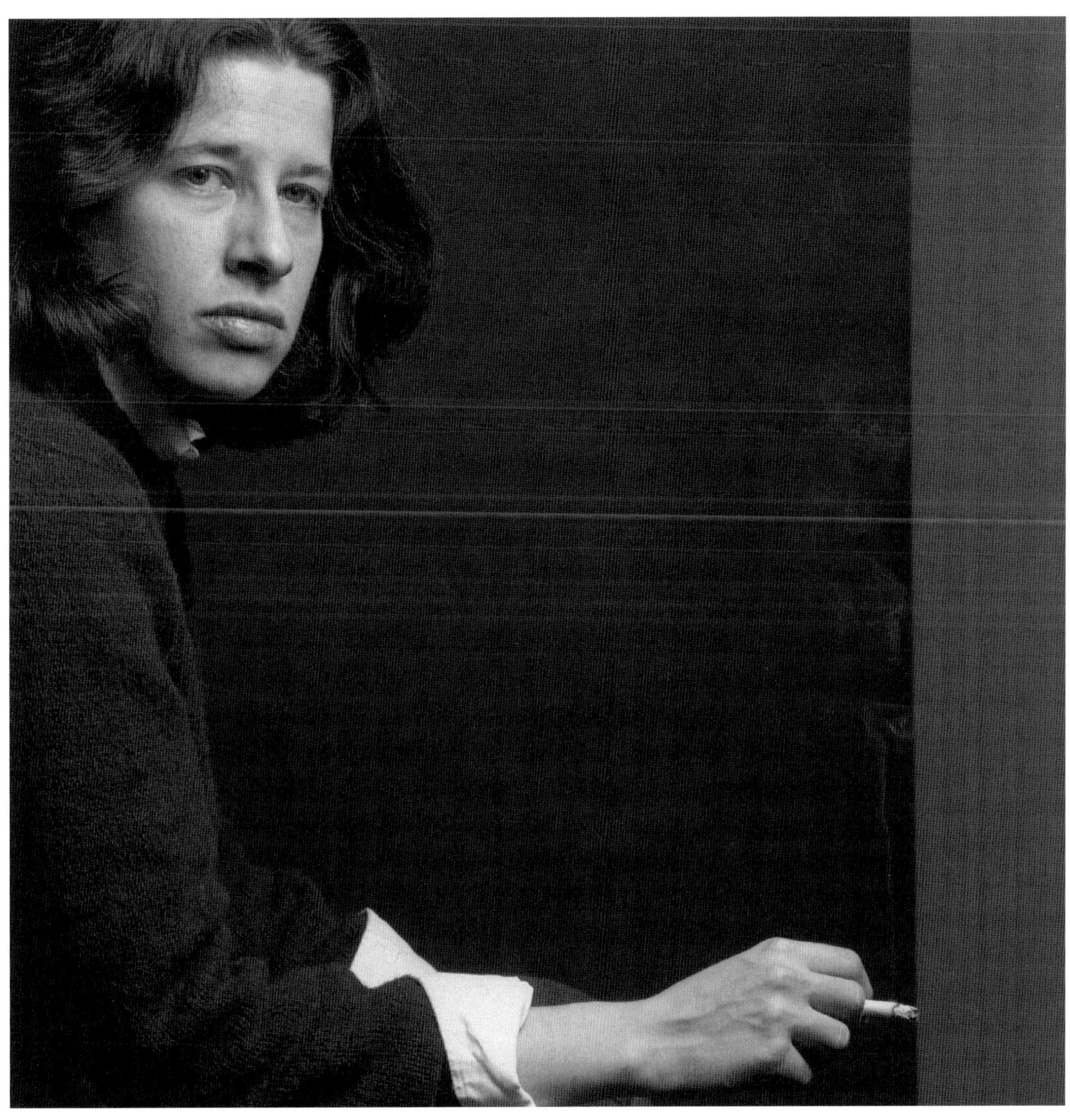

Roberta Neiman, 1980

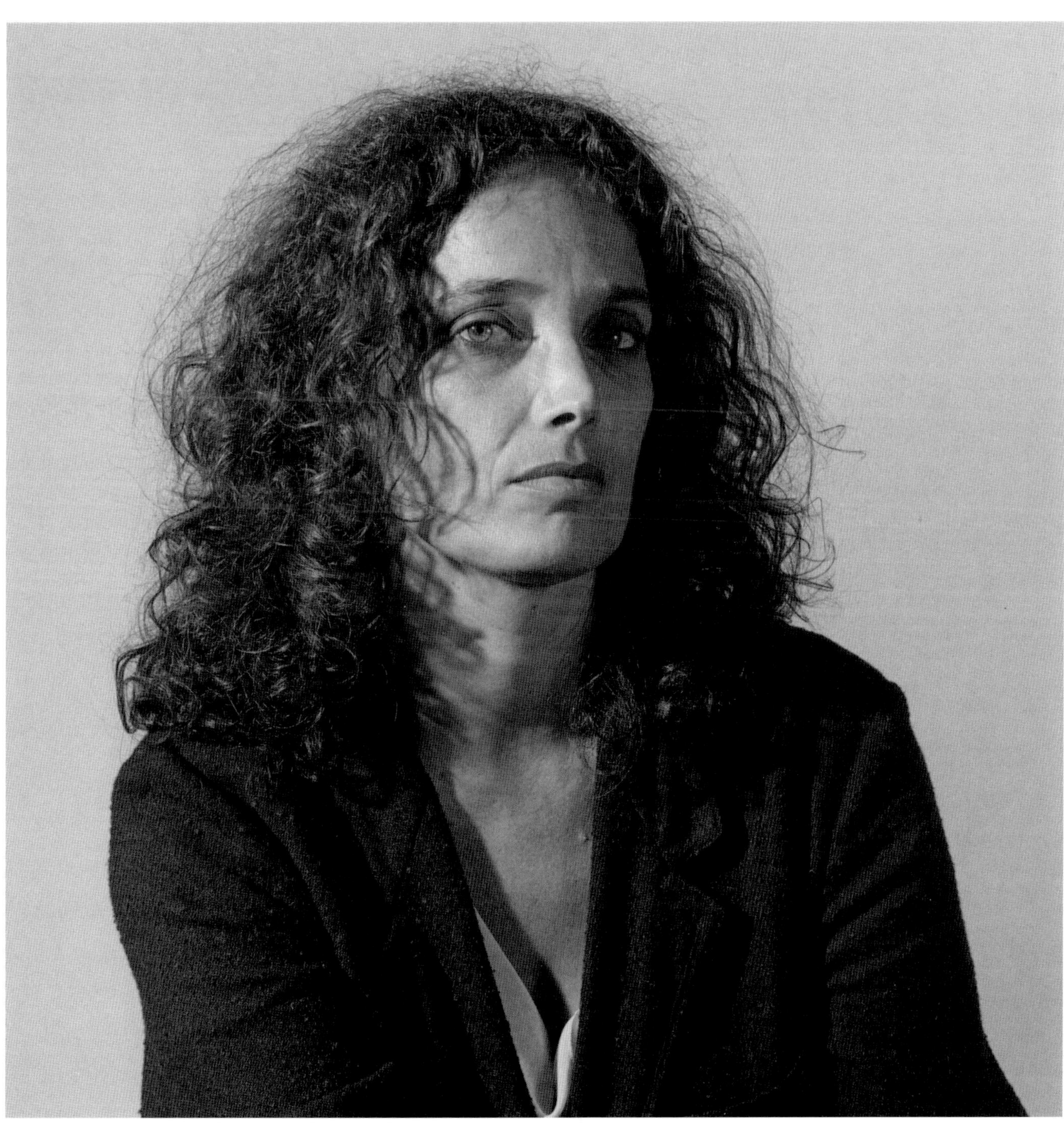

Self-Portrait, 1980

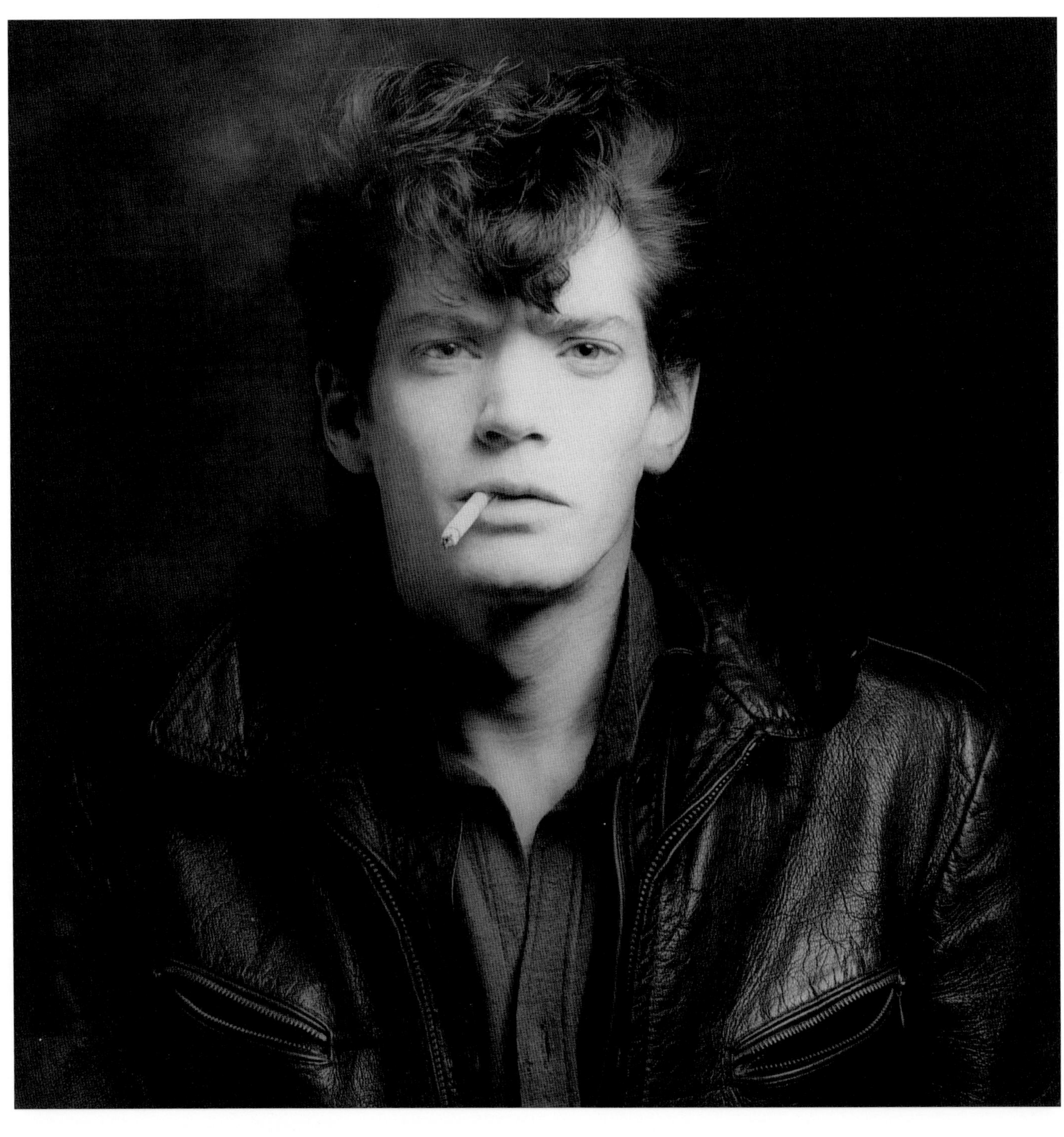

Self-Portrait, 1980

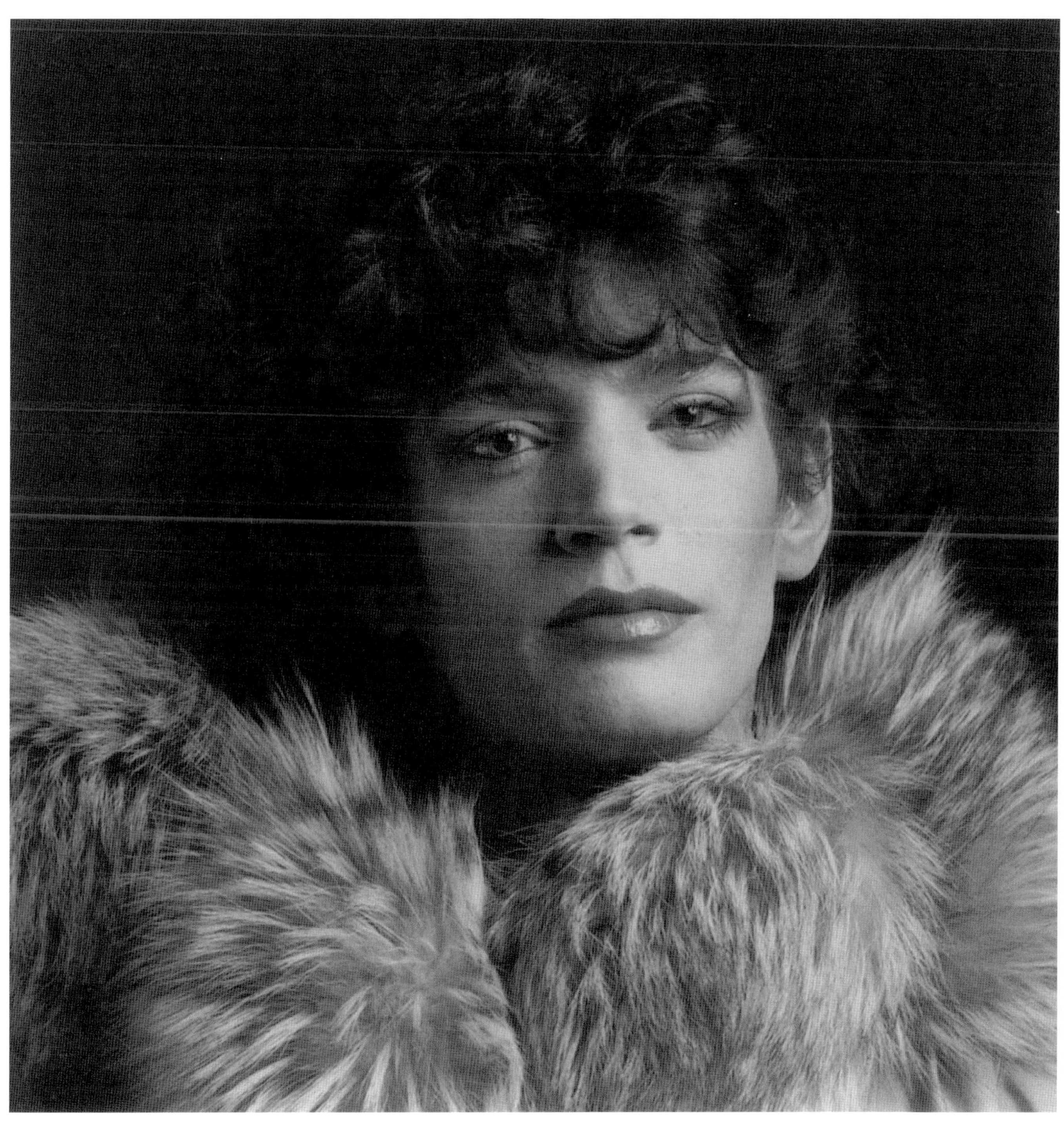

Gisèle Freund, 1980

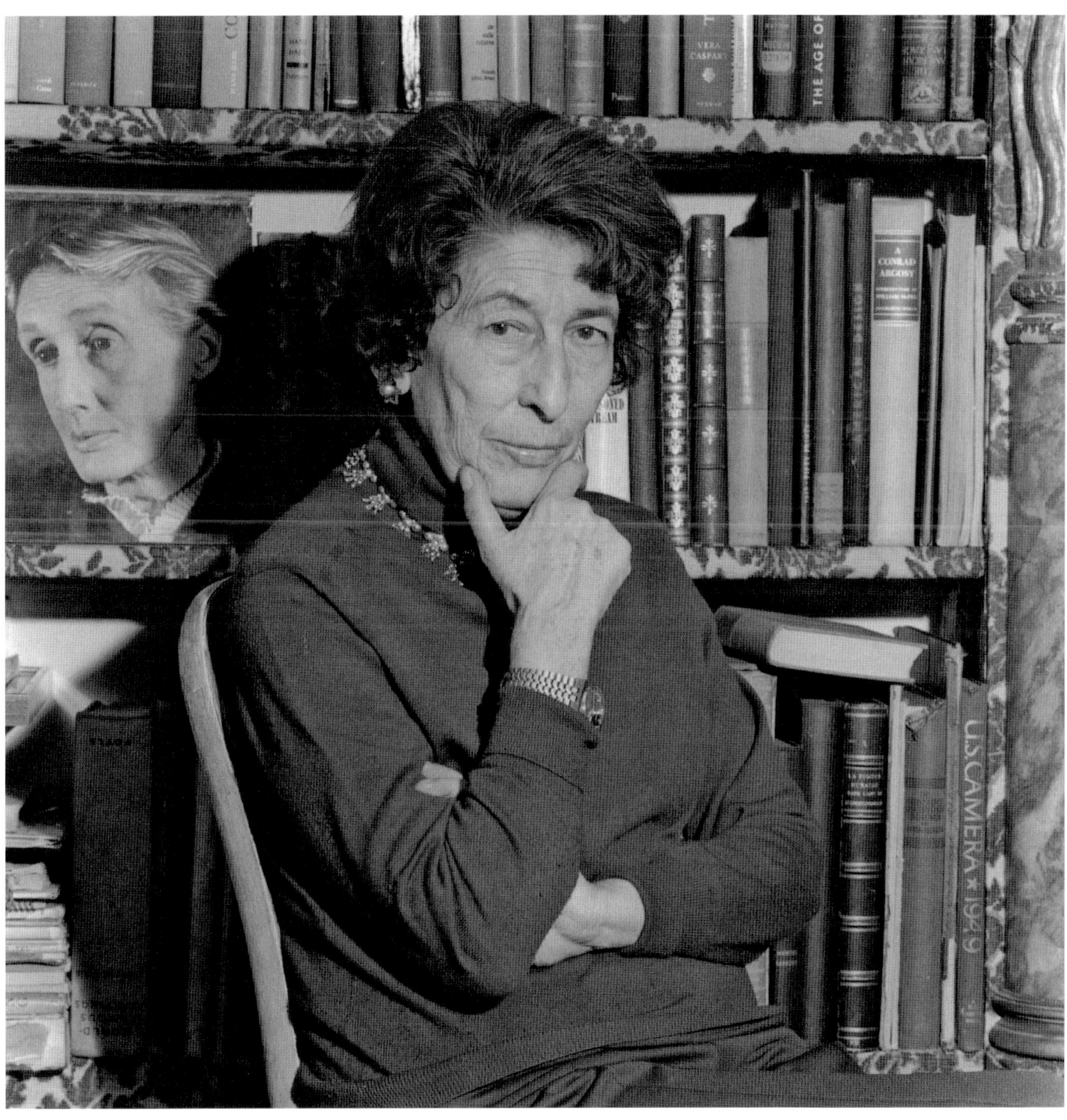

Plate 28 / Catalogue # 35

Thom Gunn, 1980

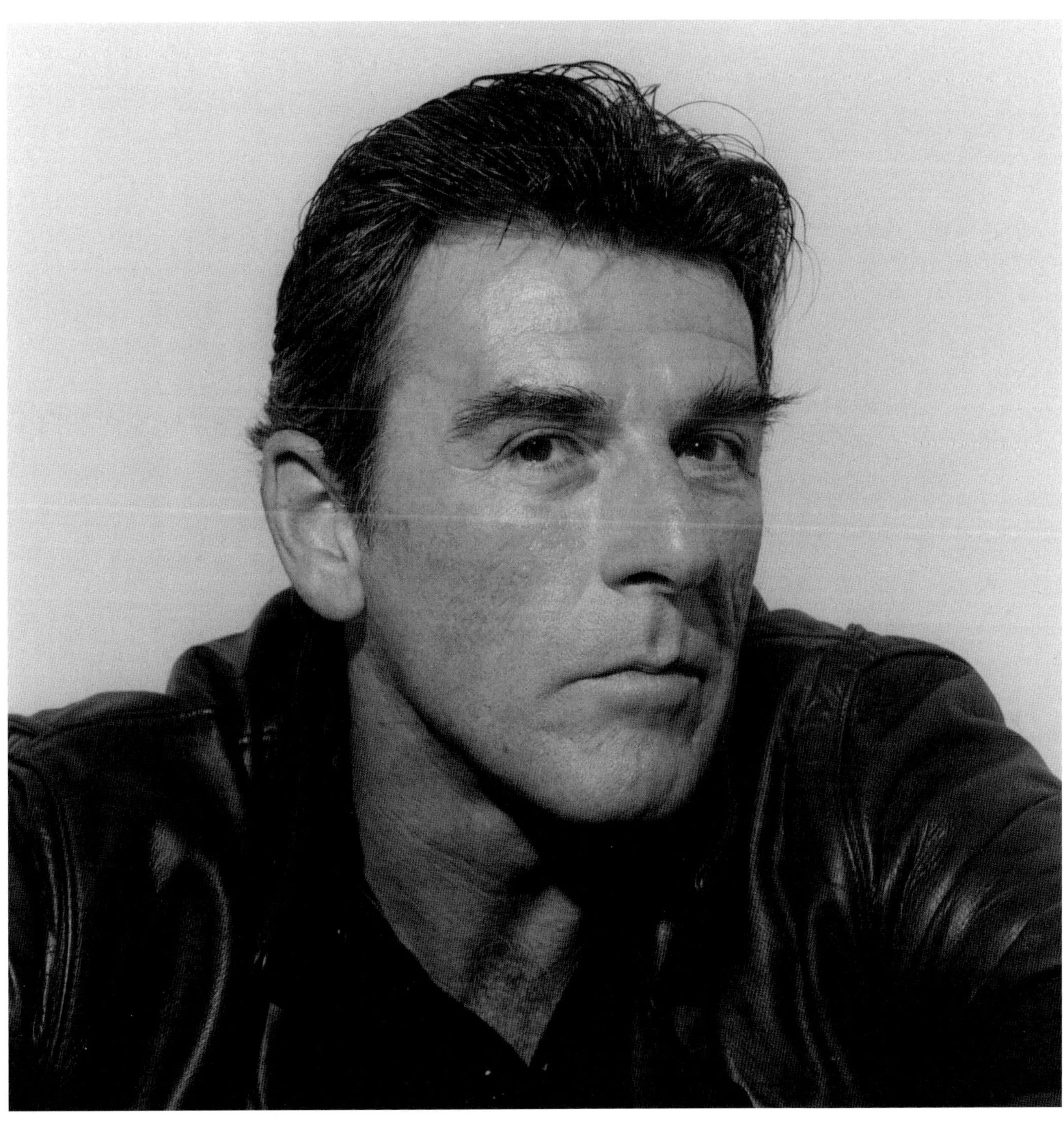

Cynthia Slater, 1980

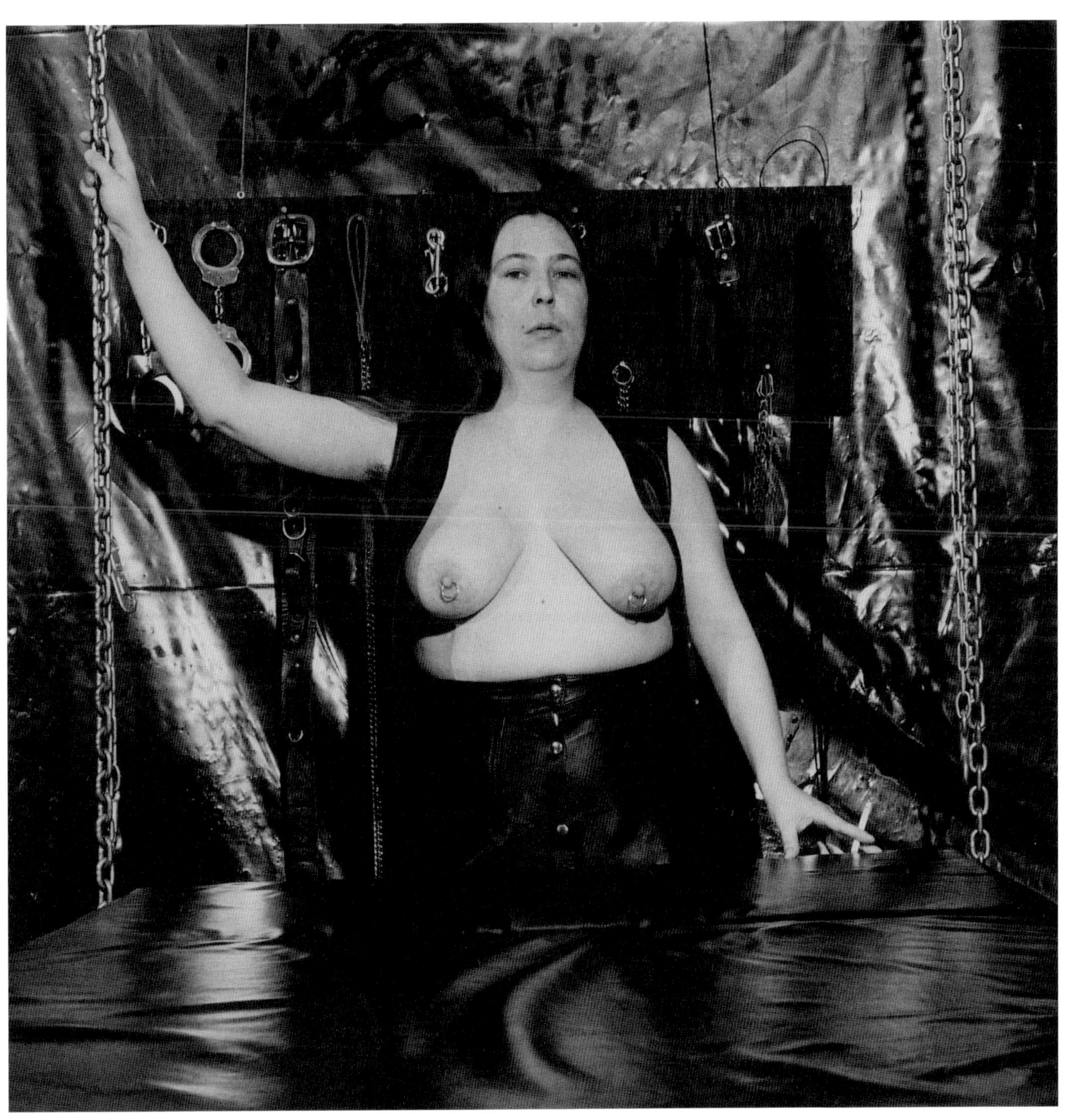

Paloma Picasso, 1980

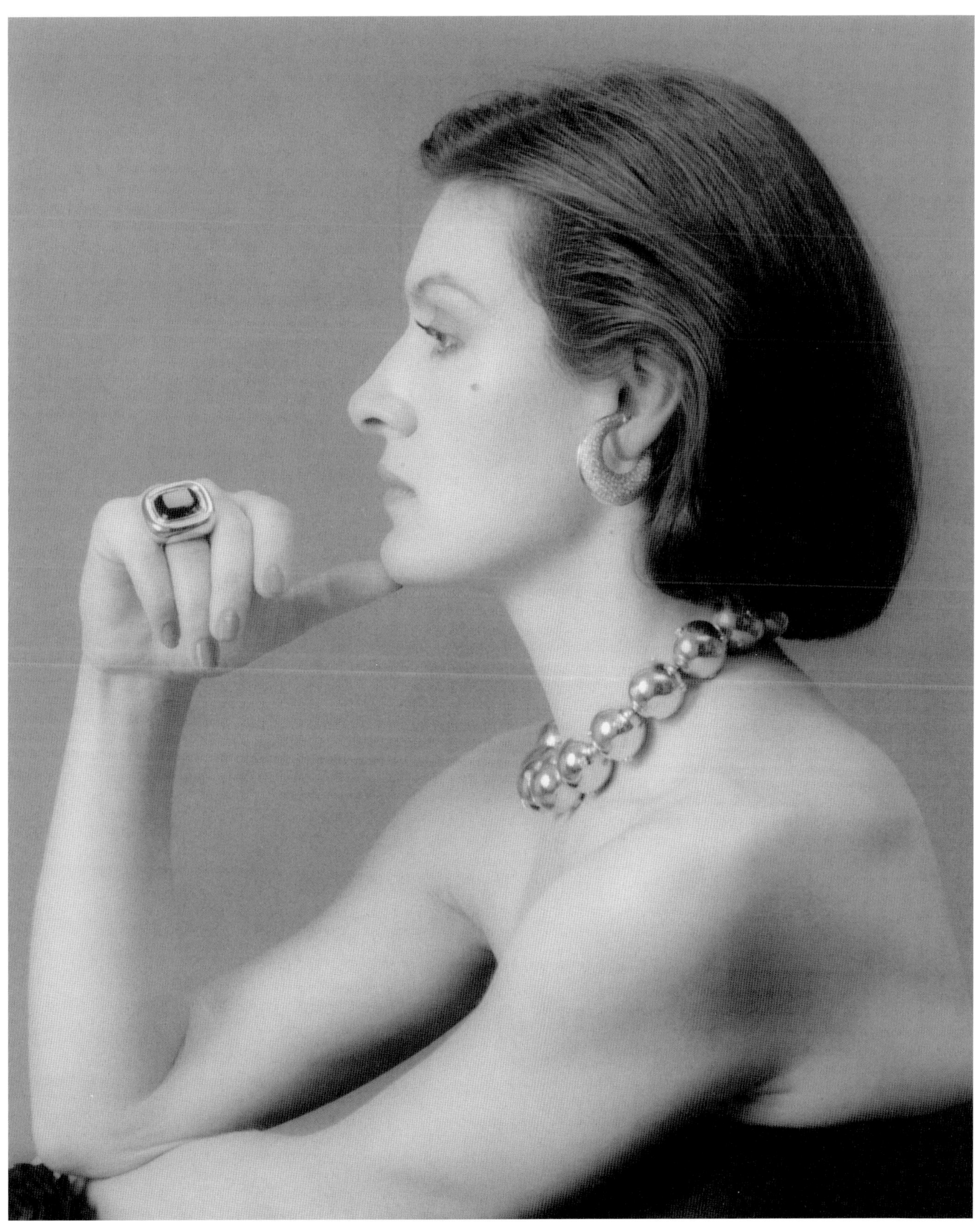

Klaus Kertess, 1980

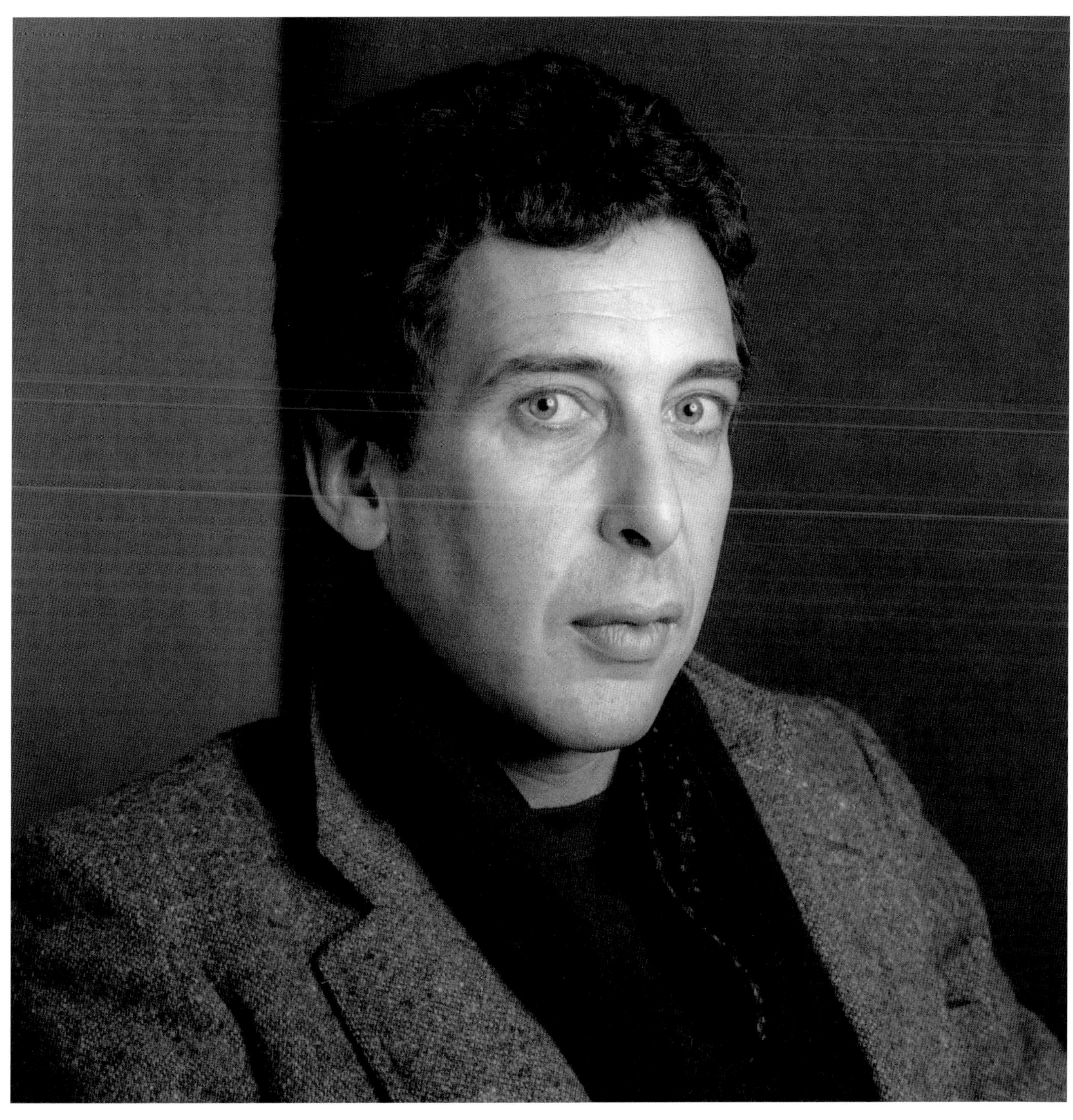

Lisette Model, 1980

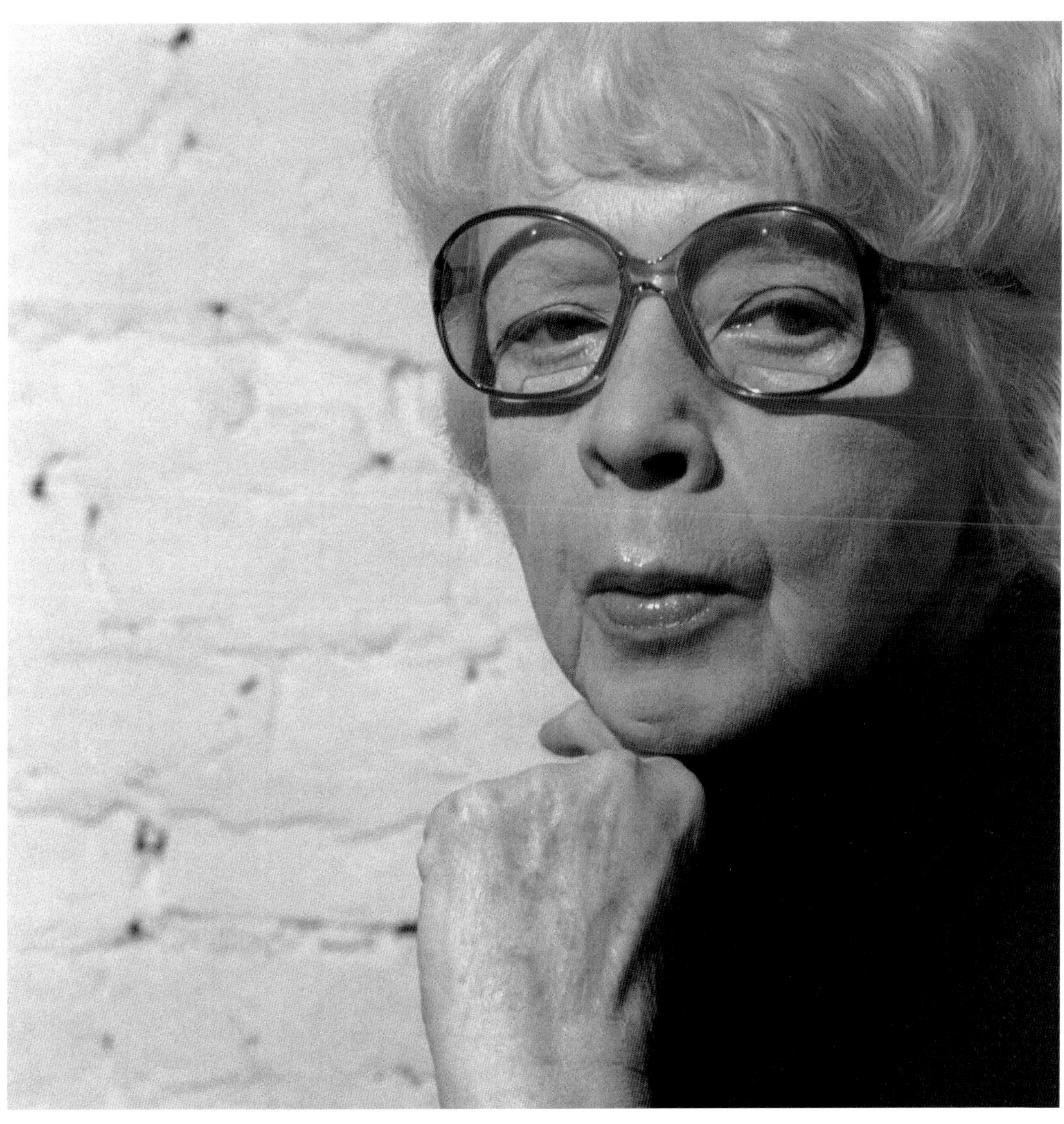

Iggy Pop, 1985

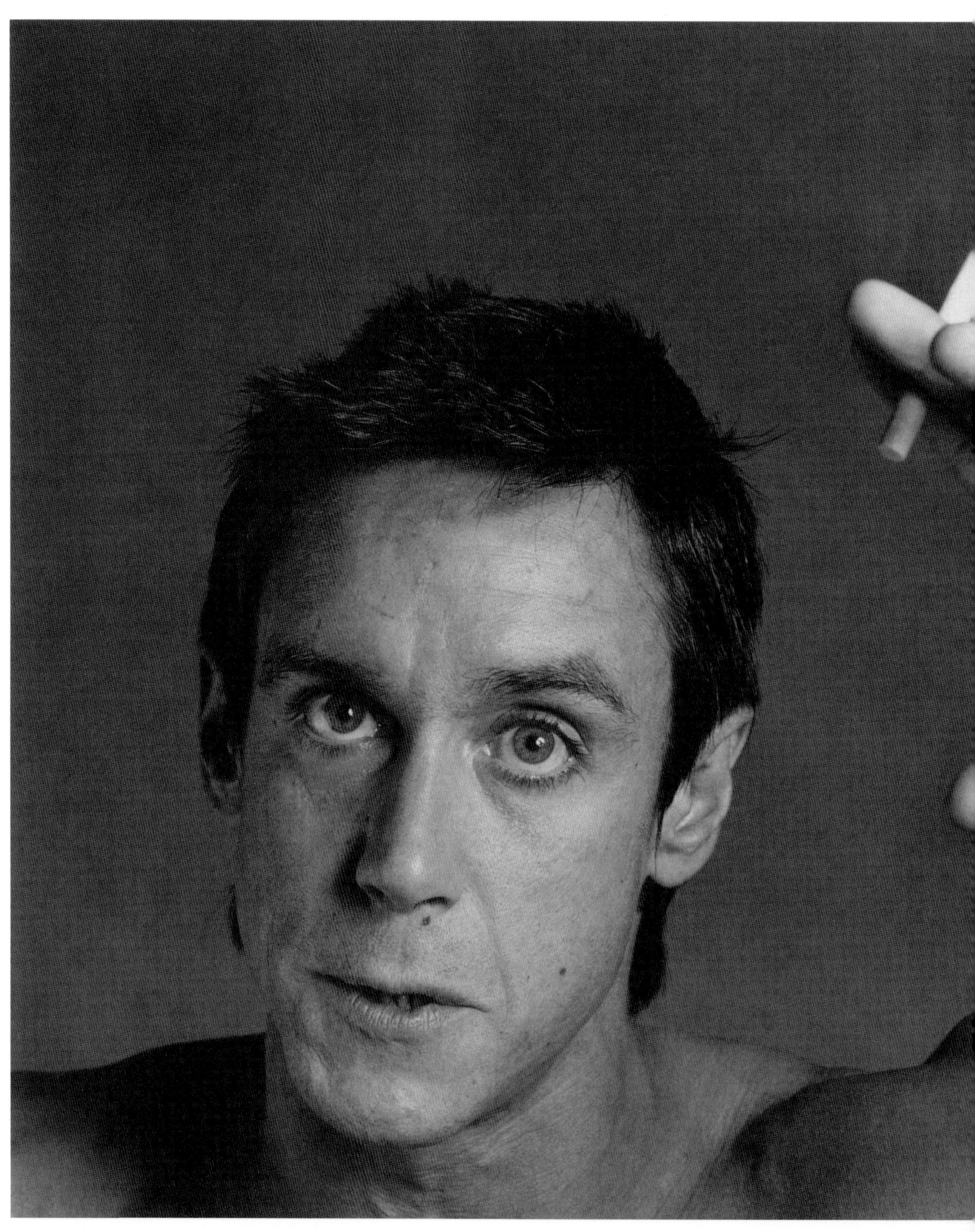

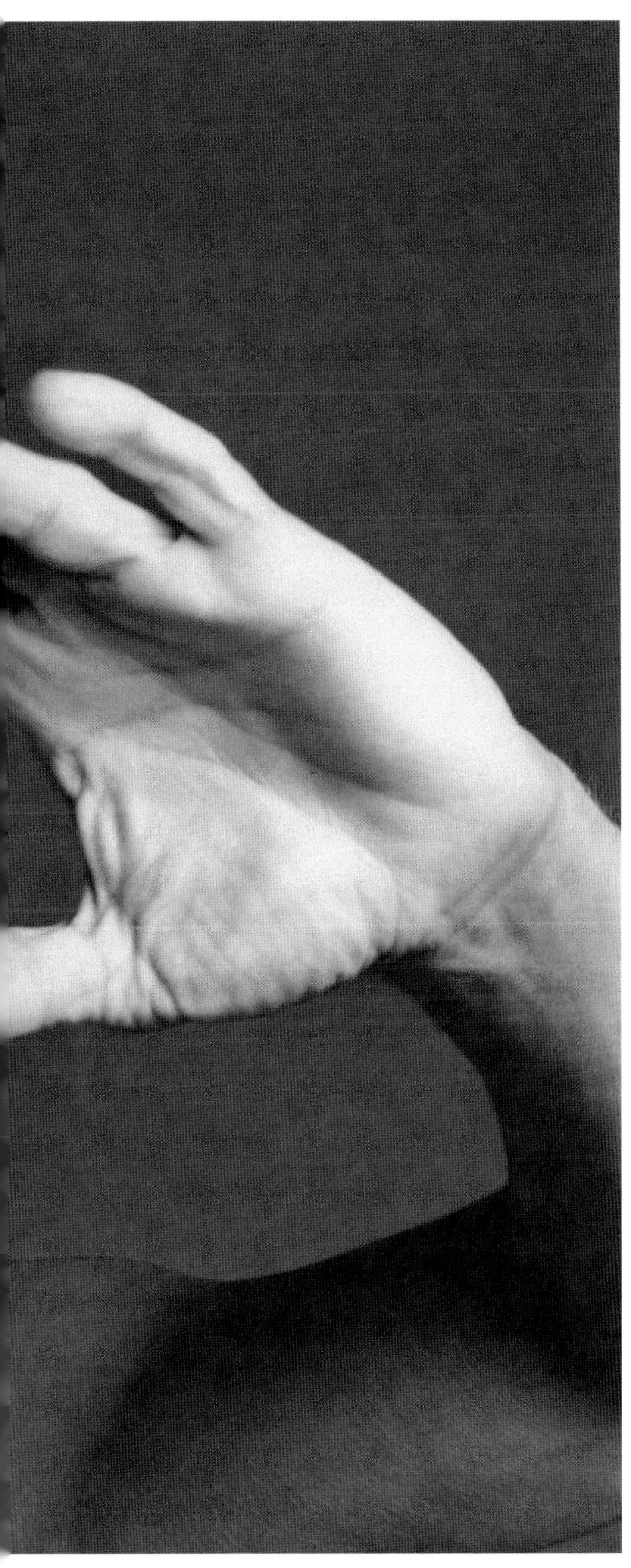

Truman Capote, 1981

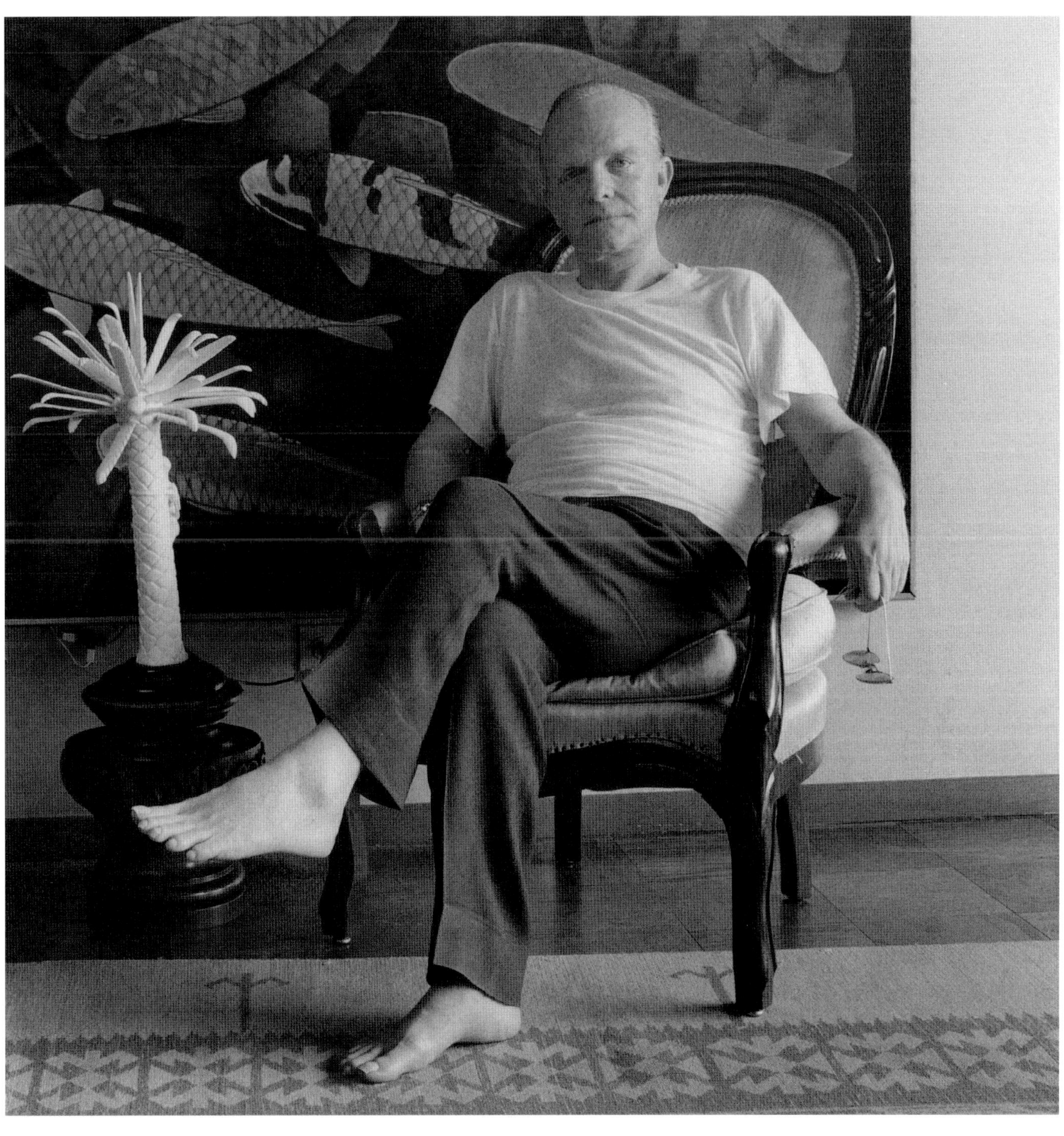

Plate 35 / Catalogue # 26

Larry Desmedt, 1981

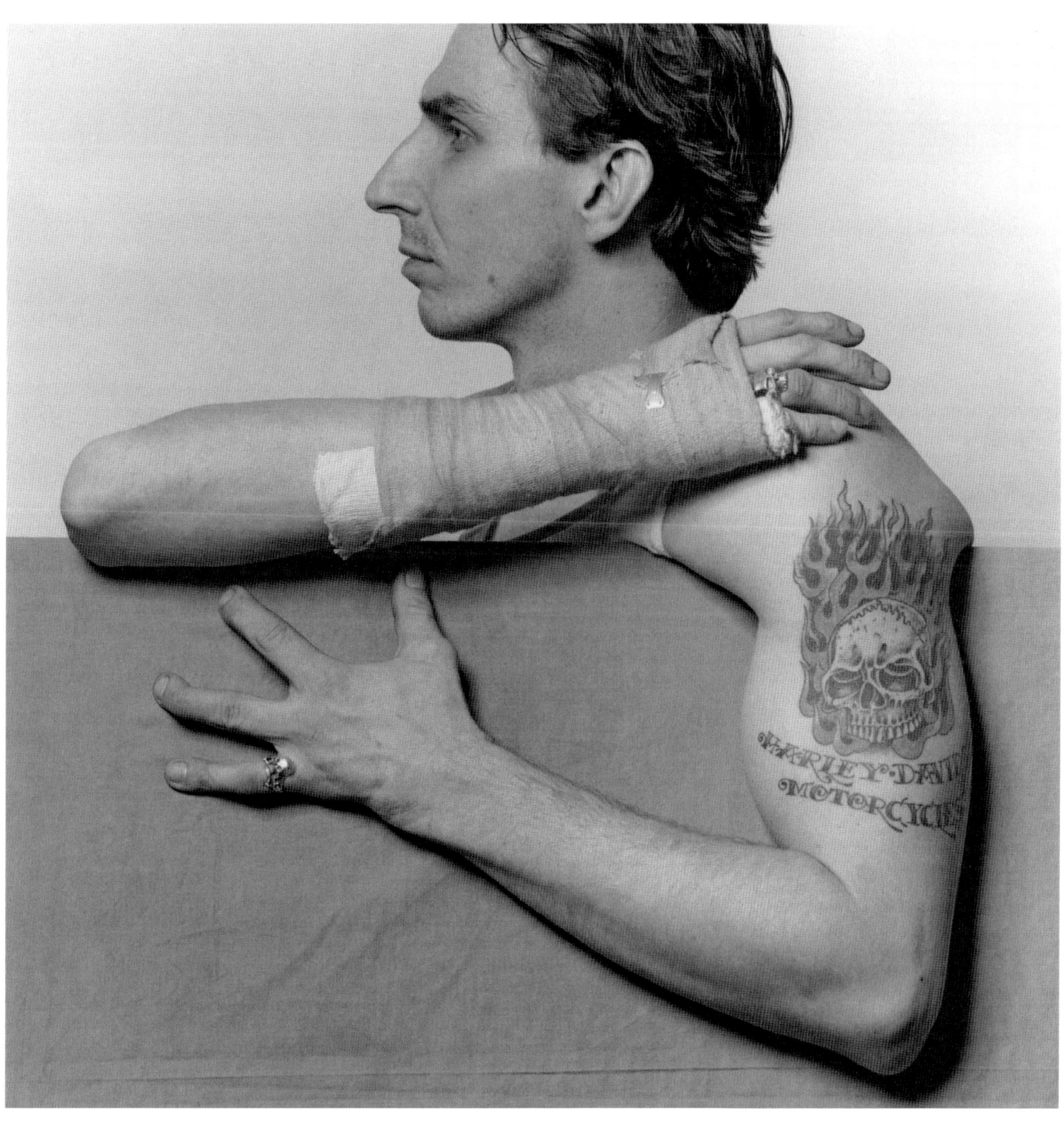

Lee Krasner, 1982

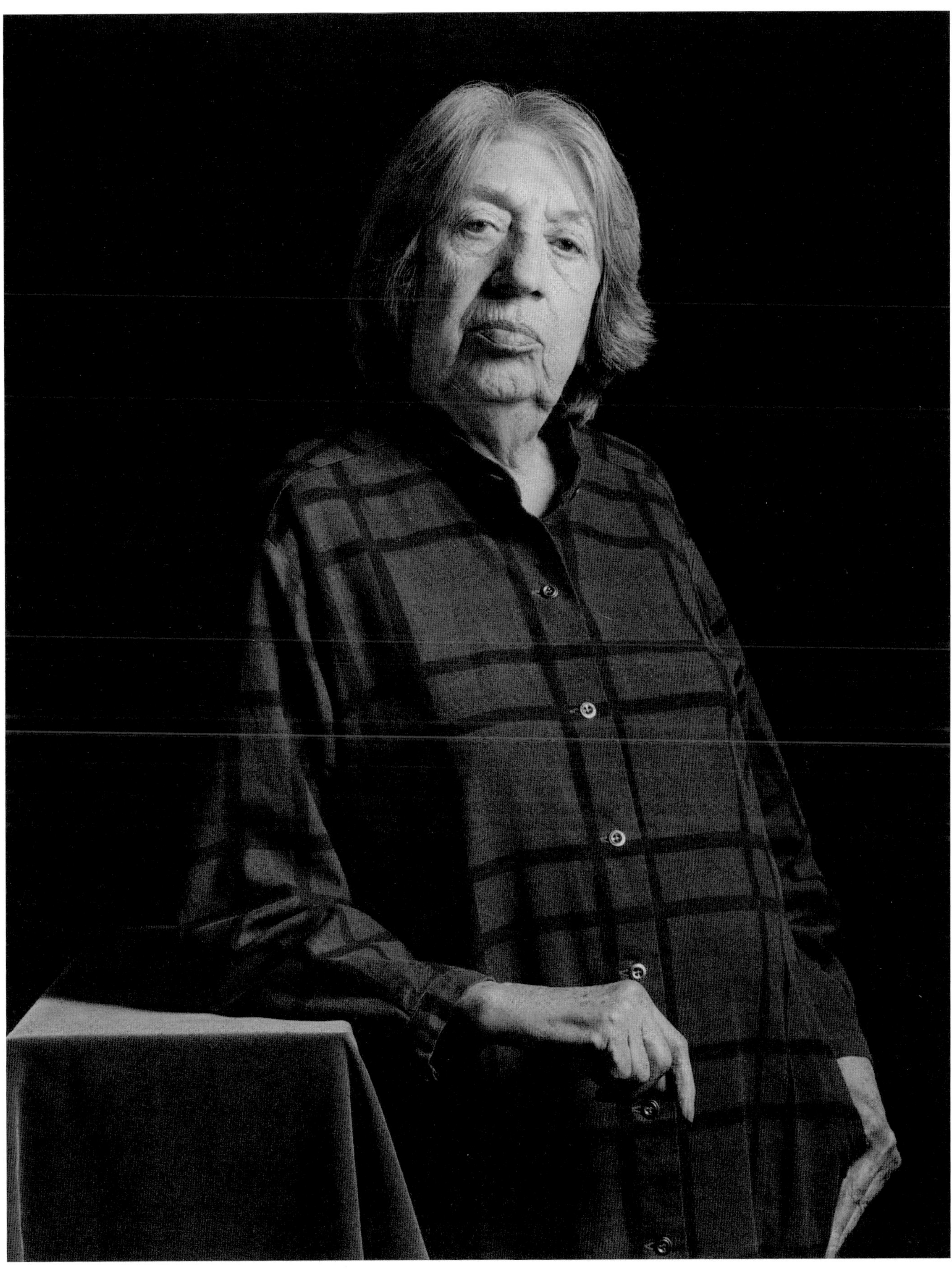

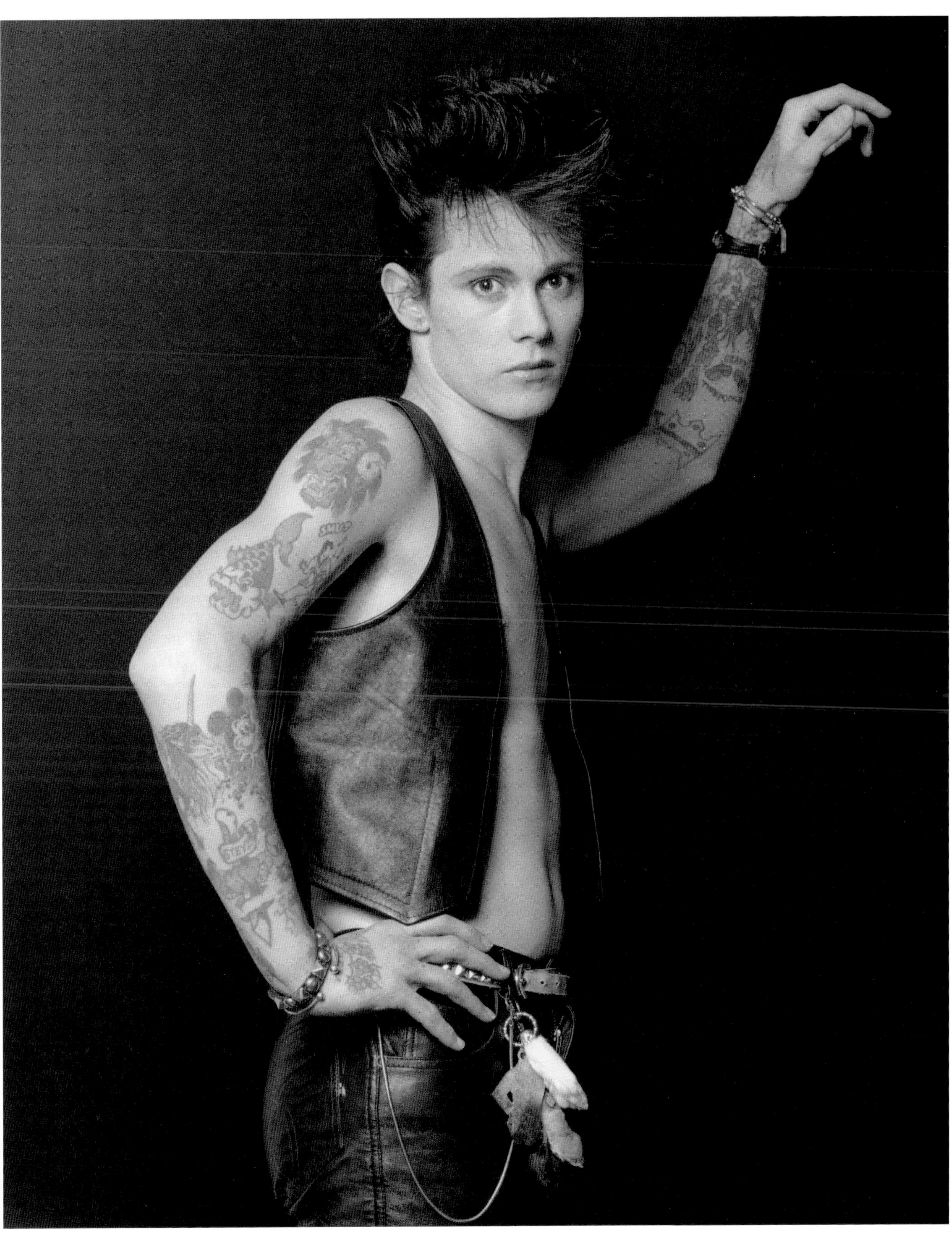

Lawrence Weiner, 1982

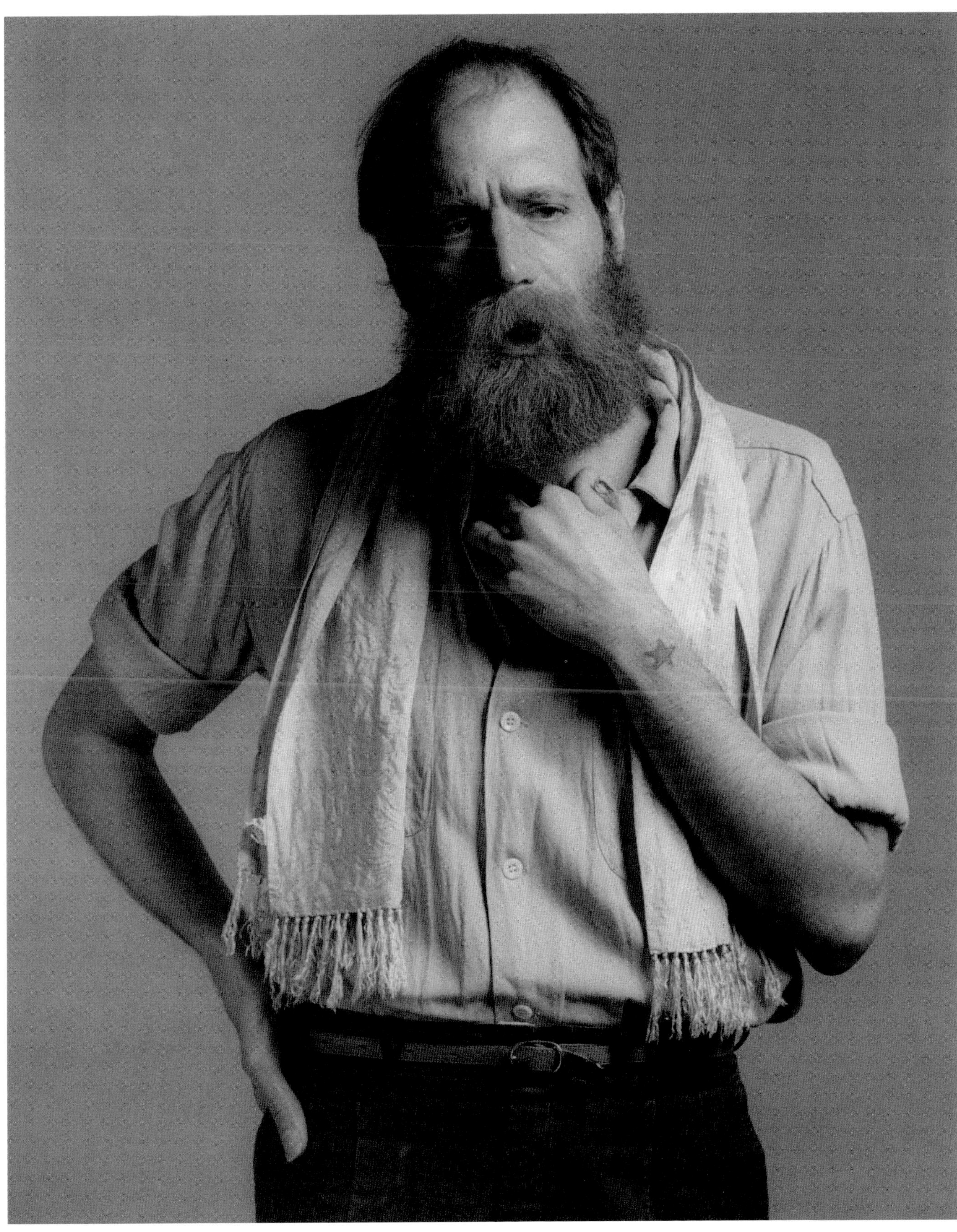

Fay Gold, 1982

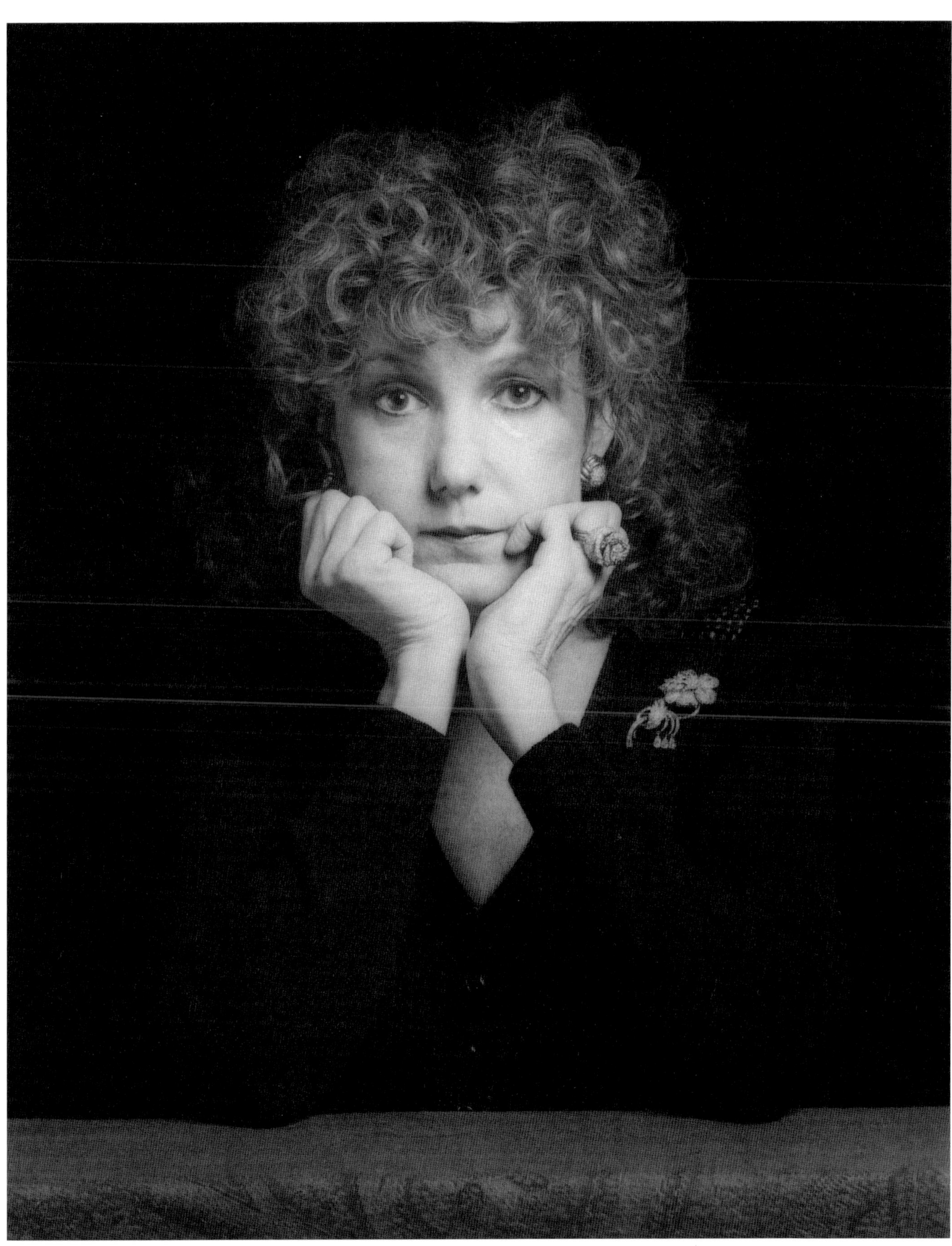

Kathleen Turner, 1982

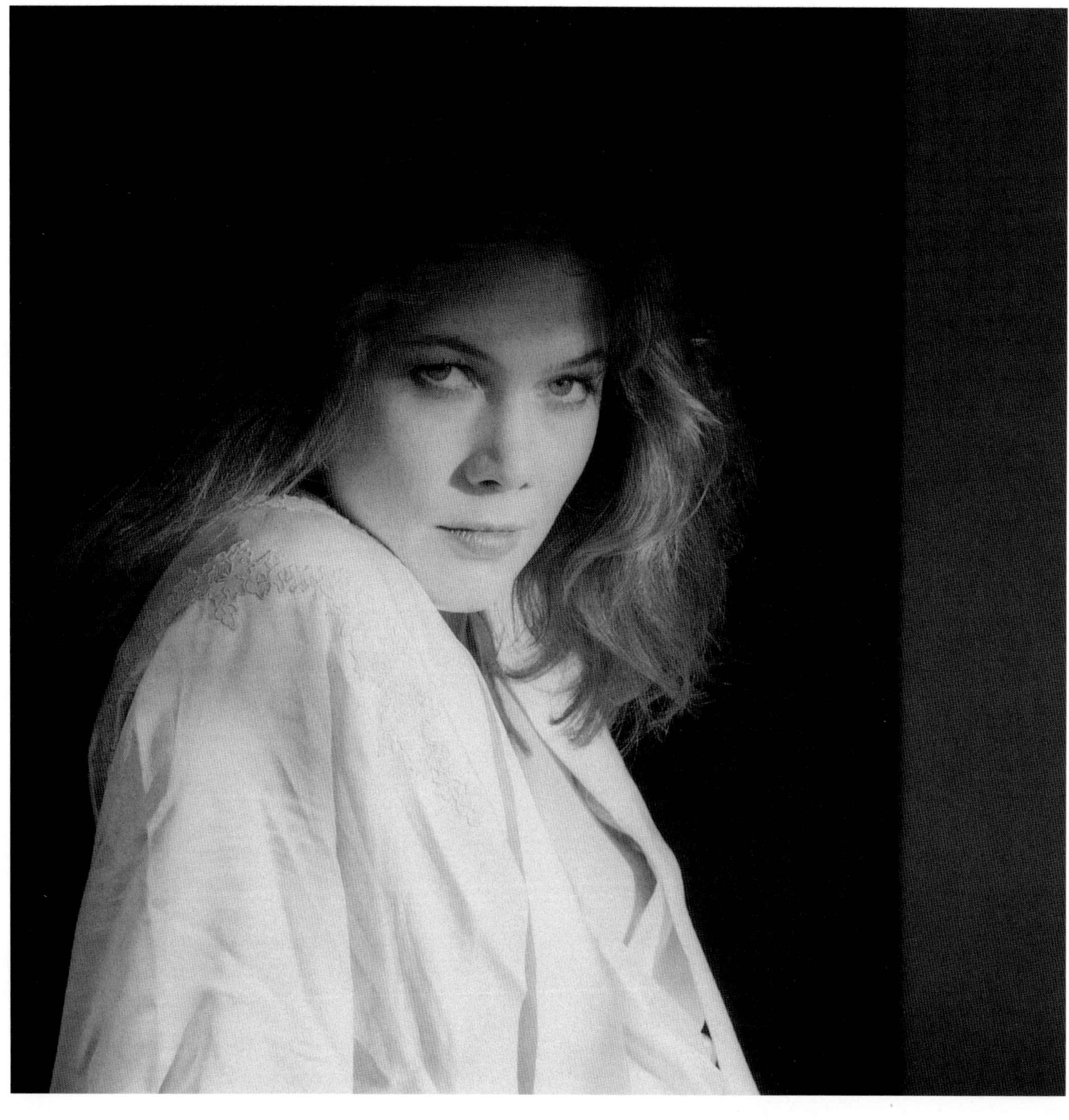

Donald Cann, 1982

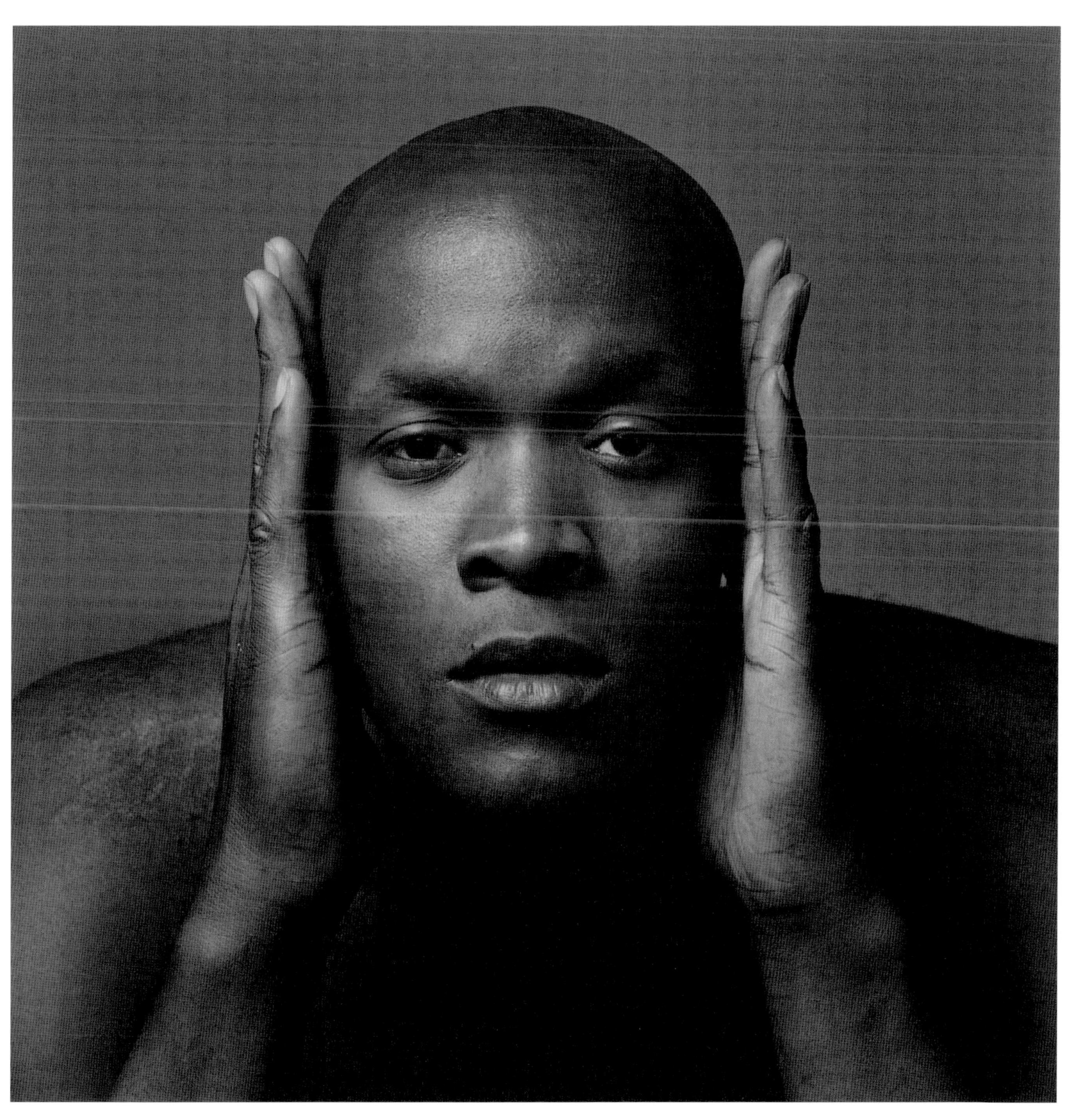

Francesco Clemente, 1982

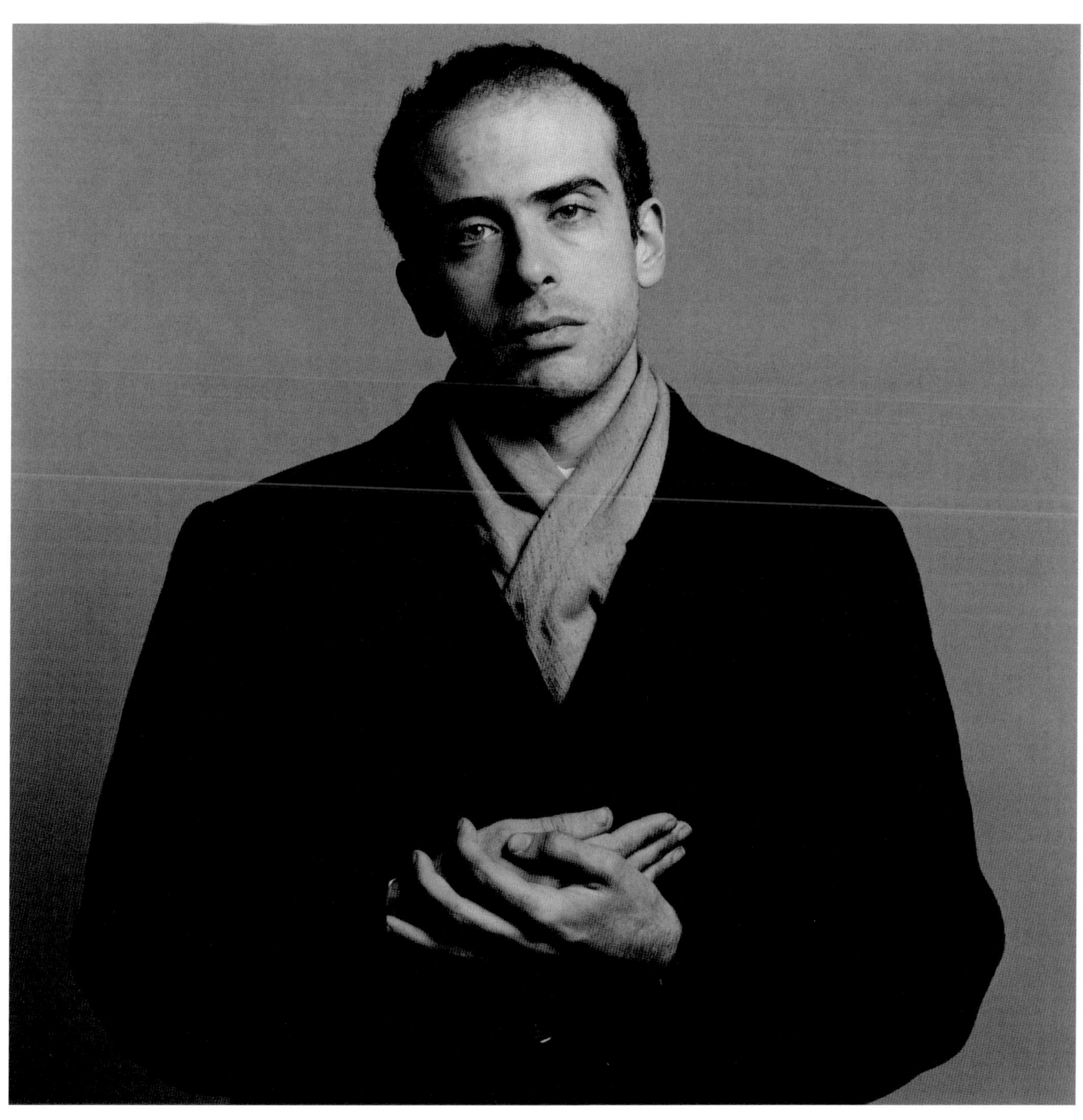

Plate 43 / Catalogue # 22

Glenn Close, 1982

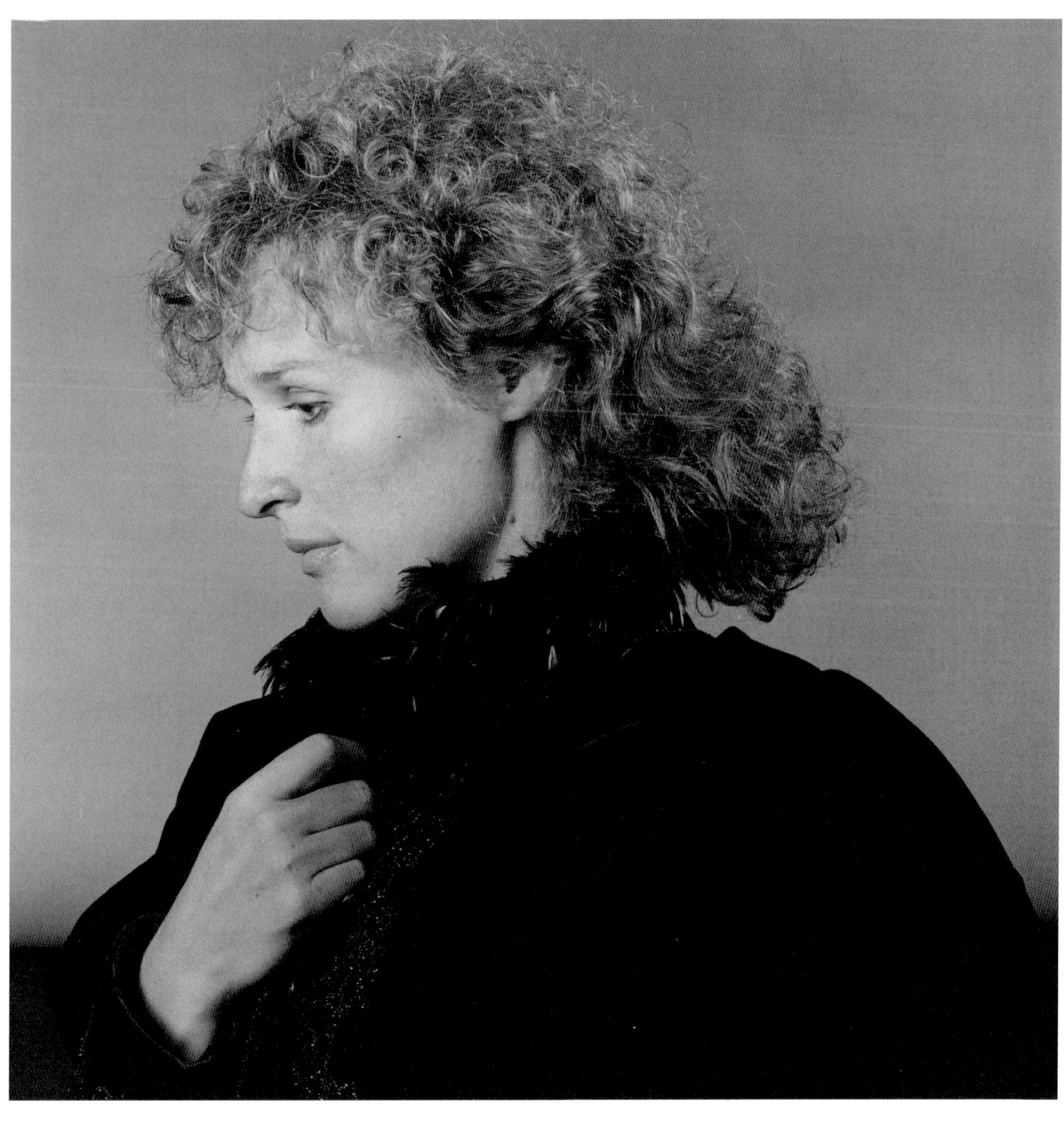

Louise Bourgeois, 1982

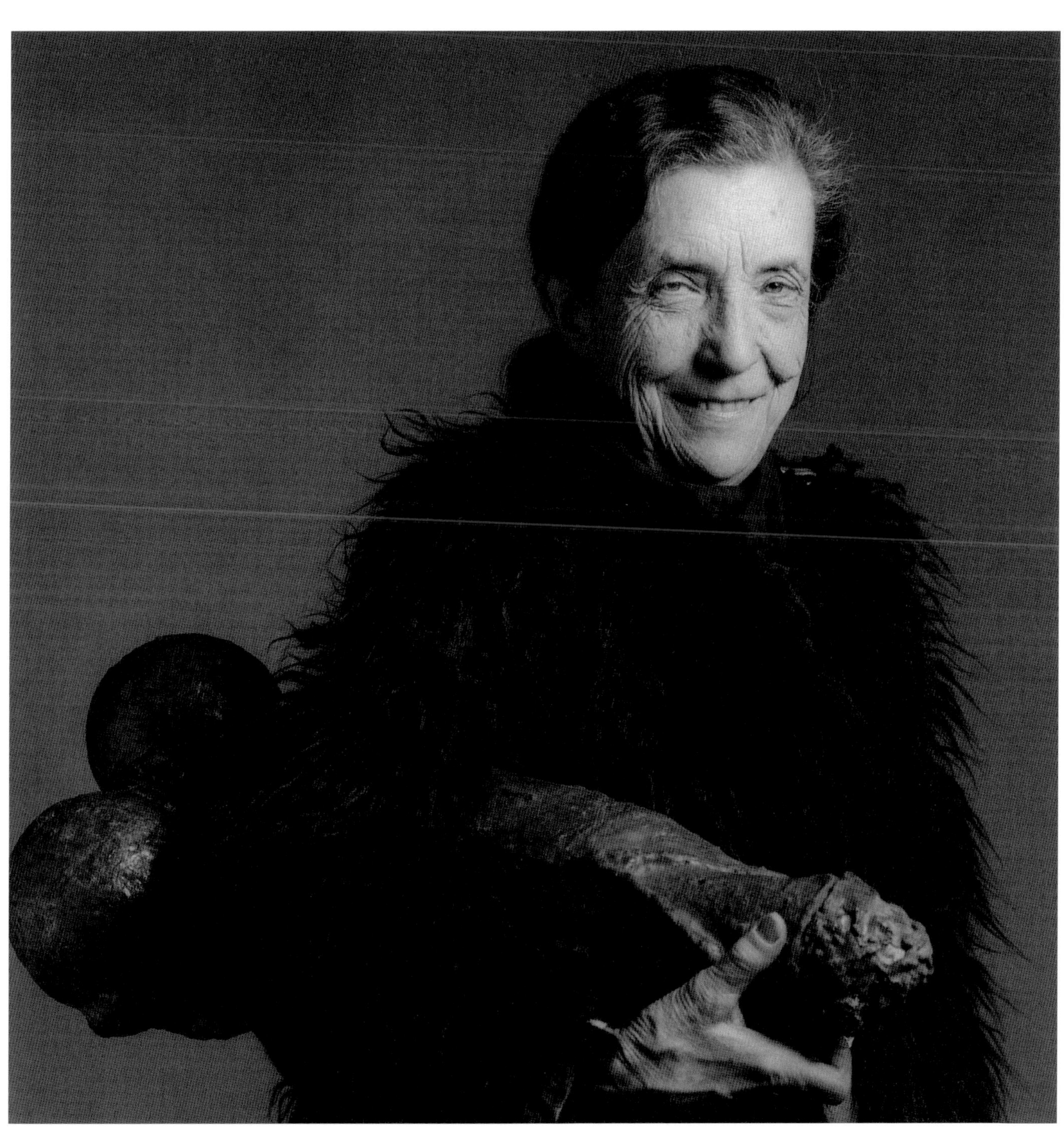

Richard Gere, 1982

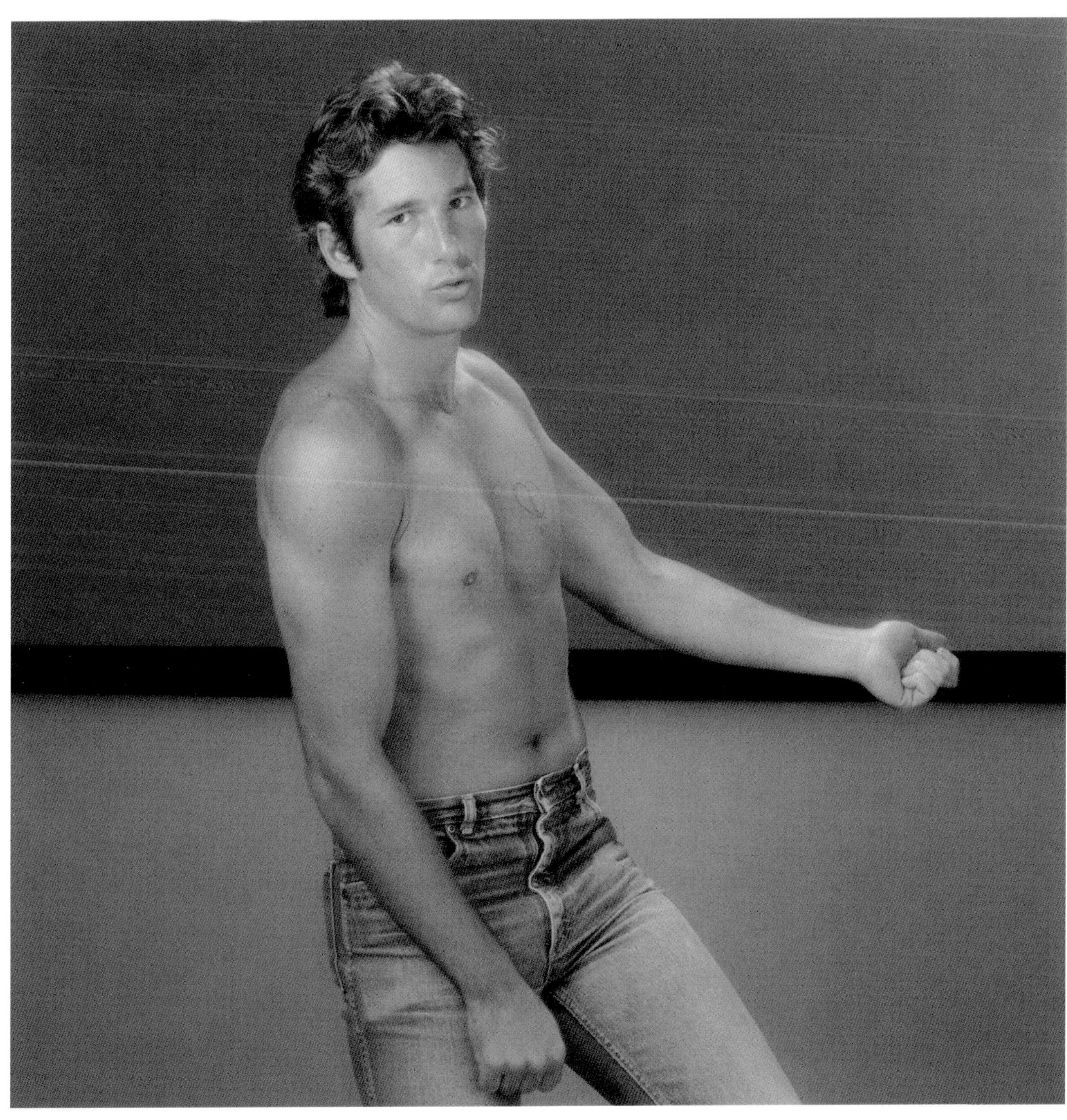

Plate 46 / Catalogue # 28 George Dureau, 1982

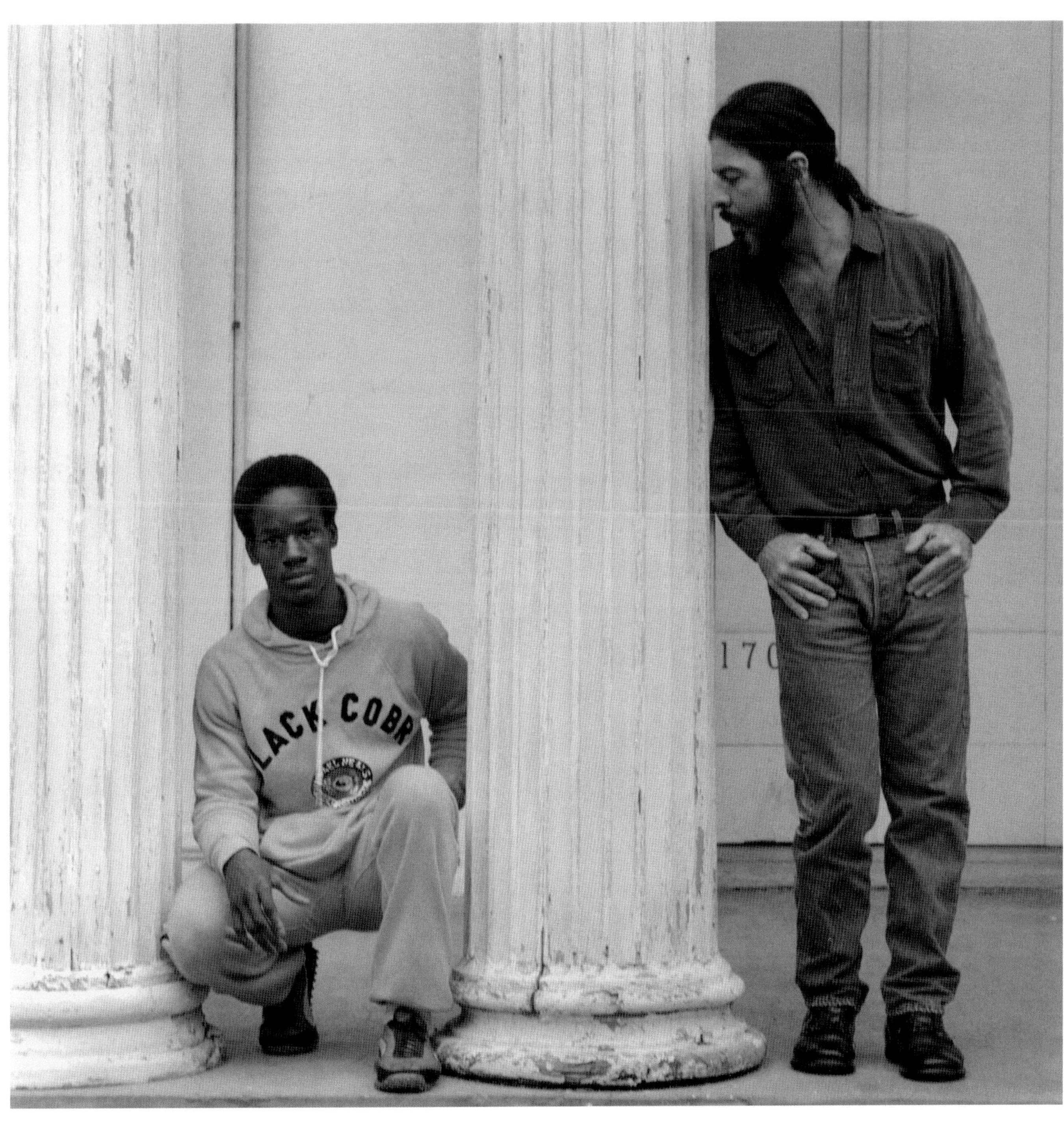

 Lisa Lyon, 1980

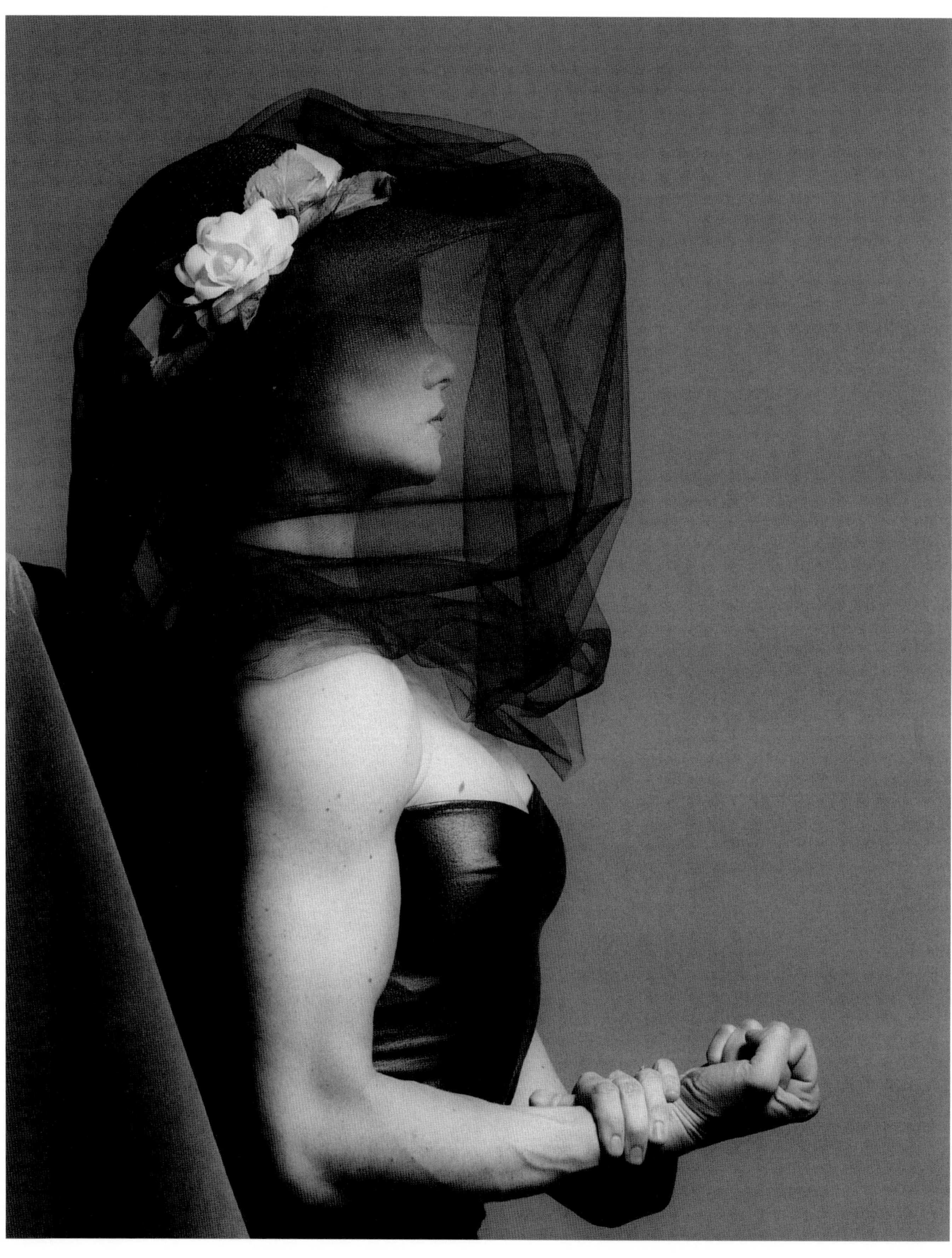

Jack Walls, 1982

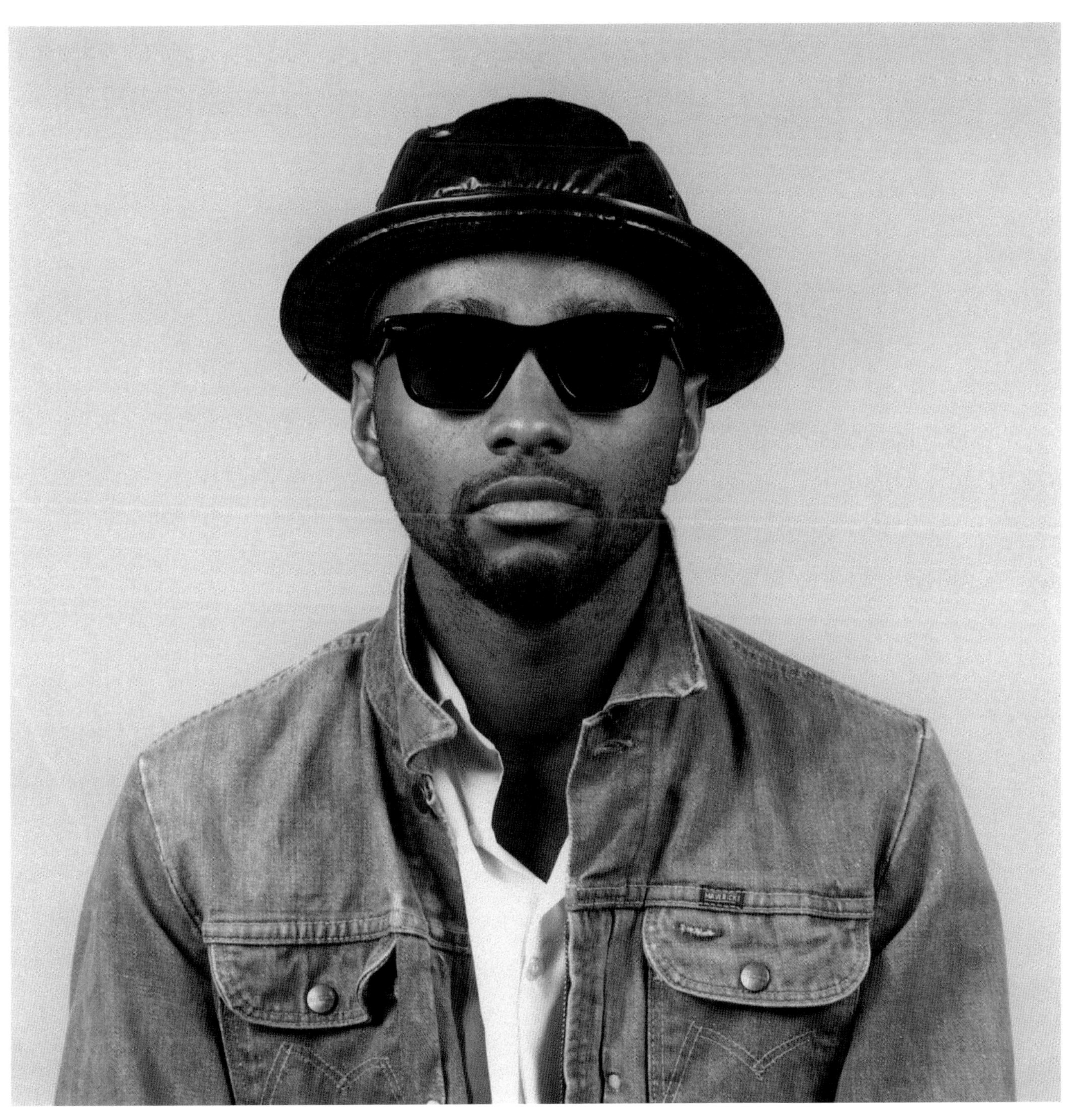

Deborah Harry, 1982

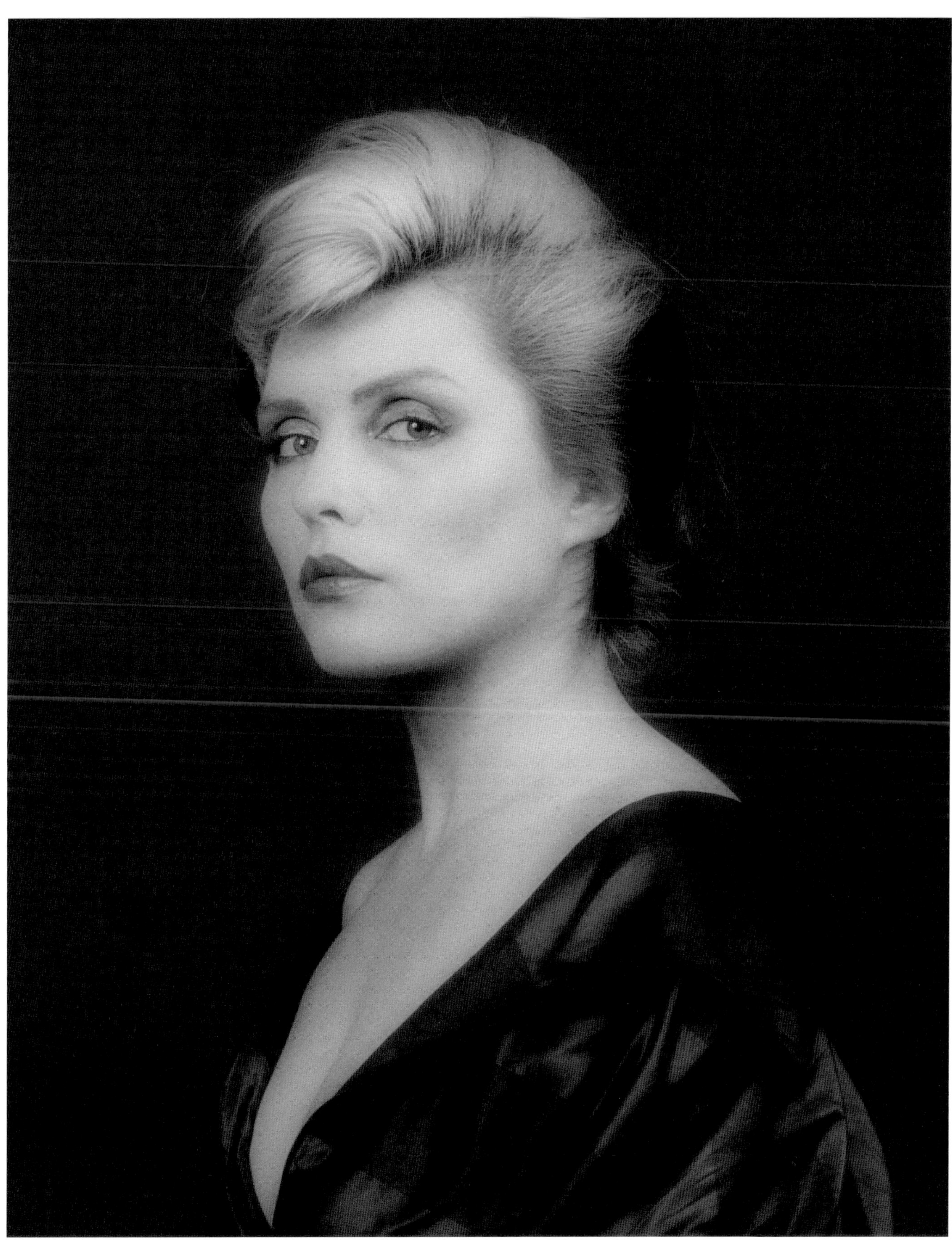

Self-Portrait, 1983

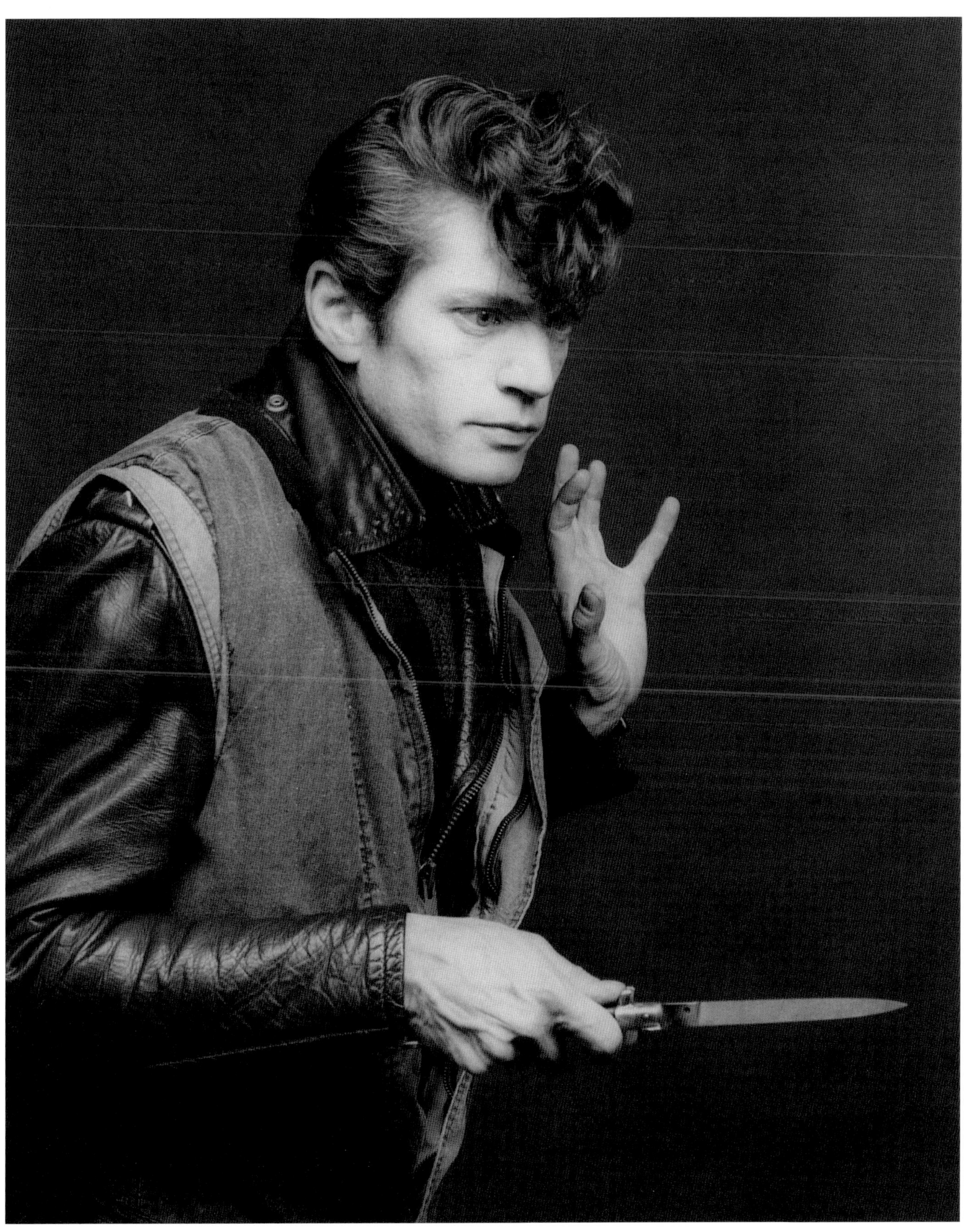

Edward Mapplethorpe, 1983

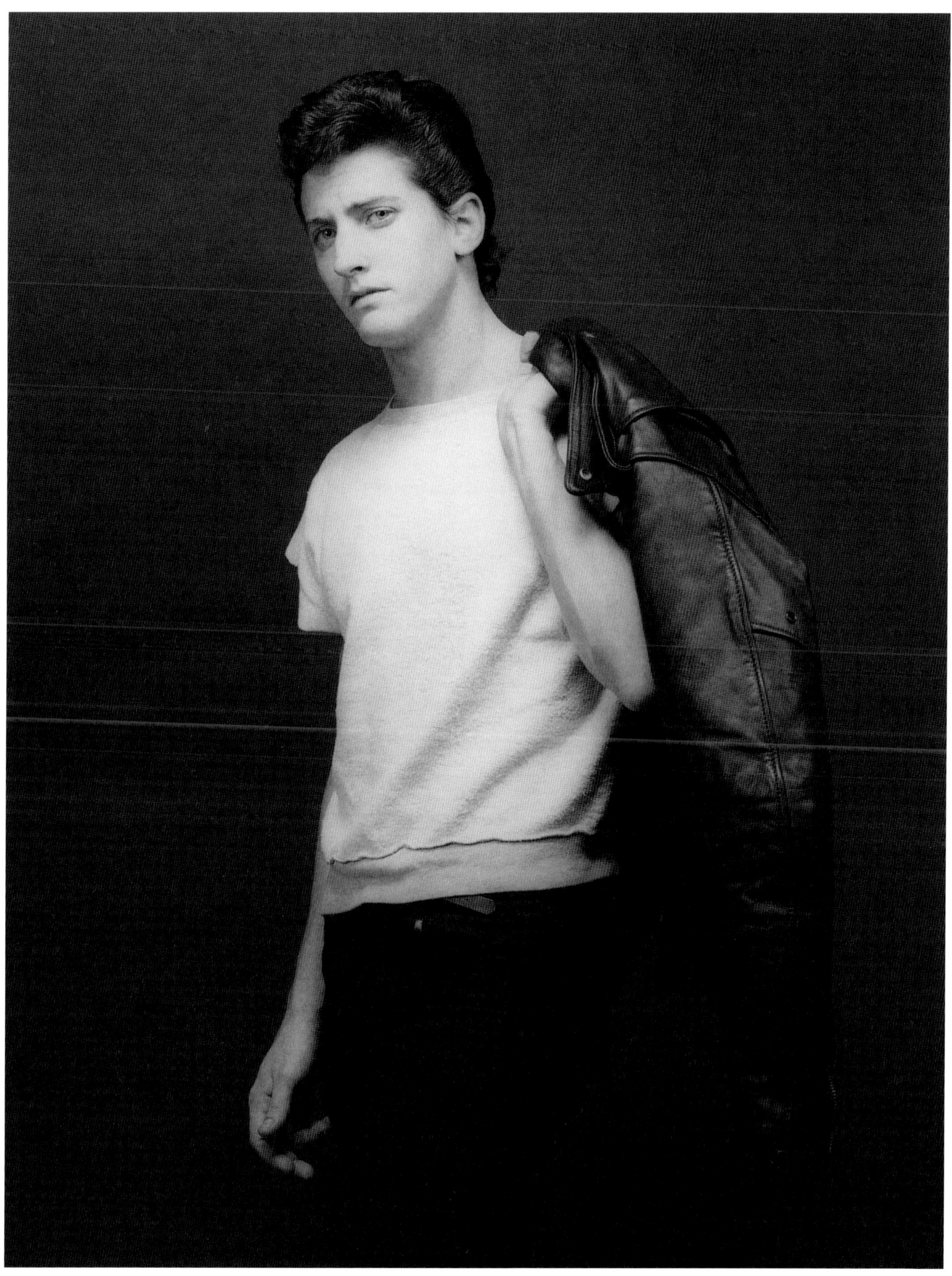

Annie Leibovitz, 1983

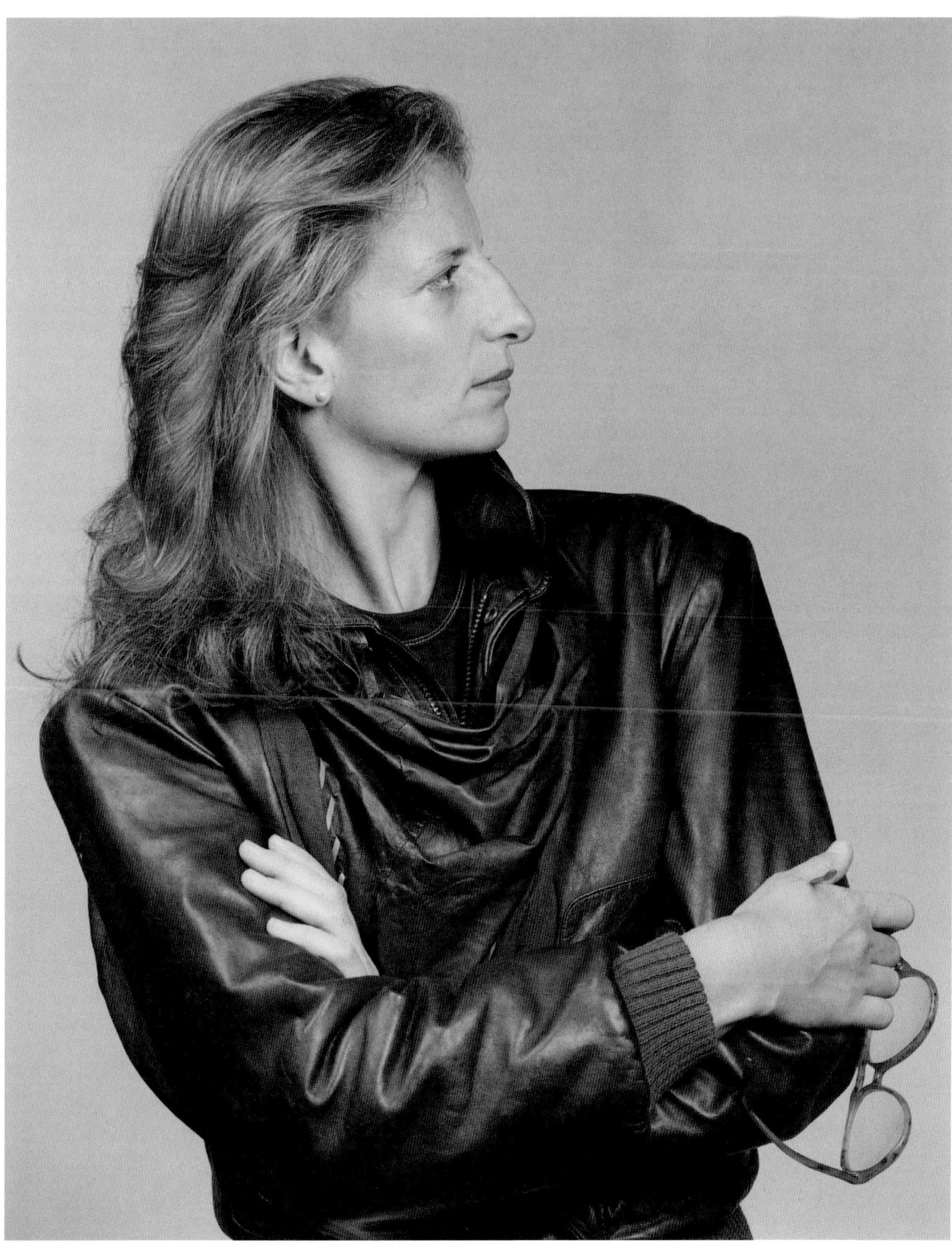

Donald Sutherland, 1983

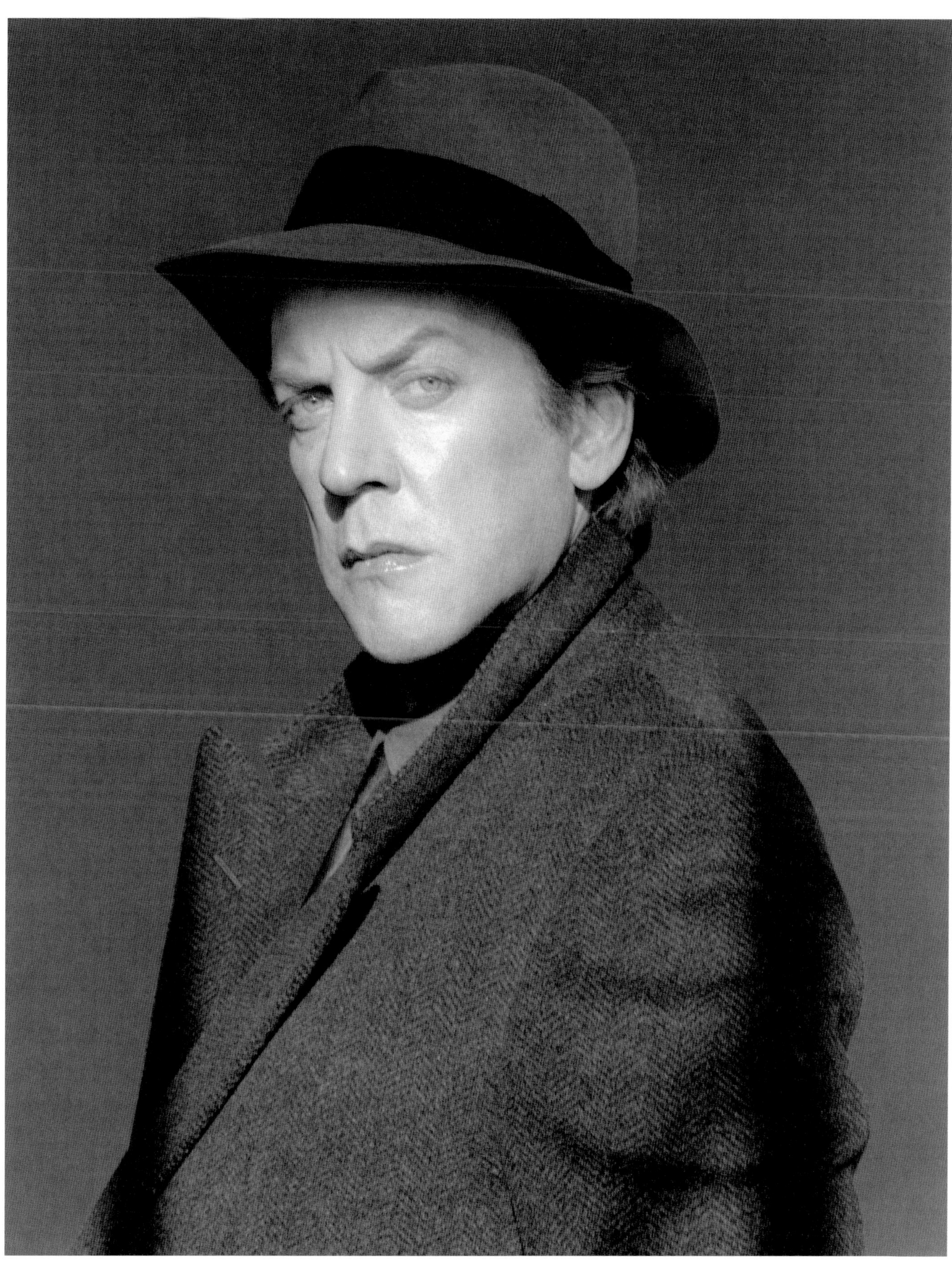

Kathy Acker, 1983

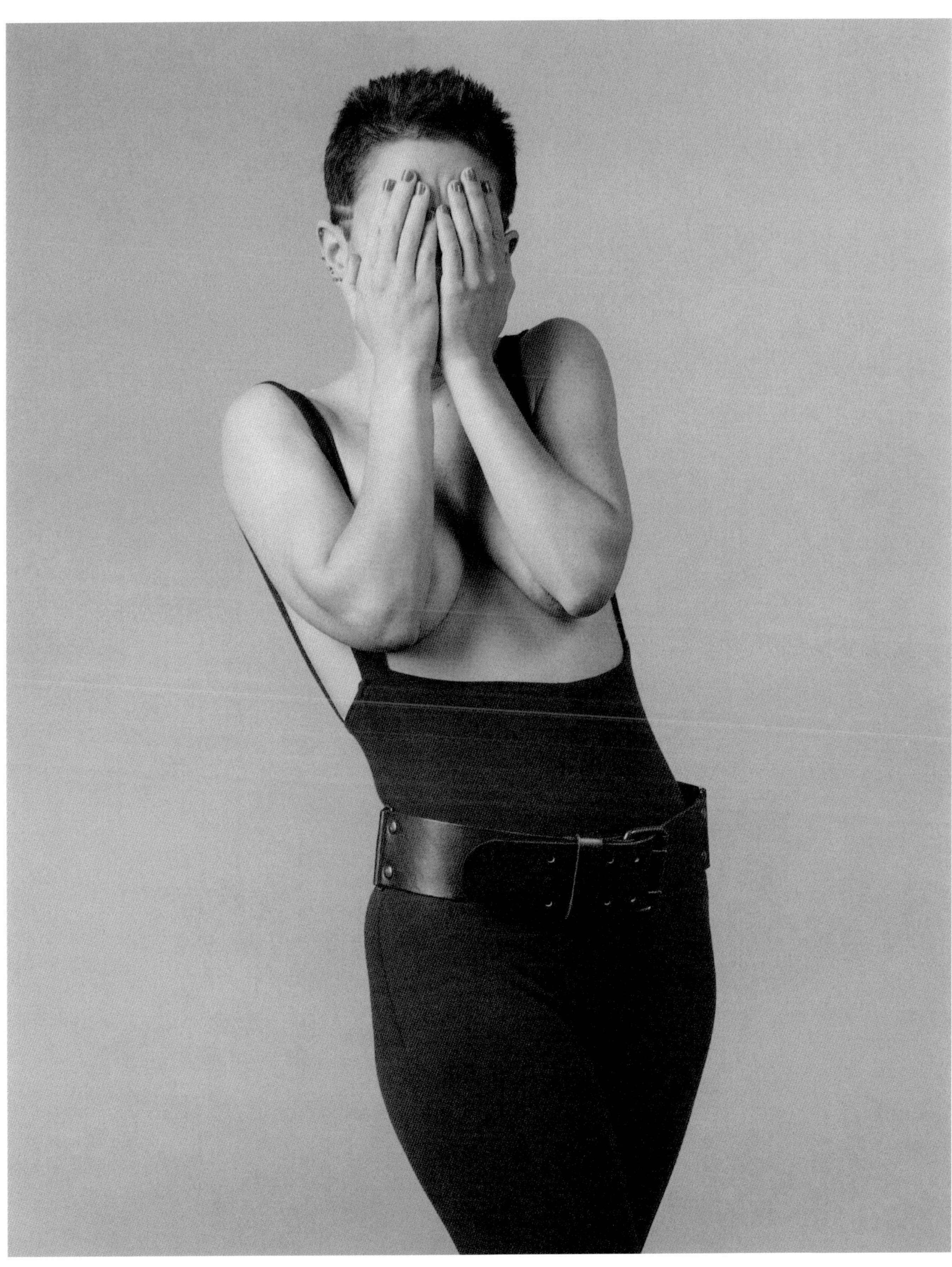

John Simon, 1983

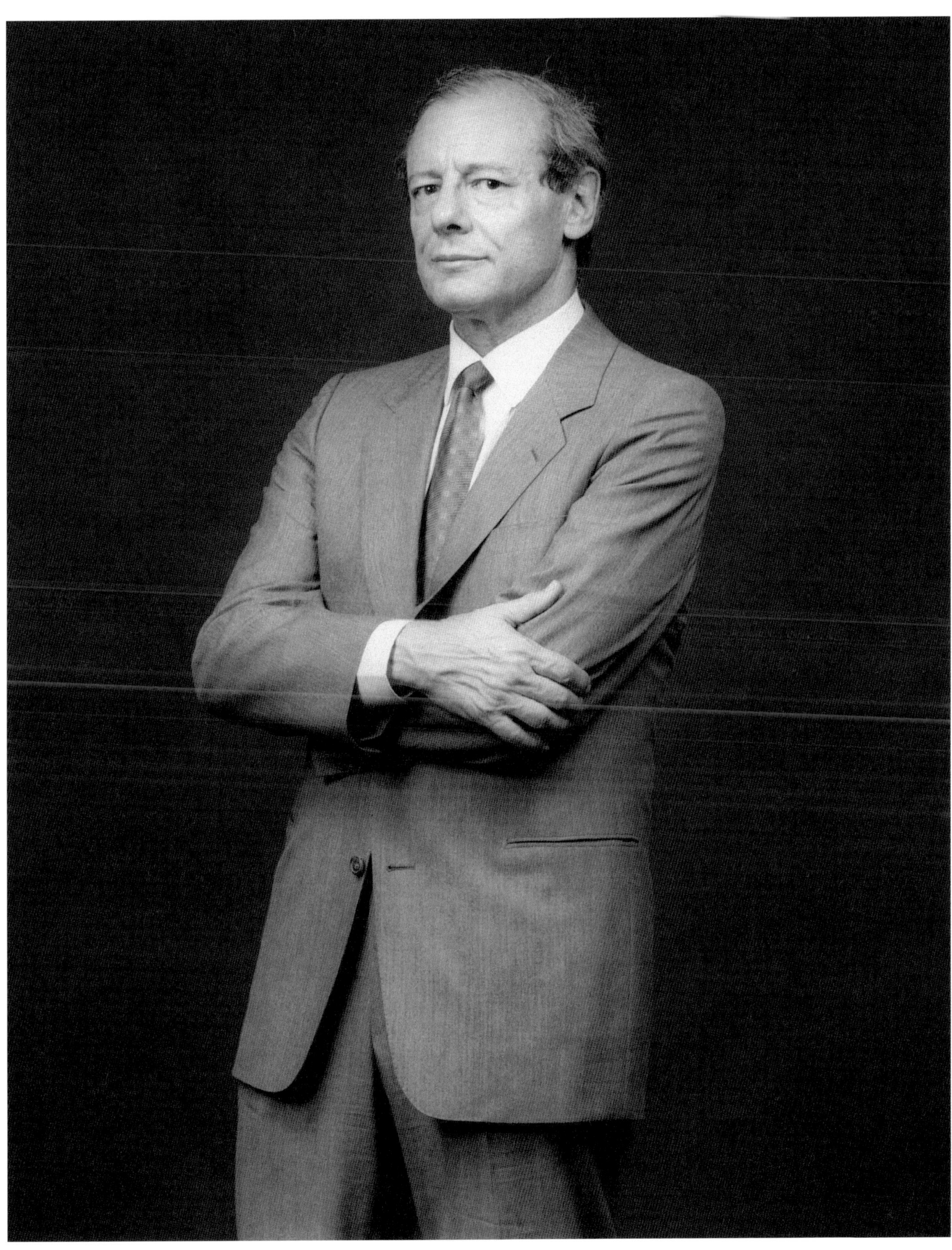

Plate 56 / Catalogue # 5

Marisa Berenson, 1983

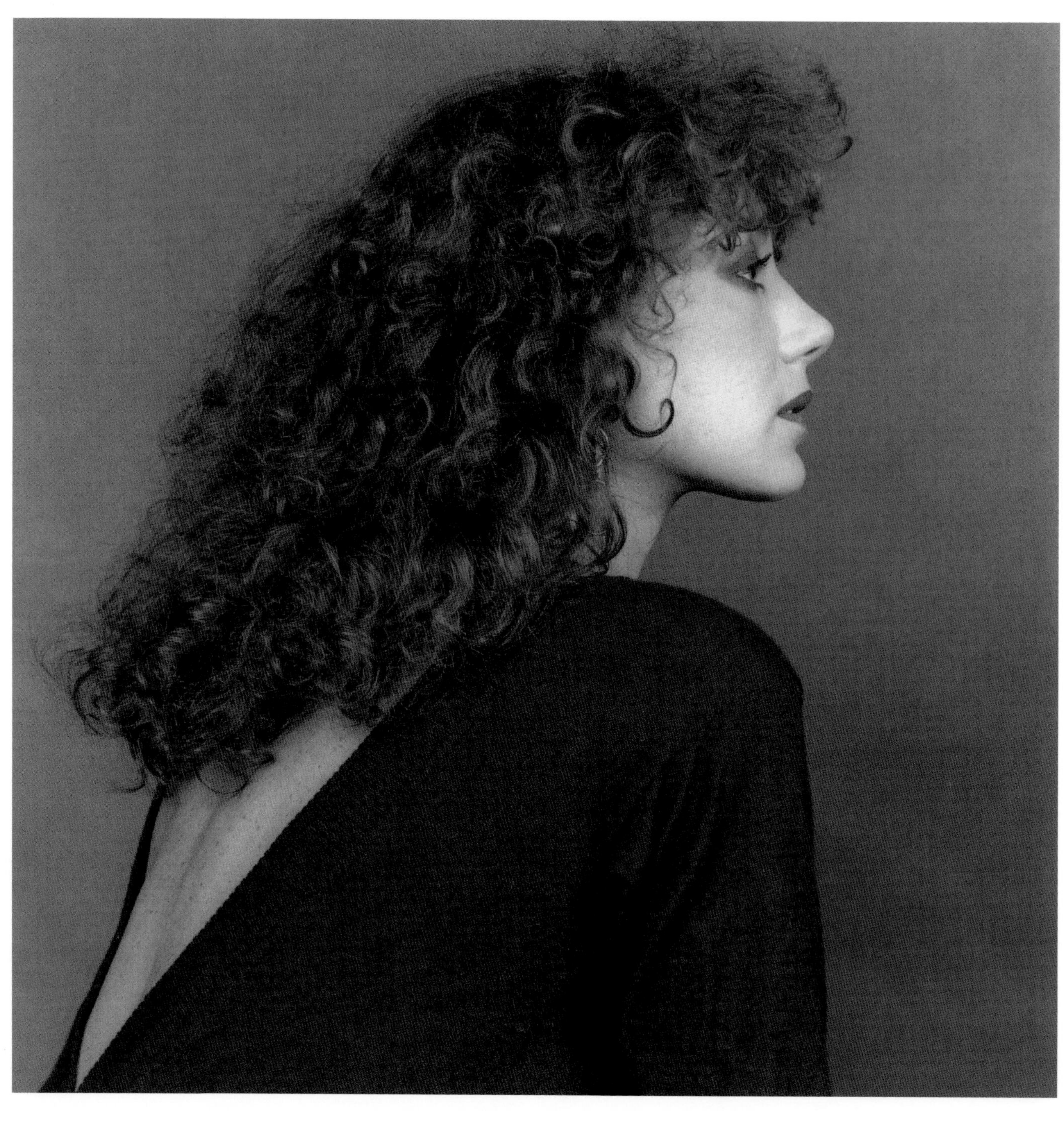

Doris Saatchi, 1983

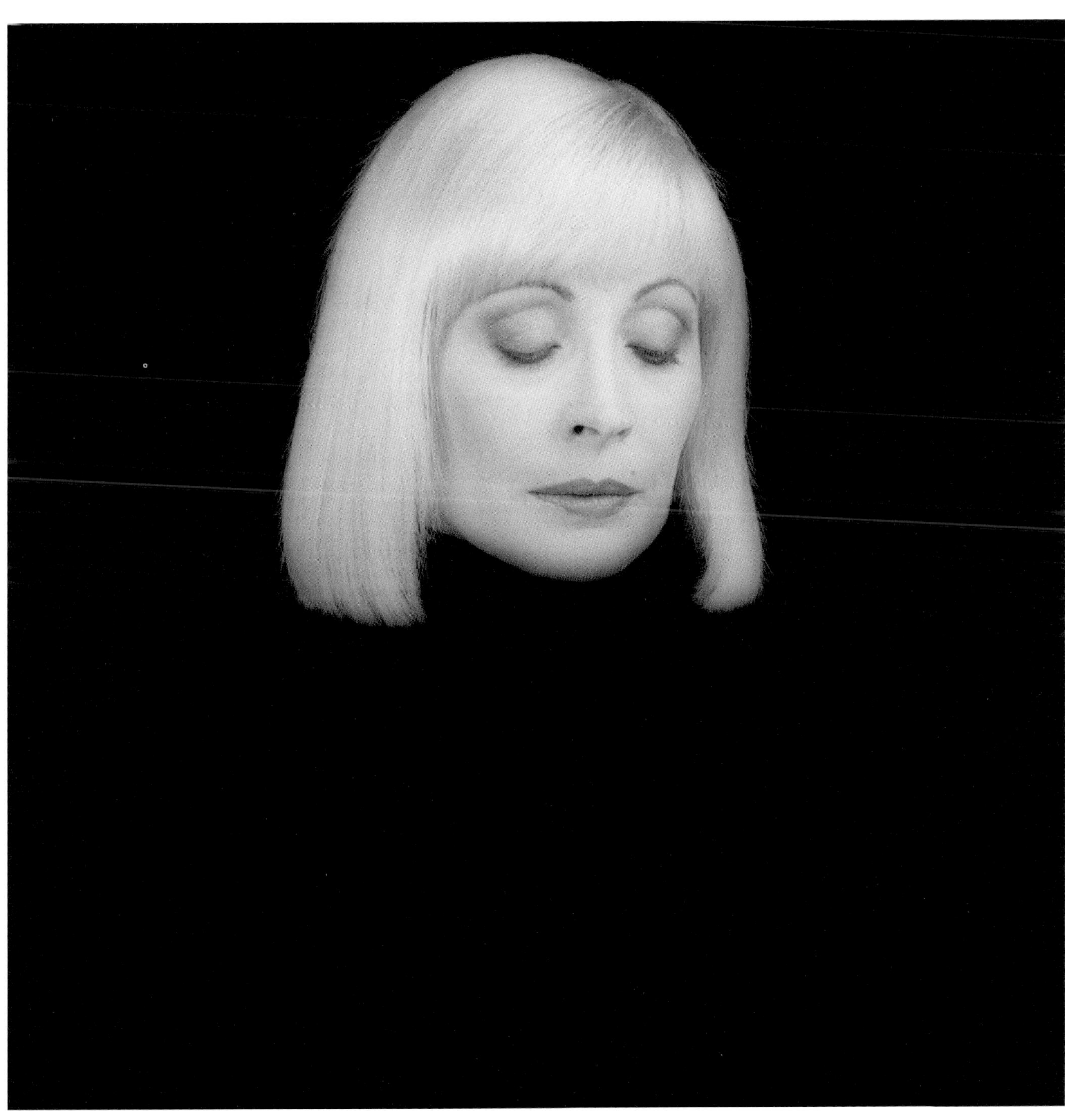

David Byrne, 1983

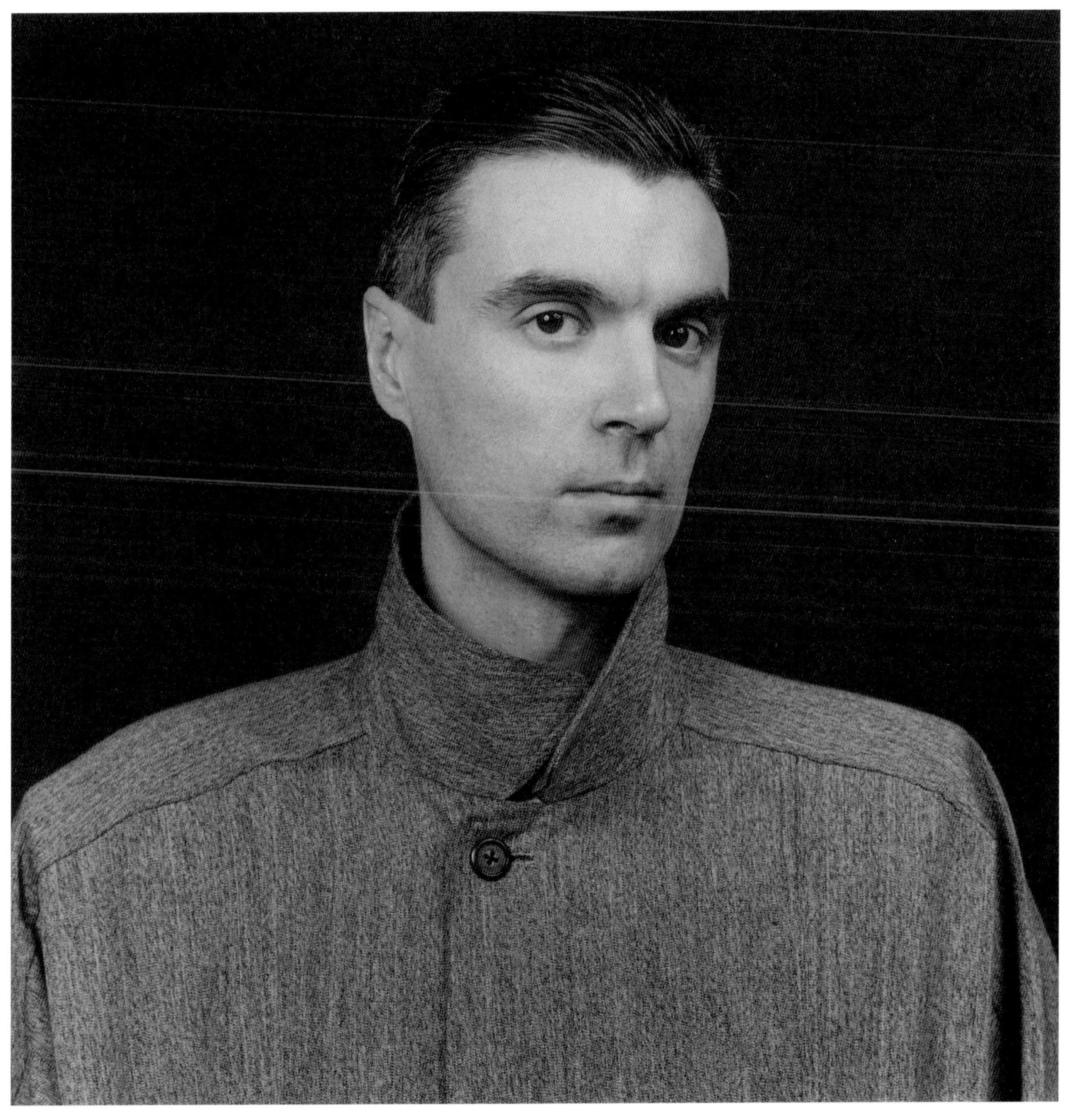

David Salle, 1983

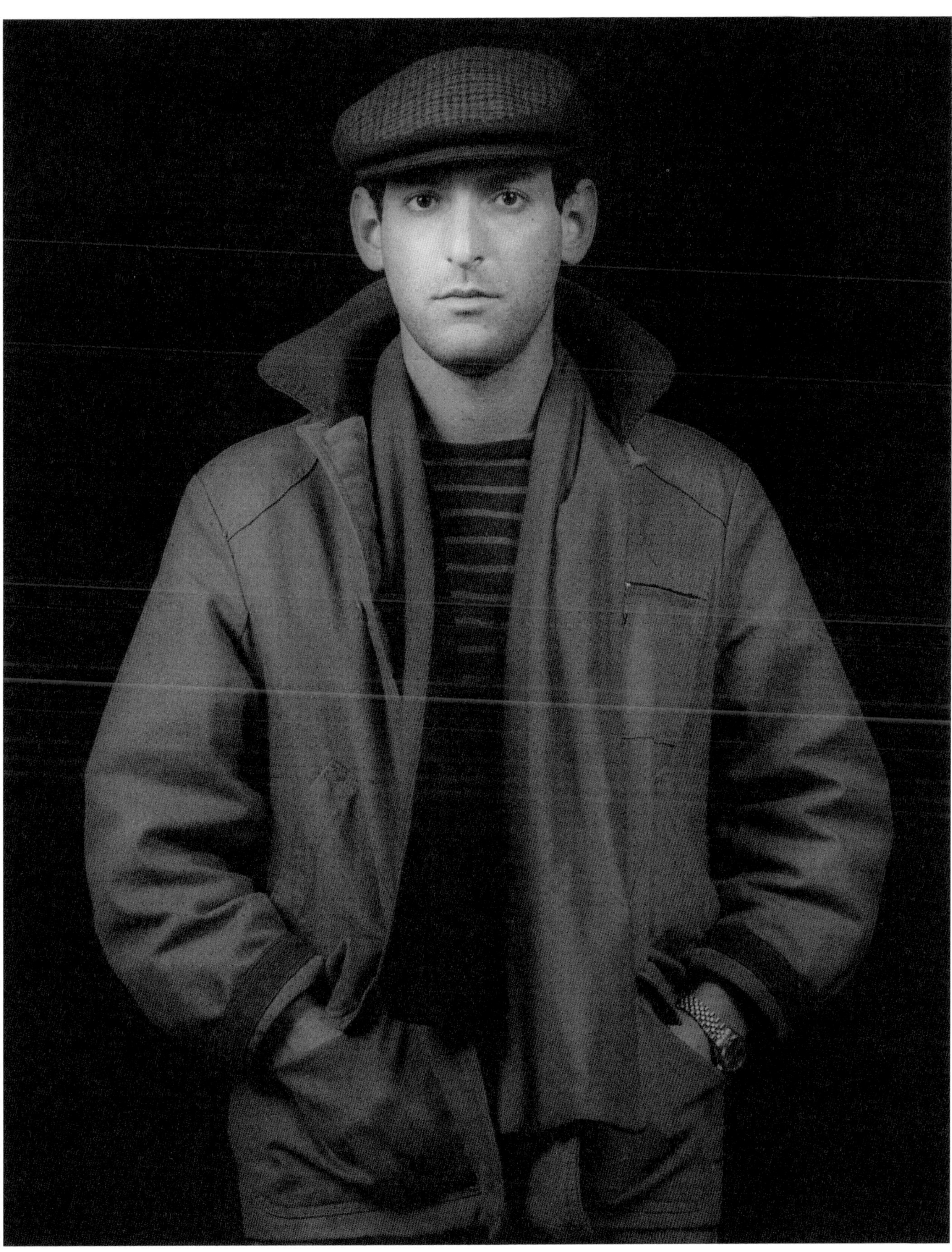

Andy Warhol, 1983

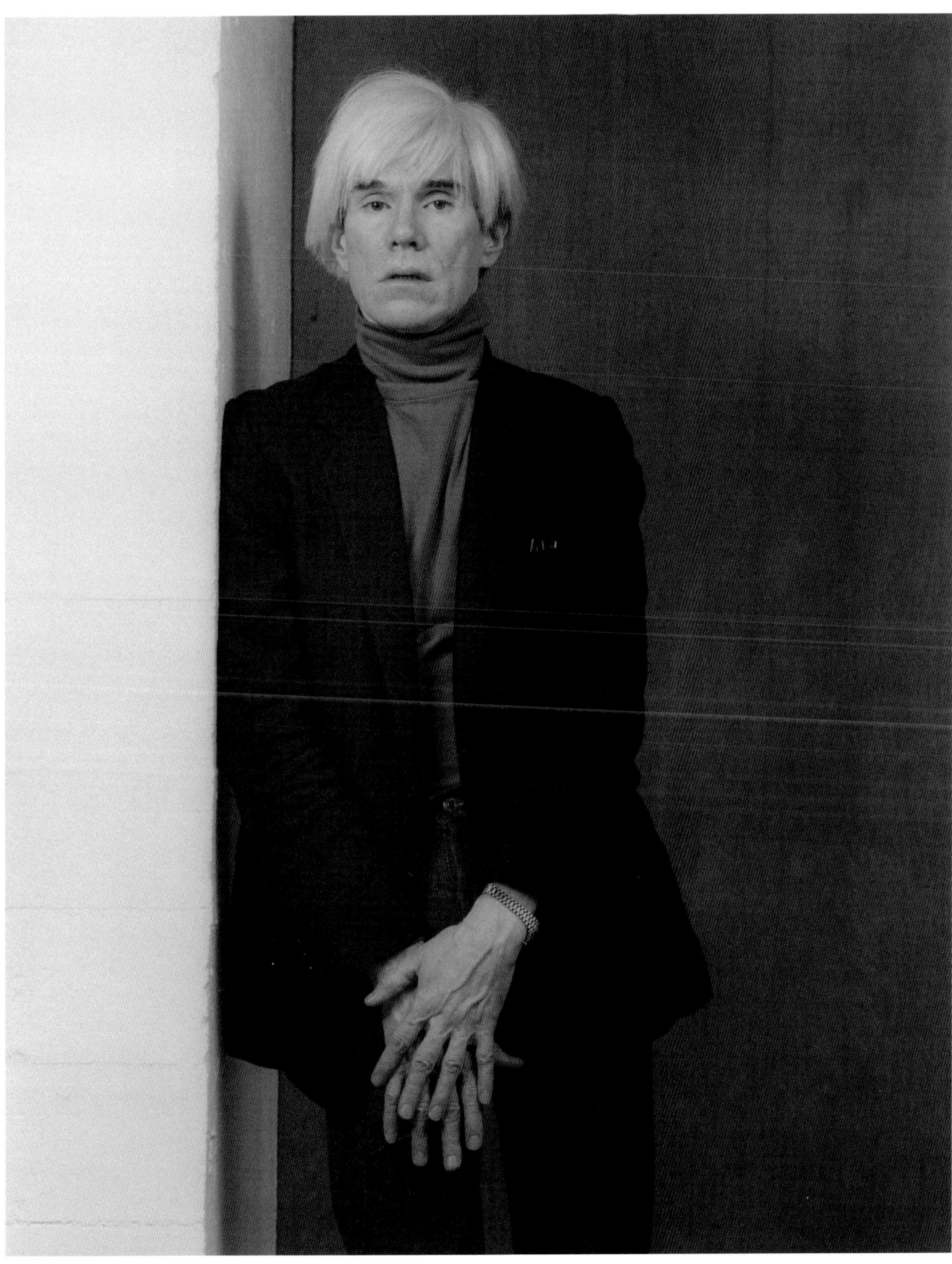

Cindy Sherman, 1983(?)

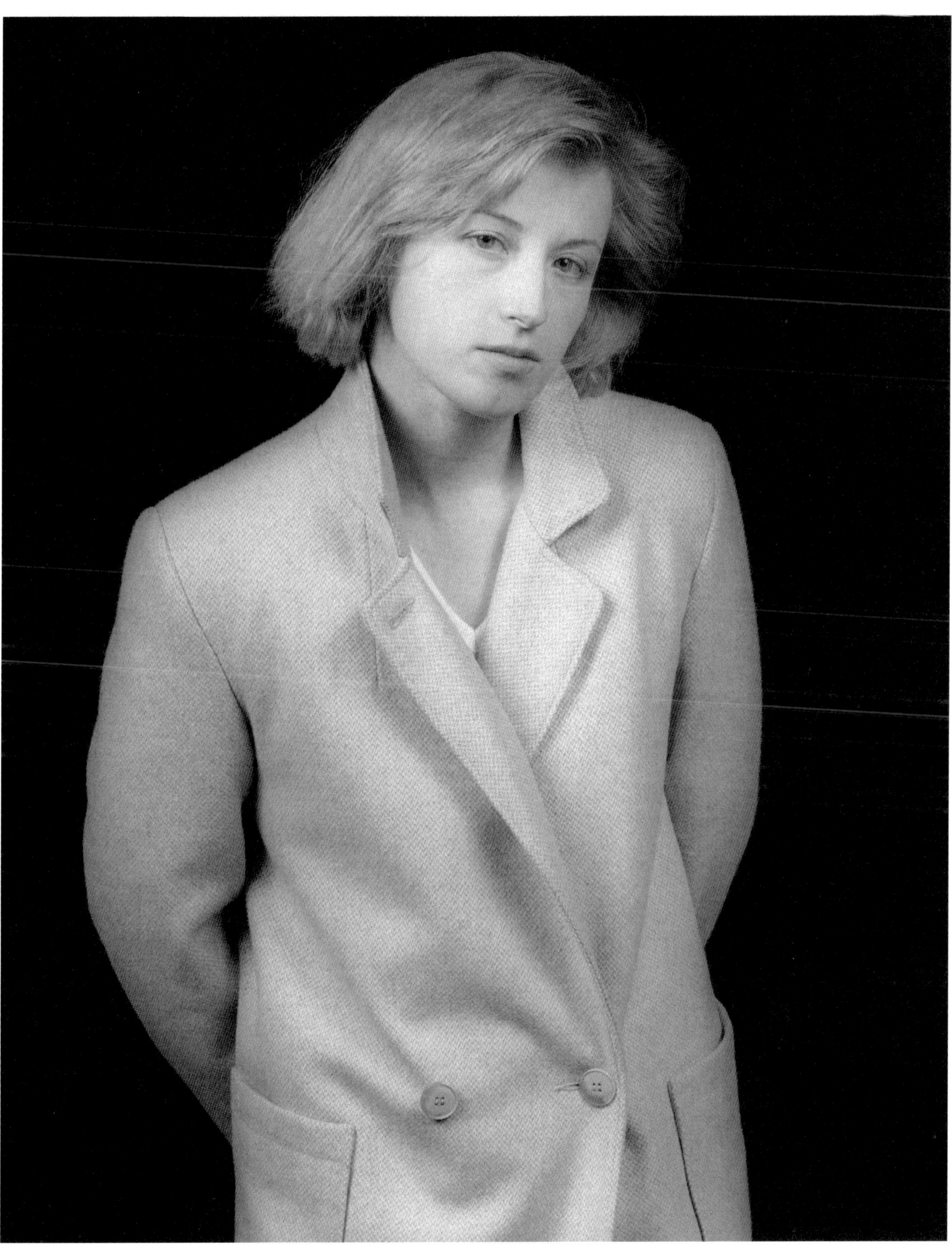

Udo Kier, 1983

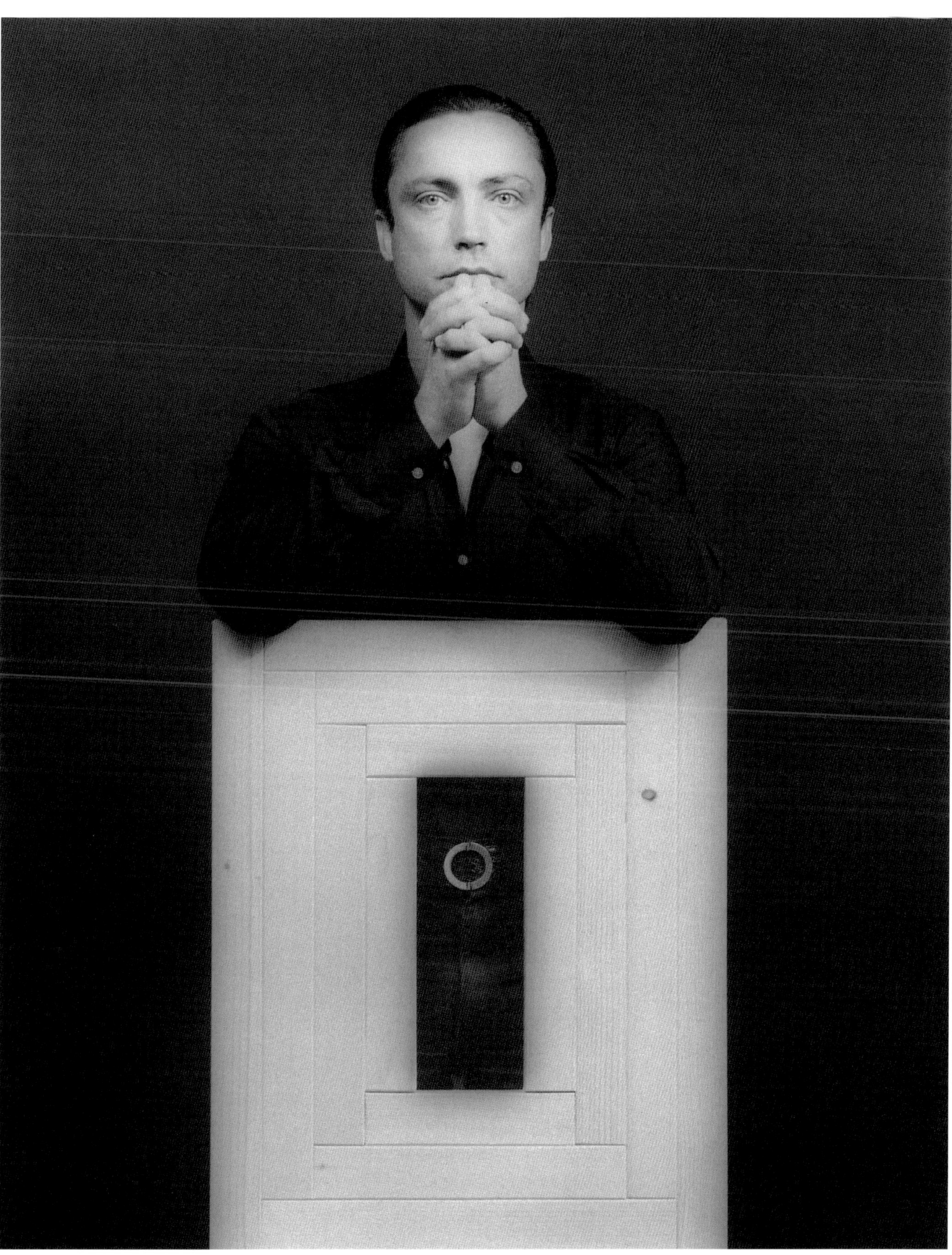

Plate 63 / Catalogue # 20 Lucinda Childs, 1983

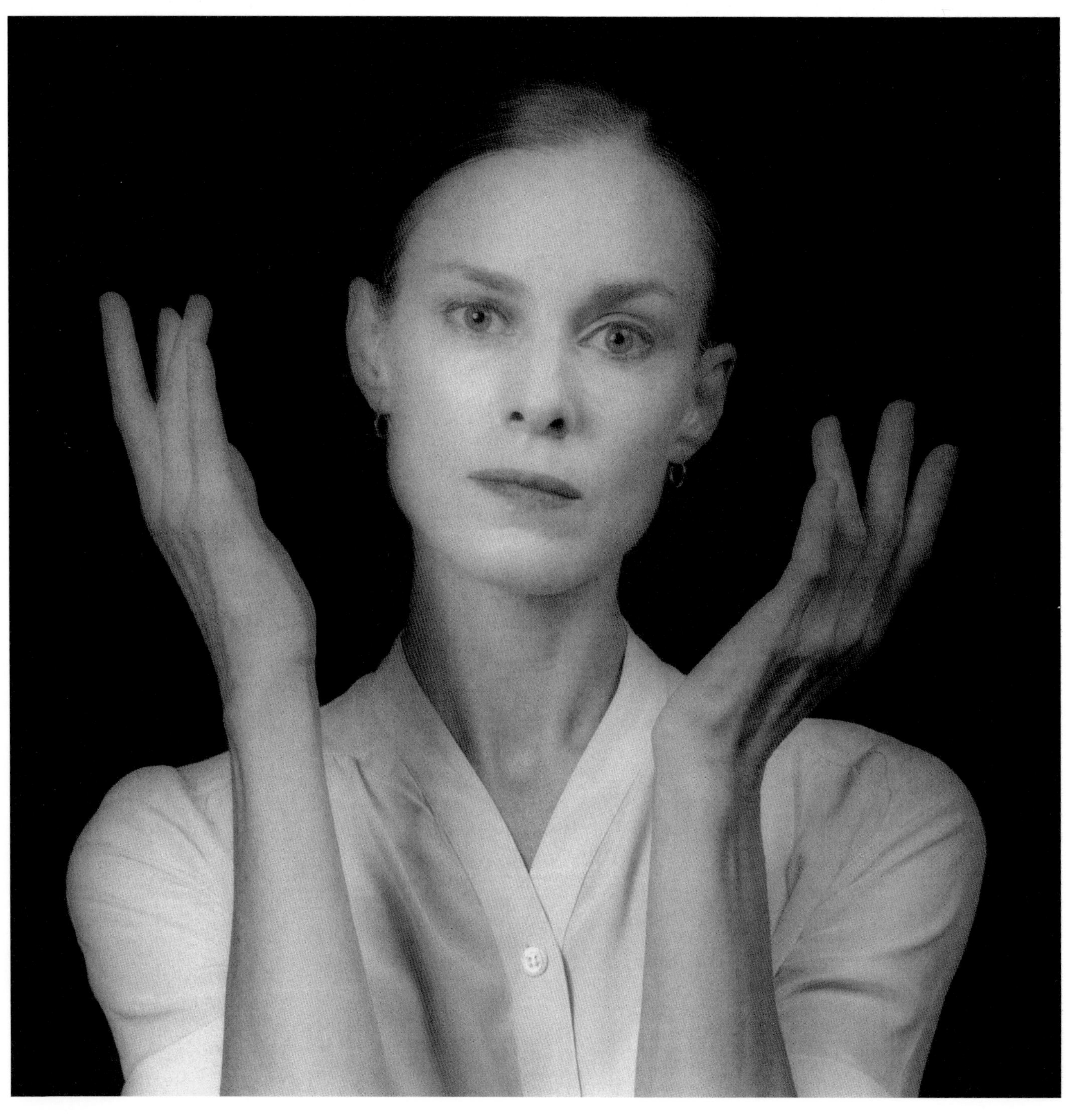

Plate 64 / Catalogue # 76

Robert Rauschenberg, 1983

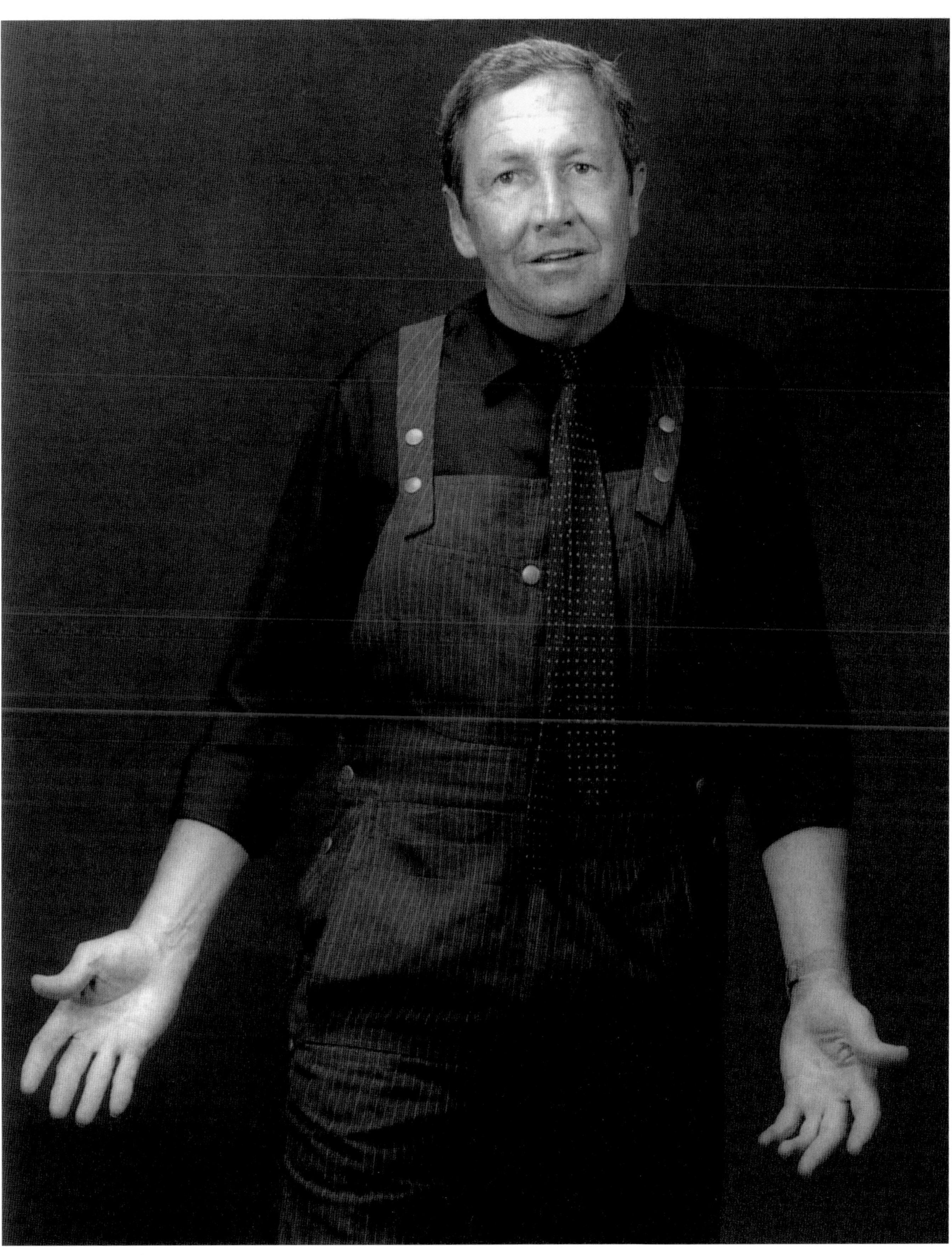

Mary Boone, 1984

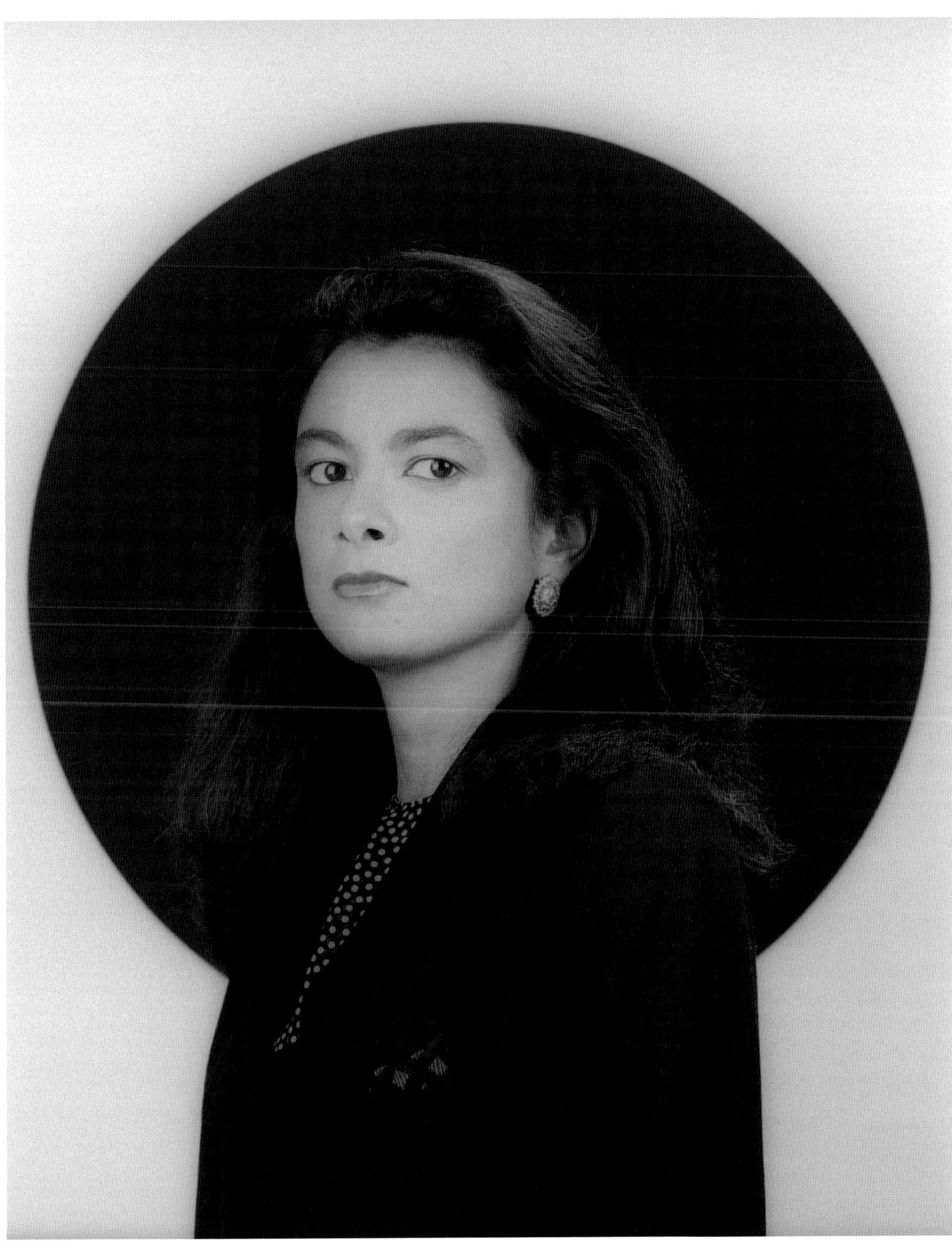

Ellsworth Kelly, 1984

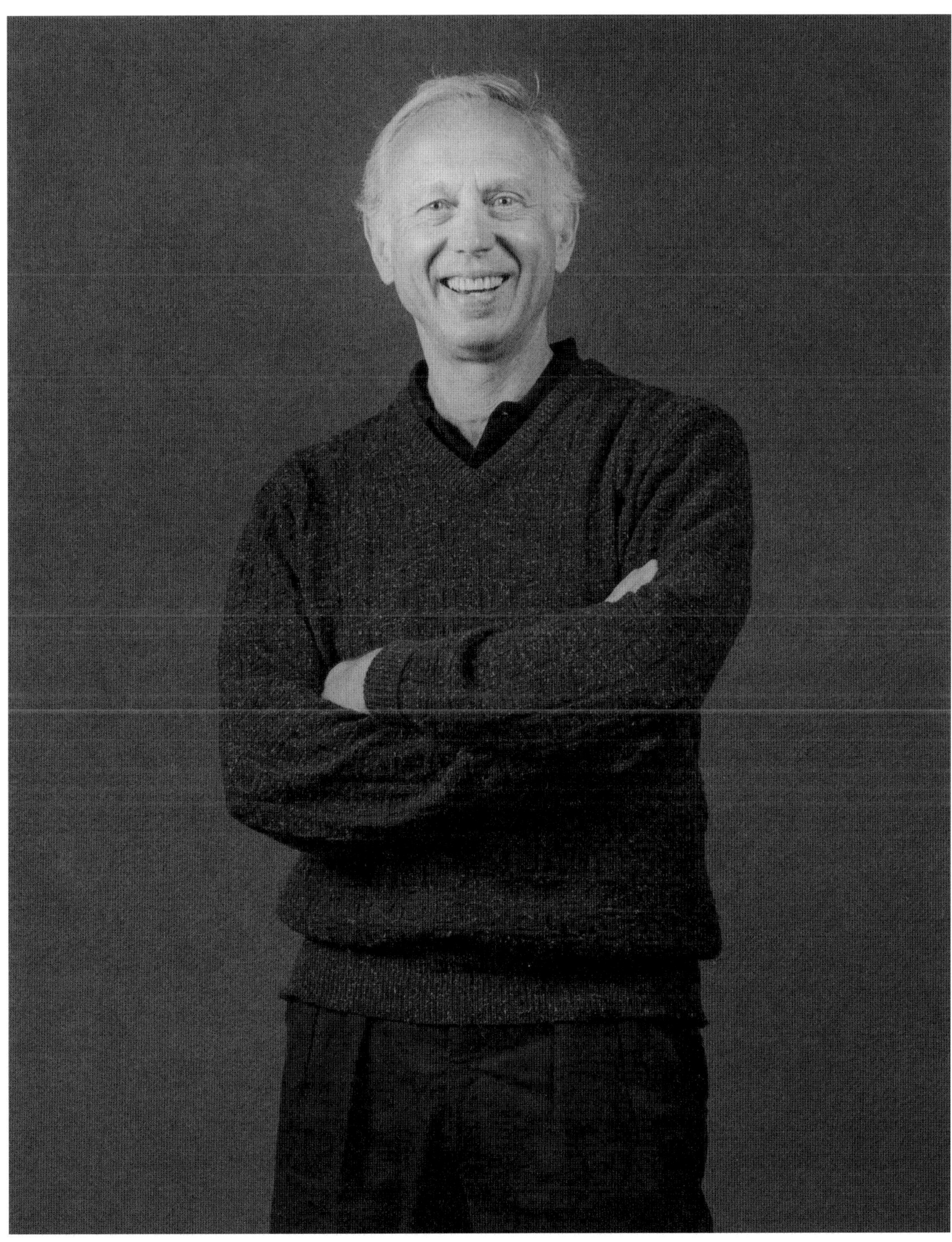

Annamirl van der Pluijm, 1985

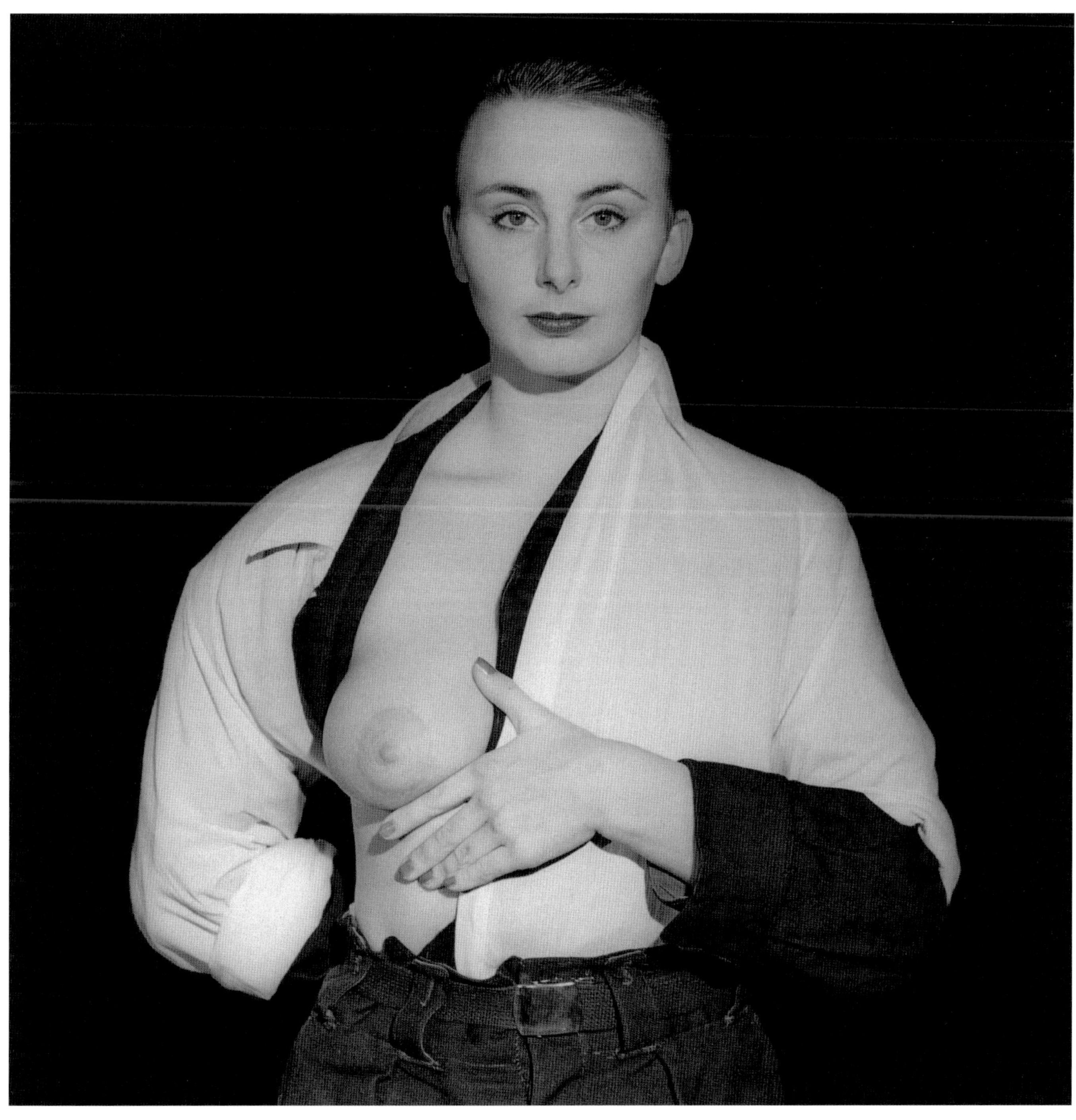

Edward Ruscha, 1984

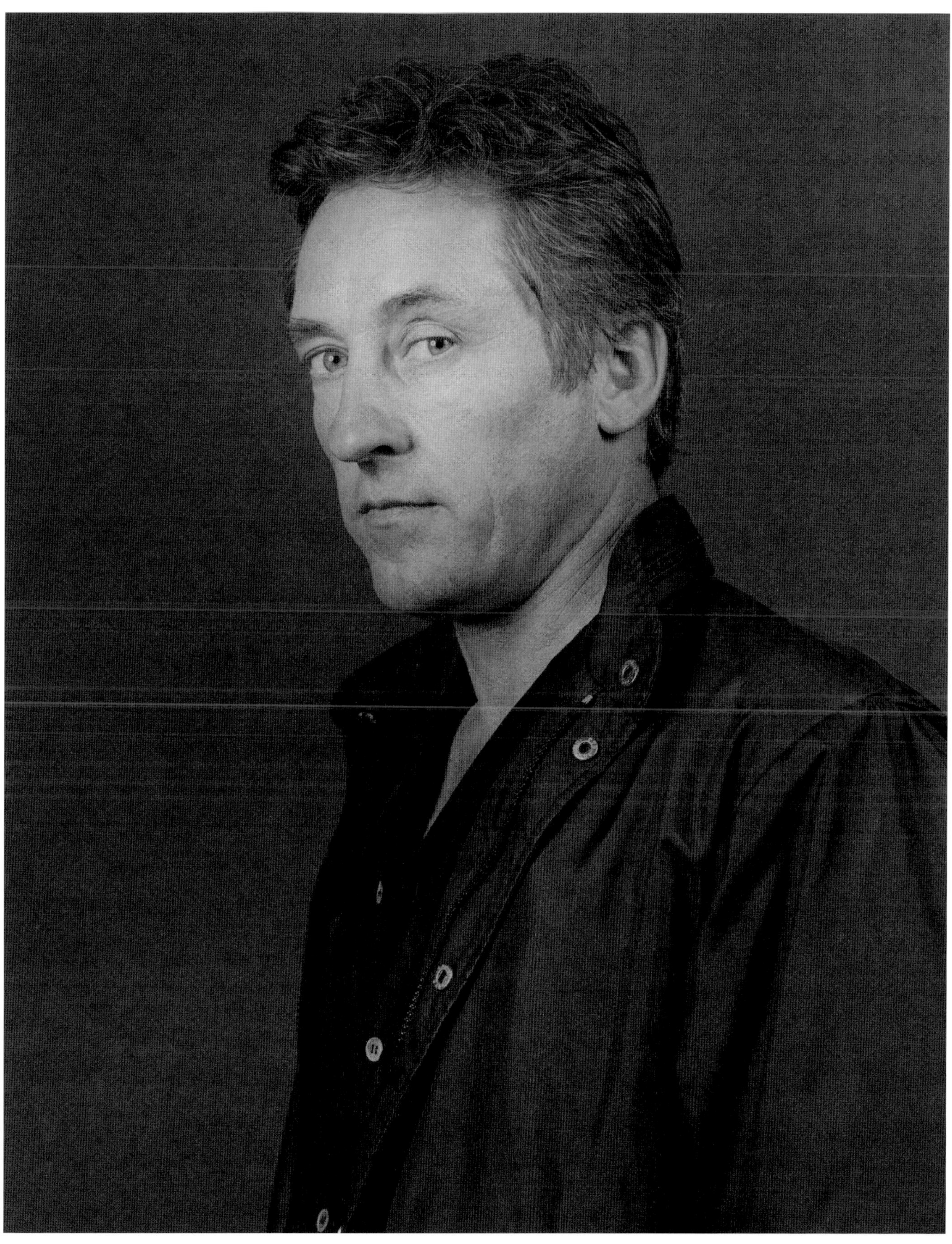

Frank Langella, 1984

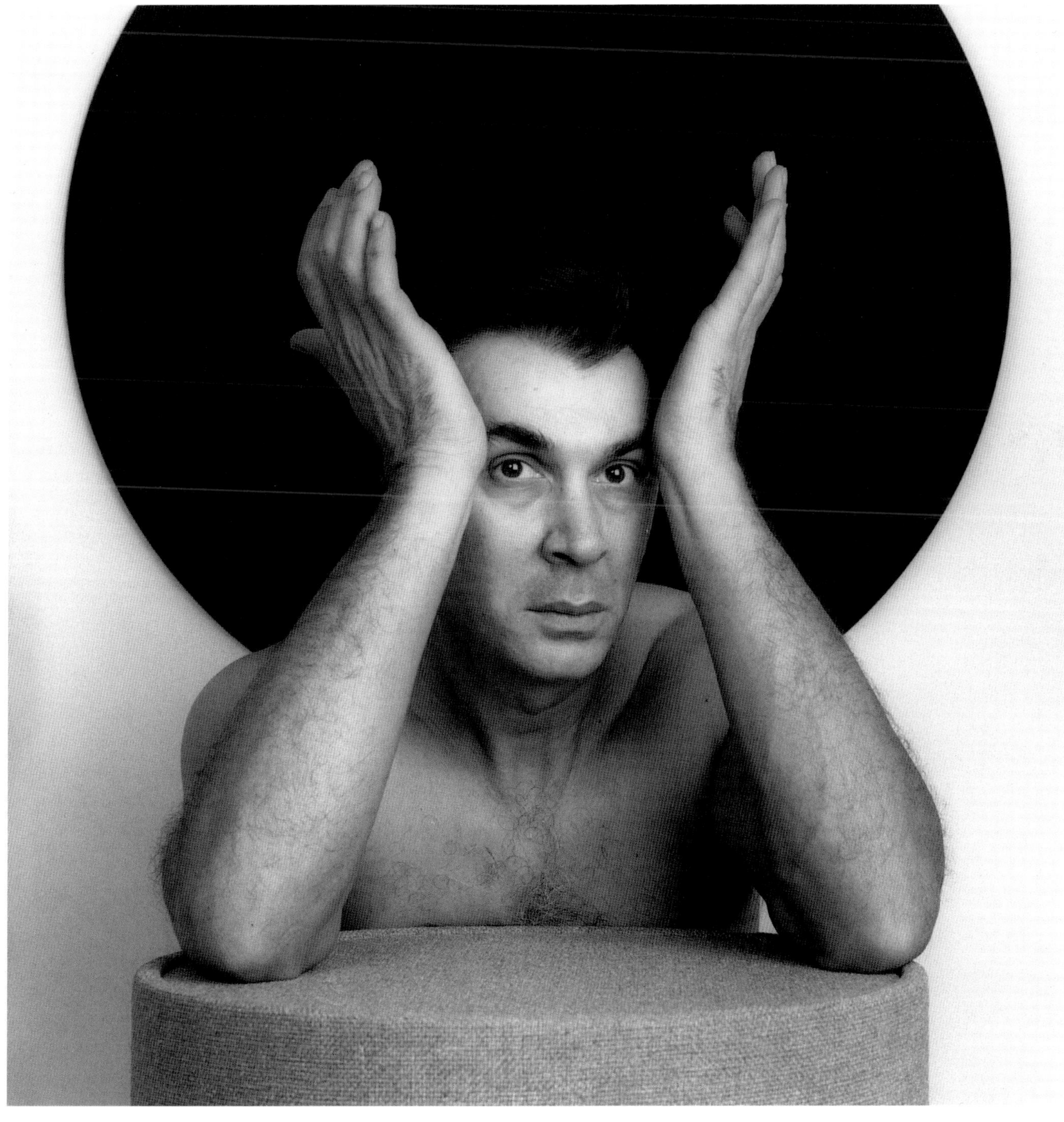

Susan Sontag, 1984

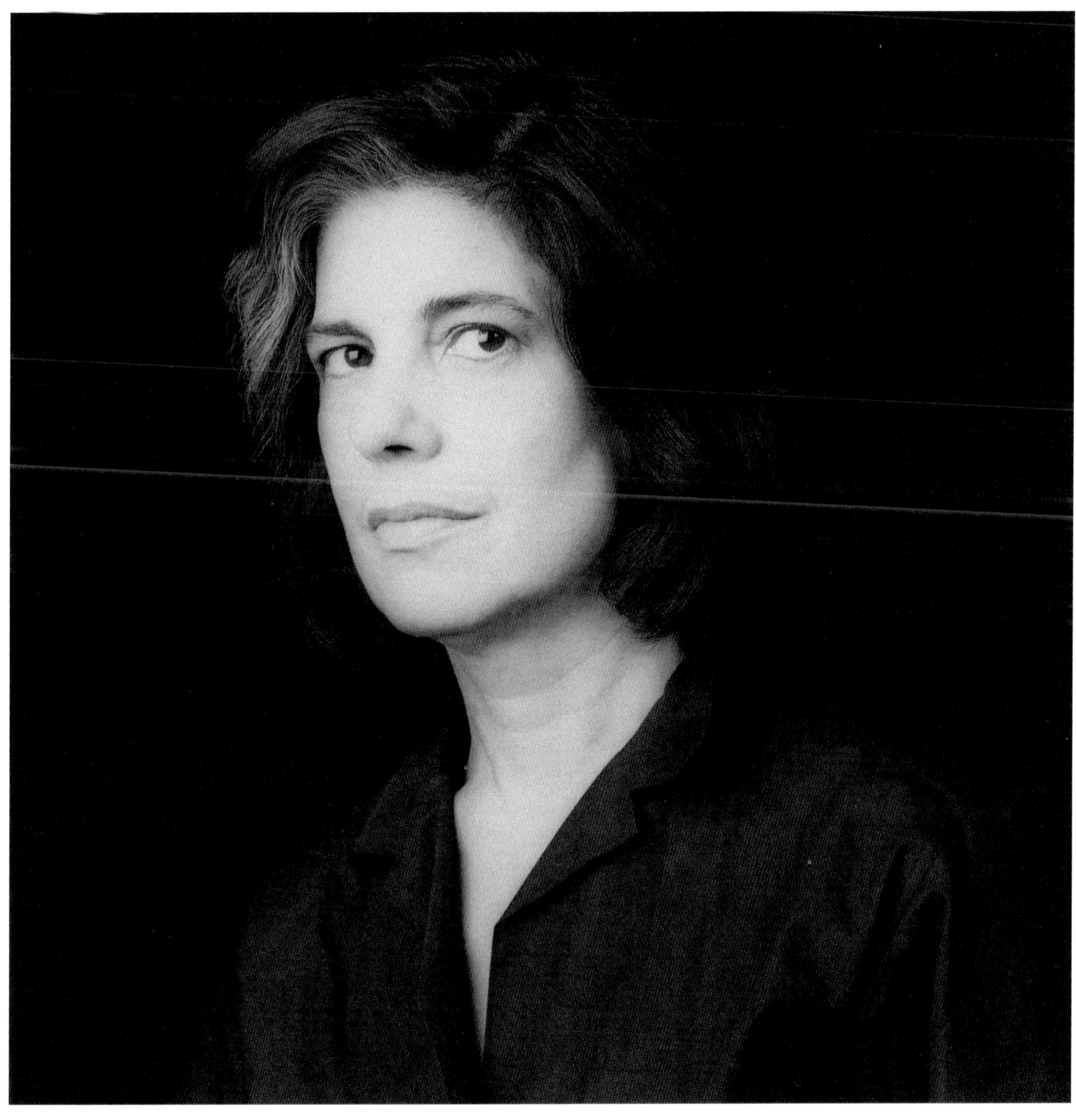

Gordon Lish, 1984

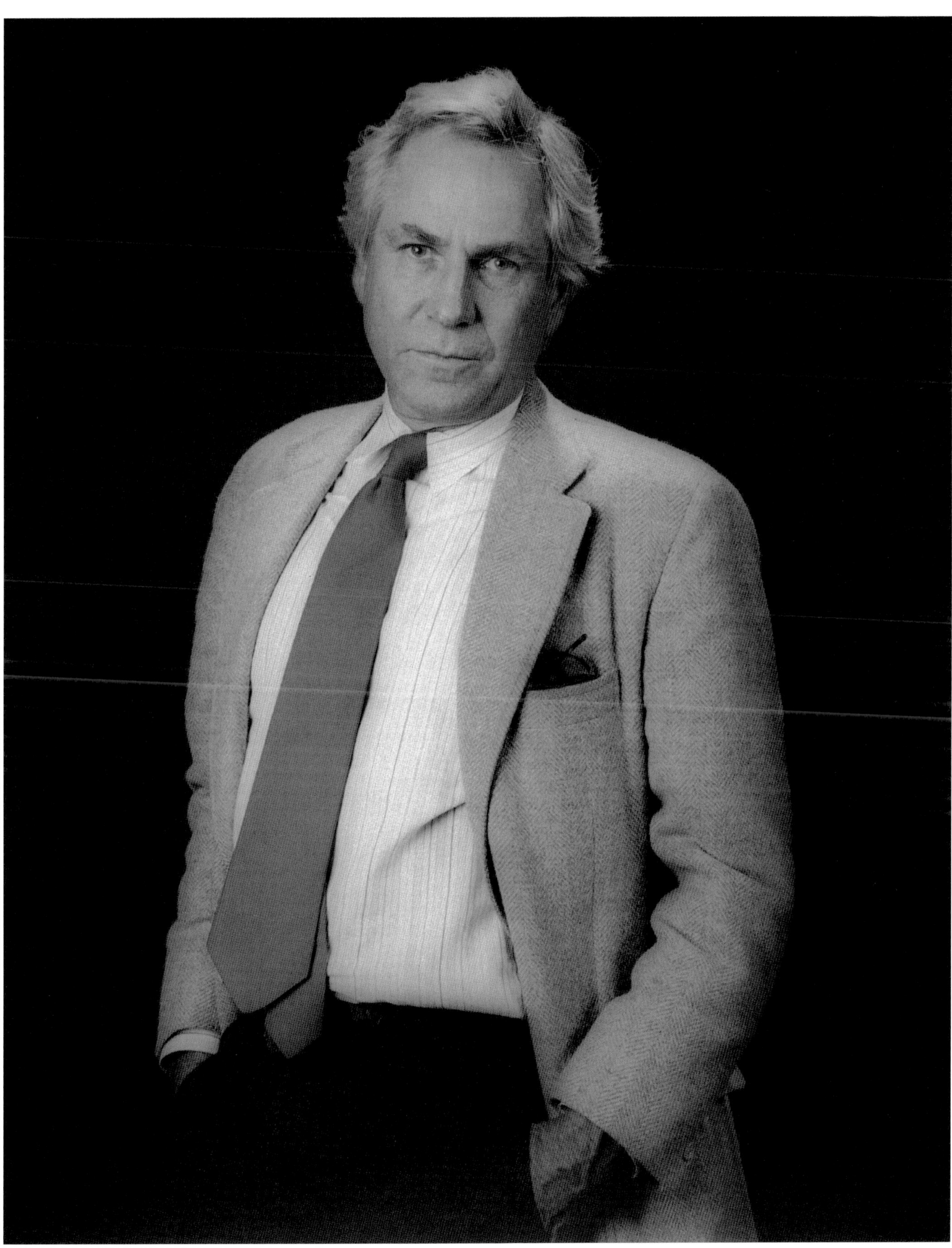

Teddy Pendergrass, 1984

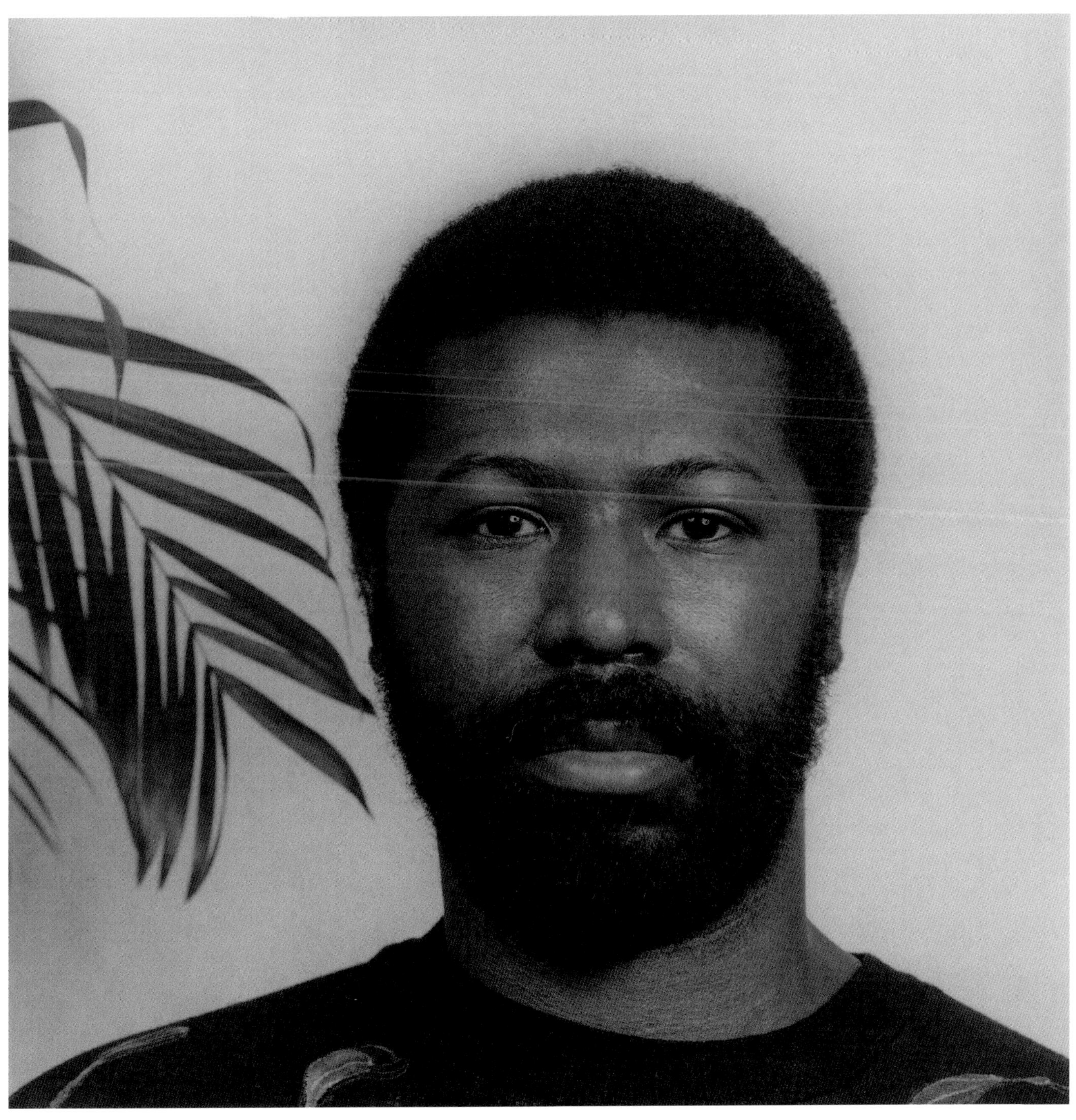

Alice Neel, 1984

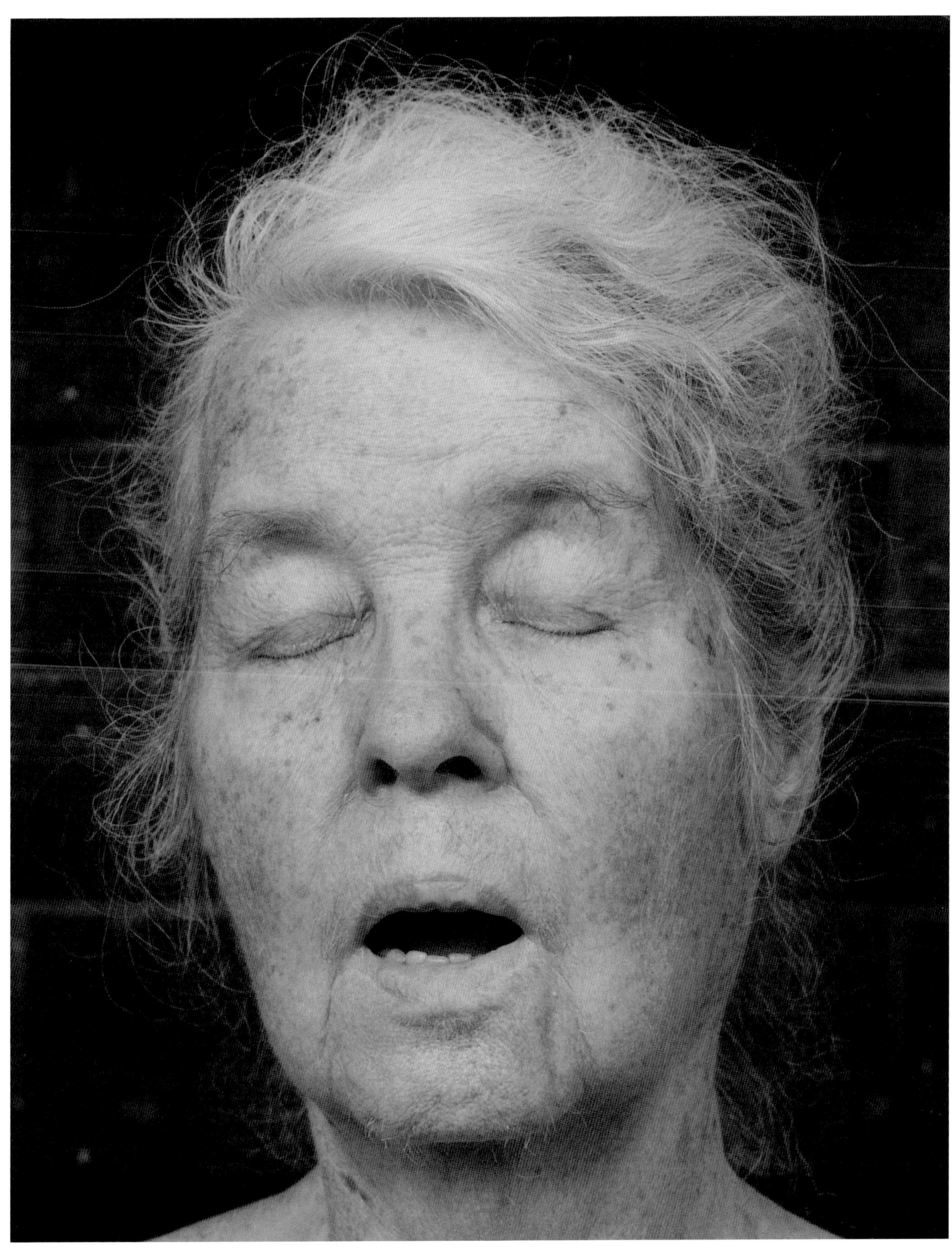

Grace Jones, 1985

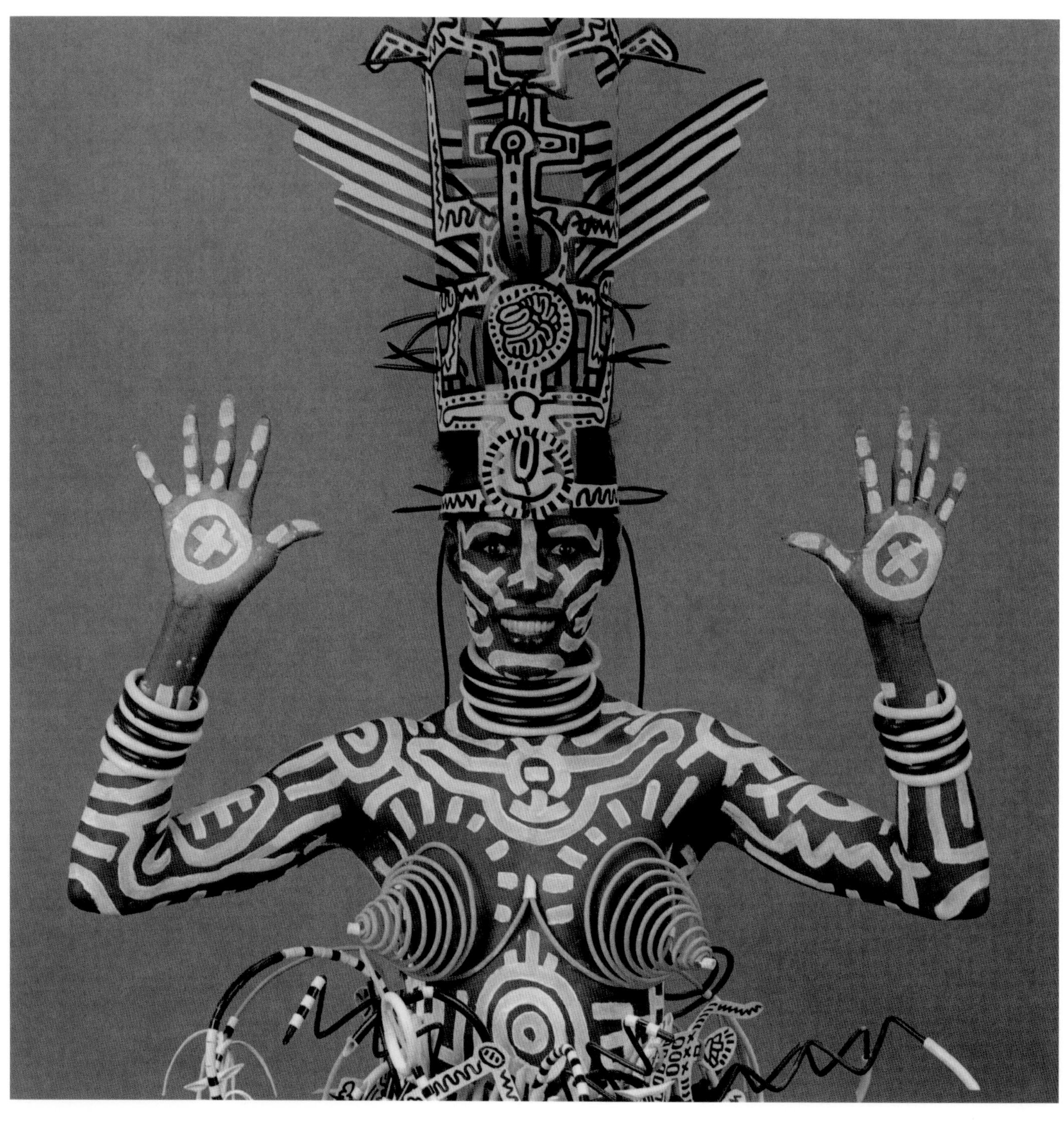

Plate 75 / Catalogue # 36

Keith Haring, 1984

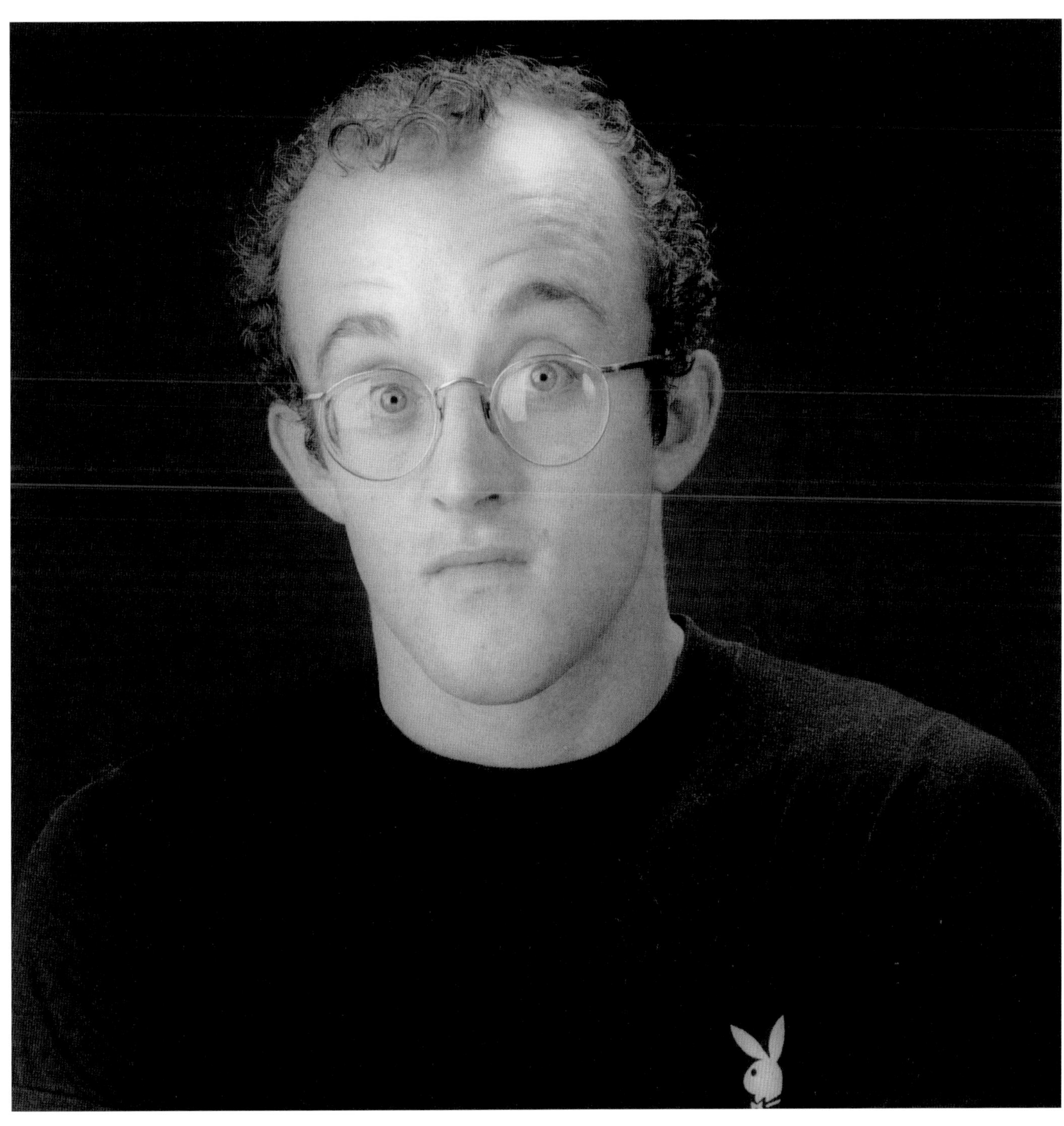

Plate 76 / Catalogue # 54 Roy Lichtenstein, 1985

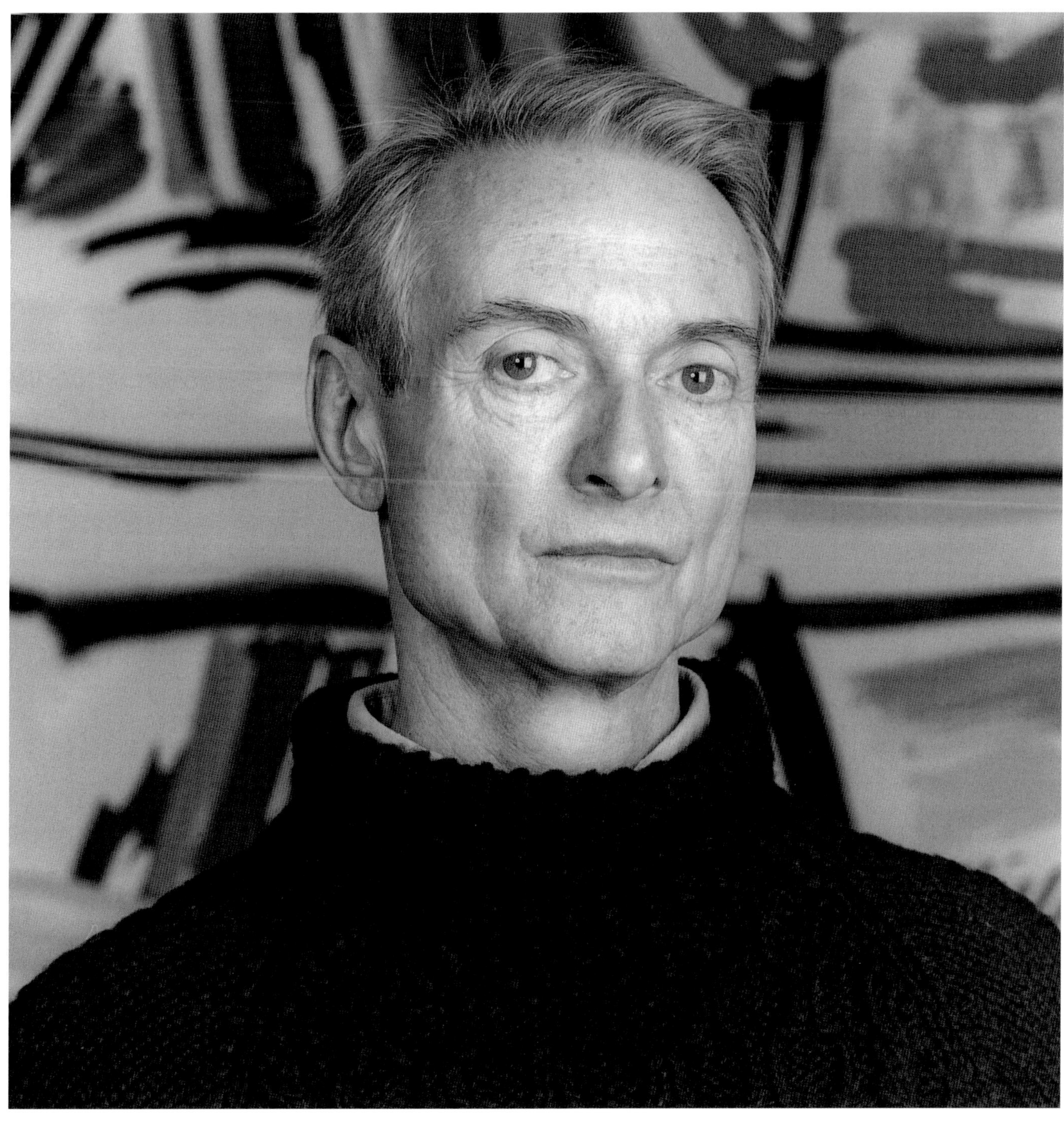

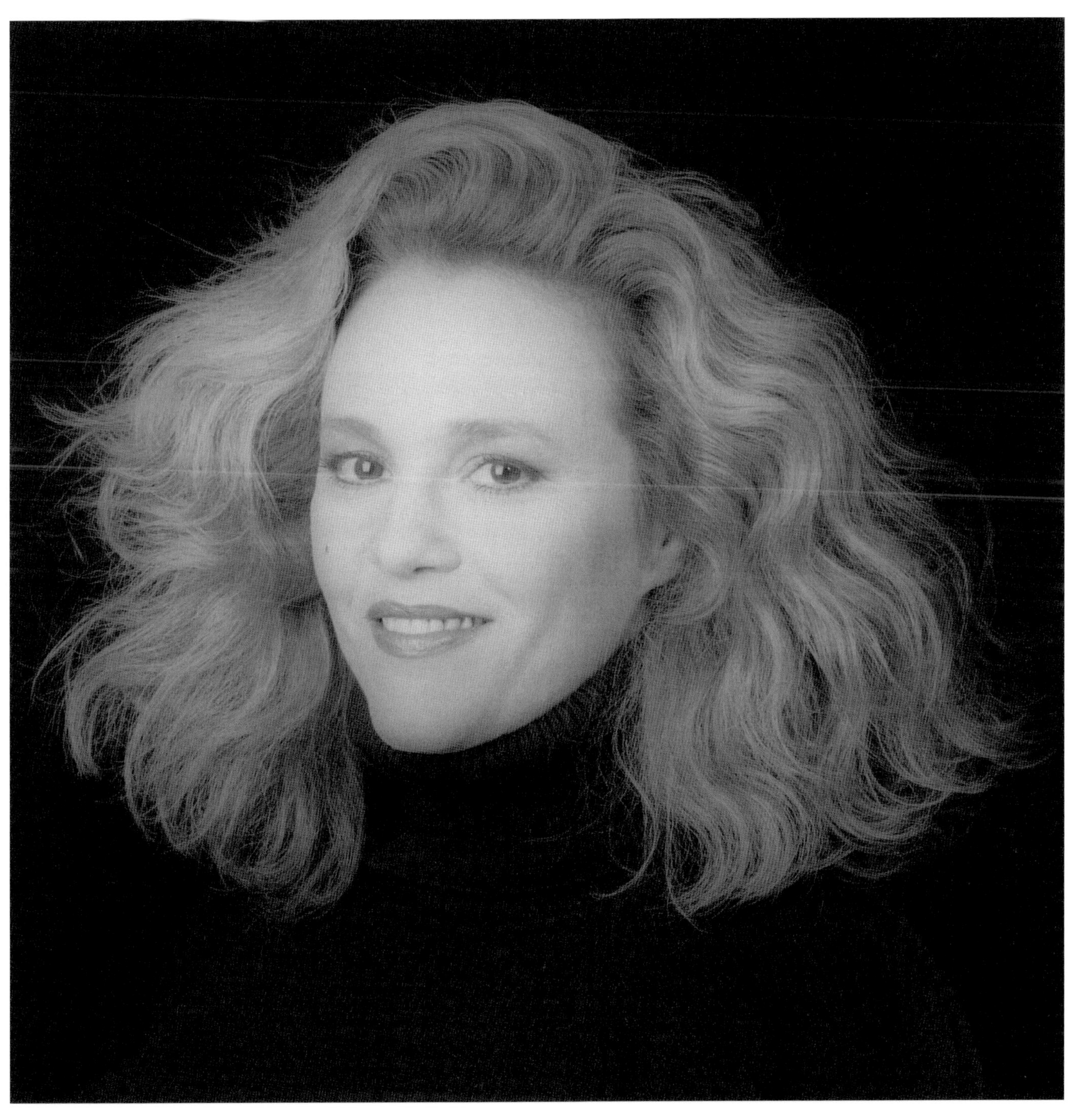

Bruno Bischofberger, 1985

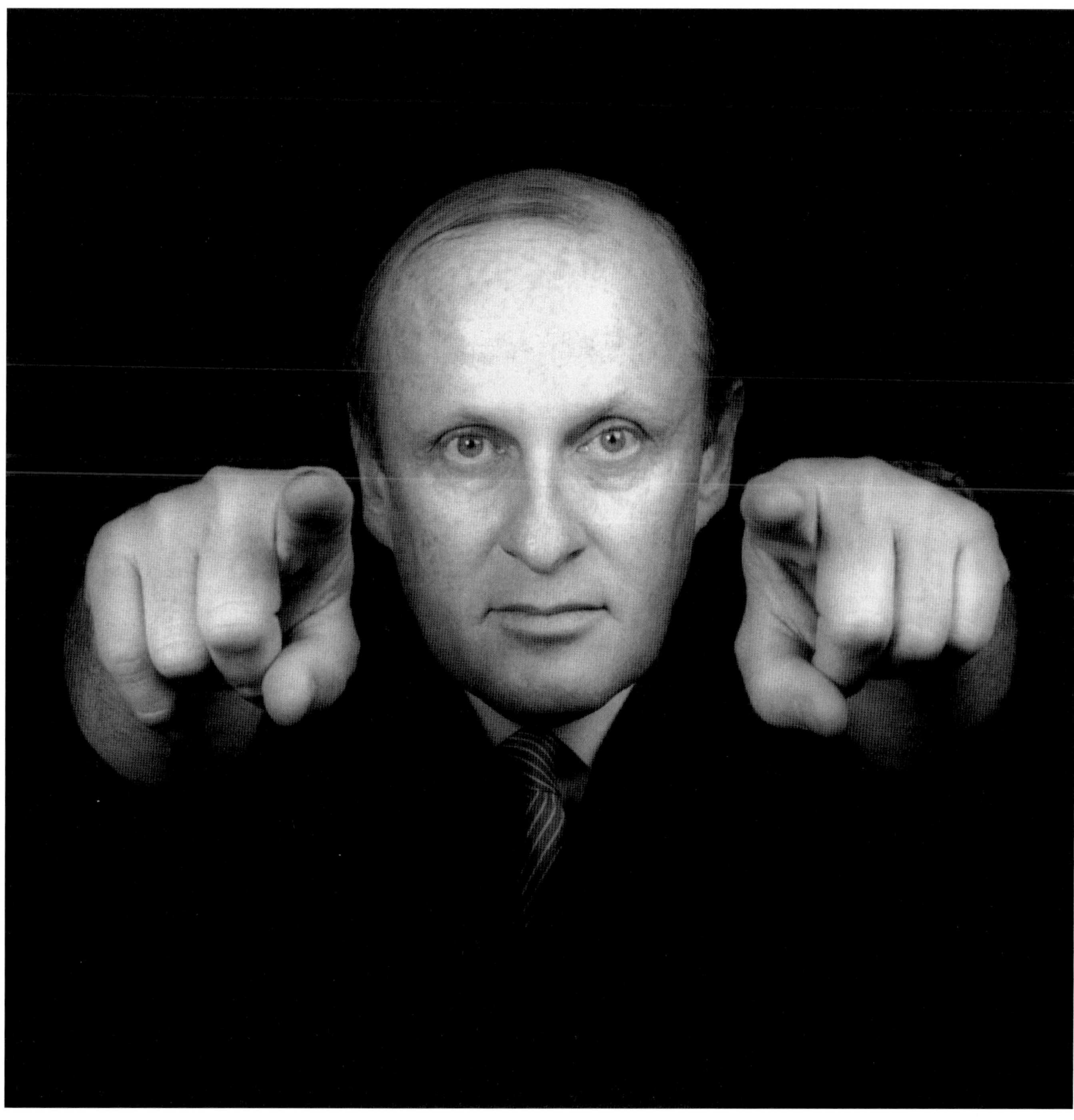

Plate 79 / Catalogue # 8 Cora Bischofberger, 1985

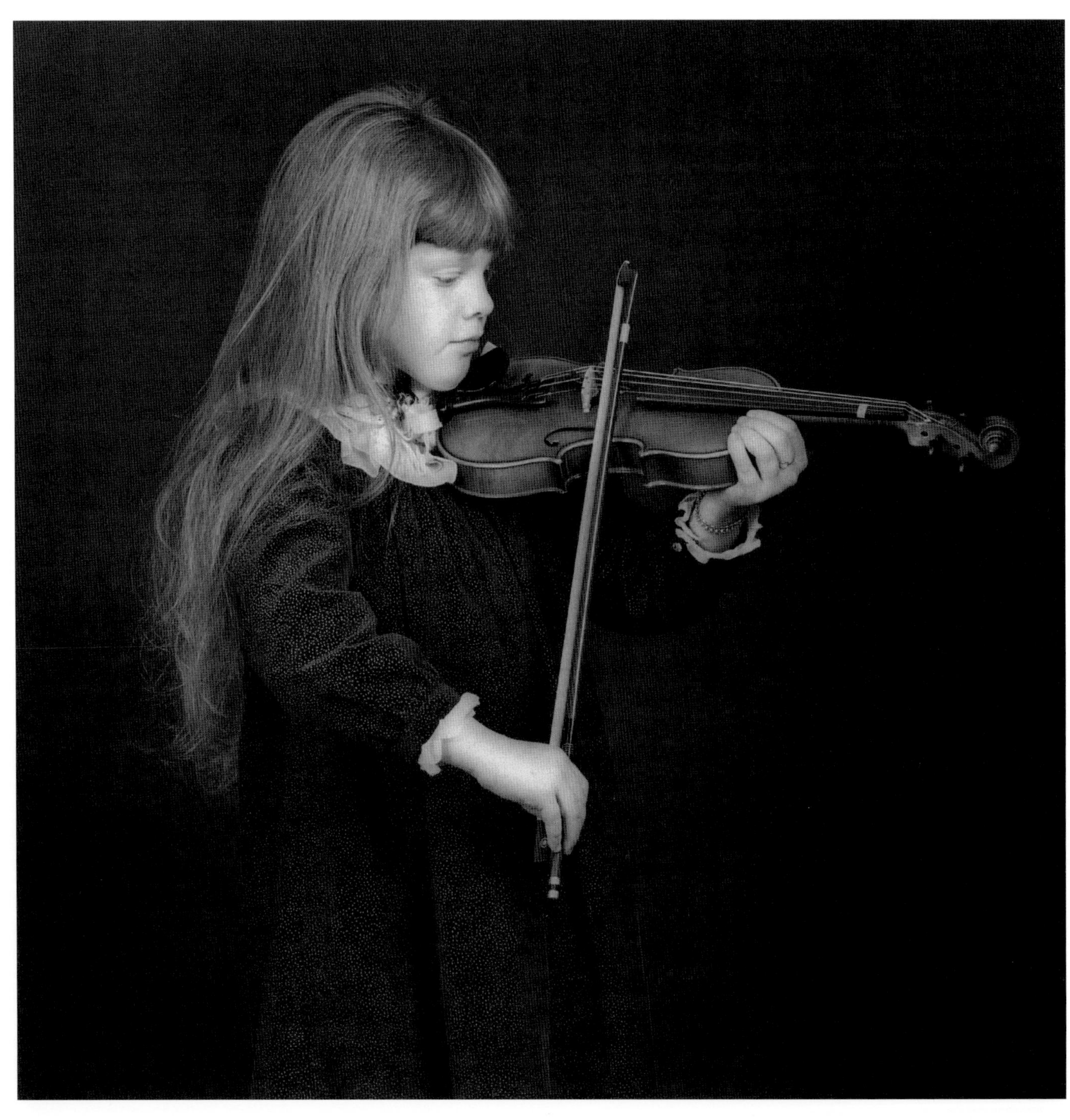

Magnus Bischofberger, 1985

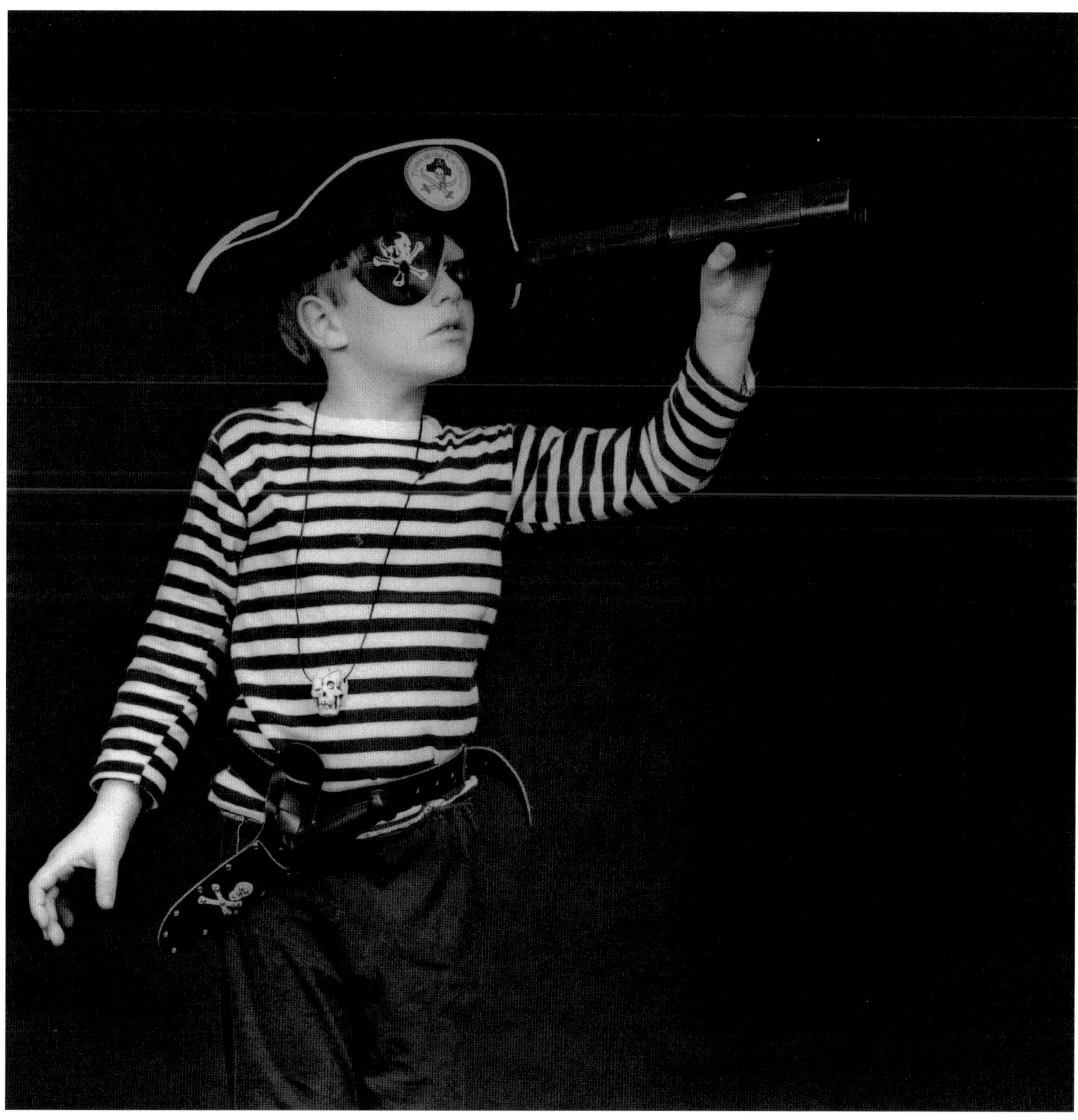

Leo Castelli, 1985

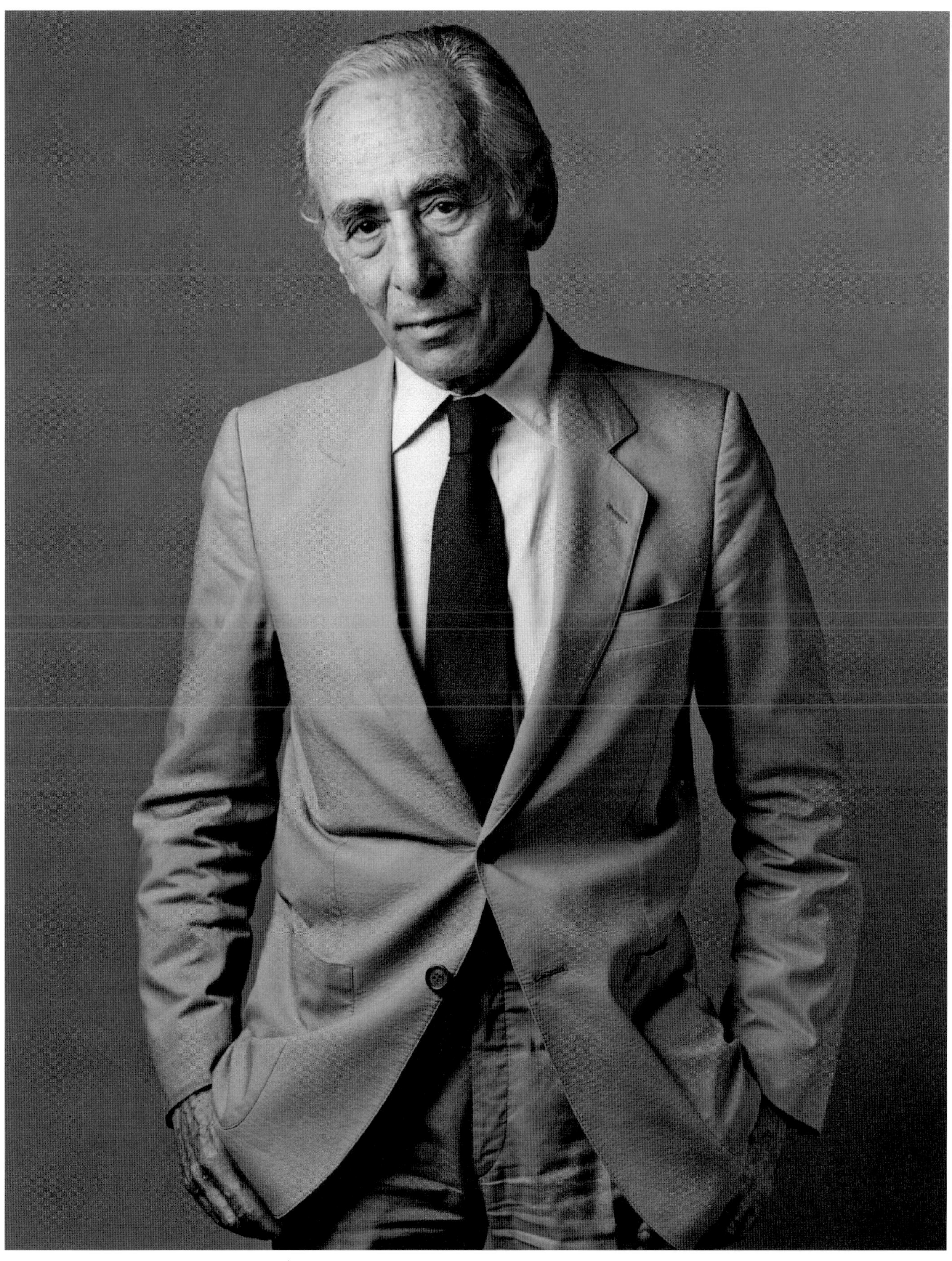

Plate 82 / Catalogue # 57

Norman Mailer, 1985

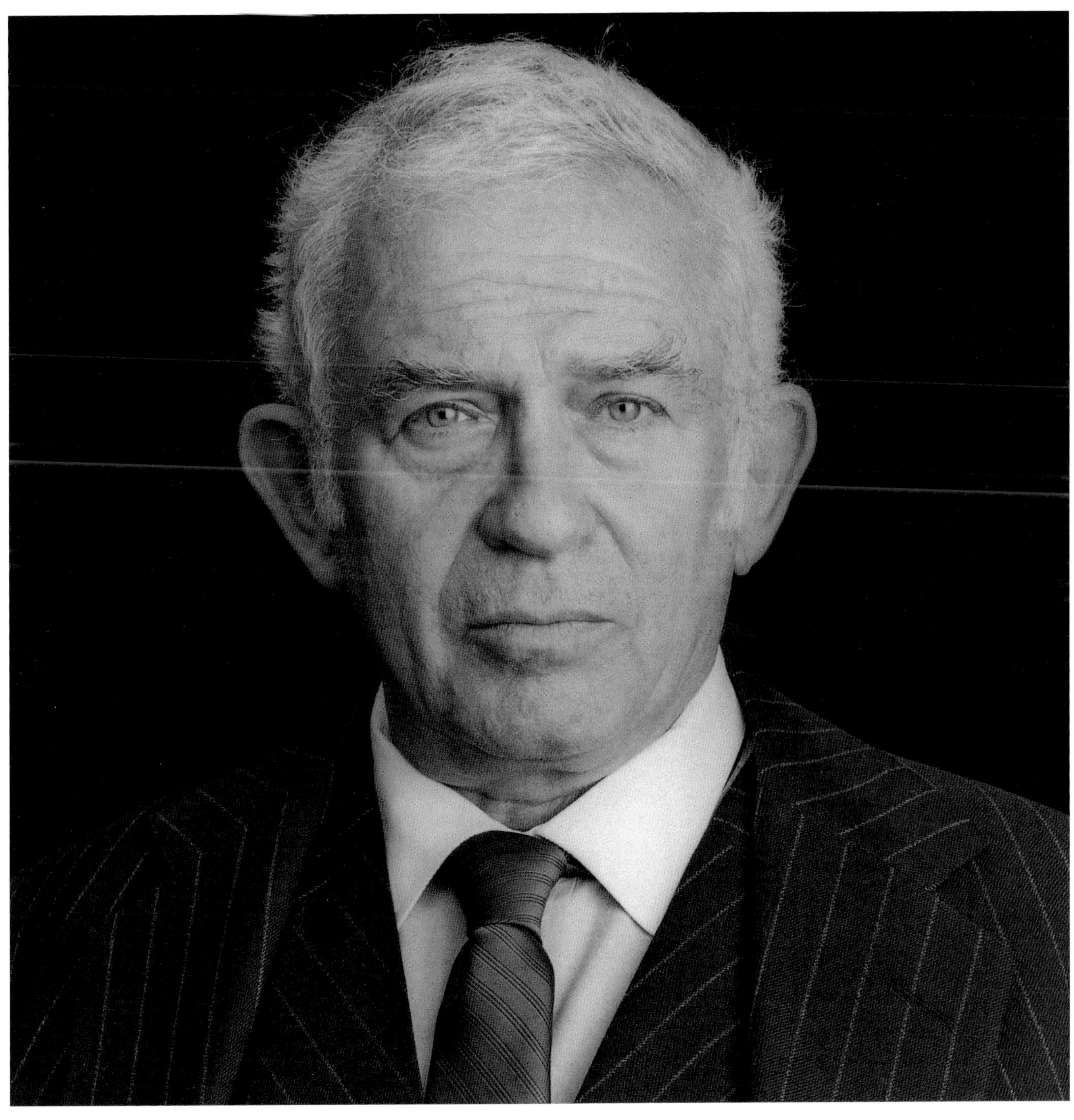

Plate 83 / Catalogue # 12 Sonia Braga, 1985

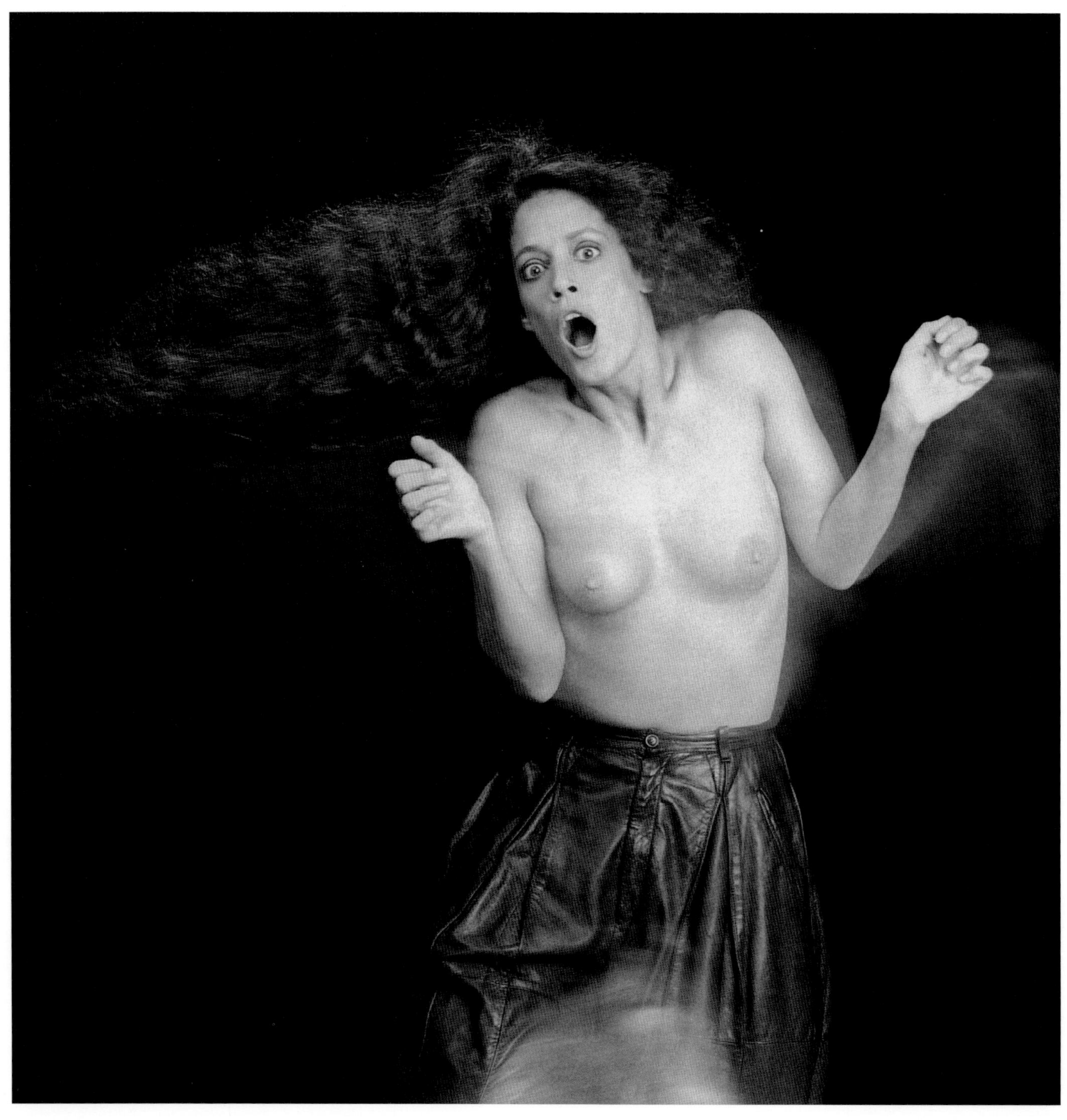

Bill T. Jones, 1985

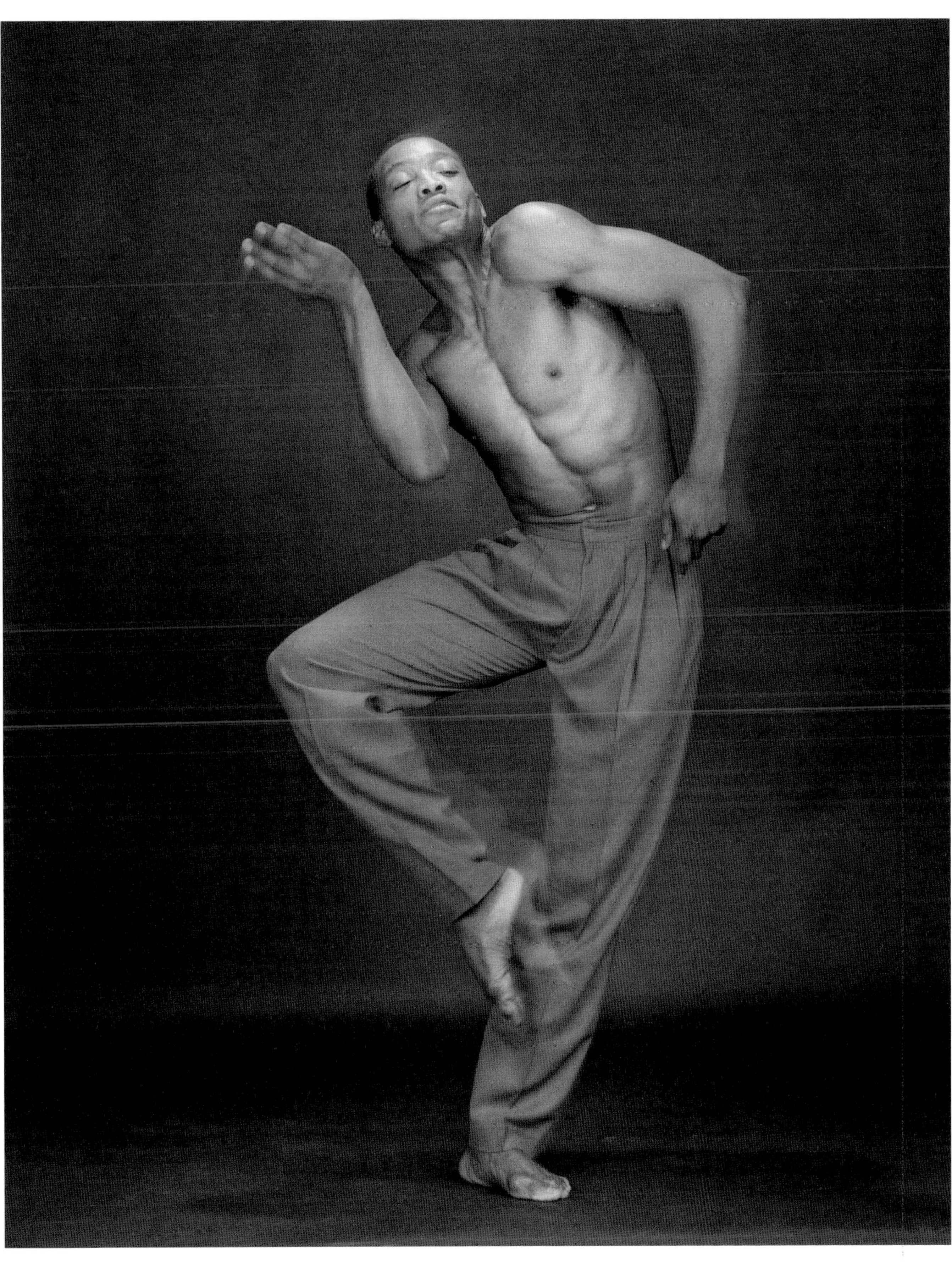

Julian Sands, 1986

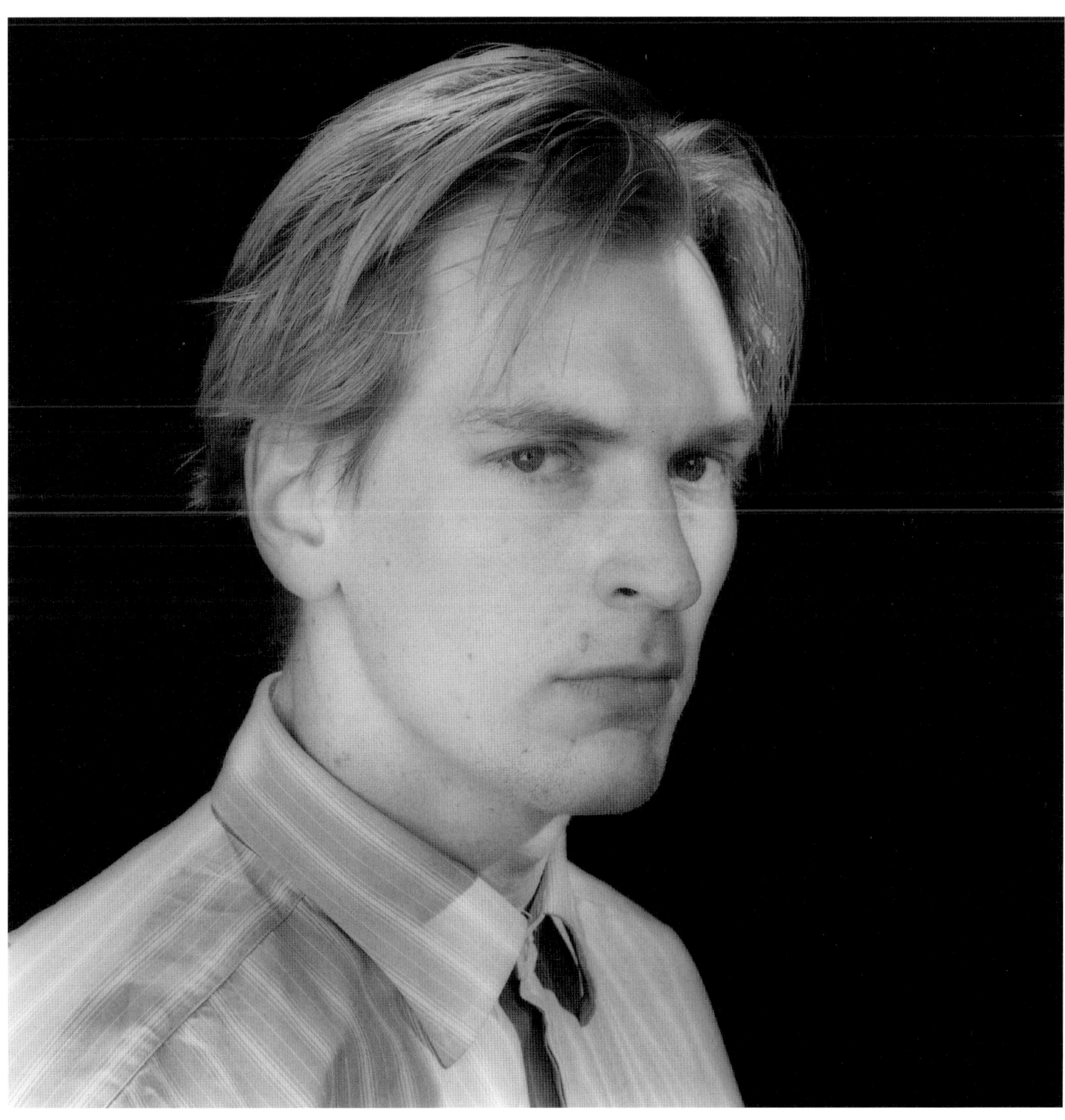

Louise Nevelson, 1986

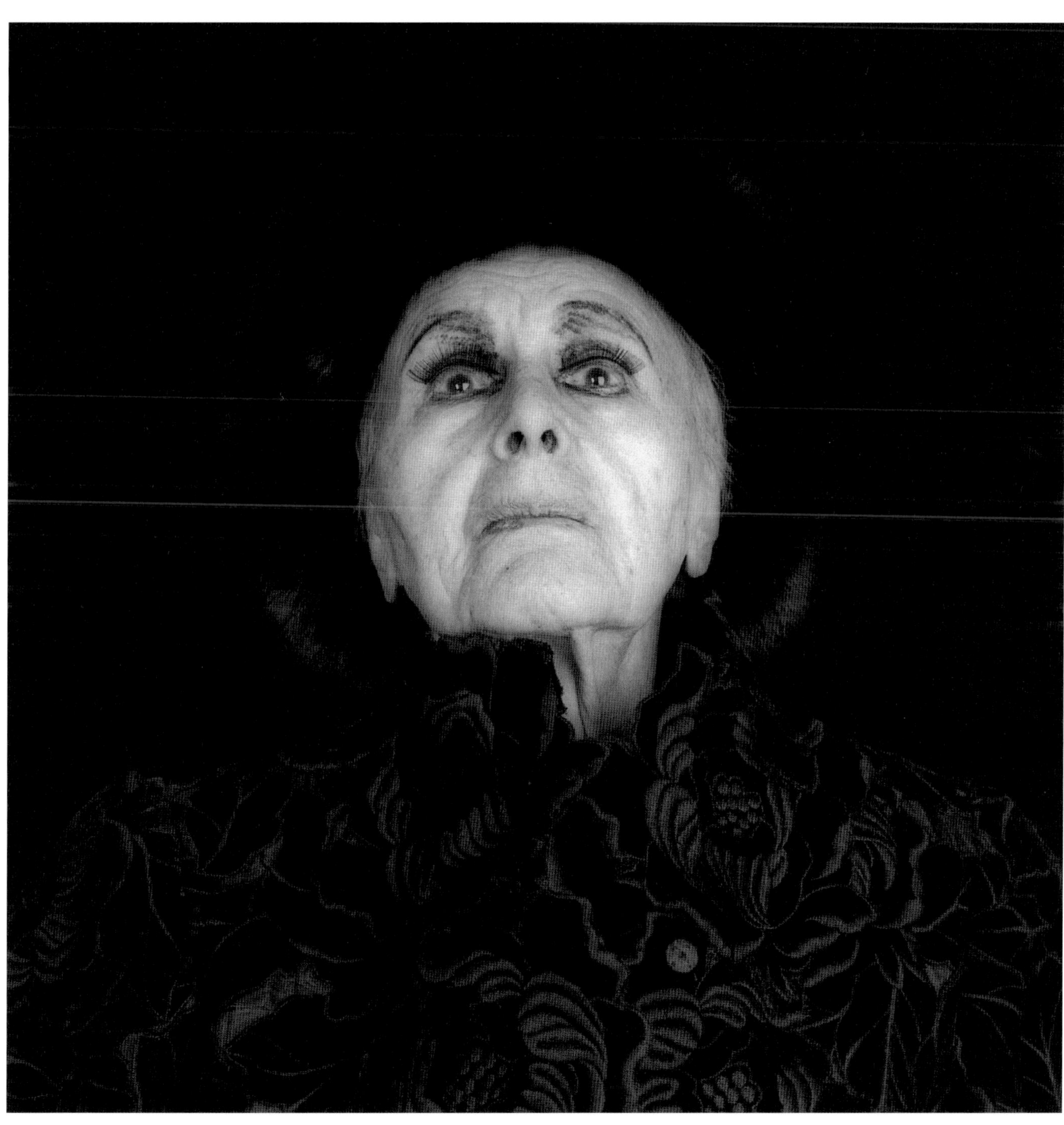

John Pope-Hennessy, 1986

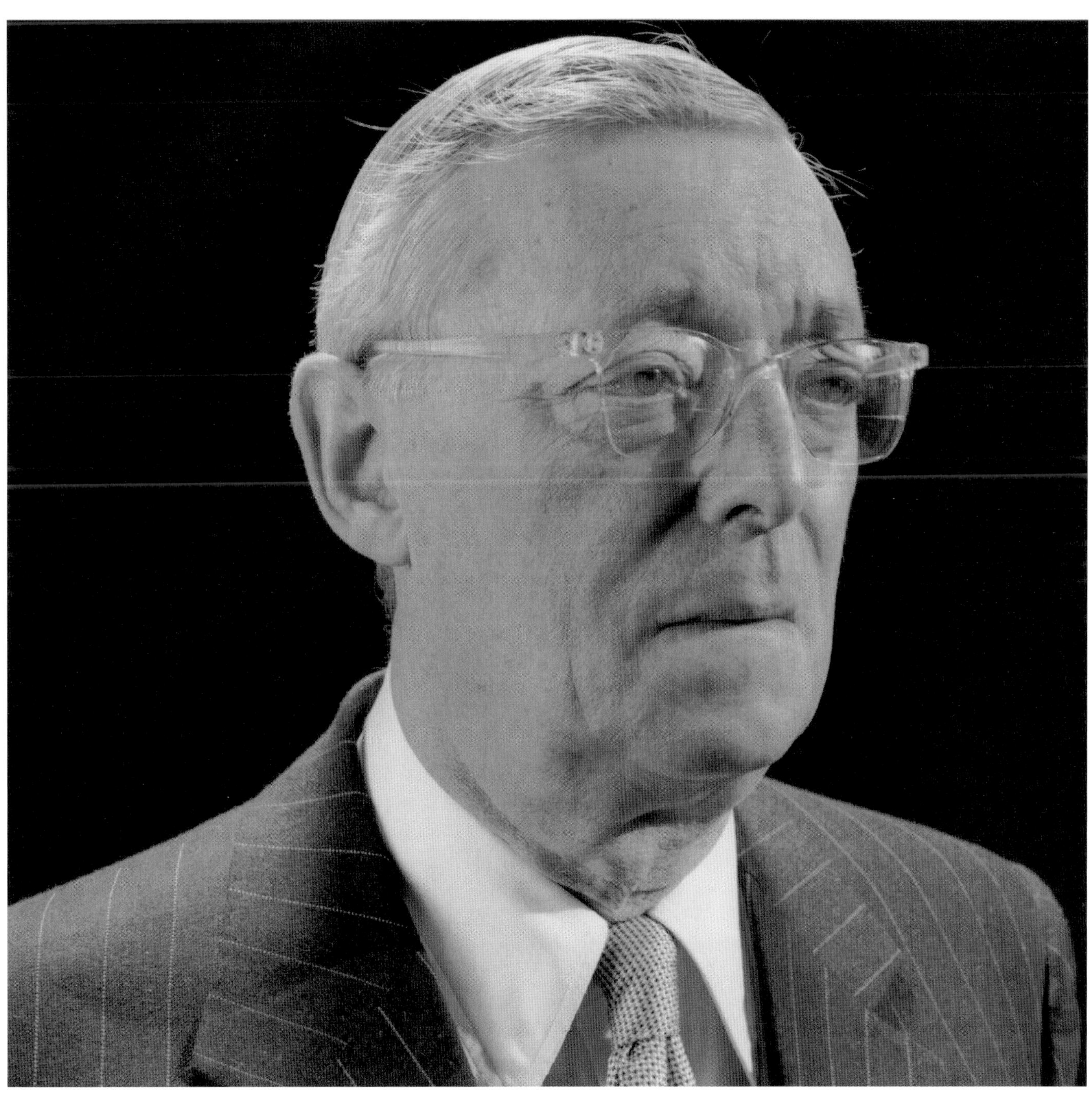

Richard Artschwager, 1986

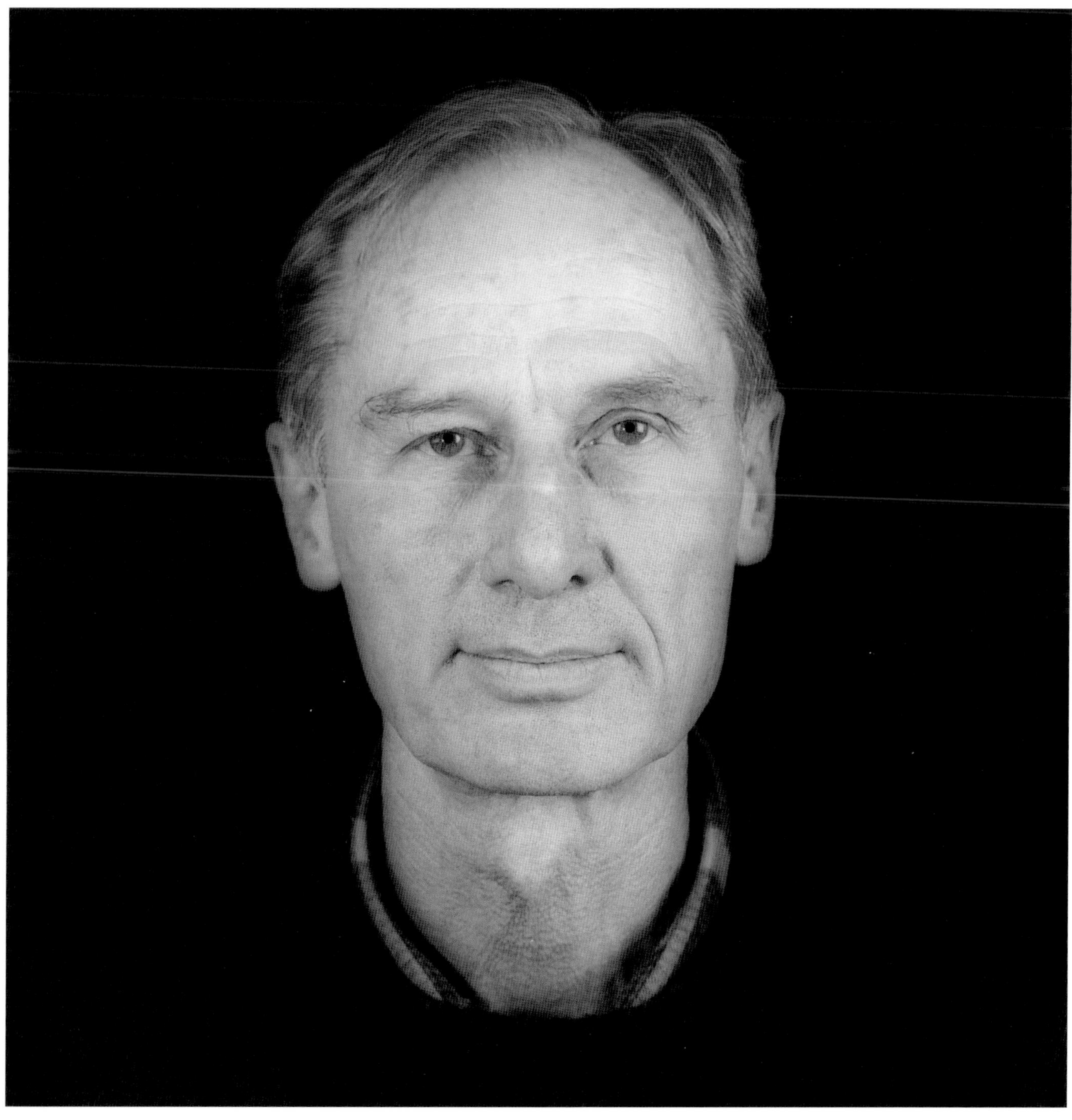

Brice Marden, 1986

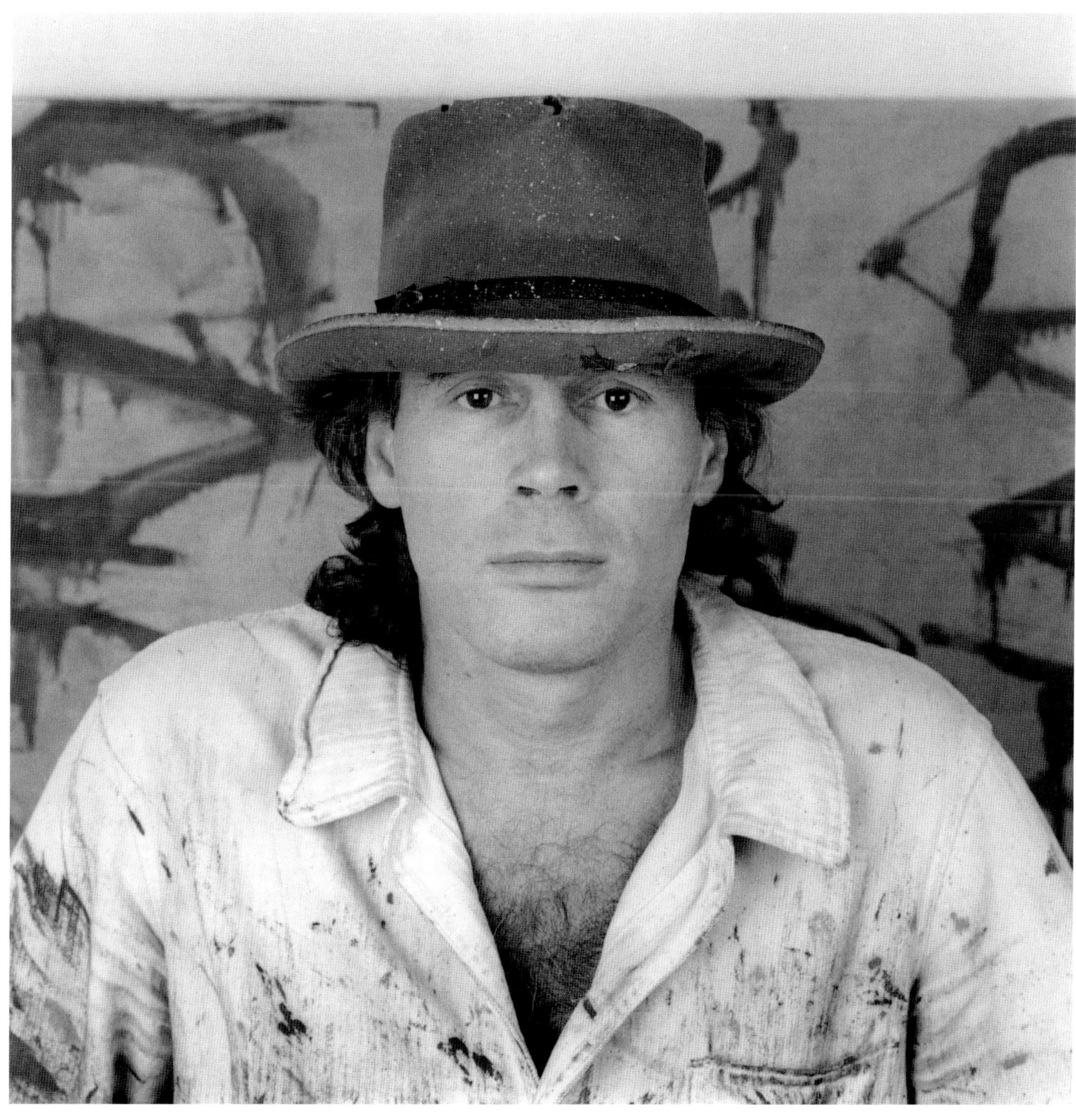

Laura Donnelley, 1986

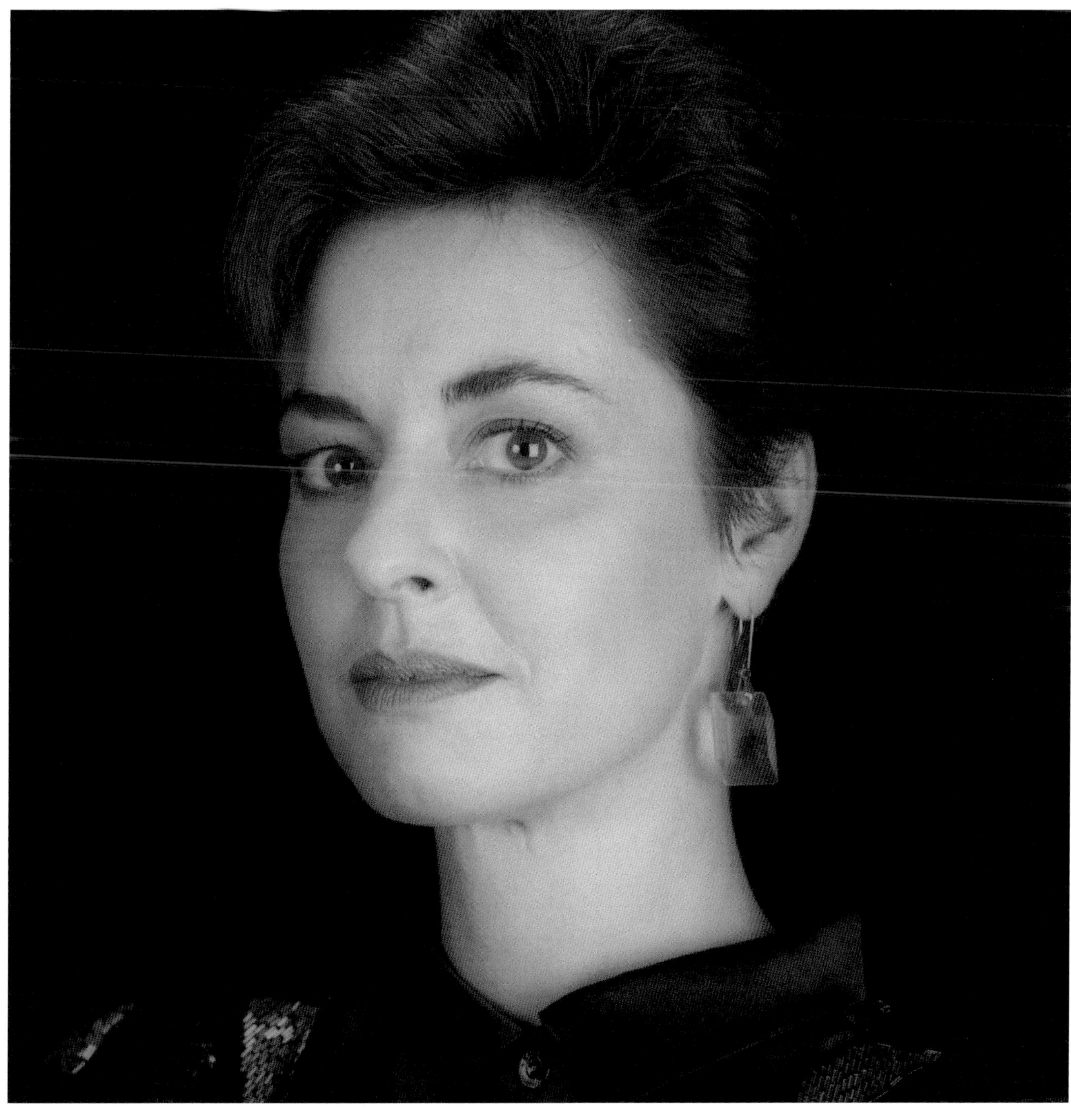

Patti Smith, 1986

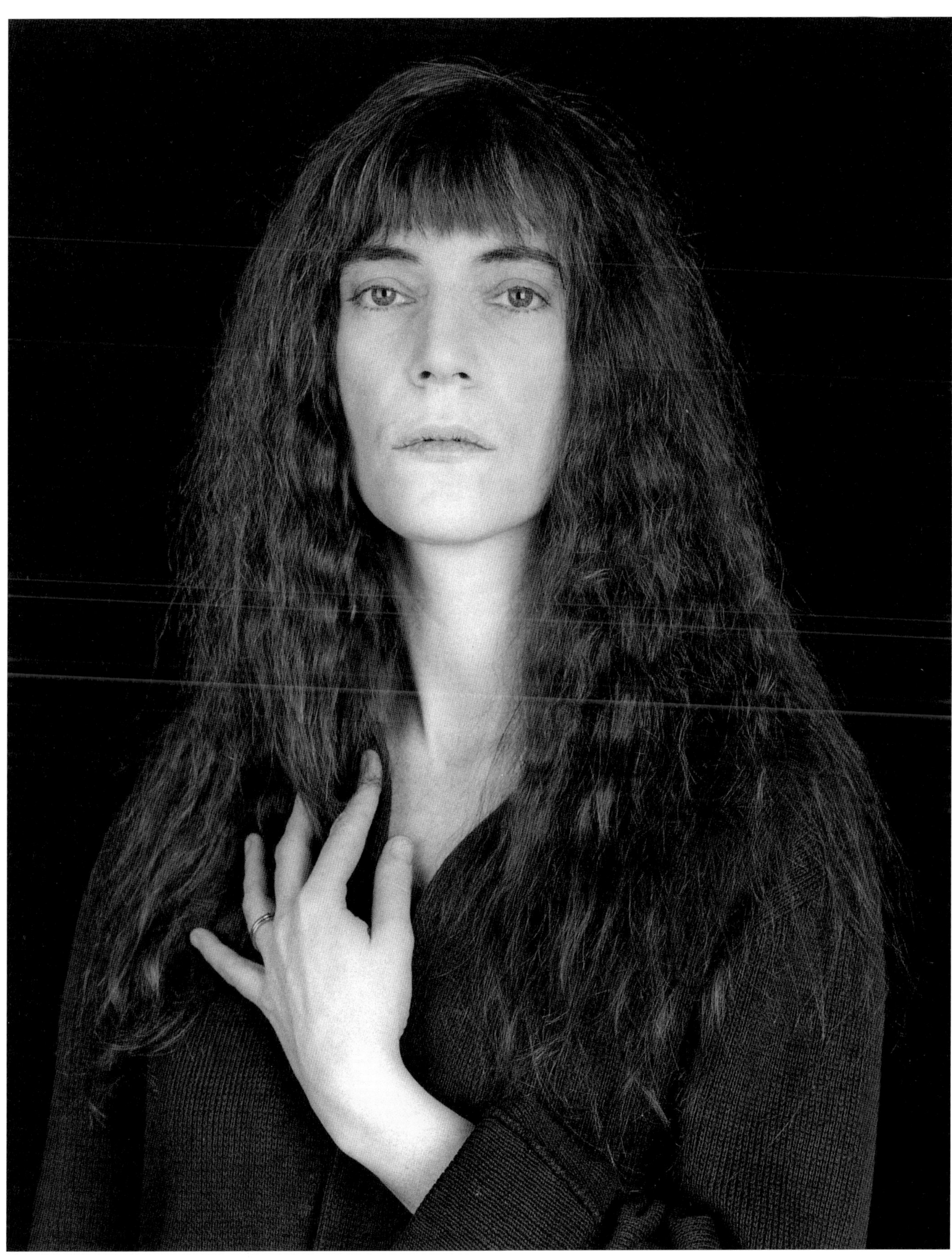

Michael Ward Stout, 1986

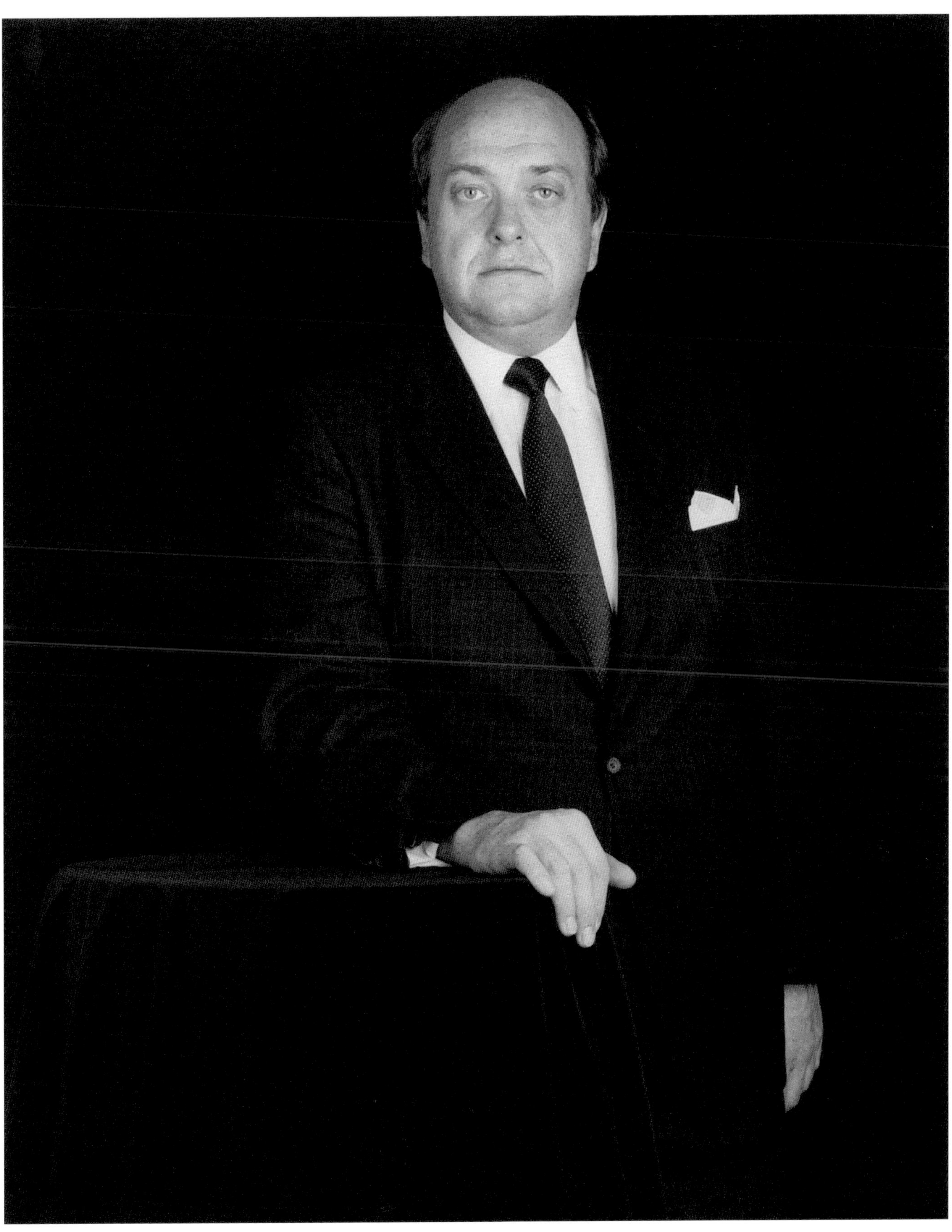

Deborah Irmas, 1988

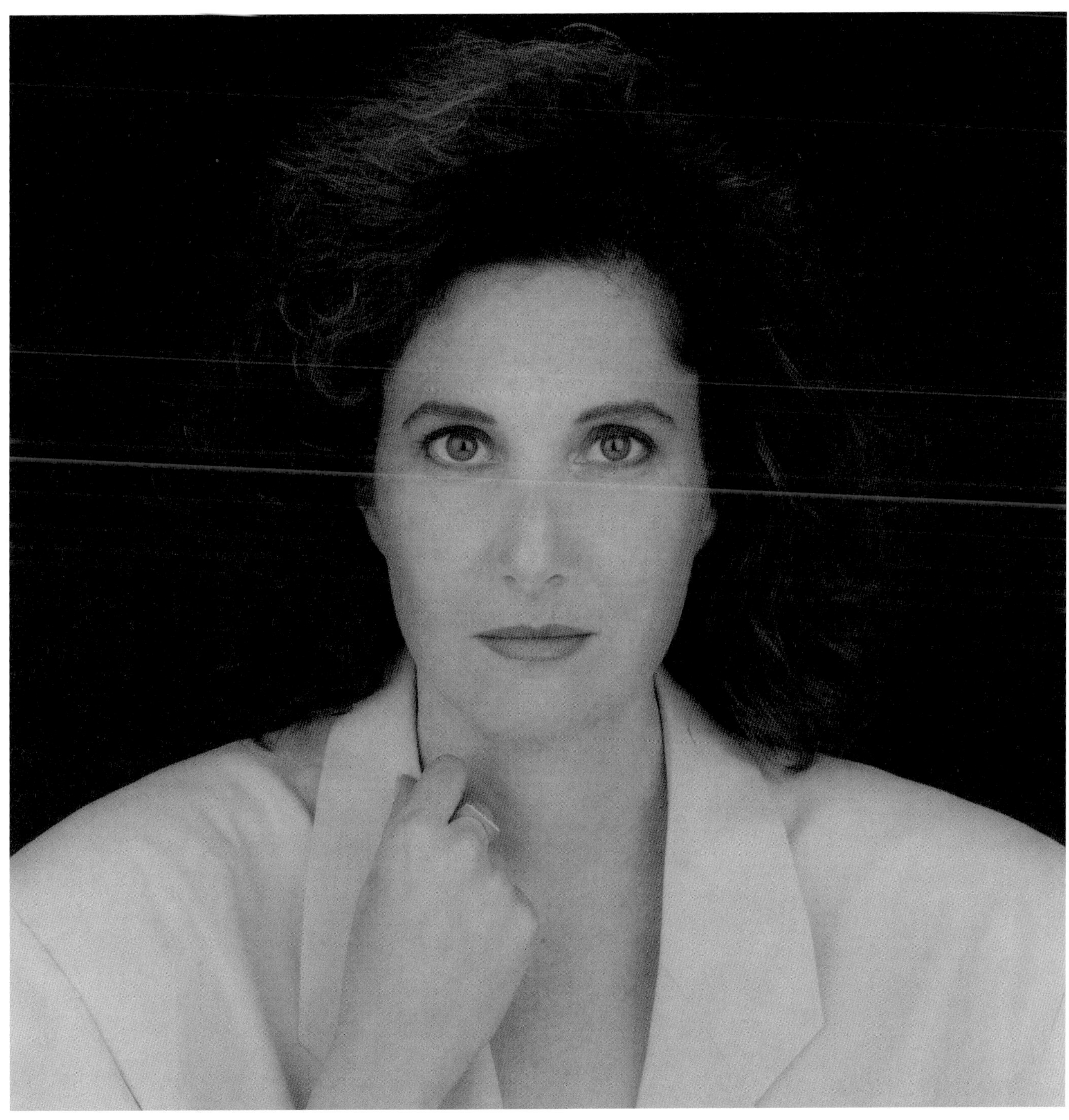

Eli Broad, 1986

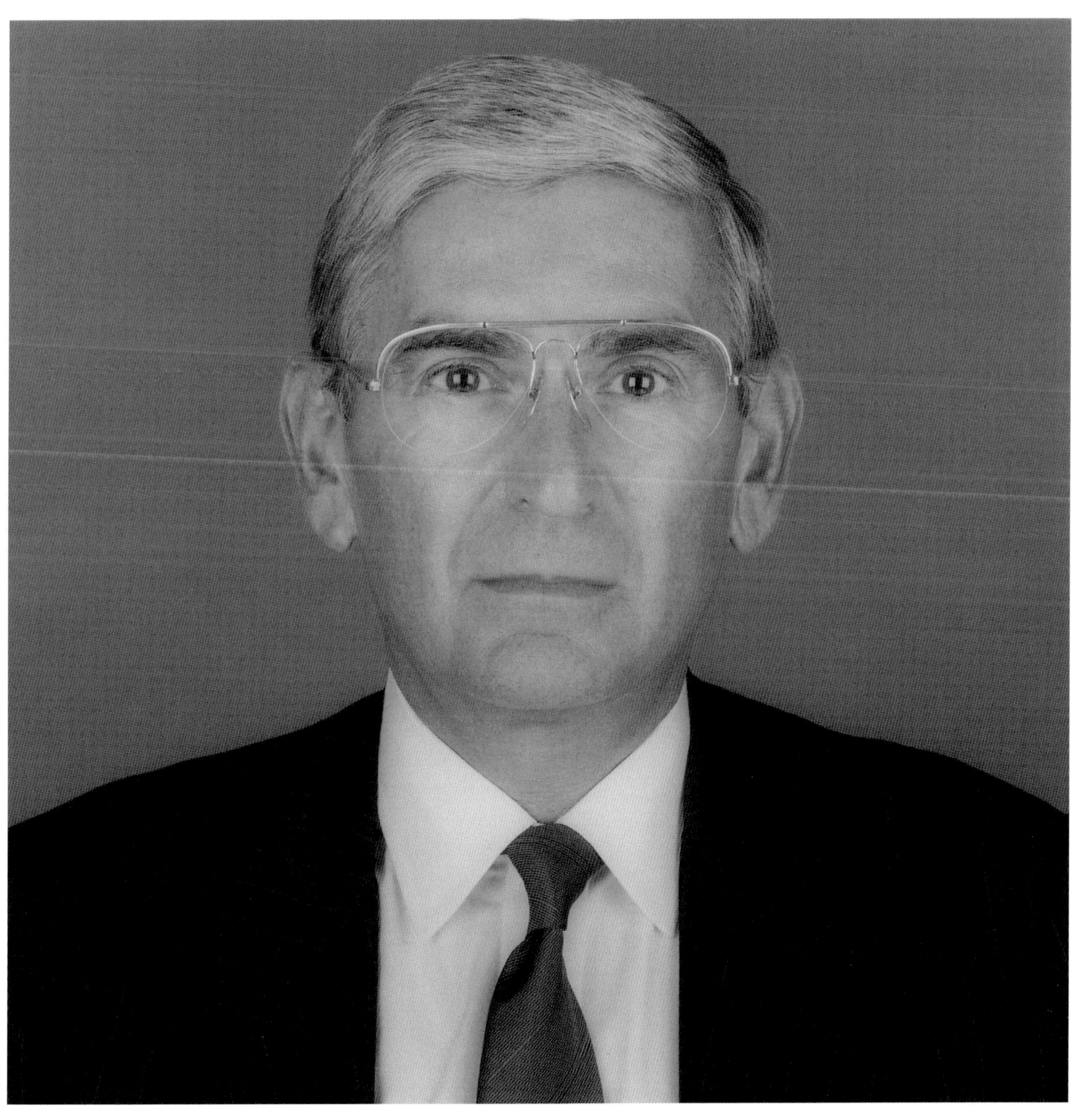

Grace Jones, 1988

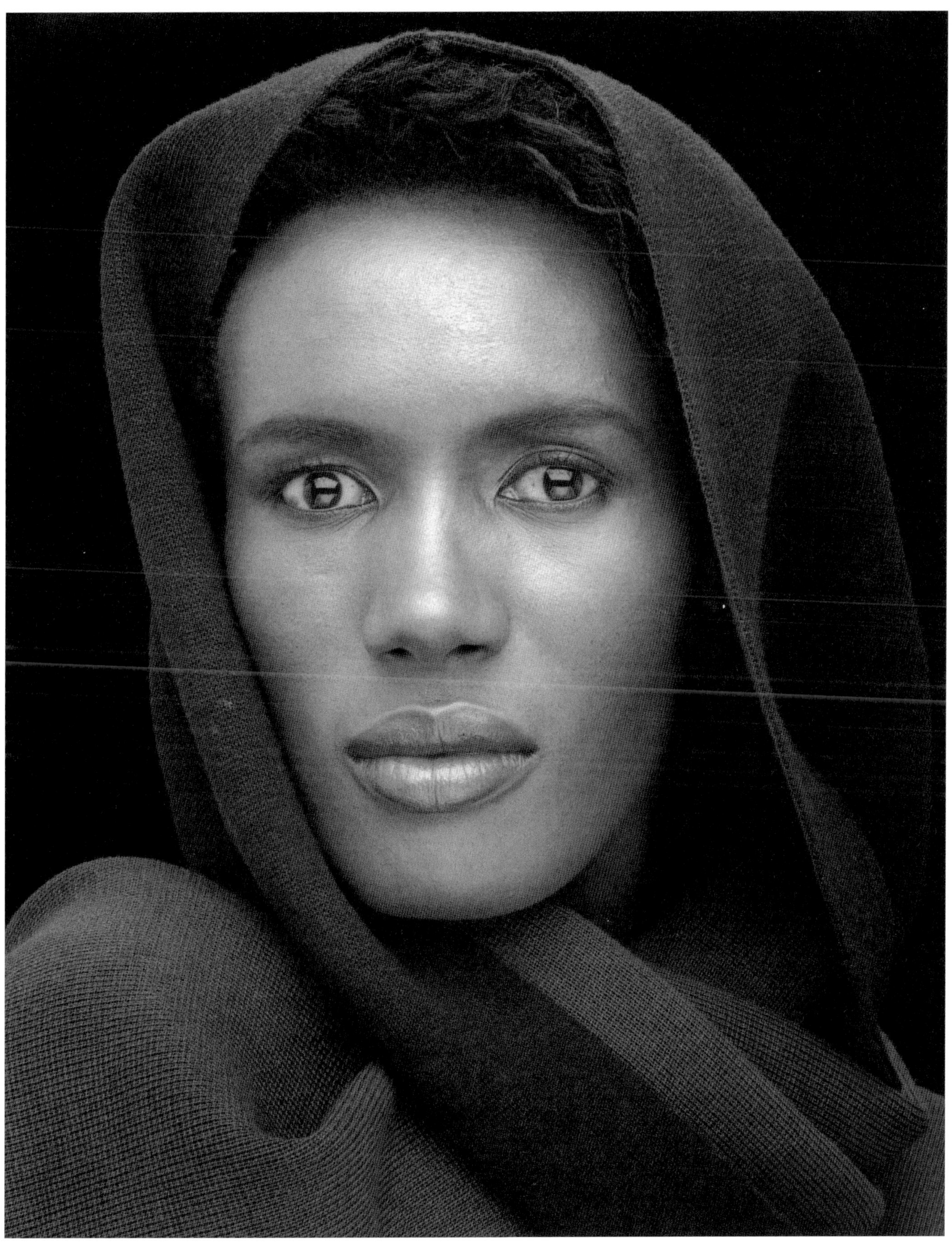

Laurie Anderson, 1987

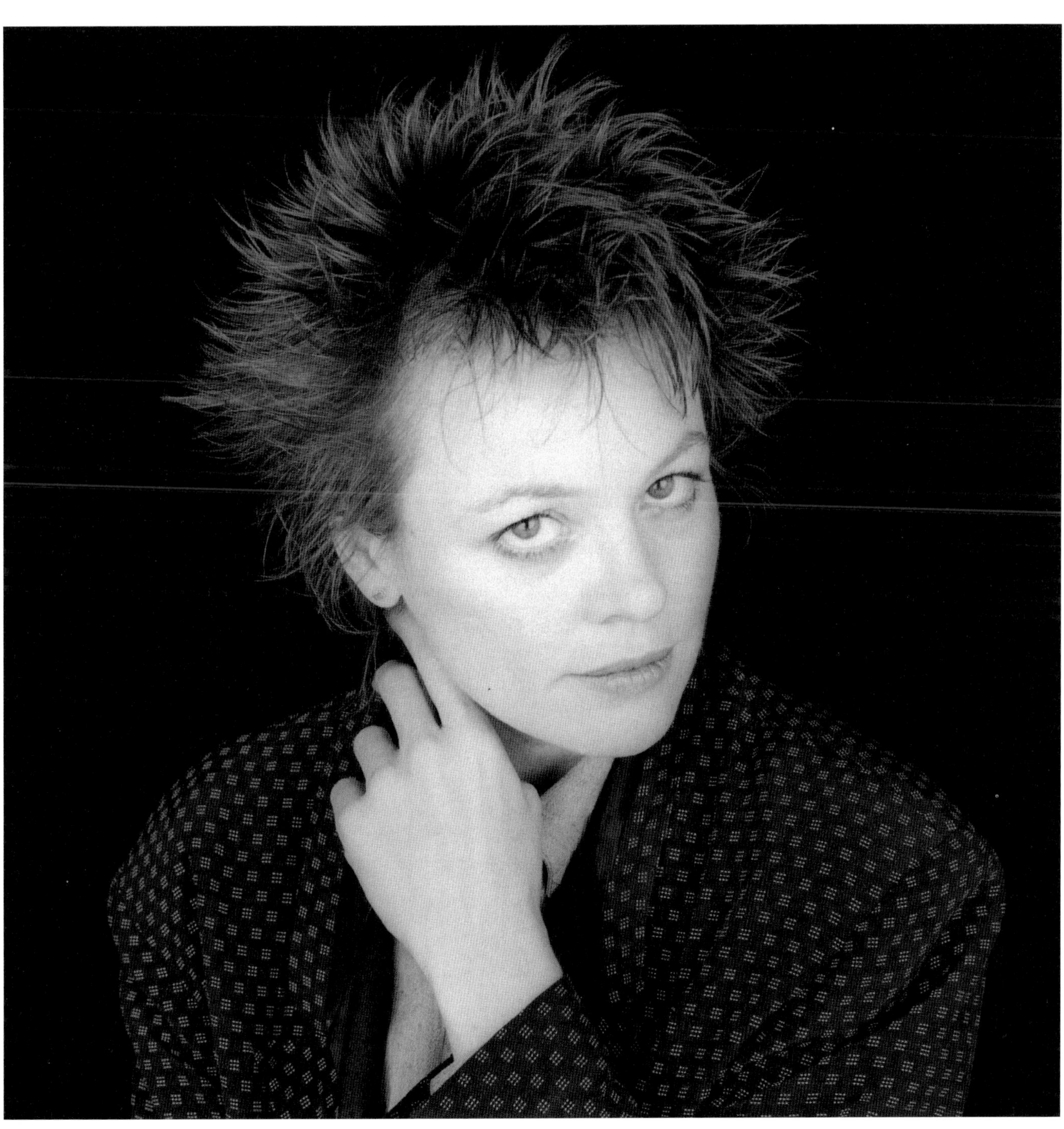

Yoko Ono, 1988

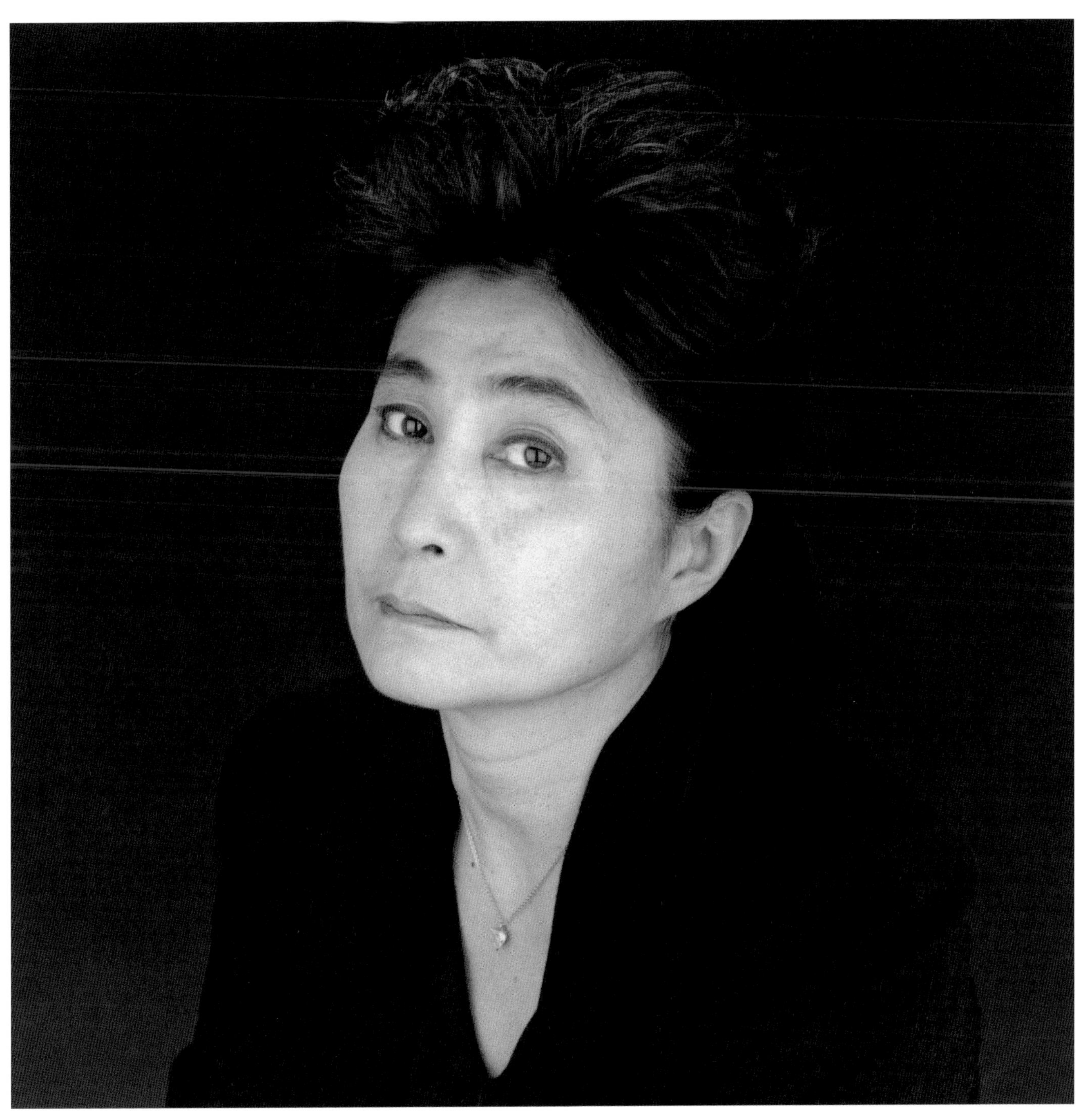

Plate 98 / Catalogue # 23 Melody Danielson, 1987

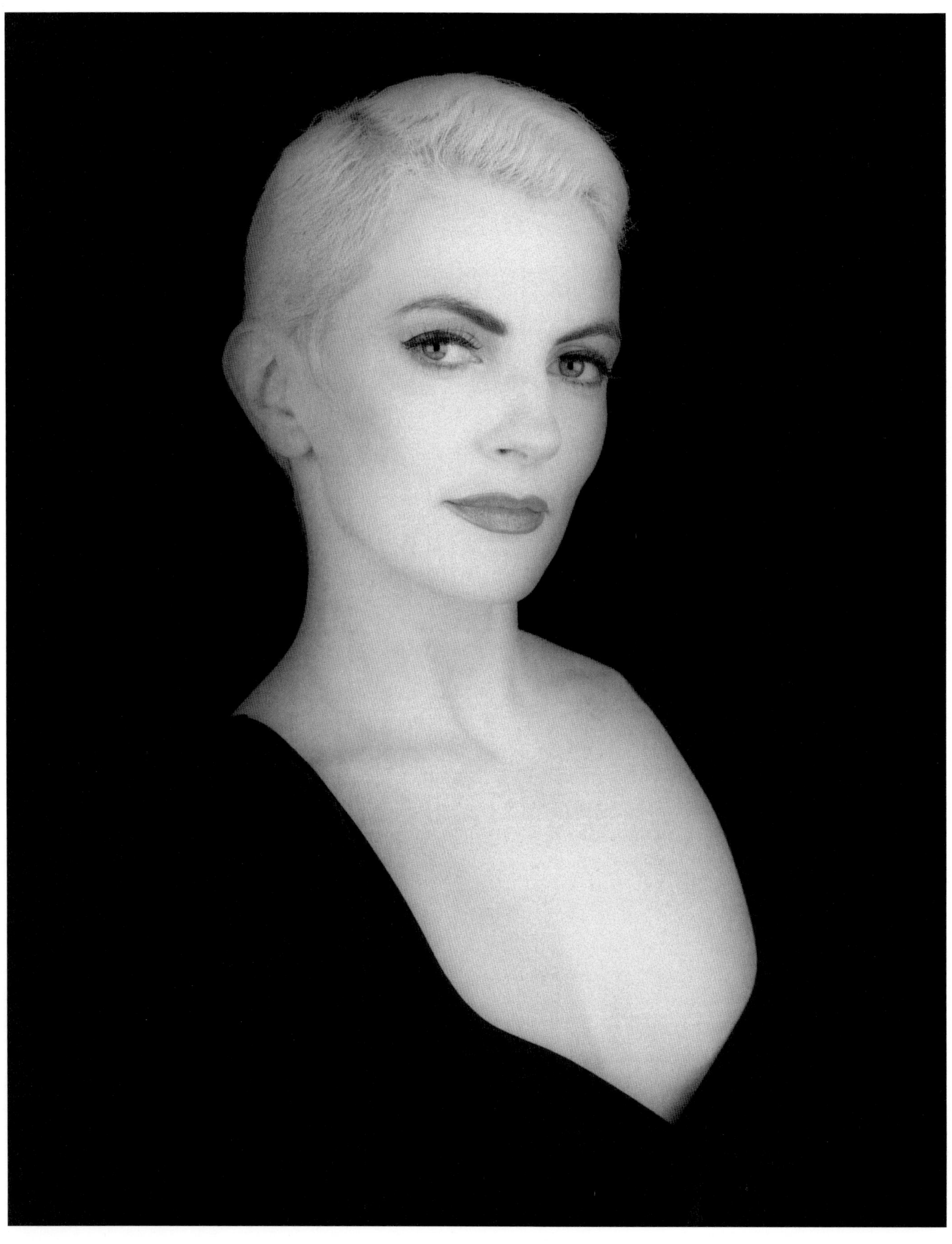

Susan Sarandon, 1988

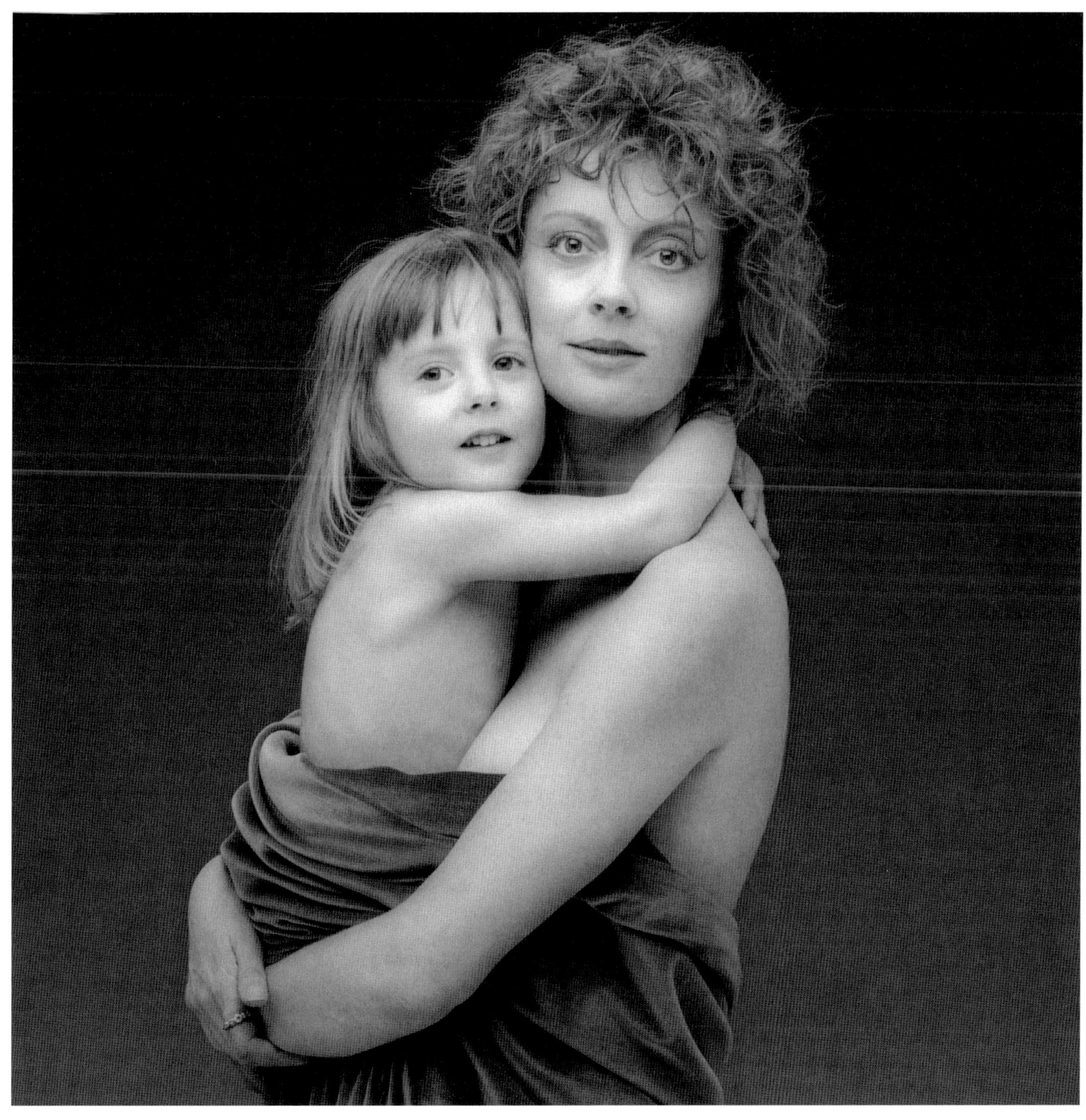

Isabella Rossellini, 1988

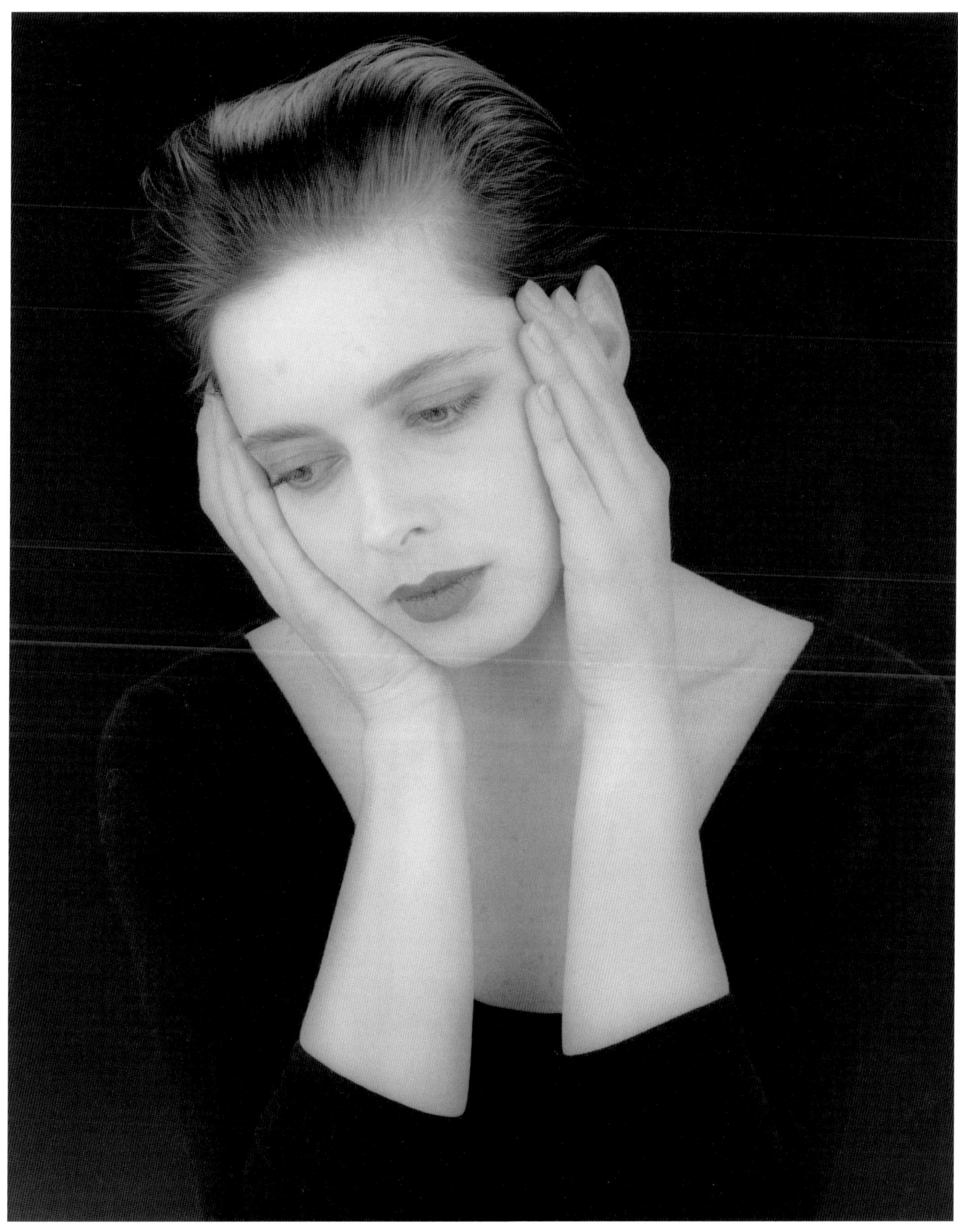

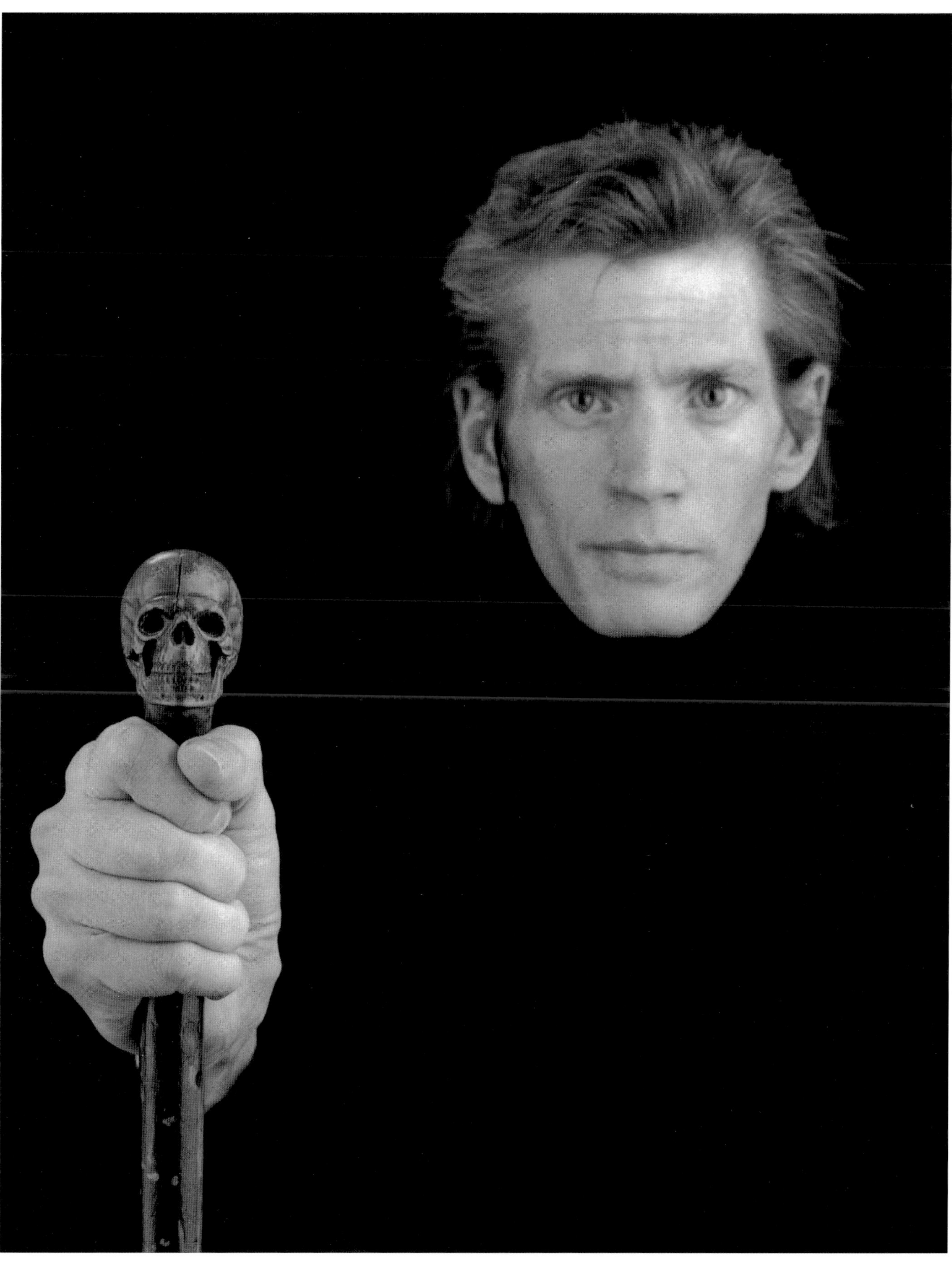

Unless otherwise noted, all works are lent by the Robert Mapplethorpe Foundation. The MAP number provided for each of those works is the inventory number used by the foundation. Dimensions are of the images and are given as height by width.

1 Kathy Acker

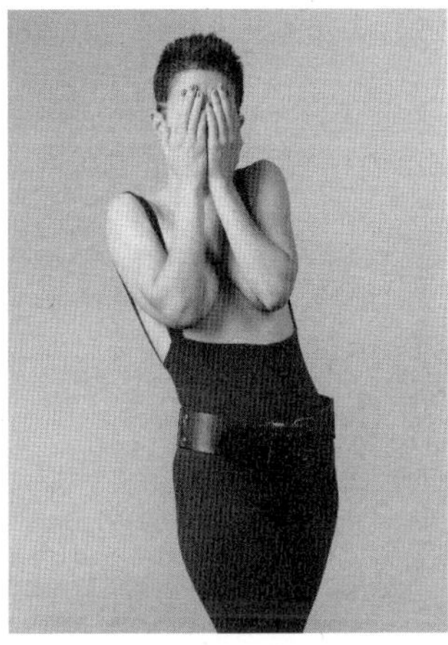

Gelatin silver print, 1983
19 1/4 x 15 1/8 in.
MAP 1125 / Plate 54

It is now unclear what brought Kathy Acker (1947–1997), the radically innovative novelist, playwright, and teacher of performance art, to Mapplethorpe's studio on this particular occasion, although a photograph he made of her at a different sitting in 1983 was published the next year in the fashion magazine The Face. He photographed her again in 1984, and in 1986 she wrote a stunning, incantatory, nearly surreal introduction to the Power of Theatrical Madness, Mapplethorpe's documentation of a Belgian dance performance. Active as a performance artist in the punk scene, Acker knew Patti Smith and, perhaps through her, Mapplethorpe. Her writing was characterized by bizarrely structured prose that was indebted to techniques used by William Burroughs and marked by the incorporation of passages that were deliberately and transparently plagiarized from famous literary classics such as Hawthorne's Scarlet Letter and by an obsessive concern with sex, blood, and violence. A feminist heroine, she was known for her unconventional if not outright wild behavior and performances, of which this image is evidence.

Having removed her upper outer garments, she posed with her arms and elbows covering her breasts and her hands covering her eyes in a warped, grown-up version of the peekaboo game one plays with babies.«1» Acker was known for her striking wardrobe and her remaining garment is svelte and unusual. Although clipped quite short, her fingernails are lacquered. Multiple minute studs are visible along the outer edge of her right ear. It is perhaps perverse to include a portrait of a vibrant person like Acker that does not show her eyes, except that it is a good example of Mapplethorpe's playing with the outer edges of what constitutes a valid portrait and, despite her obscured face, a reasonable guess can be made about her personality.

«1» Alternate readings might be that, as her eyes are covered, she cannot see her nudity in some imagined mirror or that the force of her personality was so strong that it needed to be shielded from the camera lest harm be done.

2 Mario Amaya

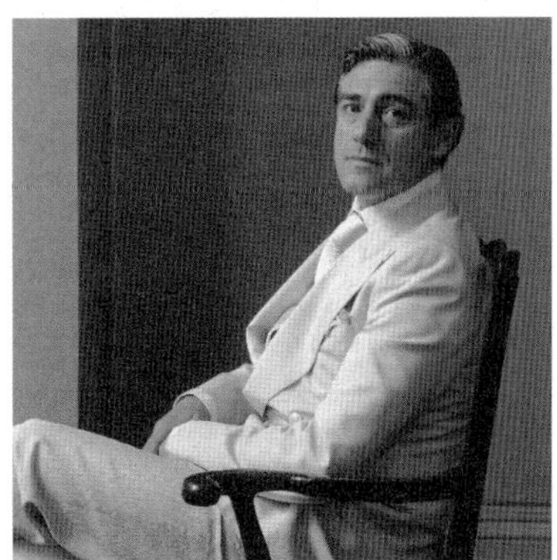

Gelatin silver print, 1978
13 1/4 x 14 in.
MAP 3.1 / Plate 10

In 1978, the year this photograph was made, Mario Amaya (1933–1986) was the director of the Chrysler Museum in Norfolk, Virginia. As early as 1970, he had bought an assemblage by Mapplethorpe for his personal collection, and he gave Mapplethorpe his first museum exhibition at the Chrysler, writing a brief, perceptive introduction to the slender catalogue that accompanied the show. There he observed that, during a portrait shoot, Mapplethorpe allowed his sitters to project fantasies of themselves while waiting for "the moment when he can fix the image that unites with his own fantasies of the subject."«1» If this was his view, then it would be interesting to know what fantasy Amaya thought he projected during his own portrait sitting and also what fantasy Mapplethorpe joined him in presenting. His seated pose was the mirror image of one that Philip Johnson assumed for Mapplethorpe's camera the same year (see plate 9), but where Johnson was all in somber hues and severe of mien, Amaya was all in whites and amiable.

«1» Mario Amaya, introduction, in Robert Mapplethorpe: Photographs, exh. cat. (Norfolk, Va.: Chrysler Museum at Norfolk, 1978), n.p.

3 Laurie Anderson

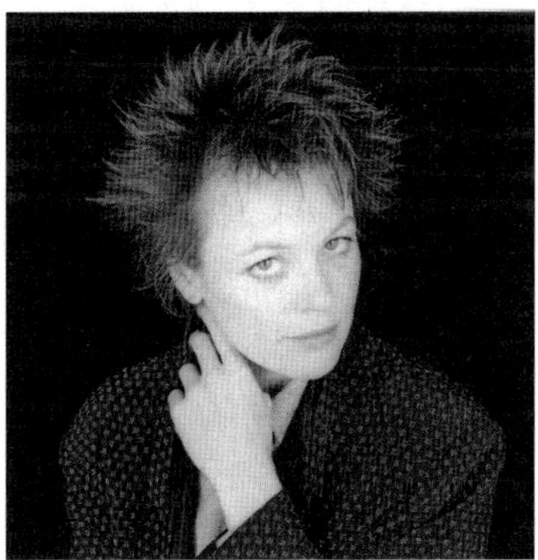

Gelatin silver print, 1987
19 1/8 x 19 1/4 in.
MAP 1814 / Plate 96

Mapplethorpe photographed the singer, musician, and performance artist Laurie Anderson (b. 1947) for a project for the BBC. This is one of two very similar portraits that Mapplethorpe editioned from this sitting. In both, the index finger of her left hand grazes her jaw, but in one, her eyes are closed, making it seem as if she is listening to music. Here, chin lowered, as if expecting something, she looks gently up toward the camera, an impression that is emphasized because so much of the whites of her eyes is visible. As she was photographed against a black background, the whiteness of her skin is conspicuous. Her artfully spiky hairdo saves her appearance from severity.

Besides appearing in her own spoken-word performances and her highly experimental multimedia productions, for which she writes the music, invents instruments, and devises visual effects, Anderson has collaborated extensively with other musicians, poets, performers, and writers, among them William Burroughs, John Giorno, Lou Reed, Wim Wenders, and Bill T. Jones (for Mapplethorpe's portrait of Jones, see plate 84). Her stage productions—from O Superman, which launched her recording career, to her current effort, Homeland—have often been a weird amalgam of the oracular, the political, and the vernacular. She has consistently exhibited her visual works, including photographs, in galleries and museums. In the 1970s, she was represented by the art dealer Holly Solomon, who also showed work by Mapplethorpe, so the singer and the photographer likely knew each other long before she came to be photographed by him. She is currently represented by the same art gallery in New York that represents the Robert Mapplethorpe Foundation.

4 Richard Artschwager

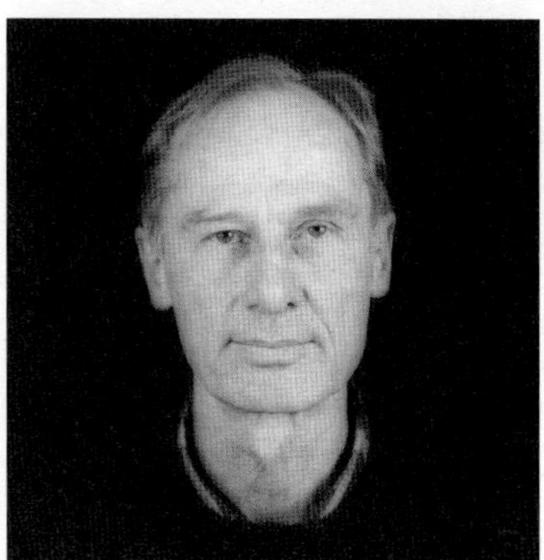

Gelatin silver print, 1986
19 1/8 x 19 1/8 in.
MAP 1754 / Plate 88

The commission from the curator Richard Marshall to photograph a group of fifty painters and sculptors, a project that was published in 1986 as 50 New York Artists,«1» brought Mapplethorpe into contact with a larger group of artists than he had previously known, most a generation older. He chose to photograph Richard Artschwager (b. 1923) against a black background, thus concentrating all attention on the artist's face. When the portrait was published, a sculpture by Artschwager, called Up and Across, was reproduced on the facing page, with a quotation from the artist in which he described the work as moving from the accessible to the inaccessible.«2» Artschwager faces the camera with level gaze and nearly without expression, presenting himself as an abstract object, somehow related to one of his sculptures.

Like Mapplethorpe, Artschwager made a portrait of the art dealer Holly Solomon, who early on did much to advance the photographer's career but, other than that, the two men had little in common.

«1» Richard D. Marshall, 50 New York Artists: A Critical Selection of Painters and Sculptors Working in New York, with photographs by Robert Mapplethorpe (San Francisco: Chronicle Books, 1986).
«2» Ibid., 19.

5 Marisa Berenson

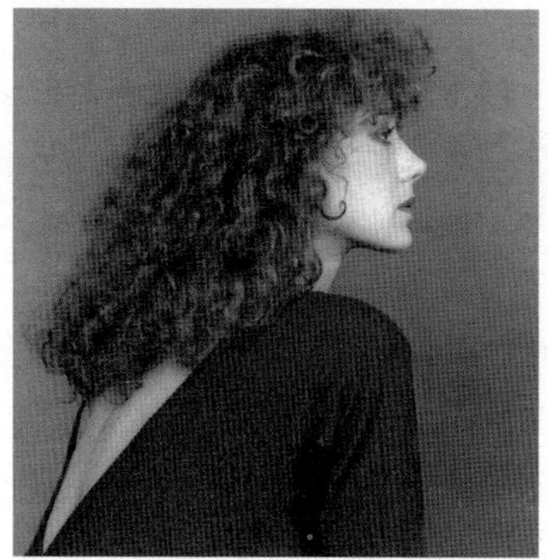

Gelatin silver print, 1983
15 1/4 x 15 1/4 in.
MAP 1589 / Plate 56

Mapplethorpe's portrait of Marisa Berenson (b. 1947) is a compositional tour de force in that her face occupies only the upper right quadrant of the image, leaving nearly half of the balance to be filled by the waterfall of her hair, which cascades down into the V-shaped spillway of the back of her dress, which ends precisely in the lower left corner of the photograph. His predilection for profile portraits—there are several, including those of Ada Wadell, Brooke Shields, Glenn Close (plate 43), Paloma Picasso (plate 30), and Annie Leibovitz (plate 52)—is derived in part from their inherent elegance and in part from his acquaintance with historical precedents. He had owned a profile portrait of Rupert Brooke made in 1913 by Sherril Schell and one of Edward Thomas made in 1904 by Frederick Evans, both of which he sold at auction in 1982. He knew, as well, about another by Julia Margaret Cameron (1815–1859), whose work he esteemed, of Julia Duckworth that Sam Wagstaff purchased at Sotheby's, London, in June 1975. In 1986 he made a profile portrait of David Salle that was published in 50 New York Artists.«1»

Mapplethorpe met the perennially stylish Marisa Berenson and her sister Berry as early as 1970, when he had just begun to make photographs, at the fashion designer Halston's apartment, but he did not take her picture until 1983. An exquisite fashion model in the 1960s, she appeared on the cover of Vogue and was often seen at Studio 54 and other chic nightclubs. She became a film actress in the 1970s, most notably starring in Barry Lyndon, in 1975, the same year that she was on the cover of Warhol's Interview magazine. This image was likely made for publication, but there are no extant records about which magazine commissioned it.

«1» Marshall, 50 New York Artists, 96.

6 Peter Berlin

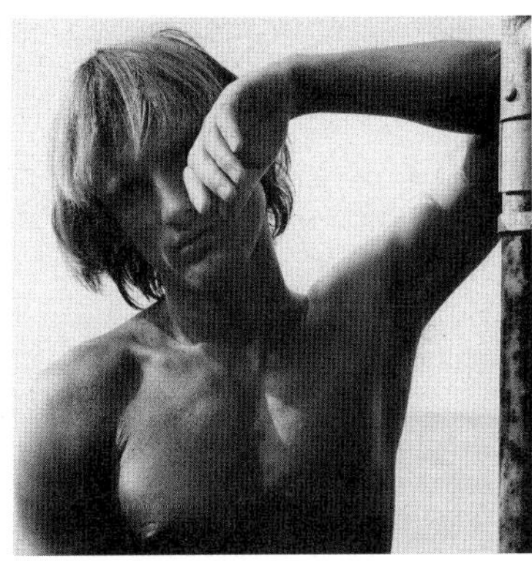

Gelatin silver print, 1977
14 x 14 in.
MAP 210 / Plate 6

The photograph is uncharacteristic of Mapplethorpe's work because his subject, Peter Berlin (b. 1942), was photographed outdoors on Fire Island in full sunlight, making the light far more harsh than in his other works and much less subject to his control. He asked Berlin, who is leaning against what appears to be a pipe, to turn out of the sun so that his face and chest are largely in shadow. By comparison with the deeply tanned skin on the rest of his body, the fingers of Berlin's left hand, which are pressed into his eye socket, are so overexposed as to seem bleached.

Mapplethorpe made other images of this sitter, but with more controlled lighting—on a deeply shaded boardwalk on Fire Island, in the Bond Street studio, and in its elevator.«1» In most of these, some of which are Polaroids, Berlin, is nude or wears either the trademark skin-tight blue jeans, which he routinely altered to be even tighter, or similarly fashioned cut-off denim shorts, often in conjunction with a military cap over his pageboy haircut. Berlin, who worked as a professional photographer in his native Germany, was notorious in San Francisco in the 1970s for parading the streets in particularly skimpy clothing of his own design and making (a few) entirely self-referential pornographic films. Mapplethorpe placed images of him in his exhibition of erotic works at the Kitchen gallery in New York in 1977.

«1» Three of the elevator Polaroids are reproduced in Sylvia Wolf, Polaroids: Mapplethorpe, exh. cat. Whitney Museum of American Art, New York (Munich: Prestel Verlag, 2007) 174, 175, 187.

7 Bruno Bischofberger

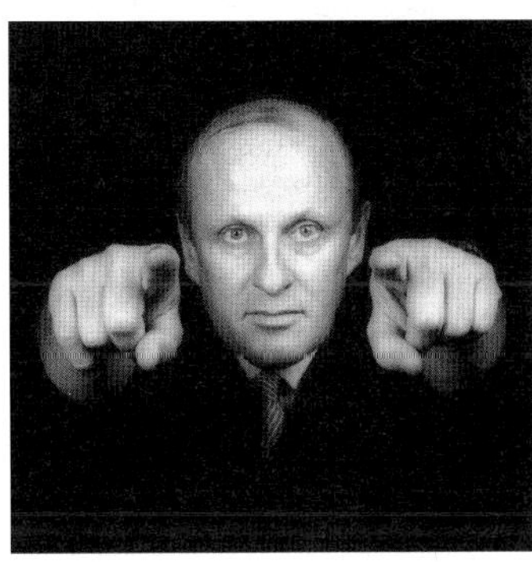

Gelatin silver print, 1985
15 1/8 x 15 1/8 in.
MAP 1760 / Plate 78

8 Cora Bischofberger

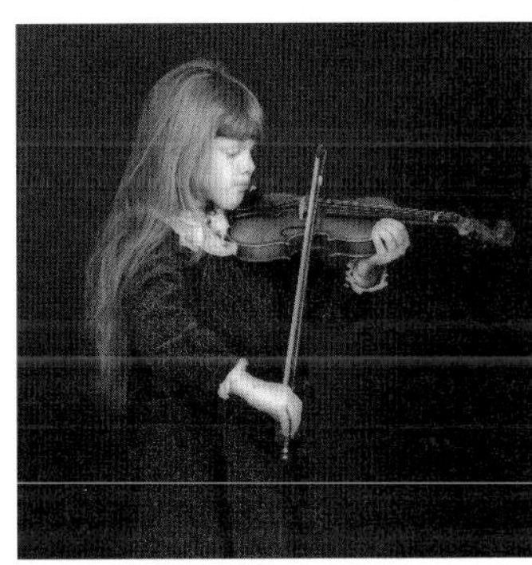

Gelatin silver print, 1985
15 1/8 x 15 1/8 in.
MAP 1761 / Plate 79

9 Magnus Bischofberger

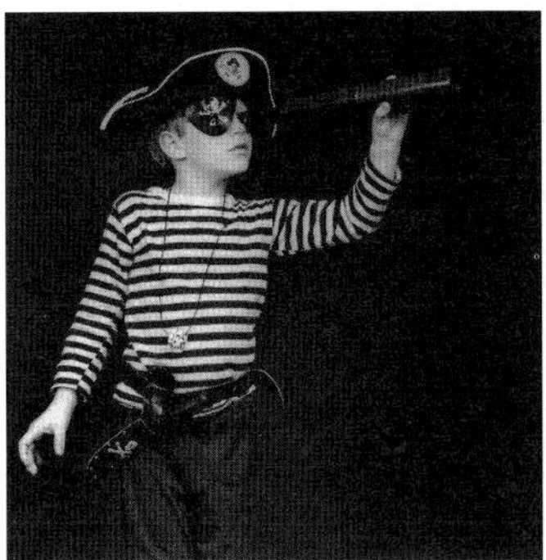

Gelatin silver print, 1985
15 3/8 x 15 1/8 in.
MAP 1762 / Plate 80

Bruno Bischofberger's dynamic pose is illustrative of the energy that has long made him a powerful force in the art world. His connection with Mapplethorpe may have been established through Interview magazine, from which Mapplethorpe occasionally received commissions. Bischofberger's gallery in Zurich exhibited work by several painters whom Mapplethorpe photographed, including Julian Schnabel, David Salle, Francesco Clemente, Jean-Michel Basquiat, and Andy Warhol,«1» whose career Bischofberger did much to further. His establishment has also extensively published the work of artists it represents.

By taking such a confrontational stance for the camera, Bischofberger virtually reversed the role of photographer and subject, seemingly assuming control of the situation and raising questions about who is looking at whom. His hands are positioned like those of Uncle Sam in a military recruiting poster, and his gaze is as intense. What seems an antagonistic attitude to the camera, and by extension the photographer, is belied by the fact that this same year he commissioned Mapplethorpe to document his collection of art glass for a book to accompany an exhibition and to make portraits of his children, Magnus, then age four, and Cora, then age five. Although Mapplethorpe thought small children difficult to photograph, as he said in a talk he gave at San Francisco Camerawork in 1984,«2» because they seldom did as they were told, these two Swiss children seem to have been very well behaved, as well as perfectly scrubbed. They've been outfitted for the occasion; his pirate costume is just as immaculate as her dress with its microscopic polka dots and frilly cuffs and collar. These photographs are charming pictures of children engaged in their own pursuits.

Mapplethorpe executed the commissions for the three portraits and the collection on the same trip to Switzerland. Bischofberger (b. 1940) took pains to be a compassionate friend in the last months of Mapplethorpe's life, once, for example, sitting with him at a dinner after a gallery opening to which he'd gone with Warhol.«3» Of the many portraits that Mapplethorpe made of art dealers, this is the most striking.

«1» For Mapplethorpe's portraits of Clemente, Salle, and Warhol, see plates 42, 59, and 60.
«2» Robert Mapplethorpe, untitled lecture, San Francisco Camerawork, San Francisco (June 12, 1984), transcript, p. 11.
«3» The incident is recounted in Kelly M. Cresap, Pop Trickster Fool: Warhol Performs Naivete (Urbana: University of Illinois Press, 2004), 125.

10 Mary Boone

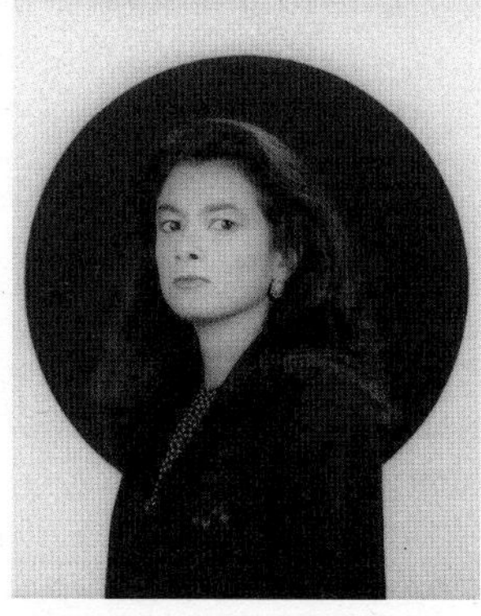

Gelatin silver print, 1984
15 1/4 x 15 1/4 in.
MAP 1494 / Plate 65

The art dealer Mary Boone (b. 1951) had known of Mapplethorpe's work from at least 1974, when she was working at the Bykert Gallery for Klaus Kertess, who had teasingly hung a Mapplethorpe nude in her office.«1» This portrait was made in 1984 for an article in Italian Vogue that dealt with art dealers in New York and included portraits of Holly Solomon, Leo Castelli, Barbara Gladstone, Ileanna Sonnabend, Anina Nosei, Paula Cooper, Daniel Wolfe, and others, most of whom, including Boone, Mapplethorpe had also photographed in 1979 for a guide book to Soho, where most of the contemporary galleries were then located.«2» By the time of this sitting, Mapplethorpe had already had solo exhibitions at the galleries of the first three of these dealers, and as he was very active socially, in part in order to advance his career, he may well have met all of the others.

With his passion for geometric forms, it is not surprising that he used a hoop to frame a sitter in 1983 and the next year asked his studio factotum, Dimitri Levas, to cut out a black circle and mount it on white seamless paper in order to use it as a background. Mapplethorpe did this for photographs of Boone, Castelli, Frank Langella, and others in 1984. Less often, he used a white circle against black seamless paper. Here he placed the camera so that the circle centers Boone's head, her luxuriant hair, and her shoulders. The white of the small flowers on her dark blouse extends the light tones of her neck to just beyond the (implied) circumference of the circle and ameliorates the overall severity of the composition. At the time, Boone represented several artists whom Mapplethorpe also photographed, including David Salle, Brice Marden, and Richard Artschwager (see plates 59, 89, and 88) and Julian Schnabel. The determination and detachment that seem evident in her expression would serve her well as her gallery thrived, moved several times, and expanded.

«1» The incident is recounted in Patricia Morrisroe Mapplethorpe: A Biography, New York: Random House, 148.
«2» Alexandra Anderson and B. J. Archer, Anderson and Archer's Soho: The Essential Guide to Art and Life in Lower Manhattan (New York: Art in America in association with Simon and Schuster, 1979), 20, 23-27.

11 Louise Bourgeois

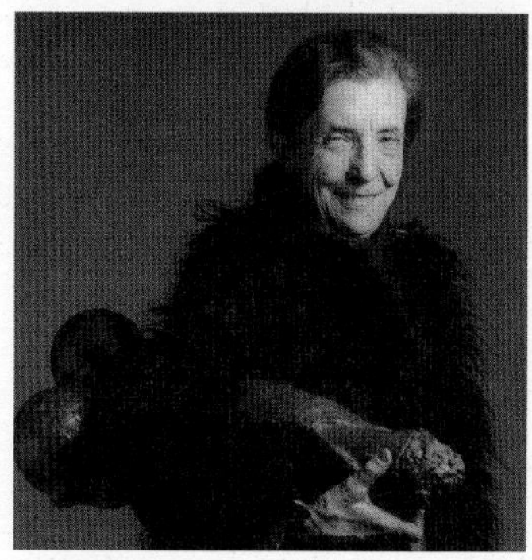

Gelatin silver print, 1982
15 1/4 x 15 1/8 in.
MAP 925 / Plate 44

Knowing Mapplethorpe, at least slightly, and certainly by reputation, the artist and sculptor Louise Bourgeois (b. 1911) armed herself by taking one of her sculptures with her when she went to his studio to be photographed for the project that became 50 New York Artists, choosing an evidently phallic work, although it is perversely titled Fillette (little girl).«1» For the photograph she tucked it under her arm but, curiously, described herself as "cradling it as if it were a baby." It was another photograph of her that was published in 50 New York Artists, although this image has been used in a Museum of Modern Art catalogue, but cropped so that only her head appears. Her smile in that photograph has been described as being one of "mischievous complicity."«2»

Bourgeois, who was born in Paris and educated there at various schools, including the Sorbonne, the École du Louvre, and the Académie Julian, moved to New York in 1938. She has had an extraordinary, decades-long career as first an artist on paper and, after about 1947, as a sculptor in various media, including wood, rubber, marble, bronze, and stainless steel. Her work has been variously described as being related to expressionism, minimalism, feminism, abstract expressionism, and, particularly, surrealism. The great critical success that has resulted in the inclusion of her sculpture in many major museums came relatively recently. Her later work includes the series, called Spiders, in which the steel insects are about thirty feet tall.

«1» Marshall, 50 New York Artists, 5. She told this story in a segment of the videotape Robert Mapplethorpe, directed by Paul Tschinkel, in the series Art/New York, no. 61 (New York: Inner Tube Video, 2006).
«2» Stuart Morgan and Alan Hollinghurst, Robert Mapplethorpe, 1970-1983, exh. cat. (London: Institute of Contemporary Arts, 1983), 15.

12 Sonia Braga

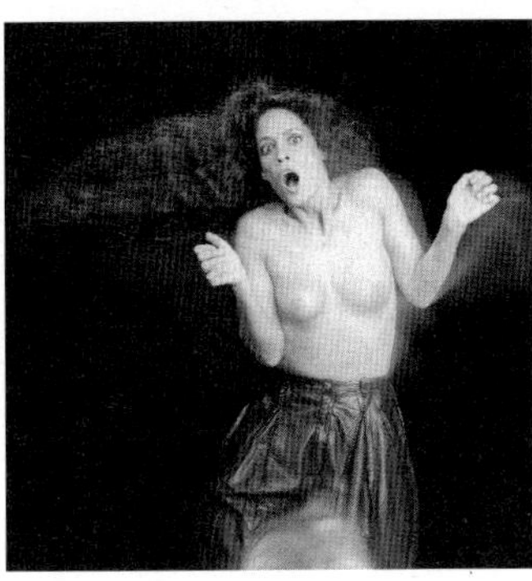

Gelatin silver print, 1985
15 1/4 x 15 1/4 in.
MAP 1621 / Plate 83

The vibrant Brazilian actress Sonia Braga (b. 1950) came to Mapplethorpe's studio with the photographer Steven Meisel, who, as part of a project for Vanity Fair magazine, had selected her to be a subject for Mapplethorpe to photograph. After the work for the magazine had been completed, Meisel departed but Braga remained. As was often the case, there was music playing in the studio, and Mapplethorpe caught Braga in the midst of a frenetic dance inspired by anger at her then-boyfriend.«1» The result is an anomaly in his work as he rarely attempted to capture motion. She was moving so rapidly that the edges of her arms and body are slightly blurred, producing an image unlike his usually preternaturally static works. This is not a conventional portrait, but it certainly gives a sense of a free-wheeling personality and energetic performer.

«1» As she recounted in a telephone conversation, March 26, 2008.

13 Eli Broad

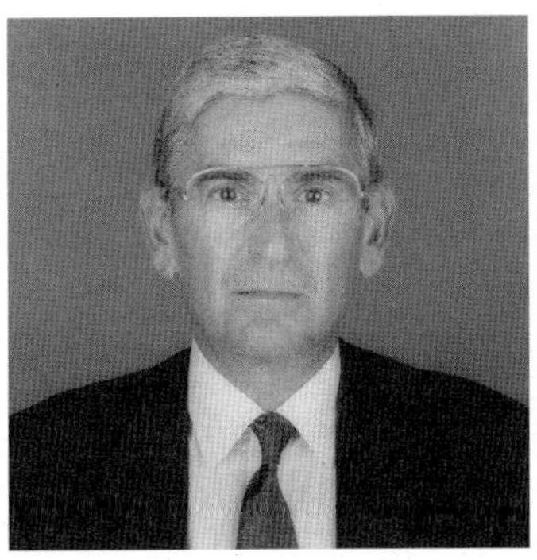

Gelatin silver print, 1986
18 3/4 x 18 7/8 in.
The Eli and Edythe L. Broad Collection, Los Angeles
Plate 94

The Los Angeles collector and patron of the arts Eli Broad (b. 1933) commissioned Mapplethorpe to make portraits of himself and his wife, Edythe. It was Mapplethorpe's invariable habit, after any portrait sitting was completed and the contact sheets prepared, to select only a few images to be printed. He made these crucial choices on his own, according to which images he felt met his exacting standards and best captured the personality of his sitters. This is one of the two images of Broad that Mapplethorpe chose to have printed from among the exposures that he made, many of which had troublesome reflections in Broad's glasses. Similarly, he chose to have printed two of Mrs. Broad and one of the two of them together from the thirty-six exposures that he made of the couple.

Broad, who is a major benefactor and trustee of many arts and educational institutions, including the Los Angeles County Museum of Art, was steadily animated throughout his sitting, but one of the two images of him that Mapplethorpe selected is this, in which the philanthropist faced the camera directly with a serious and noncommittal expression. For his sitting, Broad wore a conservative pinstriped suit, an understated, diagonally striped necktie, and an immaculately pressed, dazzlingly white shirt. His oversized glasses, so finely shaped and precisely crafted, are almost a work of art on their own.

14 William Burroughs

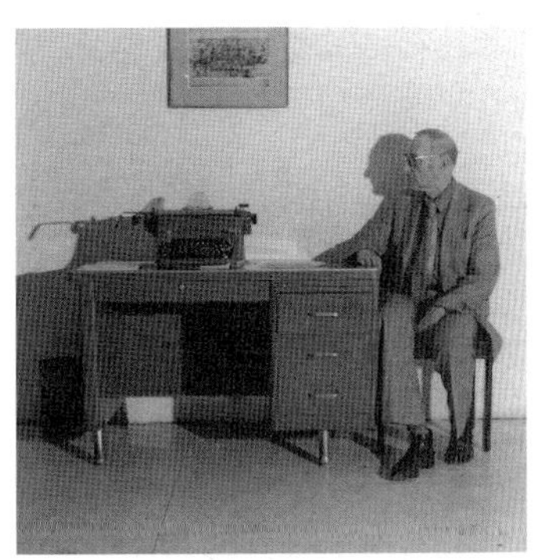

Gelatin silver print, 1979
14 x 14 in.
MAP 304 / Plate 20

William Burroughs (1914–1997), a famous and controversial American writer, whose best-known novel is Naked Lunch, was a stalwart ally of the Beat poets. Mapplethorpe's portrait of him was made in Burroughs's New York dwelling on the Bowery, which was referred to by his friends as "the Bunker," because it was a windowless conversion of part of a former YMCA gym, including the locker room and showers. In order to picture some of this Spartan setting, Mapplethorpe placed the camera unusually far from his subject, who sits on a plain office chair looking, with what seem to be mixed emotions, over to his venerable Olympia typewriter, as if it could be his muse. The top of a framed calligraphic painting by Brion Gysin above the desk establishes the upper boundary of the image, which is most strongly marked by the exactly horizontal shadows of Burroughs and his instrument that are cast by a single strong light source, which likely the photographer brought with him. The conservative sartorial style of the writer, so at odds with the quality of his writing, is evident in his muted suit, shirt, and necktie and his high-top shoes.

Burroughs was also photographed by Mapplethorpe in 1980 and 1981. A photograph from the latter year—of Burroughs aiming a shotgun—was used in 1991 as the frontispiece to his book Seven Deadly Sins, which held reproductions of paintings on Mylar and wood blocks that he had blasted with a shotgun. The macabre reference to his having accidentally shot and killed his wife in 1951 was intended. By the time Burroughs contributed to recordings with musicians such as Laurie Anderson and Philip Glass and appeared in several films, he had become, as he remains, a highly influential American cultural figure.

15 David Byrne

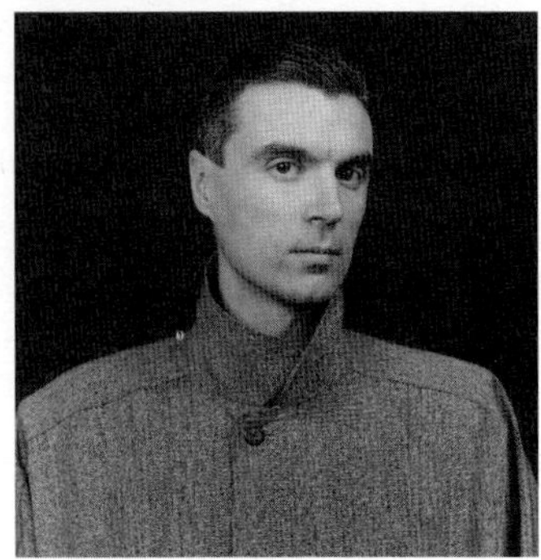

Gelatin silver print, 1983
15 3/8 x 15 1/8 in.
MAP 1069 / Plate 58

In 1974 the Scottish-born singer and songwriter David Byrne (b. 1952) founded the new-wave band Talking Heads with two other students from the Rhode Island School of Design. In 1983, the year of this portrait, Talking Heads released a studio album, Speaking in Tongues, which a critic in Rolling Stone described as finally obliterating "the thin line separating arty white pop music and deep black funk."«1» Even before the group dissolved in 1991, Byrne had branched out into other musical enterprises, writing sound tracks for movies, the score for a ballet by Twyla Tharpe, and music for a variety of theater works, including one by Robert Wilson (for whom, see plate 5). He founded a record label that produces world music and, since 1990, has extensively exhibited and published photographs and art in other media, stating in one instance that "the sublime is in the banal."«2»

For this sitting with Mapplethorpe, Byrne chose to wear an unpatterned, simple, but not closely fitted, jacket that he buttoned at its high tubular collar, concealing his slender neck. The severity of this garment has the effect of concentrating all attention on his face, on his alert and intelligent expression. His residual sideburns are raked to a point close to the top of the ears. For this bust-length portrait, he was directed to stand so that his shoulders are parallel to the picture plane and to turn his head slightly away from the camera.

Two years later Mapplethorpe photographed Byrne again, both alone and together with the rest of the Talking Heads. There is also a solo shot of at least one other member of the group, the keyboard player Jerry Harrison.

«1» David Fricke, review, Rolling Stone magazine, October 11, 1983. http://www.rollingstone.com/reviews/album/88266/review/5943976/speakingintongues (accessed May 28, 2008).
«2» David Byrne, Strange Ritual (San Francisco: Chronicle Books, 1995). http://www.lipanjepuntin.com/desc.php?UID=2008082522262269.109.186.164&id_autore=33&artist=David_Byrne (accessed August 25, 2008).

16 Donald Cann

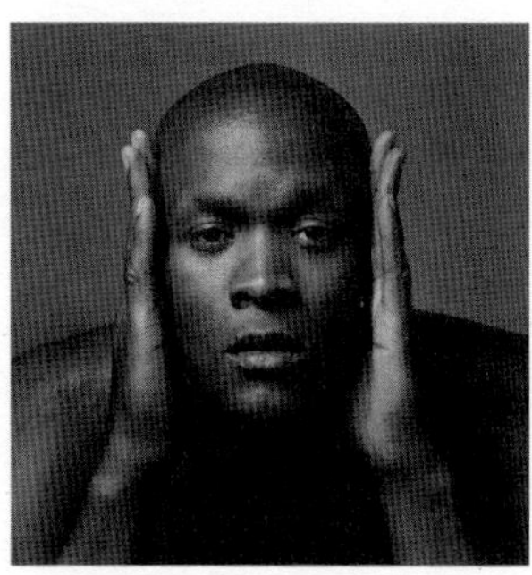

Gelatin silver print, 1982
15 3/8 x 15 1/8 in.
MAP 825 / Plate 41

Mapplethorpe made five photographs of Donald Cann, about whom nothing more than his name and the fact that he posed for Mapplethorpe are known. Two of the five are nearly abstract studies of his back and torso that recall images by Edward Weston, and one shows his head discreetly lowered and his twisted torso with his arms held behind his back.«1» The remaining two are pictures of his head alone, a relatively uncommon subject in Mapplethorpe's work. One is a profile in which Cann is wearing what seem to be dark glasses; the other is this powerful image of his magnificent head seen at very short range. He is treated with such respect and so beautifully lit that it brings to mind Edward Steichen's deservedly famous portrait of the actress Greta Garbo with her hands pressed closely to the top of her head (see fig. 1, p. 15). Just as she was noted for being remote, so, too, is Donald Cann in this portrait, despite the closeness of the camera, so close that the image could be his own view seen in a magnifying shaving mirror. He has cooperated in turning his face into an impassive sculpture.

«1» The pose may reflect the model's desire not to be identified as having posed in the nude.

17 Truman Capote

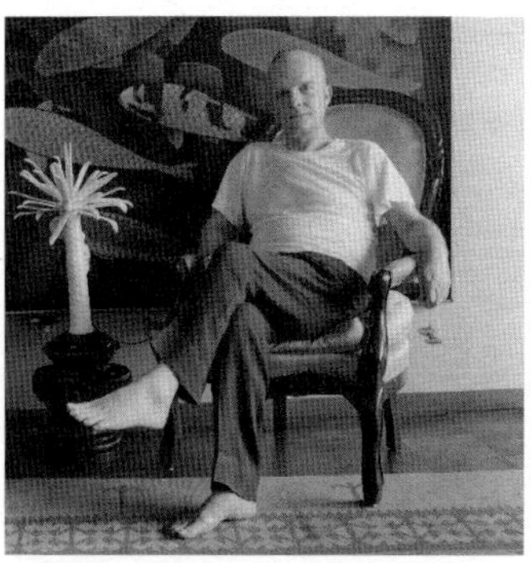

Gelatin silver print, 1981
15 3/8 x 15 1/8 in.
MAP 1099 / Plate 34

Given the fastidious quality of the prose of the writer Truman Capote (1924–1984), it might be assumed that his personal appearance would be exceptionally tidy, but as this photograph shows, it was not, at least on this occasion. As the writer Edmund White has explained, this image is not as straightforward as it might seem.«1» In order to interview and photograph Capote for After Dark magazine, White and Mapplethorpe, who were friends, went together to Capote's apartment. It was summer, the day was sweltering, the air conditioning broken, and the windows sealed. The heat explains why Capote was barefoot and wearing a T-shirt. Mapplethorpe made a double portrait of Capote and White, each sitting in one of a pair of armchairs, White on the right and Capote on the left. At some time after the magazine used that photograph, Mapplethorpe decided to create a portrait of Capote alone and to make an edition of it. He asked his studio assistant to split the negative in half down the middle, thereby excising White, to crop the remainder horizontally at the top and bottom in order to close in on Capote, and to flip the negative to improve the composition. Enlargement and the fact that the resultant, cropped part of the original negative was then printed over the whole of the sheet are the reasons that the final image is less crisp than Mapplethorpe's pictures usually are.

By the time Mapplethorpe photographed Capote, the author's life was in steep decline. A precocious writer, he was first and widely known for his short stories, but it was the publication of the best-selling novel Other Voices, Other Rooms in 1948 that made him famous, in part because of its controversial dust-jacket photograph of the author lying on a couch looking upward, some thought seductively, others, malevolently. Novellas, plays, and screenplays followed, including Breakfast at Tiffany's in 1958. But it was his nonfiction novel In Cold Blood, which was published in 1968 and dealt with the actual murders of a Kansas farming family by a pair of drifters, that cemented his reputation as a first-rate writer and confirmed the social celebrity in which he reveled. His publication in the middle 1970s of thinly veiled stories about the foibles of the rich cut off much of the social life Capote so highly valued. He appears exhausted in Mapplethorpe's portrait, and died only three years later, at the age of sixty.

«1» In a telephone conversation with the author, November 2007.

18 Leo Castelli

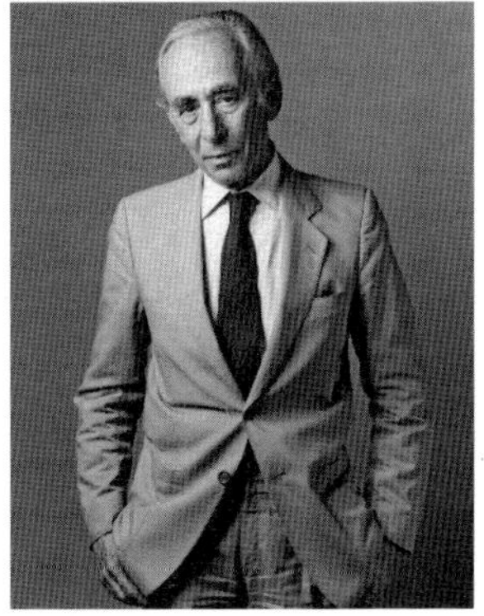

Gelatin silver print, 1985
19 x 15 1/4 in.
MAP 1587 / Plate 81

By most accounts Leo Castelli (1907–1999) was the pre-eminent art dealer of the 1970s and 1980s in New York and, although he seldom showed Mapplethorpe's work, the photographer depicted him in three different years during a span of six. The first sitting, in 1979, was for a guidebook to "life," art, restaurants, and bars in Soho. In it, Castelli was pictured as rather dour looking, but described as "ever consumed with the need to share his enthusiasms" and as maintaining "exemplary exhibition standards" in his gallery, which was then located on West Broadway.«1» He represented, at least during his first twenty-five years in business, many of Mapplethorpe's subjects, including Ellsworth Kelly, Ed Ruscha, Lawrence Weiner, Richard Artschwager, Andy Warhol, and Robert Rauschenberg.«2»

The dealer thoroughly approved of the debonair, if mildly rumpled, image of himself that he had commissioned.

«1» Anderson and Archer, Anderson and Archer's Soho, 33; image of Castelli on p. 20.
«2» See plates 66, 68, 38, 88, 60, and 64.

19 Bruce Chatwin

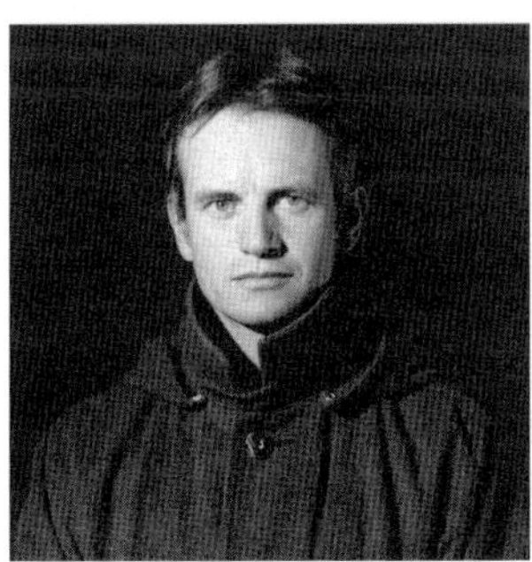

Gelatin silver print, 1979
13 7/8 x 14 in.
MAP 254 / Plate 15

Mapplethorpe photographed the British writer Bruce Chatwin (1940–1989), whom he knew as a friend of Sam Wagstaff's and with whom he had become friendly on his own. Polaroids from 1973 show that Chatwin was one of his earliest subjects. Four years after the date of this portrait, he enlisted Chatwin to write the introduction to the book of pictures that he had made of Lisa Lyon (see plate 47). The author responded handsomely, describing Mapplethorpe as having an "eye for a face (that) is the eye of a novelist in search of a character."«1» Chatwin had been an art expert at Sotheby's in London and a world-class trekker across difficult terrain in such places as the Sudan, Patagonia, and central Australia. His adventures eventually resulted in the lapidary prose of his travel books, among them In Patagonia and The Songlines, which were a blend of fiction and truth, and in his novel, Utz.

This photograph was made, in the Bond Street studio, with the aid of a single light source to the left of the camera and may have been made at night. The light does not convey the fact that the writer's hair was blond, nor does the photograph show that his eyes were a brilliant blue. His expression seems troubled, as if he were reluctant to reveal himself to the camera. Since Chatwin is wearing a loden cloth parka, it may have been chilly in the studio or there may have been an intention to portray him as the traveler he was. He died three months before Mapplethorpe did.

«1» Robert Mapplethorpe, Lady, Lisa Lyon, text by Bruce Chatwin (New York: St. Martin's Press, 1991), 9.

20 Lucinda Childs

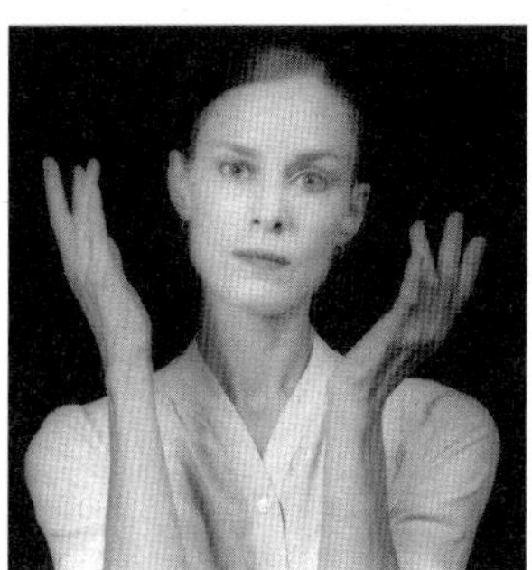

Gelatin silver print, 1983
15 3/8 x 15 1/4 in.
MAP 1233 / Plate 63

Mapplethorpe photographed the dancer and innovative choreographer Lucinda Childs (b. 1940) on several occasions, starting in 1976, when she performed in the opera Einstein on the Beach by Philip Glass and Robert Wilson (for whom, see plate 5). Here, at close range, he has let her expressive hands, which seem like semaphores, frame her face. Her left eyebrow is slightly lifted, giving her a quizzical expression, as if she were explaining a dance step and wanted to know if her listener understood what she has just finished saying. Her beautifully cut but severely simple blouse and tiny hoop earrings can be described as minimal, a word that has often, but not wholly accurately, been applied to her choreography.

In 1986, the next time he is known to have photographed her, he made three studies of her hands alone. This concentration, a kind of visual synecdoche, was wholly appropriate for a woman whose gestures are an integral part of her art. That year he also designed the light projections that were used as a backdrop for her dance production Portraits in Reflection. His collaborations with artists in other media have seldom been noted, much less described in detail. They deserve further study.

21 Francesco Clemente

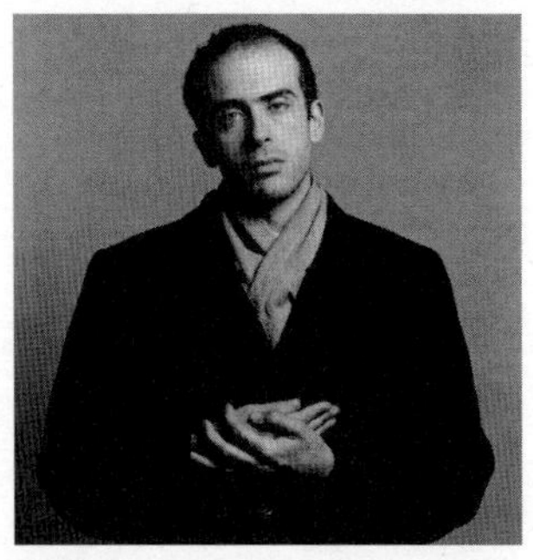

Gelatin silver print, 1982
15 3/8 x 15 1/8 in.
MAP 820 / Plate 42

A native Italian, the figurative painter Francesco Clemente (b. 1952) has lived in New York since 1981 and also in the Indian city of Chennai (formerly Madras) since 1982. Mapplethorpe owned a strangely expressive self-portrait in watercolor that Clemente did in 1976. They became close enough friends that the photographer served as a godfather to the painter's children.«1» He was a frequent sitter to Mapplethorpe for a variety of publications, including GQ in 1983, Italian Vogue in 1985, and, with his wife, Alba, for TWA's in-flight magazine, but most notably for inclusion in 50 New York Artists in 1986. The statement he made to accompany his portrait in that book included the words, "I'm interested in the body as a conductor between what we show on the outside and what we feel within. And this is reflected in our eyes, our mouths."«2»

Given that statement and the friendship of the photographer and his sitter, it is not surprising that the mood of this portrait differs from others by Mapplethorpe in that it is as intimate as it is formal. Clemente's pose is prayerful, his beautiful hands held like those of a supplicant. In other, later portraits by Mapplethorpe, he presents himself as a debonair figure in well-cut suits; here the severity of his dark overcoat and his simply wrapped scarf produce an impression of monkish simplicity. His gaze is appealingly open, even if tinged, perhaps, with sadness. His expression conveys an intentional effort to break through the mask of the persona to show himself as he believes himself to be. In this effort he had the full cooperation of the photographer. If, as Clemente once said, " a photograph is a reminder of how the person was on a certain day, in that certain light fixed,"«3» then this image is a poignant and powerful souvenir of a particularly highly charged moment.

To a degree, Mapplethorpe and Clemente, who has often been described as a poetic artist, moved in the same downtown circles and their rosters of sitters overlapped. Keith Haring, William Burroughs, and Allen Ginsberg were subjects for both artists (for the two former, see plates 75 and 20). For both photographer and painter, portraiture was an important aspect of their work but far from the only one.

«1» Mapplethorpe's role as a godfather is noted in a review of Clemente's retrospective exhibition at the Guggenheim; see Jerry Saltz, "At the Guggenheim, an Artist in Partial Eclipse," Villagevoice, October 19, 1999. http://www.villagevoice.com/art/9942,217745,9239,13.html(accessed May 28, 2008).
«2» Marshall, 50 New York Artists, 30.
«3» Francesco Clemente, interview by Ingrid Sischy, Interview magazine, July 1997. http://findarticles.com/p/articles/mi_m1285/is_n7_v27/ai_20803816 (accessed May 28, 2008).

22 Glenn Close

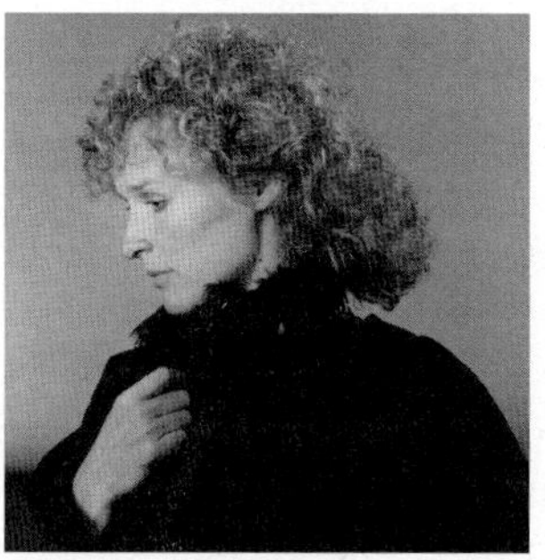

Gelatin silver print, 1982
15 1/4 x 15 1/8 in.
MAP 932 / Plate 43

In the year that the celebrated, hard-working, and award-winning actress Glenn Close (b. 1947) was photographed by Mapplethorpe, she appeared on television in The Elephant Man, performed on stage in The Singular Life of Albert Norris, and acted in her first film, The World According to Garp, which won her an Academy Award nomination. Coupled with her innate talent, the indefatigability that these multiple jobs in a single year imply has substantially contributed to her success as an actress.

Mapplethorpe chose to photograph her in profile, which necessarily cut her off from direct interaction with the camera or the viewer. Her downcast eyes are focused elsewhere and, as she hovers suspended in an indeterminate space, she is effectively objectified, served up for our delectation. We can admire the shape of her nose and the loveliness of her skin and note the contrast between the light tones of her curly blonde hair and the dark feathers at her neck, but we are not given any insight into her character. We are simply made aware of the elegant way that she has tilted her head toward her hand and the way that the photographer has placed her in the frame.

23 Melody Danielson

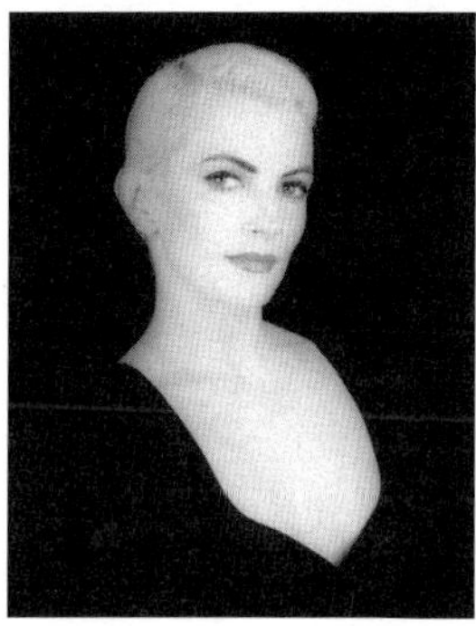

Gelatin silver print, 1987
23 x 19 1/4 in.
Collection of David Knaus
MAP 1801 / Plate 98

According to Mapplethorpe's biographer, before Melody Danielson (d. 1993) became the girlfriend of the photographer's brother Edward, a relationship Mapplethorpe encouraged, she had been a professional dominatrix, who for five hundred dollars an hour indulged the fantasies of wealthy New York businessmen.«1» Her reminiscences of her former life fascinated Mapplethorpe and prompted him to photograph her shapely legs in fishnet stockings, to lie flat on the floor to obtain a picture of her foot in a preposterously high-heeled shoe,«2» and to picture her towering over a nude male lying at her feet. Despite her plunging neckline, this decorous portrait, in contrast, has little overt sexual content, although the sitter certainly does not seem naïve. There is also a photograph of her standing next to Edward Mapplethorpe, both of them spectrally thin. All these images of her, like some of those he produced of other sitters, mark intersections of the photographer's private and public lives.

«1» Morrisroe, Mapplethorpe: A Biography, 328.
«2» In conversation (February 27, 2008), Brian English, Mapplethorpe's studio assistant, recalled the photographer's stratagem necessary to obtain the image.

24 Lynn Davis

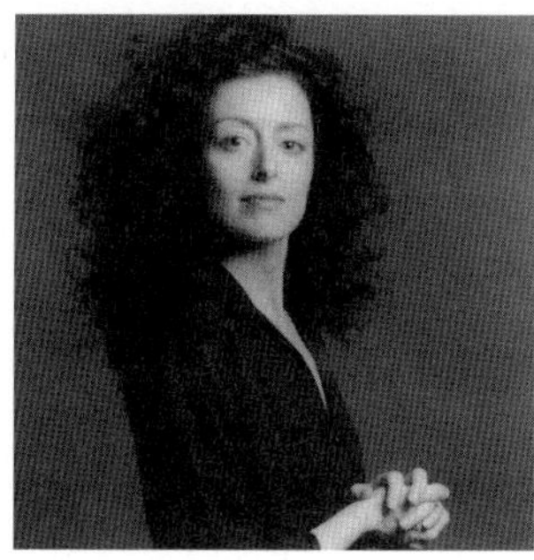

Gelatin silver print, 1979
14 x 14 in.
MAP 293 / Plate 13

Both early and late in Mapplethorpe's career, the photographer Lynn Davis (b. 1944) was a staunch friend. They met in late 1976 at a time when she was apprenticing to Berenice Abbott, working as a photojournalist, editing a small photography magazine, and making portraits and figure studies. She and Mapplethorpe became close, regularly reviewed each other's most recent works, and occasionally traded models. For a 1979 exhibition, which they shared, at the International Center for Photography, they decided to make portraits of the same sixteen sitters, including Sam Wagstaff, Marcus Leatherdale, Phyllis Tweel,«1» and of each other. These last were used on the exhibition announcement; this photograph is the one that he had taken of her.

The long line of her neck, doubled by the opening of her blouse, points to her hands, which are lightly clasped together in front of her body. She stands at nearly a right angle to the camera, but her head is pivoted back so that she looks directly toward the viewer. Her attentive gaze and her gracefully erect posture convey a sense of her having been wholly present on an occasion for which their friendship and her own experience as a portraitist had thoroughly prepared her. Her teased-out, luxuriant mane of hair explodes above and around her face, which carries an expression that combines assurance and goodwill, but is touched with vulnerability, making the portrait a combination of the august and the intimate. Their shared subject material definitively ended in 1986 when she made the first series of her ravishing black-and-white photographs of icebergs, one of which she gave to him. She has since produced minimalistic, large-scale pictures of architecture and of sacred monolithic forms, such as the pyramids, in numerous locations worldwide.

In the last two years of Mapplethorpe's life, she was a devoted friend and caregiver, accompanying him on trips to New Orleans, Amsterdam, and, finally, Boston. She has said of him that he had a European classical sensibility and represented a declining civilization in which beauty and decadence had become fascinations.«2»

«1» Other than this image of Lynn Davis, none of Mapplethorpe's portraits of these sitters that are included in the present catalogue (see plates 17, 11, and 18, respectively) appeared in the exhibition in 1979.
«2» In a telephone conversation with the author, March 8, 2008.

25 Dorothy Dean

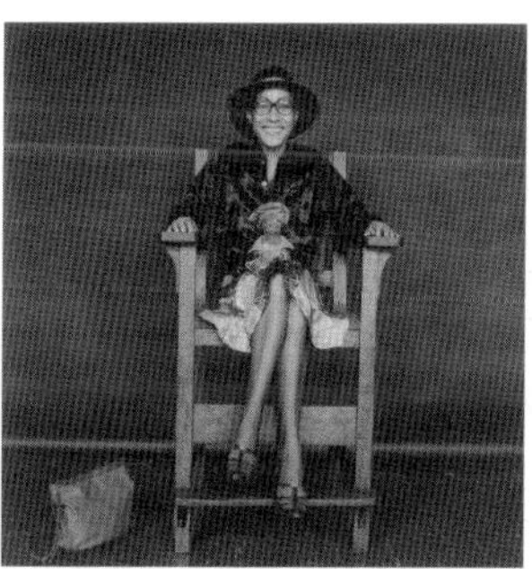

Gelatin silver print, 1974
13 7/8 x 14 in.
MAP 13 / Plate 2

Dorothy Dean (1932–1987), a Radcliffe graduate, had been a fact checker for the New Yorker, an editor for various publications, and a sought-after ghostwriter. Mapplethorpe encountered her at Max's Kansas City, then a painters' bar rather than a music venue, to which he and Patti Smith went in the early seventies. Dean, who had briefly appeared in three of Warhol's films in 1965, was a tiny woman, and, on occasion, in reference to her circle of close homosexual friends, she called herself "the spade of queens."«1»

By posing her in an Arts-and-Crafts–style chair, Mapplethorpe has accentuated her slight frame. Is she beaming at being posed dryly with an Aunt Jemima doll on her lap or because she is being pictured by an evidently rising photographer? Reflections in her oversized glasses of the Bond Street studio windows give her a secondary set of eyebrows, this time white rather than black. Her gigantic purse on the floor serves to anchor the left corner of the composition and thereby establish its overall square format. She's decorously crossed her slender legs. Her blouse, skirt, and skin are silken surfaces. The distance from the upper margin of the image to the tip of the round shape of her hat is exactly that of the tip of her toe from the floor. The photograph shows Mapplethorpe's mastery of formal composition very early in his career. His portrait of her became a transitory tombstone when it was displayed at her memorial service in 1987.

«1» Hilton Als, The Women (New York: Farrar, Straus and Giroux, 1996), 92.

26 Larry Desmedt

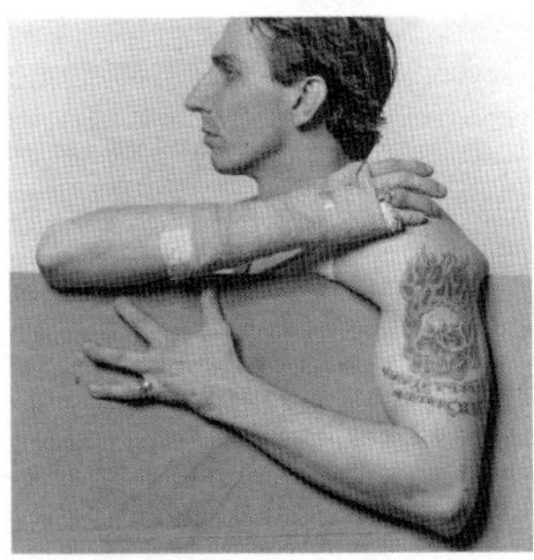

Gelatin silver print, 1981
14 x 14 1/8 in.
MAP 585 / Plate 35

The colorful and uninhibited Larry Desmedt (1949–2004), widely known as Indian Larry, from a brand of motorcycle he rode when young, was an ideal subject for Mapplethorpe. Desmedt was willing to give freely of himself to the camera and his appearance was arrestingly masculine, similar to those of the photographer's S&M sexual partners whom he had also portrayed at a slightly earlier period. Desmedt became an admired rider and builder of motorcycles as well as a movie stunt man and an actor. In 1979 he struck five poses for Mapplethorpe; twice in blue jeans and bare chested, once nude, and twice groping himself through the waistband of his long underwear. From one of these last two half-length portraits, the photographer had his studio assistants extract and print a detail of Desmedt's head tilted back in sexual ecstasy, a rare example of his reconfiguring a negative to produce a separate composition. He also made two images of Desmedt kissing another man, both wearing leather jackets.

When the biker returned to the photographer's studio in 1981 for this sitting, Mapplethorpe photographed him from one side so that he simultaneously displayed his conspicuous Harley-Davidson and flaming skull tattoo (the first of many to come), his beak of a nose, the fact that his left index finger was missing (the result of an old accident), and that recently he had been injured again and was therefore bandaged. The missing finger gives this image kinship with those images of amputees by George Dureau (for whom see plate 46), some of which Mapplethorpe owned. The skull rings Desmedt wears on the little finger of his left hand and the ring finger of his right are tokens of his bravado, his defiance of danger and death. Perhaps inevitably, he died while doing a stunt on a motorcycle. This photograph exemplifies Mapplethorpe's gift for adroitly posing a sitter and his admiration for some varieties of unconventional behavior.

27 Laura Donnelley

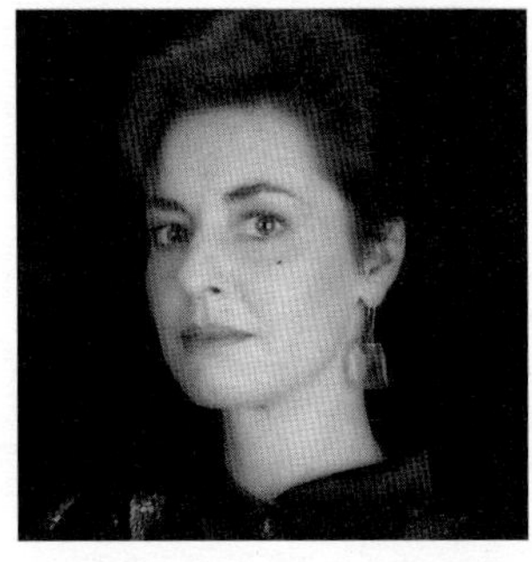

Gelatin silver print, 1986
17 7/8 x 19 in.
Private collection / Plate 90

At the urging of the art dealer Barbara Gladstone, the philanthropist, collector, and arts patron Laura Donnelley (b. 1946) commissioned Mapplethorpe to photograph her and her children, Max and Mimi Wheeler. Undecided about what she would wear and without specific instructions from the photographer, Donnelley took with her to his Twenty-third Street loft a few changes of her current favorite clothes. The makeup that the male studio technician applied to her face simultaneously emphasized her eyes and lips and homogenized her facial contours and skin, making her seem like the marble statues that Mapplethorpe sometimes pictured. Before photography started, he played on the floor with her children so that they would feel relaxed.

In the finished portrait Donnelley is not only beautiful but also completely self-possessed, although there is perhaps a trace of suspicion in the way she regards the photographer and his camera. Correlating this with her own observation that, in a form of extended narcissism, Mapplethorpe projected himself into his sitters in such a way that his portraits become self-portraits, we might speculate, perhaps, that he is regarding her with slight suspicion? Four months of intense friendship followed this portrait sitting, and Donnelly helped to underwrite the exhibition, in 1988, of Mapplethorpe's work at the Whitney Museum of American Art in New York.

Energetic and generous, Donnelley is deeply involved with the arts. She devised and funds Art Matters, a nonprofit foundation created "to assist artists who make work intending to break ground aesthetically and socially," helped develop the Aspen Museum, sits on the boards of two other cultural foundations, and is president of the Santa Monica Museum of Art.

28 George Dureau

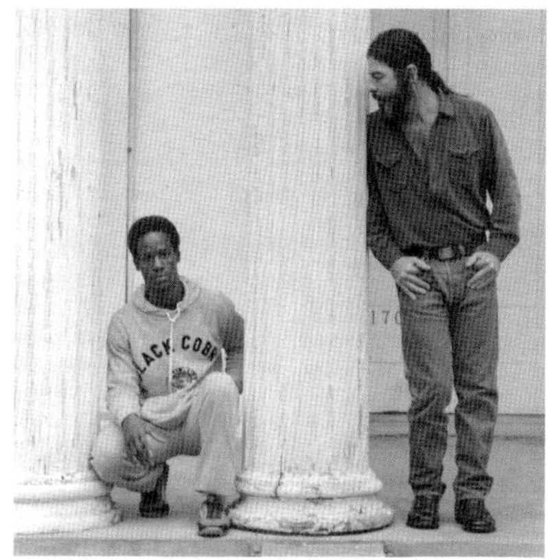

Gelatin silver print, 1982
15 1/8 x 14 15/16 in.
MAP 723 / Plate 46

There were few photographers save Lynn Davis (see plate 13) with whom Mapplethorpe was connected, but George Dureau (b. 1930) was one. A painter, photographer, and sometime sculptor, Dureau lives and works in New Orleans, and the two saw each other sedom after they first met in 1979. Because the subjects of Dureau's photographs and drawings have often been black male nudes and because Mapplethorpe acquired three dozen of Dureau's photographic images, there have been efforts to correlate their work and to declare Mapplethorpe deeply influenced by Dureau. The difference between their respective treatments of outwardly similar subjects is, however, considerable. Dureau himself thought them very different, deeming his own to be warm and empathetic and Mapplethorpe's cool and intellectual.«1» In addition, Dureau sought as models physically disadvantaged men and lit them softly; Mapplethorpe pictured his more conventionally perfect subjects in a harder and higher-keyed light.

Mapplethorpe's portrait of Dureau leaning against a battered column was made outdoors in New Orleans and shows him casually eyeing a street kid who has an alert expression and no apparent disabilities.

«1» For an extended interview in which George Dureau discussed Mapplethorpe and their differences, see Jack Fritscher, Mapplethorpe: Assault with a Deadly Camera (Mamaroneck, N.Y.: Hastings House, 1994), 232-47. For an analysis of their similarities and, particularly, their differences, see Melody D. Davis, The Male Nude in Contemporary Art (Philadelphia: Temple University Press, 1991), 69-85.

29 Marianne Faithfull

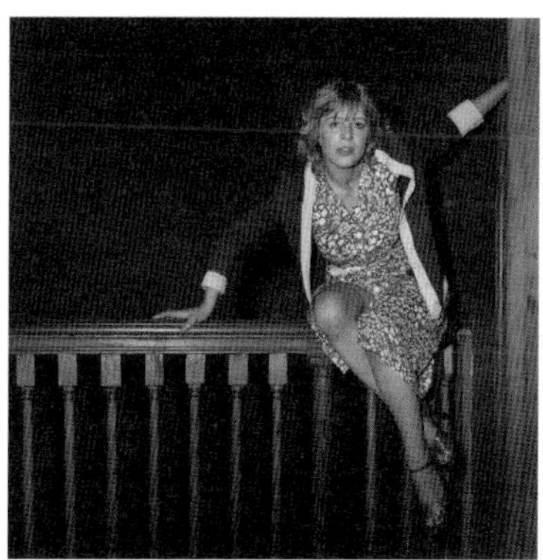

Gelatin silver print, 1976
13 3/4 x 13 3/4 in.
MAP 135 / Plate 7

As time went on, Mapplethorpe increasingly preferred to work in the controlled setting of his own studio, but earlier in his career he was able to improvise in conditions with less than ideal lighting, particularly when he was traveling. Here, apparently at night, at the top of a stairwell in London he photographed the vibrant singer and songwriter Marianne Faithfull (b. 1946). Largely because of the jaunty style of her pose with its hint of the danger of her falling, the mood was in keeping with her bad-girl reputation, a reputation that has since faded as she has continued to write and record during a long and productive career. He had made Polaroid photographs of her in 1974 on an earlier trip to London so, presumably, she was relaxed with him and his own bad-boy reputation. This sitting and her pose appear to have been spontaneous, but the camera position was calculated so that she is dynamically off-center in a highly structured composition. A somewhat more decorous variant of this image exists, in which her legs are crossed at the knees rather than the ankles, but this one has the greater intimacy, immediacy, and appeal.

30 Gisèle Freund

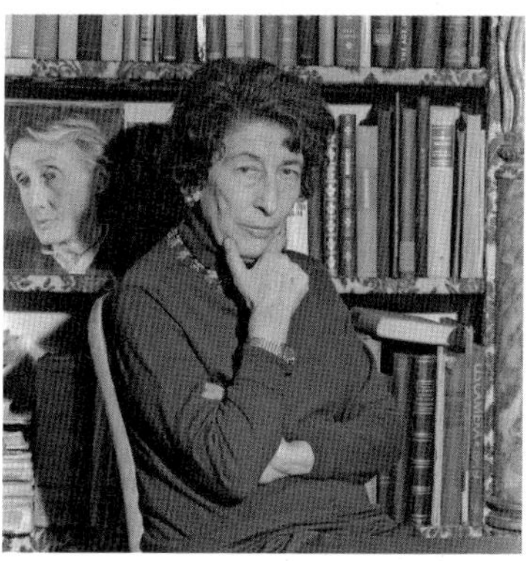

Gelatin silver print, 1980
14 x 14 in.
MAP 1763 / Plate 27

Mapplethorpe's picture of the distinguished portrait photographer Gisèle Freund (1912–2000) not only connects him directly to her but also to her own pantheon of famous sitters—an image Freund made in 1930 of Virginia Woolf, the peerless modernist English writer, rests on the fabric-covered bookshelf. It seems likely that the present photograph was made in America as all of the books on the shelves are titled in English (Freund did speak English) and one is the 1949 annual edition of U.S. Camera, which would be somewhat unlikely to be found abroad. The setting is more elaborate than those usually found in Mapplethorpe's works, even if appropriate for a subject whose great passion was reading, but the lighting is less precise than he would, perhaps, have preferred.

Freund's rise to eminence as a portraitist of the literary world was gradual. Born to Jewish parents in Germany, she fled, as the Nazis took power in 1933, to Paris, where she wrote a sociology dissertation at the Sorbonne on the effect of photography on the art of portraiture. After early work as a photojournalist, she began to photograph artists and writers, taking care to study their works before making pictures of them. Her style was characterized by its directness and lack of pretension. At the outbreak of World War II she again fled from the Nazis, this time to South America and then to Mexico. She reestablished herself as a portrait photographer in Paris in the early 1950s. Her roster of sitters included

Jean-Paul Sartre, André Gide, James Joyce, Samuel Beckett, Boris Pasternak, André Malraux, Colette, Jean Cocteau, and François Mitterand, then the president of France.

Not inappropriately, she chose to pose for Mapplethorpe somewhat as if she were herself a writer. Hand to chin, she seems thoughtful but observant, reserved but not lacking in warmth. She once stated, "When you do not like human beings, you cannot make good portraits."«1»

«1» Quoted in "Gisèle Freund, photographer...," obituary, London Times, April 1, 2000.

31 Henry Geldzahler

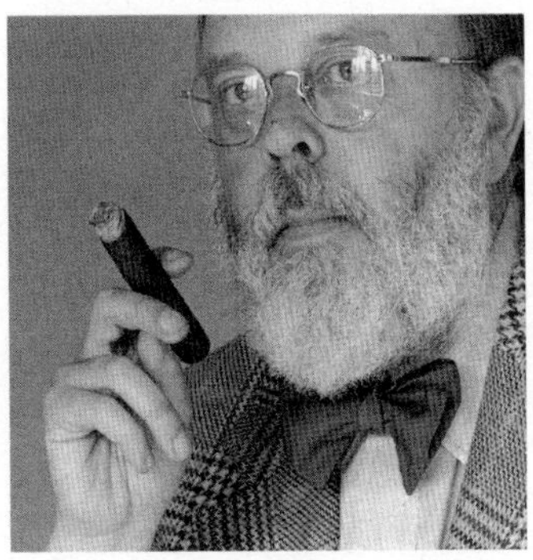

Gelatin silver print, 1979
14 x 14 in.
MAP 326 / Plate 19

Mapplethorpe had photographed the curator Henry Geldzahler (1935–1994) outdoors with his friend David Hockney on Fire Island in 1976, but in 1979 Geldzahler came to the Bond Street studio for a more formal portrait. The first curator of contemporary art at the Metropolitan Museum of Art, who, as his image attests, was a natty dresser, at least on occasion, has been described as a cherubic iconoclast because of his deceptively innocent appearance and his enthusiastic and pioneering espousal of the most important artists of the 1960s, including Jackson Pollock, Willem de Kooning, Jasper Johns, Frank Stella, Alice Neel, Larry Rivers, Marisol, and David Hockney, all of whom he befriended and by the last five of whom he was portrayed.«1» His exhibition New York Painting, 1940–1970, presented at the museum in 1969, was a landmark. Warhol filmed Geldzahler smoking one of his talismanic cigars, and Mapplethorpe, a smoker himself, included it as an essential part of the curator's image. Here Geldzahler has been photographed at close range, so that his head and shoulders fill the frame on three sides, leaving clearly defined negative space along the left side of the sheet and in its upper right quadrant. Reflections of the studio windows, the sole source of illumination, can be seen in his eyeglasses. At this period Mapplethorpe had not yet acquired sophisticated artificial lights to use for his portraiture.

«1» For Mapplethorpe's own images of Neel, Marisol, and Hockney, see plates 73, 14, and 4, respectively.

32 Richard Gere

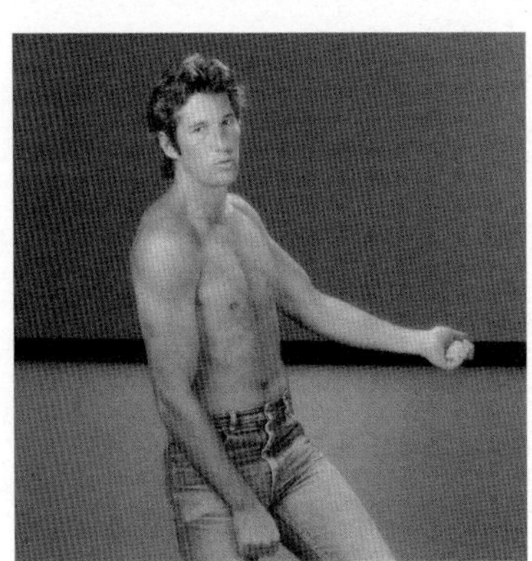

Gelatin silver print, 1982
15 1/8 x 14 7/8 in.
MAP 1098 / Plate 45

The American actor Richard Gere (b. 1949), whose career has proved to be durable and noteworthy, was photographed by Mapplethorpe in conjunction with the film Breathless, a reworking, in 1983, of Jean-Luc Godard's movie of the same title, made in 1960. With Valerie Kaprisky, his costar, and on his own, he was photographed by Mapplethorpe in Los Angeles. In keeping with Gere's reputation as a sex symbol and with the role he played in the movie, he is shirtless. He mimes the action of hitchhiking, as he did in the film, although not without a shirt, and with his left thumb stuck out rather than his right. His slightly pursed lips presumably give him additional appeal. Care has been taken so that Gere's left forearm lines up with the black strip that runs across the background wall and a hair light has been used to distinguish his dark hair from the dark background. In a more conventional and better-known head-and-shoulders shot from the same sitting, the tattoo of a broken heart that, in this photograph, is just visible on Gere's left pectoral muscle (again part of his character's appearance) has been erased, perhaps to make the image more closely resemble the neoclassical sculpture that Mapplethorpe sometimes photographed.

33 Philip Glass and Robert Wilson

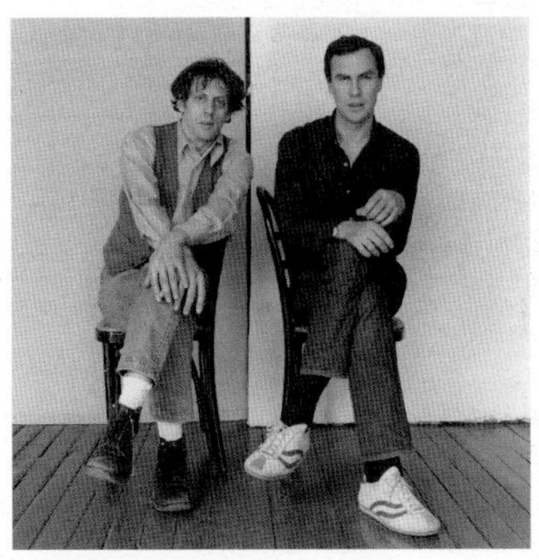

Gelatin silver print, 1976
14 x 14 in.
MAP 58 / Plate 5

This early in Mapplethorpe's career, he owned little photographic equipment save a camera and a light meter. Hence all of his portraits were made with the natural illumination from the windows on the south wall of his Bond Street studio. To make this joint picture of the composer Philip Glass (b. 1937) and the director and designer Robert Wilson (b. 1941), who were then collaborating on the first production of Glass's opera Einstein on the Beach, Mapplethorpe placed two bentwood chairs, back to back and not quite touching, on the north wall of the studio. Although Glass leans toward Wilson, both are engaged with the camera rather than relating to each other, except that they have aligned themselves in parallel fashion, which implies a sympathetic bond. Their legs are similarly crossed, their mouths are slightly open, and each holds his hands over his uppermost kneecap. Joint portraits are rare in Mapplethorpe's work, but he photographed these two together again in 1984, when they were working together on Glass's CIVIL warS, created for (but not performed at) the Los Angeles Olympics Festival. Glass also sat to Mapplethorpe in 1983 for the Brooklyn Academy of Music and in 1986 for Rolling Stone.

34 Fay Gold

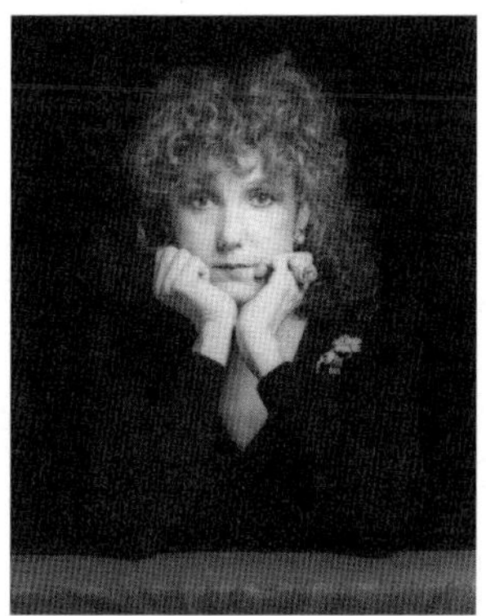

Gelatin silver print, 1982
19 1/8 x 14 15/16 in.
MAP 745 / Plate 39

Inspired by the portrait that Mapplethorpe had made in 1967 of Harry Lunn, the owner of a prominent photography gallery in Washington, D.C. and the publisher of Mapplethorpe's XYZ Portfolio, Fay Gold (b. 1932), who owned a gallery in Atlanta, commissioned her portrait from Mapplethorpe in 1982, the year in which she first showed his work. She intended to use it on the invitation to the exhibition. They had not met before she went to his Bond Street studio for the sitting. She'd chosen to wear her favorite dress, a St. John knit, and had selected her jewelry, as she'd been instructed to do by telephone before the sitting. In accordance with his usual procedure, they talked for about half an hour before he began to photograph her. Unusually, he was alone in the studio. During the course of what proved to be a very long session without help from assistants, it was he who moved the lights around and the umbrellas that reflected them.

The result is appealingly intimate. Her elbows are propped before her, so that her wrists support her chin and her folded fingers frame her mouth. The curlicues of the pin on her lapel and her ring echo the curly hair that covers her forehead. She looks steadily into the camera and the impression is given that she is comfortable in this unaffected presentation of herself although, in fact, this unforced quality may have been because, as she has explained, the picture was made at the very end of the sitting and she was exhausted.«1» She would show his photographs again in 1985, and she continues to show his works.

«1» Telephone conversation with the author, March 27, 2008.

35 Thom Gunn

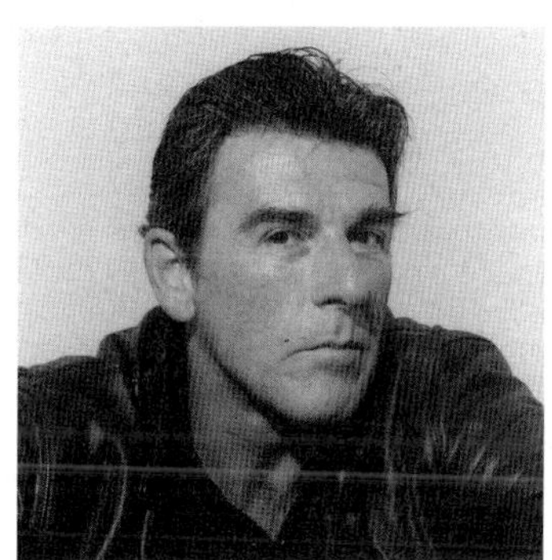

Gelatin silver print, 1980
13 13/16 x 13 3/4 in.
MAP 483 / Plate 28

Thom Gunn is one of the very few male poets of whom Mapplethorpe made a portrait.«1» An Englishman and long a teacher at Stanford University in California, Gunn (1929–2004) arrived in 1960 in San Francisco, where they met in 1978 through the magazine editor Jack Fritscher, although the photograph apparently was made in New York. Rather than receiving a commission, Mapplethorpe may have asked Gunn to sit to him as the poet did not receive a print of his image and, in 1993, paid the Mapplethorpe Foundation to use it as the cover of his Collected Poems.

Gunn's best-known early book, My Sad Captains and Other Poems, was published in 1961. His verse became freer and his subject matter darker in The Man with Night Sweats, published in 1992, when he dealt with the deaths of his friends from AIDS. His work has been described as wedding "traditional form to unorthodox themes like LSD, panhandling, and homosexuality,"«2» and these later poems can be described as taut, mournful, and casually elegiac.

In Mapplethorpe's portrait, which was likely made by artificial light, Gunn's hair is beginning to gray, and together he and the photographer have agreed to portray him as the serious man he was.

«1» The only others known to this writer are John Ashbery and John Giorno, both of whom he photographed individually in color for the jacket of a 1980 record album, issued by Giorno Poetry Systems, on which recordings of each reading from his own works are included with recordings of William Burroughs. The only known women poets he pictured were Patti Smith and Kathy Acker, both of whom were also very active in fields other than poetry. (For Mapplethorpe's portraits of Burroughs, Smith, and Acker in the present exhibition, see plates 20, 3, 91, and 54.)
«2» Wolfgang Saxon, "Thom Gunn, 74, Poet Who Left Tradition for the Counterculture," obituary, New York Times, April 28, 2004.

36 Keith Haring

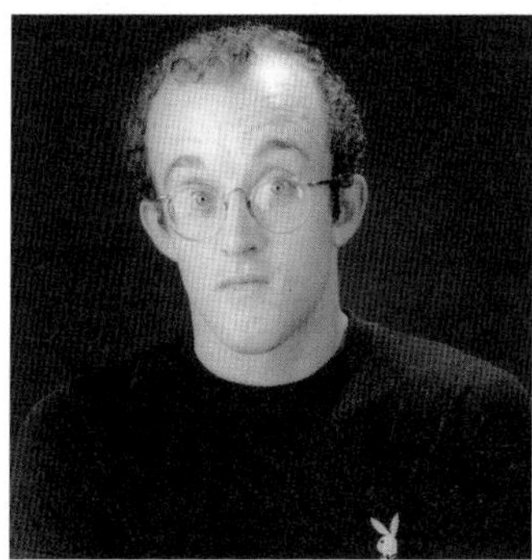

Gelatin silver print, 1984
15 1/4 x 15 1/8 in.
MAP 1463 / Plate 75

Mapplethorpe's portrait of the artist Keith Haring (1958–1990) is uncharacteristic of the photo-grapher's work in its lack of affect, which must have been a result of the interaction between the two men. For this sitting the graffiti artist-turned-painter-turned-social activist chose to wear a T-shirt decorated with the Playboy bunny emblem. This choice, evidently ironic as well as playful, must have helped to establish the tone of the photo shoot. Despite a twelve-year difference in age, a friendship existed, and in 1984, Haring painted a pottery amphora, dedicated it to Mapplethorpe, and gave it to him.

At Mapplethorpe's direction, his studio assistants had set up soft boxes to the left and right, facing the position of the sitter and meant to soften the flare of the strobe lights that were timed to coincide with the exposure. Reflections of the soft boxes can be seen in Haring's eyeglasses, and a low-power hair light was added to differentiate the top of the sitter's head from the dark background. The exposure Mapplethorpe chose to print caught Haring at a point when his eyebrows were raised to their greatest height, although the balance of his expression is amusingly and earnestly deadpan.

The photograph was originally made for and published by Interview magazine. Two years later it was selected to be included in the book 50 New York Artists, along with a comment by Haring about making art, which can also be applied to the process of being photographed: "The act of creation is a kind of ritual."«1»

«1» Marshall, 50 New York Artists, 54.

37 Deborah Harry

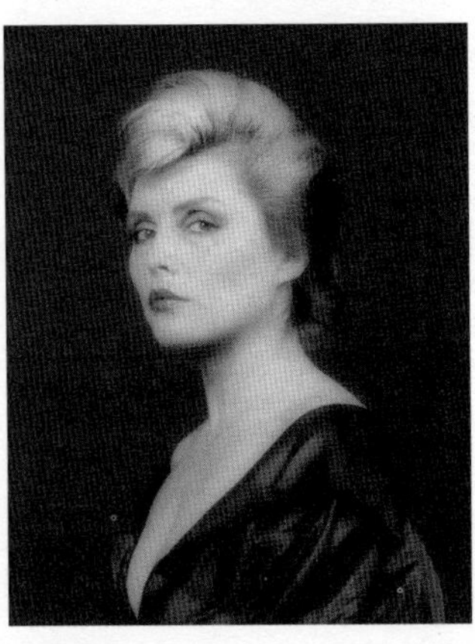

Gelatin silver print, 1982
19 x 15 1/8 in.
MAP 945 / Plate 49

Although Deborah Harry's original reputation as a punky, pouting, glamourpuss is reflected in the portrait Mapplethorpe made of her in 1978, his camera turned her into a film goddess in 1982. By this time, she had released a solo album but was still the singer for Blondie, the group that had made her considerable reputation and had recently released its sixth studio album but was on the edge of dissolution. Harry (b. 1945) had a wide range of pursuits, among them an interest in writers of the Beat generation, which led to her friendship with William Burroughs (plate 20).«1»

The image is a successful, classic portrait of a beautiful woman. In order to animate the portrait, Mapplethorpe suggested that she stand angled away from the camera and then turn her head partway back toward it, so that she looks out of the sides of her eyes at it. This kind of angled pose, which he often employed, was also used by the great nineteenth-century Parisian portrait photographer Nadar, some of whose pictures Mapplethorpe owned and with whose work his has other affinities, among them the use of utterly plain backgrounds. It was a particularly adroit choice of pose for picturing this singer as it so effectively shows her pronounced cheekbones and the line of her jaw. For the occasion, her eyes and mouth have been painstakingly made up. The sheen of her dark, broadly striped dress is matched by the gleam of her lips and the highlights in her carefully brushed hair. Her poise, glamour, and intelligence have enabled her long career as a singer and an actor, on stage and in films.

«1» Victor Bokris, Beat Punks (Cambridge, Mass.: Da Capo Press, 2000), 171-78.

38 Carolina Herrera

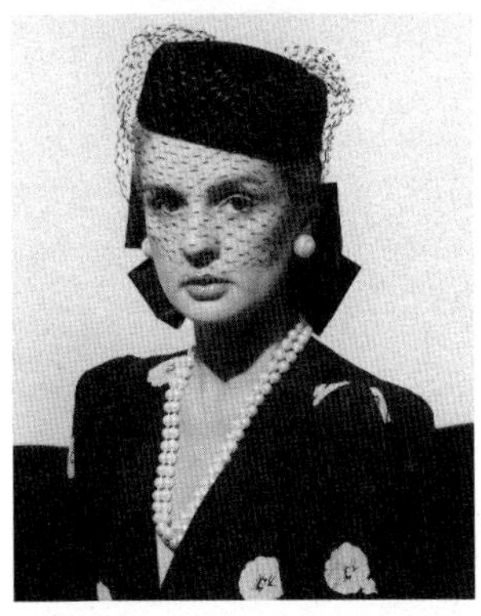

Gelatin silver print, 1979
18 x 14 in.
MAP 450 / Plate 16

At the time Mapplethorpe photographed the Venezuelan-born aristocrat Carolina Herrera (b. 1939), she was on the point of transforming herself from a chic socialite into a successful fashion designer.«1» The clothes and accessories she wore for the sitting are elegant; the expression on her face resolutely neutral, save perhaps for her slightly wary gaze. The image is cool in tone, even severe, partly because it was made using tungsten light, which is somewhat harsh, and partly because of the sharp contrast of the crisp black silhouettes of her hat and bow against the dead white background. Neither her veil, with its oblong flecks and their shadows on her face, nor the perfectly delineated necklace, every pearl with a highlight, significantly softens the overall effect. Only the shapes of the flowers on her dress and the fact that her head is not precisely centered on the sheet lessen the rigor of the image, and even the degree to which it is to the left of center is calculated. Although the chilly result was produced by both the photographer in his choice of light, pose, and backdrop, and by his sitter in her choice of impeccable clothes, it is the apparent detachment of this kind of image that has engendered criticism of Mapplethorpe's portraiture as lacking warmth and depth. Its formal perfection and polish cannot, however, be denied.

«1» Her husband, Renaldo Herrera, sat to Mapplethorpe two years earlier, and she would sit to him again when he was working on the book that became Some Women (Boston: Bulfinch Press), which was published in 1989, after his death.

39 David Hockney

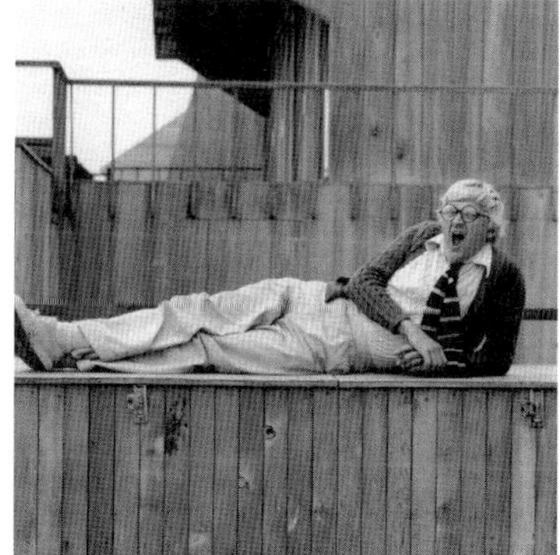

Gelatin silver print, 1976
13 3/4 x 13 3/4 in.
MAP 42.1 / Plate 4

Later in his career as a portrait photographer, Mapplethorpe strongly preferred to work in the controlled environment of his studio. This early picture of David Hockney (b. 1937), the English painter who often lived in California, stretched out on the deck of a house on Fire Island on a hazy day, proves that the photographer could achieve impeccable results outdoors as well, particularly when, as here, there were strong architectural elements to establish a formal geometry. For the setting, Mapplethorpe appropriated the exterior of the house next door to that of John White, where Hockney and Henry Geldzahler (see plate 19) were staying. He photographed them together and separately. Even though Hockney chose to wear a necktie, which although characteristic for him was extraordinarily formal garb for Fire Island at any season by day or night, he was likely a relaxed sitter, in part because he and Mapplethorpe were well acquainted. They had first met in about 1970 at the Chelsea Hotel, when the photographer was living with Patti Smith (plate 3).«1» In 1971 Mapplethorpe took a Polaroid of Hockney with the painter Francis Bacon, and Hockney made a drawing of Mapplethorpe and inscribed it to him; in turn, Mapplethorpe gave the Englishman a Polaroid of a male nude.

Always alive to the possibility of the unconventional in portraiture, Mapplethorpe has shown the painter in the middle of a yawn; sleepy, but not asleep, as the cigar in his left hand indicates. He would photograph Hockney outdoors again eight years later, but on the West Coast rather than the East. In that same year, he would make another photograph of a man yawning, this time his frequent model Ken Moody.

«1» See the biographical sketch of Mapplethorpe at www.alisonjacquesgallery.com that accompanied an exhibition in London of Mapplethorpe's work that was curated by Hockney and Charlie Schieps in 2005 (accessed March 31, 2008; biography page no longer available).

40 Deborah Irmas

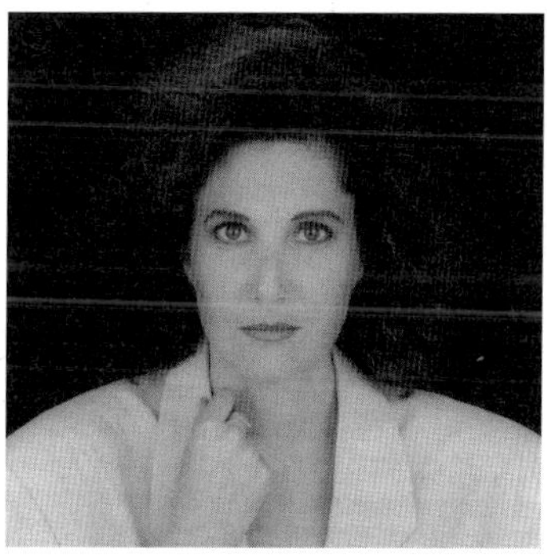

Gelatin silver print, 1988
18 x 19 in.
Collection of Deborah Irmas / Plate 93

The first person whom the photo historian, curator, and documentary film producer Deborah Irmas (b. 1950) encountered when she arrived at Mapplethorpe's Twenty-third Street loft in May 1988 was a woman who was a make-up artist and hairdresser. Her ministrations included the application of a virulent coral-colored lipstick, which, she assured her subject, would appear to be understated in a black-and-white image. Once she had finished working on Irmas, Mapplethorpe appeared, suggested that his sitter's hair be fluffed up some more, approved the result, and proceeded with the sitting.

In the pupils of Irmas's eyes, to the left and right of their centers, there can clearly be seen the trapezoidal reflections of the soft boxes that temper the glare of the strobe lights that are timed to flash at the moment the film in the camera is exposed. An irregularly shaped dark area in her eyes, between the trapezoidal shapes, must be the inverted image of the photographer and his camera. There appears to have been a separate hair light. Her well-spaced eyes are so wide open as to invite comparisons with those of Bambi, but she had been told to keep them open, and, despite her nervousness at being formally photographed, her overall expression bespeaks self-possession.

Mapplethorpe knew, from the gallery that represented him and through which the sitting had been arranged, that Irmas was advising her parents, Audrey and Sydney Irmas who were forming a collection of photographers' self-portraits and had already acquired one of him in drag. So, when the portrait session was over, he volunteered to show her his most recent. This proved to be the photograph with the cane with skull finial (plate 101). The Irmases acquired this second self-portrait and donated it with the rest of their collection to LACMA in 1992.

41 Philip Johnson

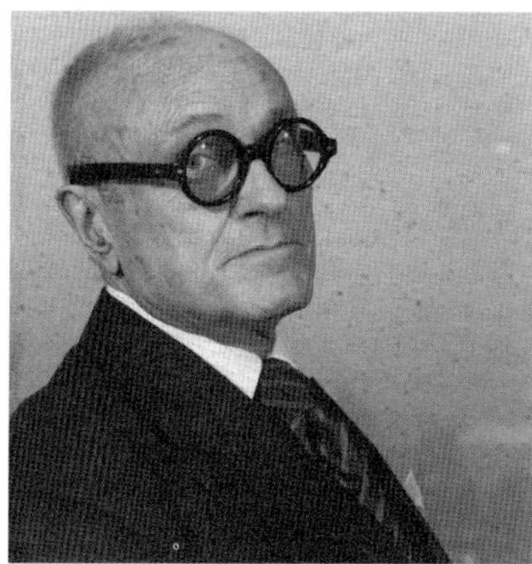

Gelatin silver print, 1978
14 1/8 x 14 in.
MAP 69 / Plate 9

In twentieth-century portraiture, black, heavy-framed round eyeglasses can be a clue that the subject is an architect—a marker used much as symbols of their martyrdom identify medieval saints. Such eyewear was long a personal trademark of the immensely influential architect Philip Johnson (1906–2005), who, like I. M. Pei, adopted the style in emulation of Le Corbusier. The rest of Johnson's garb is extremely restrained but impeccable. The photograph, made in Johnson's office in front of a window that was spotted with pearlescent drops of rain, was lit by a single source above and to the sitter's right.

The placement of the head and shoulders on the page would be more reminiscent of a sculptural portrait bust if the clean, sloping line of Johnson's chest were not interrupted by the triangle of his pocket handkerchief. The photograph very closely resembles that of another from the same session in which the architect is seen from a greater distance, and it becomes clear that he is sitting upright in an armchair with his arms stretched along its armrests, his wrists bent slightly, so that his hands resemble the paws of a sphinx.

42 Bill T. Jones

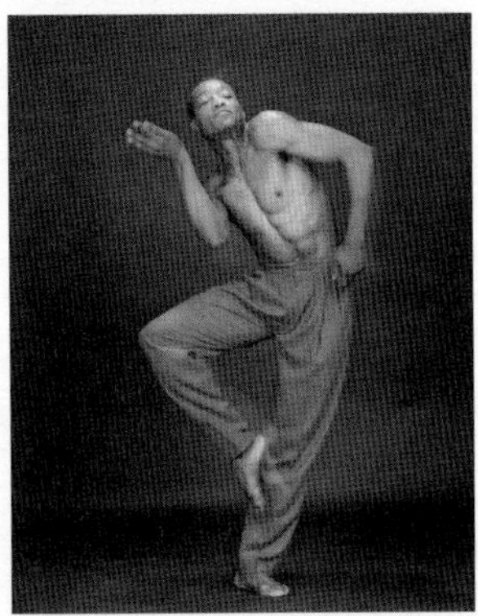

Gelatin silver print, 1985
19 1/8 x 15 1/4 in.
MAP 1616 / Plate 84

Mapplethorpe rarely tried to capture people in motion but did so intentionally in 1985, when he photographed the dancers Gregory Hines and Bill T. Jones, and spontaneously when he saw the actress Sonia Braga gyrating in his studio (plate 83). His photograph of Jones (b. 1952) is particularly appealing because of the dancer's exuberant nonchalance. Camera drag is visible in the doubling of his right foot and the blurring of the edge of his left forearm, because Jones was moving too fast for the camera exposure to freeze his motion. At the same sitting Mapplethorpe made a number of studies of Jones, including some of the dancer at rest.

Jones is a highly accomplished dancer and a prolific choreographer for the company he founded with his late partner, Arnie Zane, and for many other companies. He has also directed plays and operas and written memoirs and a children's book on dance. His work has won many awards and he has several honorary doctorates. This portrait of a dancer dancing conveys much of the attractive energy that has made these accomplishments possible.

43 Grace Jones

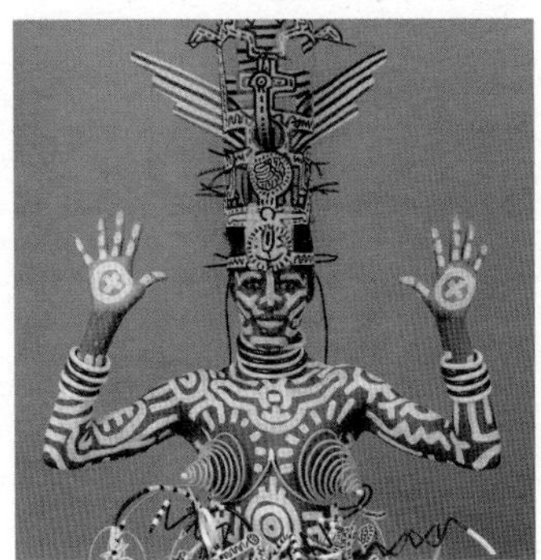

Gelatin silver print, 1985
15 1/8 x 15 1/16 in.
MAP 1447 / Plate 74

Keith Haring painted Grace Jones's body in tribal patterns, which were closely related to his characteristic linear graphic style, for two appearances at the celebrated downtown alternative disco, the Paradise Garage, in 1985.«1» The results were so striking and successful that the singer and painter collaborated again in 1986 for the video that accompanied the release of her hit song "I'm Not Perfect" on her album Inside Story and for the film Vamp. Her towering rubber headdress and a small portion of the stage of the club were also painted by Haring, who had been introduced to Jones by Andy Warhol (for whom, see plate 60). She, too, had been photographed by Warhol. In collaborating with Haring, she was very much a participant in the process, not simply a blank slate. She has often made radical alterations to her appearance, once having her hair shaved into a flattop.

Of his photographs of Jones in this quasi-tribal get-up, Mapplethorpe chose to make editions of ten prints of two views of Jones's hand gestures and one of a full-length dance pose. The costume was intended, at least by Jones and Haring, to be an overt reference to the early comedic performances in Paris of the black American singer, dancer, and entertainer Josephine Baker in the 1920s.«2» The image is not a portrait in any conventional sense, but can be deemed to be a portrait of a performance or spectacle. (For a portrait proper, see plate 95.)

«1» The club was in New York on King Street, a block south of Houston, between Hudson and Varick Streets.
«2» It has been suggested, improbably, that the wire coils that ensnare Jones's breasts were inspired by a sculpture of Baker by Alexander Calder that has similar coils (www.english.emory.edu/Bahri/GraceJones.html; accessed August 19, 2008).

44 Grace Jones

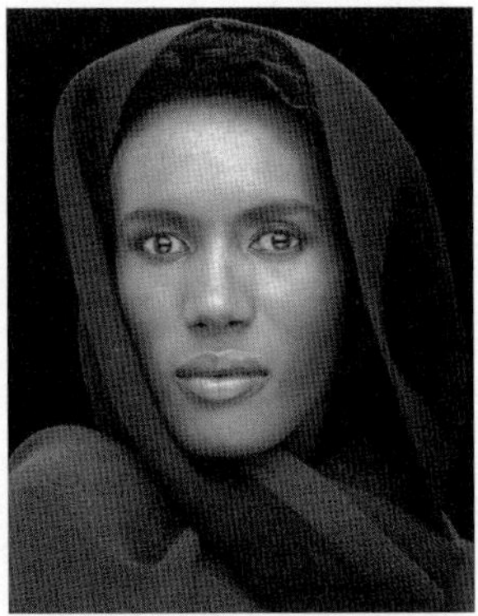

Gelatin silver print, 1988
23 x 19 1/4 in.
MAP 1907 / Plate 95

Through his activities as a collector of photographs, often in tandem with his patron, Sam Wagstaff (plate 17),

Mapplethorpe was well acquainted with the work of his predecessors in the nineteenth century and the first half of the twentieth. Both men owned work by Julia Margaret Cameron, the great maker of portraits from the world of the arts in Victorian England. Although it has rarely been noticed, Mapplethorpe's photographic pantheon would come to roughly resemble Mrs. Cameron's; this softly glowing portrait of the extremely successful singer, fashion model, and actress Grace Jones (b. 1952) with her head swathed in dark fabric recalls some of Cameron's close-in images of women with similarly wrapped heads (see fig. 3, p. 18). The photograph was made for Splash magazine.

For an entirely different portrait of Jones, see plate 74.

45 Madeline Kahn

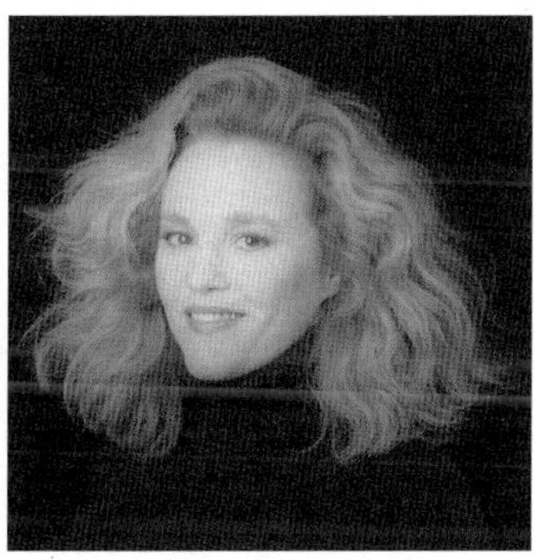

Gelatin silver print, 1985
15 3/16 x 15 3/16 in.
MAP 1507 / Plate 77

The comedienne Madeline Kahn (1942–1999) is best remembered for her roles in three films by Mel Brooks, including Blazing Saddles. In 1985 she starred in Clue, which was released at the end of the year in which the photograph was made. Here Mapplethorpe was photographing her for the Italian edition of Vogue magazine, so there was a clear effort to make her seem as glamorous as possible. This effort was abetted by the make-up artist and hairdresser, who were employed in Mapplethorpe's studio on a regular basis for portrait sittings. In order to soften the overall effect of this portrait, in the darkroom Mapplethorpe's printer used a diffuser in the enlarger between the light source and the negative. This produced an image with softer shadows and smoother skin textures, both of which flattered the sitter. This finished photograph is thus the product of at least five people: Mapplethorpe, one or more studio assistants, the cosmetician, the hairstylist, and the darkroom technician.

46 Ellsworth Kelly

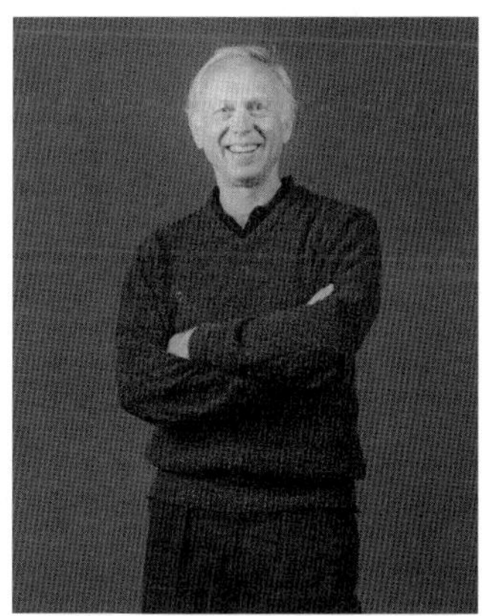

Gelatin silver print, 1984
10 3/4 x 8 1/2 in.
Dagny Corcoran Collection
MAP 1368 / Plate 66

The East Coast artist Ellsworth Kelly (b. 1923), whose work, although ultimately extracted from the natural world, is more apparently closely related to both hard-edge and minimalist painting, was photographed in Los Angeles at the same dinner party at which Mapplethorpe photographed Ed Ruscha (plate 68). Kelly, who at that time was having an exhibition of his painted aluminum sculpture at Margo Leavin's gallery nearby, seems to have genuinely been having a good time and could perhaps be among the most amiable of all of Mapplethorpe's sitters, save for the fact that, when he was photographed in 1986, for inclusion in 50 New York Artists, his expression was wholly serious. The difference can be attributed to the setting and occasion. This was informal, postprandial, and social, the other, formal, midday, professional, and meant to be part of a serious book that included a portrait of the artist, an example of his work, and a brief artist's statement.«1»

«1» Marshall, 50 New York Artists, 64.

47 Klaus Kertess

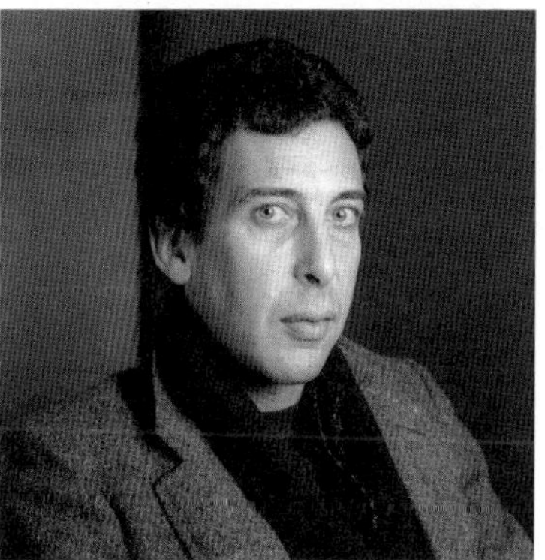

Gelatin silver print, 1980
13 3/4 x 13 7/8 in.
MAP 438 / Plate 31

As a writer about contemporary art and a curator for numerous exhibitions, including the Whitney biennial in 1995, Klaus Kertess (b. 1940) has been phenomenally productive for decades. When he was running the radically innovative Bykert Gallery in New York at the end of the 1960s, Brice Marden (see plate 89), one of the painters he showed, introduced him to Mapplethorpe and the two became friends. For a while they were neighbors on Bond Street and, in 1974, two photographs by Mapplethorpe were shown at Bykert.

Kertess had moved elsewhere by the time Mapplethorpe asked him to sit for this photograph, which was intended to be included in a book of portraits that Mapplethorpe was then planning. As the photographer vetoed beforehand the curator's choice of a favorite old overcoat, Kertess presented himself in a tweed jacket and a silk-lined wool scarf. This grazes his jawline because of his turned-up collar, which, in turn, creates the only cast shadow in the image. Despite his astuteness and their friendship, he was surprised to find how directorial, even dictatorial, Mapplethorpe was about the exact angle toward the camera he should hold his head and about his expression. As it is, Kertess looks out at us with characteristic luminous intelligence and sensitivity.

48 Udo Kier

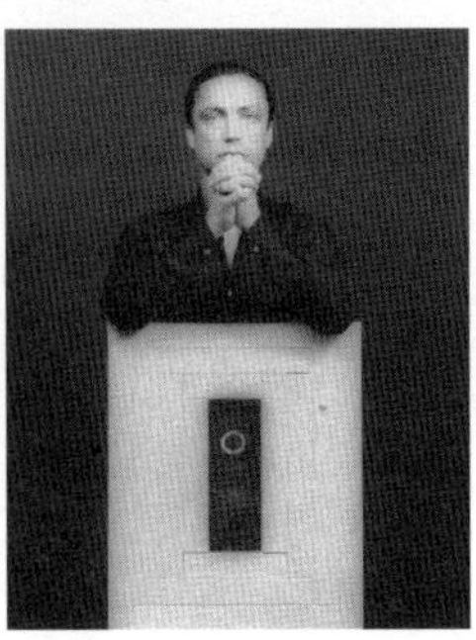

Gelatin silver print, 1983
19 1/4 x 15 1/4 in.
MAP 1072 / Plate 62

Just after Kier was born in 1944 in Cologne, bombs started falling on the hospital but he survived. Although sometimes described as a specialist in playing vampires and villains, he has, over a long career as a movie actor, played a great variety of roles in more than seventy films in Germany and the United States. Here, Mapplethorpe impishly used a layered mat to improvise a frame for Kier's round belt buckle. He instructed the actor to prop his elbows on the top edge of the mat and then fold his hands in such a way that his thumbs rest precisely on the parting between his upper and lower lips. The V of his unbuttoned shirt points down while his thumbs point up. The pose and prop combine to make the resultant image very roughly resemble an ancient Greek herm, a type of fertility statue in which a human head tops a solid but slender vertical block from which an erect phallus protrudes midway up its height. Although a belt buckle decorously replaces the phallus, the effect is mischievous and oddly unsettling despite the level, clear-eyed gaze of Kier's widely spaced eyes.

49 Lee Krasner

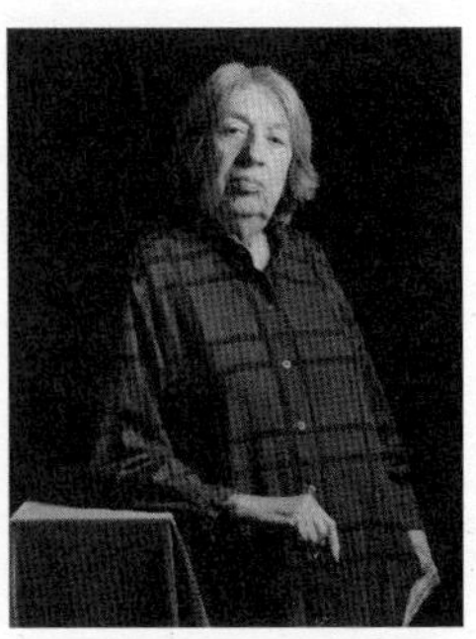

Gelatin silver print, 1982
19 x 15 1/8 in.
MAP 930 / Plate 36

Perhaps because they were two generations older than he, Mapplethorpe seems not to have photographed any of the abstract expressionist painters except Lee Krasner (1908–1994) and Willem de Kooning. The de Kooning portrait was specifically commissioned for a book on New York painters and, as Krasner was not part of the circles in which the photographer normally moved, it is likely this portrait was also a commission, although for another project.«1» Krasner was very much a painter in her own right before she married Jackson Pollock in 1945, during their marriage, and after his death in 1956. When she posed for Mapplethorpe at age seventy-four, while resting her elbow on a velvet-covered pedestal, she uncompromisingly presented herself as she was, without makeup, save lipstick, and wearing a simply patterned, nearly shapeless garment. Her face is lined, her hands age spotted. She seems to be appraising the photographer and the way he went about depicting her.

«1» It is possible that Mapplethorpe's connection to Krasner was made through Sam Wagstaff, who had purchased an important Jackson Pollock, The Deep, from her after Pollock's death. Wagstaff's correspondence with Krasner can be found in the Archives of American Art at the Smithsonian Institution, Washington, D.C.

50 Frank Langella

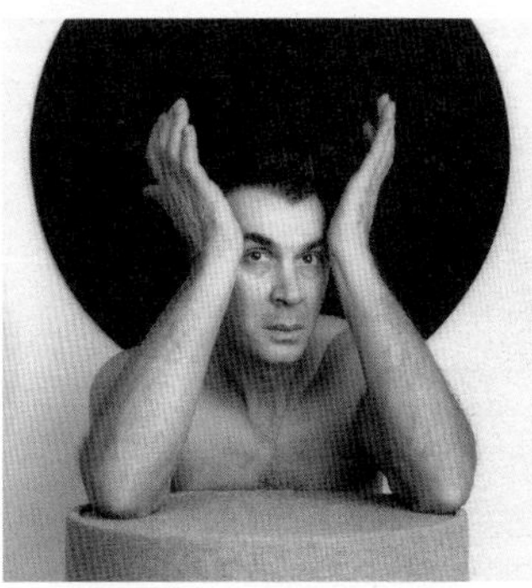

Gelatin silver print, 1984
15 3/16 x 15 1/4 in.
MAP 1453 / Plate 69

The records of the Mapplethorpe Foundation indicate that this photograph was made to be used as an advertisement for a play. In June of 1984 the immensely gifted and hard-working actor Frank Langella (b. 1940) opened in a revival of Noël Coward's Design for Living (1933), playing a sophisticated painter; in November he opened in a revival of Arthur Miller's After the Fall (1944), playing a troubled lawyer. Because the actor was photographed without a shirt, it seems at least somewhat more probable that the picture was made to publicize the second of these two plays, although that conjecture doesn't wholly explain the absence of the shirt.

Langella, who is most famous for playing Dracula, was photographed against the circular cutout with a black paper background that Mapplethorpe employed extensively during 1984 when making nude studies and portraits such as that of the art dealer Mary Boone (plate 65). Exceptionally, given Mapplethorpe's love of pure geometric form, the upper part of the circle is cut off at the top, as it is in another image from this sitting, in which the actor's head is collapsed forward onto the round pedestal and hidden by his crossed arms. Here, his elbows rest on the pedestal, his wrists press on his temples, and his hands extend upward like antlers, the outside edges of which echo the circumference of the black background circle. This gesture, his wide-open eyes, and unsmiling lips combine to make him seem exasperated or beset by woes. Manifest expressions of feeling are rare in Mapplethorpe's portraiture. As this was intended as an advertisement for a play, it is clear that Langella was portraying a character rather than simply sitting for his portrait.

51 Marcus Leatherdale

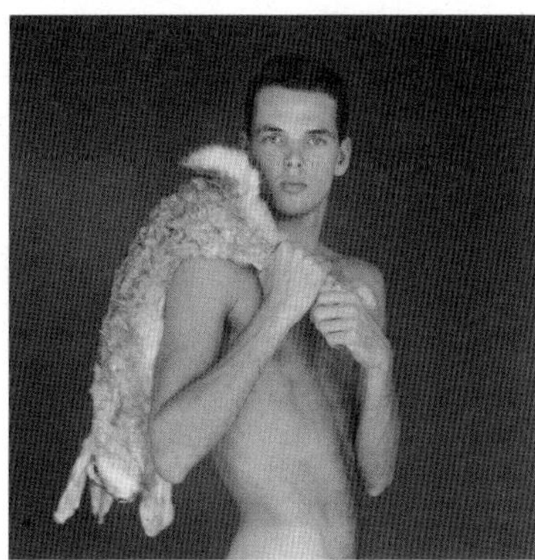

Gelatin silver print, 1978
13 13/16 x 13 3/4 in.
MAP 308 / Plate 11

Leatherdale (b. 1952), a fledgling photographer at the time, was working for Mapplethorpe as a studio assistant when he was asked to pose. The younger man wanted, he recently explained, his body to be photographed so that the result would resemble one of Mapplethorpe's still lifes rather than one of his nudes. Thinking of traditional painted still lifes that included the carcasses of hanging game, Leatherdale purchased a large rabbit from a local butcher. In the first photographs from the session, the rabbit was suspended from a cord parallel to his nude body, but here he slung the dead animal over his shoulder as if it were a trophy of the hunt.«1» The photograph is an uneasy contrast of textures, the flesh of the rabbit against the flesh of the man gently illuminated from below by light reflected up from the studio floor. The powerful line set up by the back of the corpse of the rabbit continues through and across Leatherdale's knuckles and hands and down his left forearm to the elbow. The circle that is roughly implied by this line is carried by momentum across his abdomen and back past its starting point upward along his right arm. A stabilizing counterweight to this circular motion is provided by his head with its widely spaced eyes, strongly marked grooves between nose and mouth, and full lips and by the level intensity of his gaze. Altogether this is a strange and arresting image, not quite to be classed as a nude, nor as a still life, but perhaps best described as a portrait, even a dual portrait, of rabbit and man. As a rabbit is neither sword nor shield, there is no reference here to physique photographs in the little magazines of the 1950s or 1960s, with which Mapplethorpe was familiar, in which, to legitimize the images of naked men, models were pictured with props intended to reference the classical world.

In his own photographic practice, Leatherdale went on to make a series of portraits that Details magazine published and titled "Hidden Identities." He described these as exploring "the possibilities of covert portraiture . . . hiding the features but focusing on the subject's personal style and star quality."«2» Mapplethorpe assiduously explored similar questions about the extent to which facial features can be concealed and personality still conveyed.

«1» Mapplethorpe would continue the theme of dead game as still life by photographing a single suspended dead pheasant in 1984. This image is, however, more reminiscent of nineteenth-century British records of bagged game than of seventeenth-century Dutch still lifes.
«2» Leatherdale's statement about "covert portraiture" and a selection of examples of his images that fall under that rubric can be found at http://www.marcusleatherdale.com under the heading "New York Photographs" and subheading "Hidden Identities" (accessed May 28, 2008).

52 Fran Lebowitz

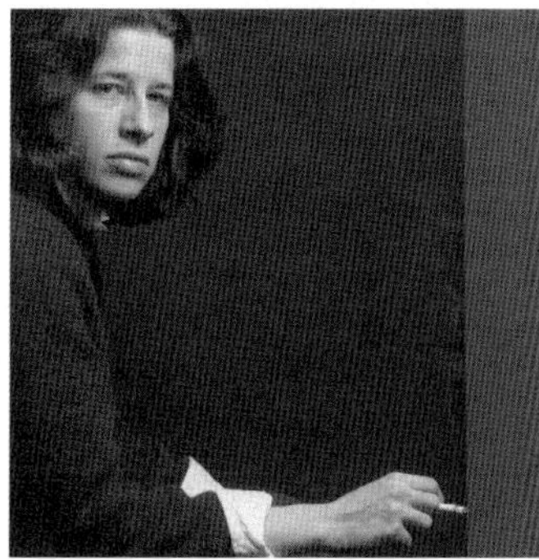

Gelatin silver print, 1980
13 7/8 x 13 7/8 in.
MAP 424 / Plate 23

The stylish American author Fran Lebowitz (b. 1950) regards the camera with what seems to be distrust. She and Mapplethorpe had been friends for some years, and her wariness is simply part of the sardonic attitude toward the world that informs her humorous writing. "Vegetables," she holds, "are interesting but lack a sense of purpose when unaccompanied by a good cut of meat."«1»

This photograph is as carefully composed as any of her well-wrought one-liners. The cigarette in her hand is as much a part of her persona as are the man's shirts she habitually wears, and the tip of the ash is lined up precisely with the edge where the background color shifts from black to gray.

«1» A collection of her apothegms may be found on line at http://www.quotationspage.com (accessed May 30, 2008).

53 Annie Leibovitz

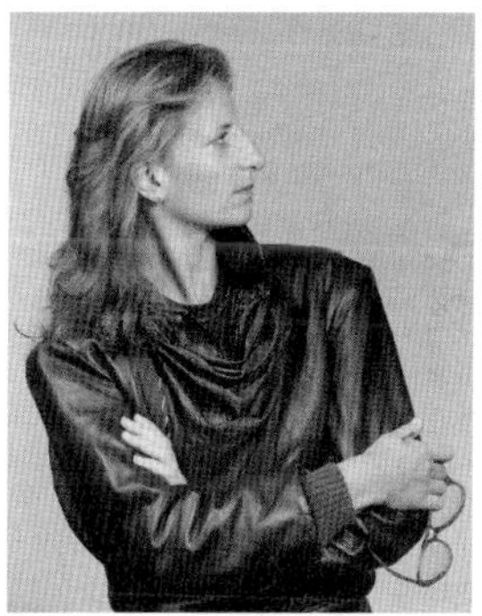

Gelatin silver print, 1983
19 1/4 x 15 1/4 in.
MAP 1095 / Plate 52

Although the work of the portrait photographer Annie Leibovitz (b. 1949) has been described as displaying a close collaboration between the photographer and her subjects, that cannot be said to be very evidently the case here. Mapplethorpe owned a profile portrait made by her in 1982 of the singer and guitarist Peter Tosh with his hair brushed forward, completely covering his face, an image that paralleled his own interest in portraits with hidden faces. That the two photographers were friendly is indicated by her affectionate inscription to him on a print of the double portrait of John Lennon and Yoko Ono that she had made in 1980, shortly before Lennon was murdered.«1»

Perhaps she removed her glasses at his request, in order to better show her remarkable profile. He often chose to make profile views of his sitters, correctly thinking that they led to elegant results. This is a good example, even though her eyes are not shown to advantage. Her face seems not to be made up and she wears a softly draped black leather jacket, the color of which may be the reason Mapplethorpe photographed her against a white background.

Leibovitz, whose work has been widely published and exhibited, first became famous because of the numerous assignments that she executed for Rolling Stone magazine, for which she was the chief photographer from 1973 until 1983. Since then, she has extensively photographed celebrities for Vanity Fair, often displaying great inventiveness, sometimes coupled with humor, in her images. Whoopi Goldberg, for example, is lying in a bathtub filled with milk, and the artist Christo is so thoroughly wrapped that he would be unidentifiable were it not for the caption.

«1» For Mapplethorpe's portrait of Yoko Ono, see plate 97.

54 Roy Lichtenstein

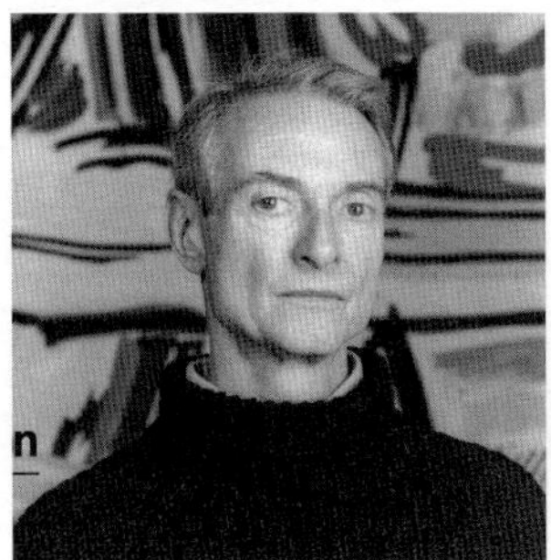

Gelatin silver print, 1985
19 1/8 x 19 1/8 in.
MAP 1637 / Plate 76

Mapplethorpe photographed the important pop artist Roy Lichtenstein (1923–1997) for 50 New York Artists, a book that gave Mapplethorpe the fortunate opportunity to picture many of the most prominent painters and sculptors of the 1980s.«1» Richard Marshall, the curator who devised and wrote the publication, has stated that Mapplethorpe was thrilled to photograph Lichtenstein, whose work he admired.«2» Lichtenstein, who is pictured in his studio in front of one of his canvases, appears very much present for the occasion. His crow's-feet seem to be extensions of his eyebrows, and his head and neck are isolated from his dark turtleneck sweater as if he were a classical sculpture in two different kinds of colored marble.

Lichtenstein's best-known paintings are images directly derived from single comic book panels, which he greatly enlarged and rendered in a style as flat as the originals. His first one-man show at Leo Castelli's gallery in 1962 was an immediate success and his career soared.«3» Gradually, his subject matter evolved away from pop art sources to include wider cultural references and painting styles of the past, but his treatment of all these remained consistently even, smooth, and flat. His work, which is represented in numerous museum collections, is a landmark in the history of twentieth-century art.

«1» Marshall, 50 New York Artists, 68.
«2» In a telephone conversation with the author, late November 2007.
«3» For one of Mapplethorpe's portraits of Castelli, see plate 81.

55 Gordon Lish

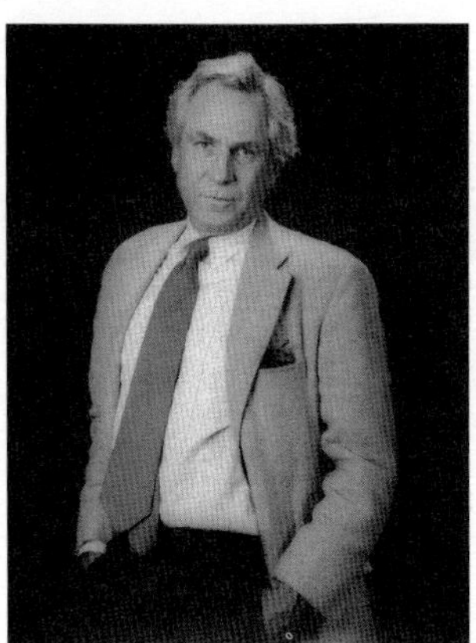

Gelatin silver print, 1984
19 1/8 x 14 15/16 in.
MAP 1409 / Plate 71

Gordon Lish (b. 1934) first made his name as an influential editor at Esquire, later, as an editor at the publisher Alfred A. Knopf, and subsequently, as a novelist. He brought to bear his exacting intelligence on the manuscripts of numerous writers, but particularly those of Raymond Carver, whose early work he substantially shaped. Bristling with testosterone, he regards Mapplethorpe's camera with stern impatience. As a stalwart of the literary establishment, he was outside the photographer's customary circle of sitters, most of whom were drawn from the visual arts, the theater, cinema, and design. Lish was photographed for the London Sunday Times, which commissioned Mapplethorpe, very occasionally, to portray an eclectic selection of people, including the poet Allen Ginsberg in 1978 «1» and the filmmaker Kenneth Anger in 1985.

«1» The portrait of Ginsberg is described in a letter of April 10, 1978, from Mapplethorpe, who was in Boulder, Colorado, to Jack Fritscher in San Francisco. No print or reproduction of it is now findable, despite inquiries to the London Sunday Times and two of its former picture editors. Neither the Mapplethorpe Foundation nor the Ginsberg Trust has any information about its existence. See Fritscher, Assault, 31-32.

56 Lisa Lyon

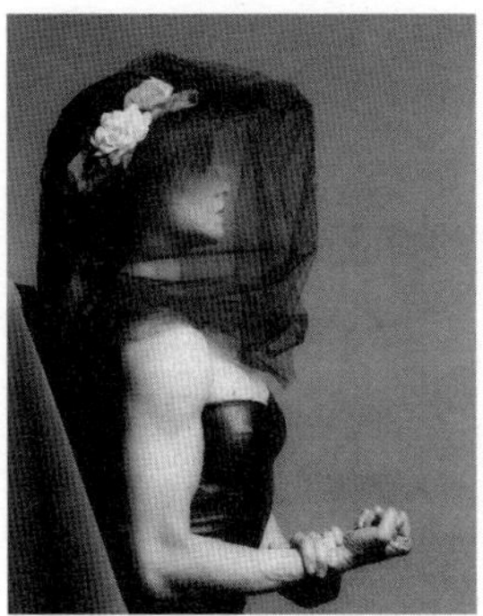

Gelatin silver print, 1980
19 1/8 x 14 7/8 in.
MAP 773 / Plate 47

Mapplethorpe's interactions with the model and bodybuilder Lisa Lyon

(b. 1953) were intense and complicated. They met at a party in New York in 1979 to which she'd worn a black rubber outfit that perfectly showed the physique that had won her the First World's Women's Bodybuilding Championship.«1» The next day he began to photograph her and, between 1980 and 1986 but mostly in 1981 and 1982, he made more than two hundred separate images of her that he turned into editioned prints. Many of these came into being because she convinced Viking Press to publish a book of Mapplethorpe's photographs of her made in a variety of places, ranging from Joshua Tree, California, to Jamaica.«2» Mapplethorpe, who was infatuated with Lyon, and she with him, described the book as a novel without a real story.«3» In the introduction, Bruce Chatwin enumerated some of her roles: "Lisa posed as bride, broad, doll, moll, playgirl, beach girl, bike-girl, gym-girl, and boy-girl; as frog-person, mud-person, flamenco dancer, spiritist medium, archetypal huntress, circus artiste, snake-woman, society woman, young Christian, and kink."«4» For some, she is elaborately costumed. The simplest is no more than Lyon's shadow on a wall. Many are nudes. Collectively, the clothed photographs can be thought of as weirdly analogous to Cindy Sherman's smaller series Untitled Film Stills, which were made a few years earlier, but with broader, if less clear, referents. (Tomoko Sawada's far more recent and restrained photographs also come to mind.) Many of these collaborations embody fantasies thought up by either the photographer or his model or both together.

In this photograph, Lyon's delicate profile is visible through the cloud of black veil that tumbles from her wide-brimmed hat, which has a wreath of white flowers around it. Below are her bare shoulders, muscular arms, and a shiny black bustier. The slightly sinister aura created by the costume and the strength of the pose necessitate the considerable negative space that the figure dominates. This is not an ordinary human nor is this an ordinary portrait; effectively, it is a portrait of an imaginary person.

Lyon was pictured by many other photographers in a variety of guises. Perhaps her oddest impersonation was her bare-breasted but luxuriantly bearded impersonation of the god Hercules for Joel-Peter Witkin. She gave Mapplethorpe, who owned other photographs by Witkin, a print of it.

«1» For an account of their relationship, see Morrisroe, Mapplethorpe: A Biography, 230-33 and many additional references.
«2» Mapplethorpe, Lady, Lisa Lyon.
«3» In an interview broadcast on the television program Arena, produced and directed by Nigel Finch (BBC Television, 1988).
«4» Mapplethorpe, Lady, Lisa Lyon, 14.

57 Norman Mailer

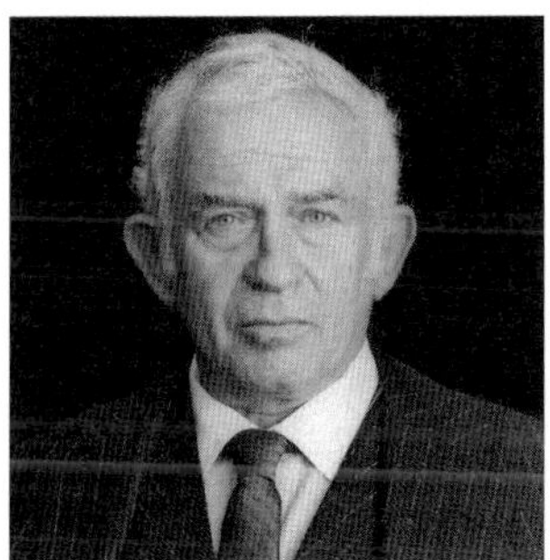

Gelatin silver print, 1985
15 1/4 x 15 1/8 in.
MAP 1599 / Plate 82

The personality of the formidable American writer Norman Mailer (1923–2007) was so outsize that it might have been almost presumptuous to attempt to capture it in something as static as a photographic portrait but, as Vanity Fair requested that Mapplethorpe do so, he complied. At the same sitting, he also made pictures of Mailer's sixth wife, Norris Church, and of the couple together. For the occasion, Mailer chose to wear a white shirt and a conservative suit and tie. In accordance with his consistent preference, his sideburns are long. He seems to have become an elder statesman with a piercing gaze that perhaps hints at his reputation, when younger, as a contentious maverick and untidy brawler. Save for the intensity of his eyes, the image of the writer is very restrained, but it is a great portrait of an important cultural figure.

Mailer's first novel, The Naked and the Dead, which was drawn from his experiences in World War II, was highly praised and sold very well, making him instantly famous. He wrote thirteen more works of fiction and twenty others on a variety of subjects including Marilyn Monroe, Pablo Picasso, and, often, politics. He won the Pulitzer Prize twice: for Armies of the Night, a partially fictionalized narration of the protest march on the Pentagon in 1967, and for The Executioner's Song, an account of the murderer Gary Gilmore's efforts to be punished for his crime. A thoroughly engaged public figure, Mailer was a founder of the Village Voice newspaper, a mayoral candidate in New York City, and an opponent of women's liberation. He covered six national political conventions and could be counted on to express controversial opinions during his frequent appearances on television talk shows. But his paramount importance, as he insisted, was as a writer. Among the other writers whom Mapplethorpe photographed were Truman Capote, Bruce Chatwin, Edmund White, Brad Gooch, Christopher Isherwood, Fran Lebowitz, and William Burroughs.«1»

«1» For images of Capote, Chatwin, Lebowitz, and Burroughs, see plates 34, 15, 23, and 20.

58 Edward Mapplethorpe

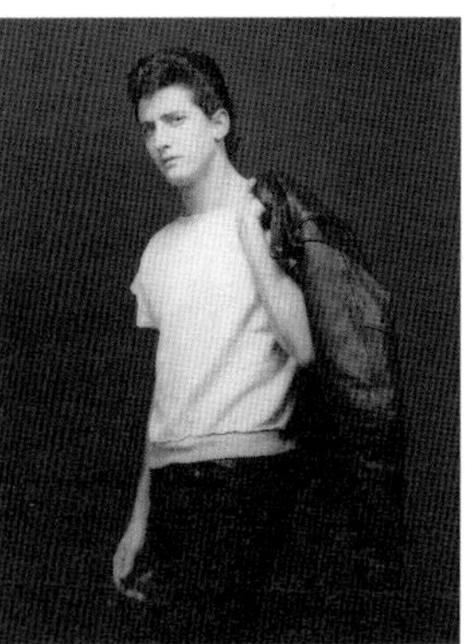

Gelatin silver print, 1983
19 1/8 x 15 1/4 in.
MAP 1303 / Plate 51

Edward Mapplethorpe (b. 1960) was only three when Robert, who was thirteen years older, moved away from their parents' house permanently and thereafter had little contact with the family. In 1982, Edward had just finished college, where he had studied photographic lighting and darkroom techniques. Robert then hired Edward as a studio assistant, and he proceeded to apply what he had learned to his older brother's practice. As a result, Mapplethorpe's photographs became more polished in their overall appearance and their lighting more sophisticated. Simultaneously, Edward began to make his own photographs, but when he placed some of these in an exhibition in which Robert was also showing, the latter persuaded him not to use their common surname. Edward Mapplethorpe became Edward Maxey and stayed so until well after his brother's death. He continued to work in the studio until 1984 and then moved to Los Angeles. Three years later, in 1987, as his brother's health deteriorated, he returned and lived with Melody Danielson (see plate 98). He remained with the studio until Mapplethorpe's death. Since then, he has been a successful photographer. Among his recent works are chromogenic and black-and-white lithographic prints and cameraless photograms.

In this portrait, he wears simple clothes—the inside-out sweatshirt with cut-off sleeves, black jeans, and black leather jacket—and his hair is sleekly oiled and brushed. His expression is less than relaxed, and the fingers of his right hand are tensely curved. The only other portraits of him that Robert Mapplethorpe editioned as prints are one with Edward wearing a black jacket and photographed against a white background rather than a dark one and a dual portrait, with Melody, made in 1988.

59 Self-Portrait

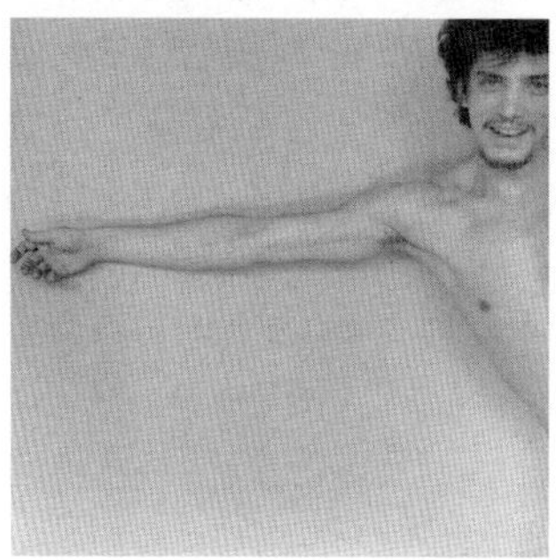

Gelatin silver print, 1975
14 x 14 in.
MAP 138 / Plate 1

Although Mapplethorpe's pose is reminiscent of a crucifix, the spirit of the photograph is playful because of his gleeful expression. Earlier, he had made numerous Polaroid self-portraits, often nude, but this is his first in a large format, and it is more lighthearted than those that followed. There would be many in the course of his career, from Polaroids at its beginning to some later in drag and in a variety of tough-guy poses. At the end of his life, there were others that are devastatingly honest in their depiction of the ravages of AIDS. Even if the mood of this piece, which was made at night, is jaunty, his calculated placement of the figure along the right edge with the index finger of his right hand just touching the left margin gives the image formal structure.

The image is playfully reminiscent of, but not dependent on, the work of the pictorialist photographer F. Holland Day (1864–1933), who, in the late 1890s, portrayed himself as Christ in elaborate tableaux of the crucifixion and in a series of seven self-portraits with varying, appropriately exaggerated, expressions and entitled 'The Seven Last Words of Christ.' When this picture was made, Mapplethorpe may not yet have known the work of the pictorialist, but later he owned a portrait by Day of a nude youth.«1» In another parallel to Mapplethorpe, Day also made (relatively discreet) studies of black male nudes. Mapplethorpe was born a Catholic; Day became one only on his deathbed.

«1» See Christie, Manson & Woods International, The Collection of Robert Mapplethorpe, sale cat., New York, October 31, 1989, lot 46, p. 33.

60 Self-Portrait

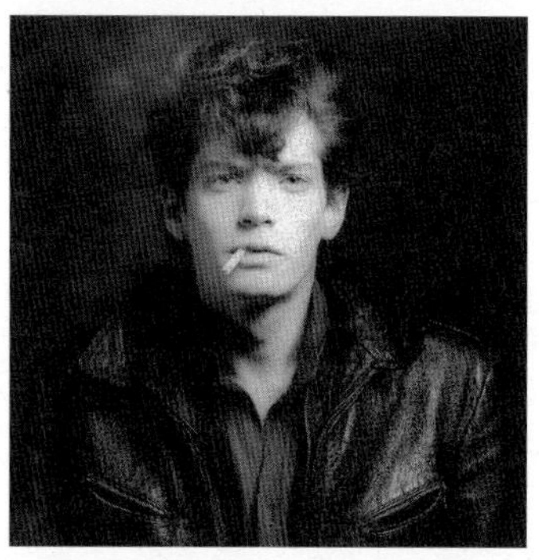

Gelatin silver print, 1980
14 x 14 in.
MAP 434 / Plate 25

61 Self-Portrait

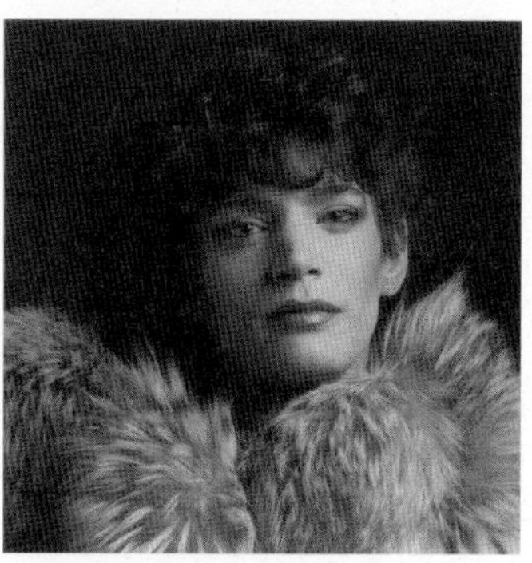

Gelatin silver print, 1980
14 x 14 in.
MAP 384 / Plate 26

From the time Sandy Daley, Mapplethorpe's earliest tutor in photography, lent him a Polaroid camera in 1970, he made self-portraits. In many of the earliest, he explored and displayed varieties of the autoeroticism with which he was experimenting.«1» Collectively, the images document a stage in his sexual development, but most are not intentional self-portraits in the full sense of the term and do not show his face. Their fetishistic content resembles the photographs of Pierre Molinier (1900–1976), one of whose works Mapplethorpe owned, but his are not as elaborately staged as are those of the Frenchman and do not include elaborate female attire. After receiving a Hasselblad camera from

Sam Wagstaff in 1976, the first image Mapplethorpe made that can perhaps be considered a self-portrait is the infamous photograph that shows him with a whip inserted in his anus and twisting awkwardly around to look at the camera. Made in 1978, it is his last-known overtly sexual picture of himself, unless the bare-chested, bust-length self-portrait of 1980, for which his face was made up, can be deemed to be sexual. An image of the back of Mapplethorpe's head, made in 1981, is more an exercise in geometry than a self-portrait: from the corners of the picture, four diagonal lines converge toward its center, wholly dominating the composition. Two are lines of piping on the back of his jacket; the other two, lines in a painting behind him.

Mapplethorpe made a number of self-portraits in 1980 of which these two are examples. In one, a straightforward presentation of his day-to-day appearance on the street, he faces the camera directly. He wears an open black leather jacket, the breast pockets of which are unzipped, over a plain flannel shirt with an abbreviated collar. Seemingly casually, his hair is tousled over his forehead, and he is lit primarily from the upper right. There is a conscious intention to present himself as he ordinarily wanted to be seen.«2»

In contrast, in the self-portrait in drag, he presents himself as he never wanted to be seen, except in this photograph. Its existence is a natural outgrowth of the myriad images that he was making of Lisa Lyon at the time(see plate 47), in various roles that they invented. Because this picture is taken at such close range, it is more intimate than those of her. Unlike his older contemporary in the downtown art scene, the portrait photographer Peter Hujar, Mapplethorpe was apparently not interested in photographing the radical drag performance artists of the period, so to have portrayed himself as a woman was to move into unfamiliar territory, but using his customary rigorous approach.«3»

The drag self-portrait is lit in the same way as that with the leather jacket, with a principal light source above and to the right. Again, the background is dark, but the camera is closer. Where the leather jacket is restrained, the (rabbit?) fur collar that cushions his face here is exuberant. One of the cosmeticians whom he employed for women's portraits likely helped to apply his makeup. To have made these two portraits, of a seemingly ordinary, butch downtown guy and a drag queen, is for a man who was often described as being sweet and shy, a pictorial tour de force of shifting identity and public self-display.

After 1980, there are twelve more self-portraits that he editioned. He photographed the back of his head in 1981. In 1982, he showed himself wearing a skinny necktie and a black leather jacket. From 1983, there are four images, in two of which he posed in front of flat geometrical devices of his own devising and two in which he holds a switchblade knife. In 1985, he editioned two of himself, one with his head in motion, the other with little devil's horns on his head; in 1986, one in a dinner jacket. In 1988, he made three, one with a skull-headed cane (plate 101), another in which he wore a bathrobe, and a third of his eyes alone.

«1» For a selection of these Polaroid images, see Richard D. Marshall, introduction, Robert Mapplethorpe: Autoportrait (Santa Fe, N.M.: Arena Editions, 2001); and Wolf, Polaroids, plates 54-55, 92-99, and 138-45.
«2» This picture is described by David Joselit as superimposing an exaggerated convention on the body of the artist, one of "sullen, rough masculinity" (Joselit, "Robert Mapplethorpe's Poses," in Janet Kardon, Robert Mapplethorpe: The Perfect Moment, exh. cat. [Philadelphia: Institute of Contemporary Art, University of Pennsylvania, 1989], 19).
«3» Among Mapplethorpe's sitters there seems to be only one male, named Aira, in female attire. Among the sitters that both Hujar and Mapplethorpe portrayed are Susan Sontag, Andy Warhol, Fran Lebowitz, William Burroughs, Robert Wilson, and Lynn Davis, who knew the two photographers very well.

62 Self-Portrait

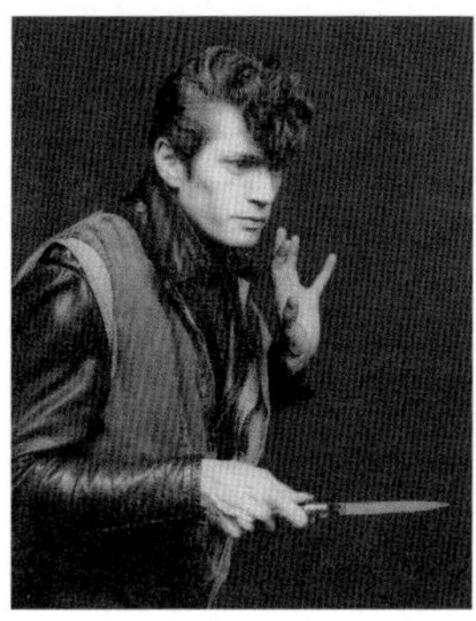

Gelatin silver print, 1983
19 1/4 x 15 1/4 in.
MAP 1277 / Plate 50

This self-portrait with a switchblade knife can be considered as a corollary to the many photographs Mapplethorpe made earlier of Lisa Lyon enacting various roles. He plays the part of a knife-wielding street tough who wears a denim overlay over a canvas vest over a black leather jacket over a sweater, which is presumably over a T-shirt. Had it been five years earlier, save for the knife, he's outfitted as he would have been if he were en route to a gay S&M bar in winter. This kind of macho clothing for gay men was copied from that of straight biker outlaws. In fact, by the time this photograph was made, Mapplethorpe usually sought other nighttime venues with different dress codes.

As instruments of violence and power, and as phallic symbols, knives had enough fascination for Mapplethorpe that they appear in his images relatively often. In 1979 he made a side-view photograph of Frank Diaz with his muscular forearm raised as if he were ready to stab someone with the knife he grips in his fist. From 1984 there is a half-length color portrait of Mapplethorpe's studio assistant, the young Spaniard Javier Gonzalez, with a knife pointed to the left, and an image of Chris Hoffman with a stiletto. Knives were not exclusively associated with men; he photographed Lisa Lyon in 1982, once silhouetted in a circle of light with an upraised dagger and once in a pose similar to that taken by Diaz. From 1985 there is a radical still life of a carving knife stuck into a watermelon as well as a study of a flower blossom and a thin blade and, from 1989, the image of a tomato run through by a knife. (Revolvers and rifles appear infrequently; only in pictures of Jack Walls and Lisa Lyon in 1982 and of Dennis Speight and of himself in 1983.)

An incongruous detail in this photograph is that, although his eyes are intensely focused, they are directed below the place where his knife is pointed and where we might logically assume his unseen target to be. His left hand is held up defensively. Appropriately for this imaginary scenario, there is visible tension in his right cheek, but given the photographer's mordant, mocking sense of humor, there remains a possibility that even though the picture was carefully composed, this kind of role-playing was not entirely intended to be taken seriously.«1»

«1» It is indicative of his intention to get a satisfactory image that, according to his studio records, he made fifty-six exposures to obtain this picture.

63 Self-Portrait

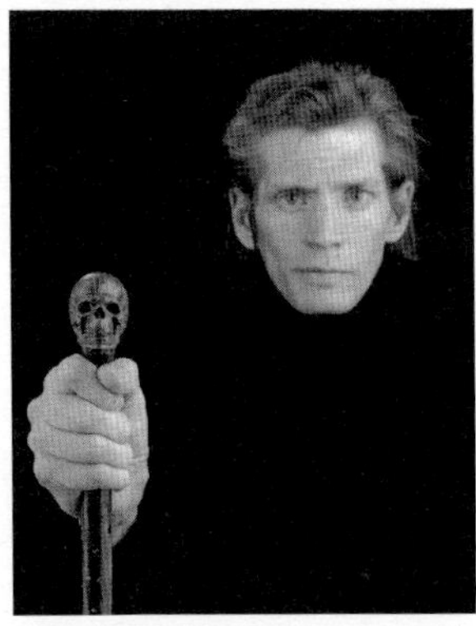

Gelatin silver print, 1988
22 3/4 x 19 in.
MAP 1860 / Plate 101

Mapplethorpe's self-portrait in which he grasps a skull-headed cane with his right hand was made in the spring of 1988. Although the camera is focused on the cane rather than on his ravaged face, which is thereby slightly softened, the photograph is devastatingly frank about his prematurely aged appearance. Even so, he is still handsome. The image marked the height of his honesty about himself and his illness. He was brave to have made this admission of his own mortality. Although at this point he needed assistance to move around, once the camera had been set up and a preliminary exposure made of the cane by itself, he went back to his bedroom to change into a black turtleneck sweater, so that his head would float against the black background in diagonal juxtaposition with the skull and his hand.«1» Fully half of this daring composition is black, which represents the culmination of his long-term predilection for increasingly dark work. His obsession with the skull as an obvious symbol of mortality dates back to his student days at Pratt in the 1960s, but here he forcefully and fittingly employs one to mirror his present distressing condition. Because of its candor and composition, this photograph can be considered to be a masterpiece. In the only other portrait of himself that he made before his death in 1989, at the age of forty-two, he sits in an armchair. Wearing an expensive silk bathrobe, he appears pale and exhausted, and his hands and feet are skeletal.

«1» He was, of course, wholly aware that, in the history of art, skulls obviously and invariably represent death, as they do in popular culture, as, for example, in the jewelry worn by his sitter Larry Desmedt (plate 35). Earlier in his career, he had made an edition of an image of a human skull.

64 Brice Marden

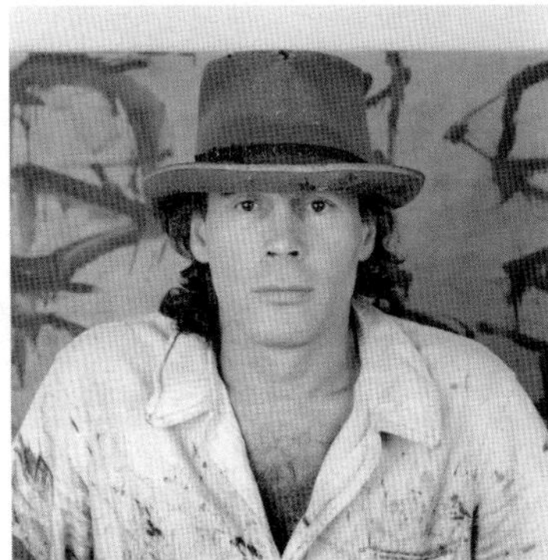

Gelatin silver print, 1986
19 1/4 x 19 1/4 in.
MAP 1628 / Plate 89

Mapplethorpe's connection to the painter Brice Marden (b. 1938) was arguably stronger than to any other artist of the period. They may first have met at the legendary bar and restaurant Max's Kansas City, which Mapplethorpe frequented with Patti Smith when they could afford to go out. Starting in 1975 Mapplethorpe photographed Marden, his wife, Helen, his son, Nick, and his daughters, Melia and Mirabelle individually in various years. In 1980, he made a group portrait of the whole family sitting on a couch. The present portrait was made, for the book 50 New York Artists, in Marden's studio in front of one of his canvases.«1» Although his hat and coveralls are spattered with paint, there seems to be none on his face. He regards the camera calmly and unpretentiously, content to be present for an occasion in familiar company.

After training at Boston University, where he received a bachelor's degree, and at Yale, where he earned a master's degree, both in fine arts, Marden moved to New York in 1963. At first, his early paintings were of nearly monochromatic rectangles. Gradually, they came to be single dense colors on separate, adjacent panels, each rendered in a muted palette specific to his work. These oils were rubbed with beeswax to give them their characteristic sheen. Concomitantly, he made even-toned charcoal or graphite drawings. His first solo exhibition in New York was at Klaus Kertess's Bykert Gallery in 1966, a year when he also began to be employed as Robert Rauschenberg's assistant, whose work does not seem to have influenced his own.«2» Marden's paintings became more complex when he began to assemble rectangular blocks of color into compositions that might be elegant, minimalist evocations of the uprights and lintels of Stonehenge. More recently, he has overlain monochromatic fields of color with ribbons of meandering lines that were at first clearly related to Asian calligraphy but have become increasingly loose and independent. His work has been consistently exhibited and is widely collected.

In an interview in 2006, Marden

commented that Mapplethorpe was "a driven person,"«3» a remark that was descriptive and not intended to be critical.

«1» Marshall, 50 New York Artists, 76.
«2» For Mapplethorpe's portraits of Kertess and Rauschenberg, see plates 31 and 64.
«3» Interview recorded on the videotape Robert Mapplethorpe, directed by Paul Tschinkel, in the series Art/New York, no. 61 (New York: Inner Tube Video, 2006).

65 Marisol

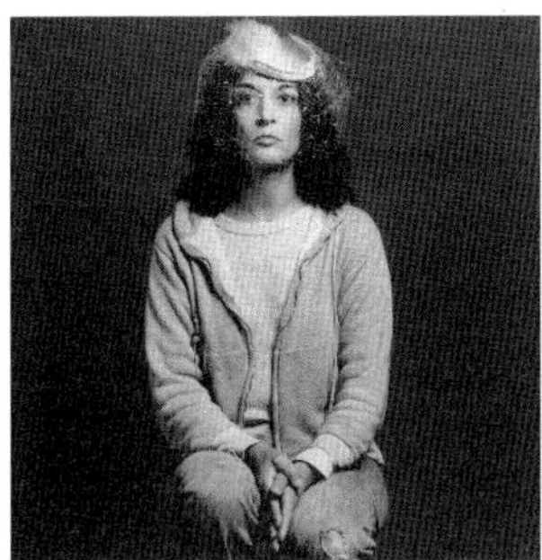

Gelatin silver print, 1979
13 3/4 x 13 3/4 in.
MAP 327 / Plate 14

Born of Venezuelan parents in Paris in 1930, the sculptor Marisol attended several art schools before studying painting with the abstract expressionist Hans Hofmann. In about 1951 she turned to sculpture, which has remained her principal medium, although she also makes etchings and lithographs. Her sculpture has frequently been made from found pieces of wood that she then paints with imagery that is drawn from popular culture and links her work to pop art.

In the Bond Street studio there were three rolls of pull-down sheets of seamless paper in black, white, and gray to be used as backgrounds behind sitters. Mapplethorpe chose the "Thunder Gray" roll for his photographs of Marisol, likely to contrast with her black hair and white clothes. The sculptor, who is known for her silences, solemnly stares, wide-eyed, straight at the camera. The formality of her jaunty satin and feather hat with its cloud of veil and her elaborately made-up eyes are at odds with the informality of her garments. She wears jeans with a hole in the left knee, a long-sleeved thermal undershirt, and an unzipped, hooded sweatshirt, her wristwatch visible beneath a cuff. The impression she gives of self-contained reserve is emphasized by the way she gently interlaces her hands between her knees.

66 Lisette Model

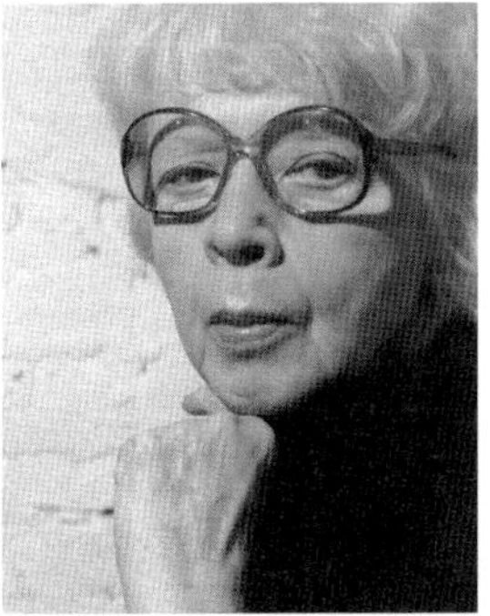

Gelatin silver print, 1980
13 3/4 x 13 3/4 in.
MAP 406 / Plate 32

Judging by the white painted brick in the background, Lisette Model (1901–1983), the portrait photographer, posed in front of the west wall in Mapplethorpe's Bond Street studio. In order to avoid distracting reflections in her oversized eyeglasses, the light source has been placed high and to one side. This produces somewhat exaggerated shadows from her glasses frames on her face. Less pronounced shadows show us that she is wearing bifocals, the left lens of which magnifies the size of her left eye to a point where it seems overpowering.

Model, who was born in Vienna, studied music composition there and then voice and painting in Paris before settling into a career as a photographer, first in France, later in the United States. Her approach to her work may be inferred from her statement that she had a great love for the snapshot because, of all photographs, it comes closest to the truth. Its apparent disorder and imperfection is its appeal and style.«1» As well as regularly producing fashion work for Harper's Bazaar, she made candid photographs in the streets of New York and taught photography at the New School for Social Research, where her most famous pupil was Diane Arbus. For that reason, this portrait links Mapplethorpe to Arbus, another important twentieth-century photographer, whose work he undoubtedly knew, although his style cannot be said to be directly indebted to hers, even though he owned three of her photographs. Nor was he particularly influenced by Model. Other noted photographers whom Mapplethorpe pictured are Gisèle Freund in 1980 (plate 27) and Horst in 1986.

«1» Youtube, Masters of Photography—Lisette Model, http://www.youtube.com/watch?v=3Aeocmdatio (accessed August 20, 2008).

67 Alice Neel

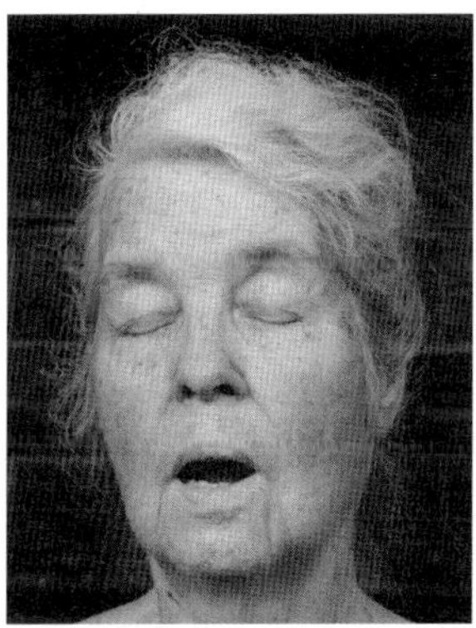

Gelatin silver print, 1984
19 1/4 x 15 1/8 in.
MAP 1444 / Plate 73

Toward the end of this sitting, after Mapplethorpe had photographed the portrait painter Alice Neel (1900–1984) at a distance, he moved in to do a close-up. As he started to make a new exposure, she spontaneously and surprisingly closed her eyes and opened her mouth. He was impressed by her gesture and, because he was consistently interested in pushing the boundaries of portraiture, he chose to make an edition of this image as well as one of a more conventional picture from the same sitting, in which Neel sits upright in a chair close to a brick wall, eyes open and gazing firmly at the camera. Herself a maker of forceful portraits, she would have been aware of how unflinchingly and shockingly intimately she was about to be portrayed, eyes open or closed. Her face resembles a death mask, and, in fact, she died only a few months after the photograph was made. The image is one of Mapplethorpe's most impressive. Its strength derives largely from the courage of his sitter, who was, at eighty-four, wholly without vanity.

68 Roberta Neiman

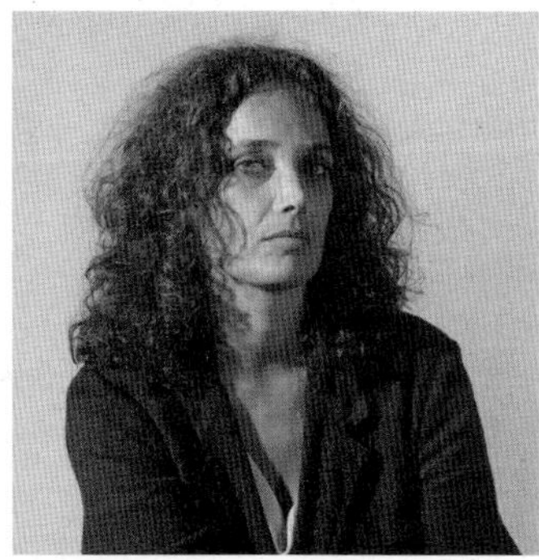

Gelatin silver print, 1980
13 7/8 x 14 in.
MAP 470 / Plate 24

The photographer Roberta Neiman knew Mapplethorpe through three friends, the art dealer and curator Clarissa Dalrymple, with whom she shared a loft that Mapplethorpe sometimes visited, and the photographers Elaine Mayes and Lynn Davis. He made portraits of all four women (for a portrait of Lynn Davis, see plate 13). At his request, Neiman and her son Greg came to the Bond Street studio, which she remembered as rather dark and elegant, to be photographed. Clad in her habitual uniform of black jacket and white blouse, she posed against the west wall in light that was fading. Because the photograph was made with available light, augmented only with a reflector, it more closely resembles a photograph by Nadar, the nineteenth-century French portraitist, than it does Mapplethorpe's later work, in which natural light was supplemented, or entirely supplanted, by electric light. As usual at this period of his career, there was a studio assistant, in this case Marcus Leatherdale (see plate 11).

Neiman's life has long been both geographically and professionally peripatetic. She shifted back and forth to Los Angeles, Aspen, Nova Scotia, New York, and Mexico, and worked, in turn, in a gallery, in film production as a photographer, as an art director, and as an interior designer, but with her own photographic practice a constant. Her book Ever Since Durango is an evocative, minimalistic visual diary of some of these travels.«1» With her inherently torrid appearance, she would be not out of place in a film noir. Mapplethorpe's portrait might have been taken in a scene toward the end of such a movie, her guarded expression the result of weariness and disquiet occasioned by events in the course of the story. The photographer has sensed and seized on this internal turbulence to make this image more, and unusually, emotionally expressive, even though, as always, he wished to produce a flattering portrait.

«1» Roberta Neiman, Ever Since Durango (New York: Passenger Press, 1977).

69 Louise Nevelson

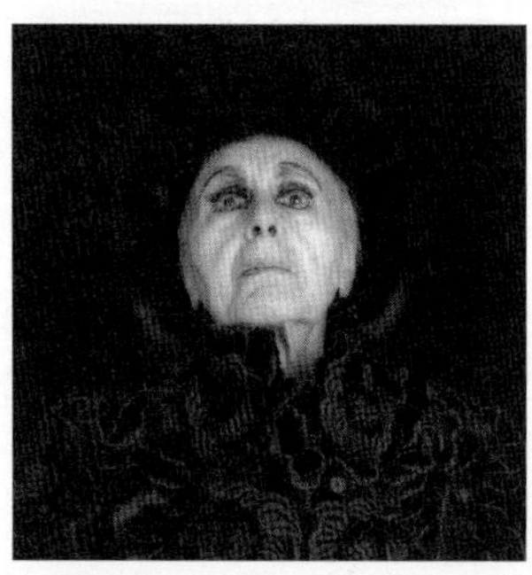

Gelatin silver print, 1986
19 1/4 x 19 1/4 in.
MAP 1630 / Plate 86

Although she was eighty-seven at the time the photograph was made, the formidably imposing sculptress Louise Nevelson (1899–1988) had no hesitation in staring the camera down. Her appearance, from her round fur hat to her wild, elaborate, and unusual eye makeup, is calculated to make a striking impression, which Mapplethorpe was happy to reinforce by placing his camera low, so that she appears even more forceful and strong willed as her head emerges from the riot of dark blossoms on her high-collared coat. This is an important example of subject and photographer working together to achieve a common goal. The photograph was made to be included in 50 New York Artists, but a less theatrical pose made at the same sitting was selected for publication.«1»

Mapplethorpe recognized the dramatic power of this image and chose to print it at a somewhat larger scale than usual. The difference was not great, a matter of four inches in each direction, but he had become interested in bigger pictures, which presumably had more wall power, and increasingly he asked his printer, Tom Baril, to make these larger prints.

«1» Marshall, 50 New York Artists, 84.

70 Yoko Ono

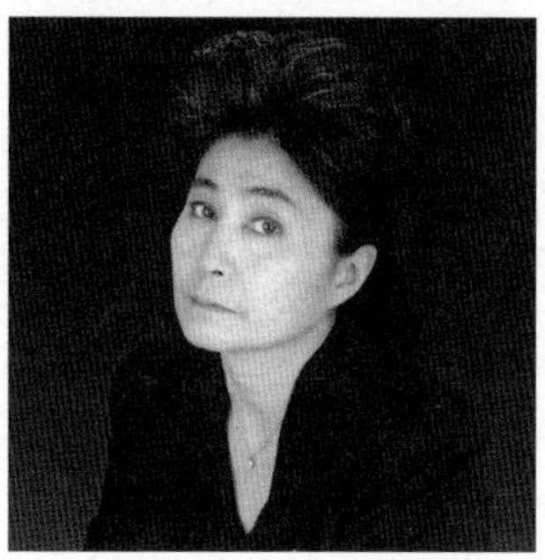

Gelatin silver print, 1988
19 1/4 x 19 1/4 in.
MAP 1952 / Plate 97

The conceptual artist and musician Yoko Ono (b. 1933), who is also well known as having been the wife of John Lennon, agreed to be photographed for inclusion in Mapplethorpe's book Some Women, but subject and artist do not seem to have established a meaningful connection when they met. Although the photographic result has a chilly elegance, she seems merely present and not wholly engaged in the process. Her expression can even be read as detached if not distrustful, although Joan Didion, who wrote a perspicacious introduction to the book, thought that Ono was the only one of the sixty or so subjects who were included in the publication to have presented herself as "'modern,' entirely in charge of herself, a woman who has negotiated the demands of sex and celebrity to appear before us as a middle-aged survivor, with sensible lapels, clear eyes, blown hair."«1»

Some Women, despite its understated, deadpan title, is a compendium of formal portraits, nudes, and fashion shots. About it, Didion, clearly referring to Mapplethorpe's rigorous control of the results, commented, "There is something interesting in all this, and willful, and the will is not that of the subjects."«2» Made at varying dates from 1981 to 1988, the images depicted women with a variety of occupations, including actresses, models, artists, agents, writers, and designers of glass, clothes, and interiors. The ages of the sitters varied from girlhood to old age. It was Mapplethorpe's last major project and did not appear until after his death in early 1989.

«1» Mapplethorpe, Some Women.
«2» Ibid.

71 Teddy Pendergrass

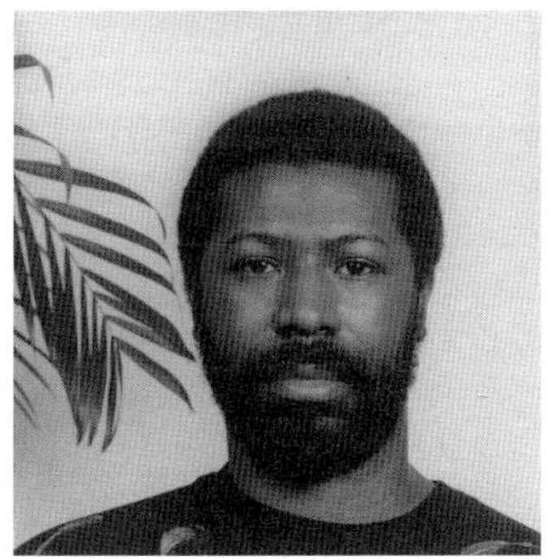

Gelatin silver print, 1984
15 3/16 x 15 5/16 in.
MAP 1462 / Plate 72

This nearly unembellished image of the rhythm-and-blues singer Teddy Pendergrass (b. 1950) was likely intended to be a record album cover but seems not to have been used for that purpose. Originally a drummer, Pendergrass became a singer in the early 1970s for Melvin and the Blue Notes. He left in 1976 in order to embark on his own career. Propelled by his smooth, melodious voice, a highly successful solo career ensued. Among his many seductive hit songs were "Close the Door" and "Turn off the Lights." Five platinum albums followed in succession, but in 1982 a devastating automobile accident left him paralyzed from the waist down. He has continued to record but has largely given up public performances. Much of his energy is directed toward raising money for a foundation that he set up to benefit the survivors of spinal cord injuries.

In Mapplethorpe's portrait, Pendergrass faces the camera foursquare, lit primarily from the left. To soften the image, the photographer has, uncharacteristically, provided a houseplant, making a slight context for the sitter. Some album covers by Mapplethorpe that were realized include those for Patti Smith in 1975 (see plate 3), for the group Television in 1977, for Joan Armatrading in 1984, and for Taj Mahal in 1986.

72 Paloma Picasso

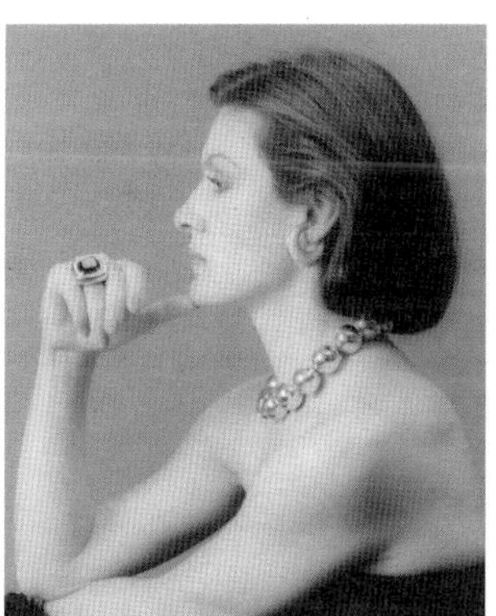

Gelatin silver print, 1980
18 x 14 in.
MAP 1588 / Plate 30

Mapplethorpe photographed the jewelry designer Paloma Picasso (b. 1949) for Tiffany's, where her jewelry, which is very conspicuously on view in this picture, was (and still is) sold. The daughter of Françoise Gilot and the painter Pablo Picasso, she founded a company that also makes perfume and evening wear. Her head and shoulders have been carefully positioned on the sheet, her eyes are not engaged with the camera, and her ring, bracelet, and earring are prominent. Judging by the even quality of the artificial lighting, it was probably made elsewhere than in Mapplethorpe's Bond Street studio.

73 Annamirl van der Pluijm

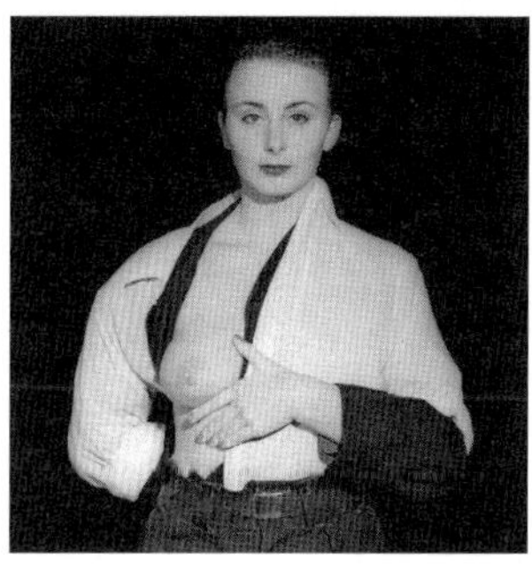

Gelatin silver print, 1985
15 1/4 x 15 1/4 in.
MAP 1920 / Plate 67

In January of 1985, Mapplethorpe went to Antwerp in order to document a performance piece, The Power of Theatrical Madness, by the radically innovative Belgian director and choreographer Jan Fabre. Between 1984 and 1986, the piece traveled widely in Europe, the United States, Australia, and Japan. When it appeared in New York, a reviewer described van der Pluijm as "a calmly riveting dancer-actress."«1» Presumably during a rehearsal that was conducted so that Mapplethorpe could make a series of images at several stages of the spectacle in order to roughly outline the performance, she and the other dancers were photographed performing a variety of actions, while clothed or nude.

As this picture was made while the actress was playing a part, even if the character was defined by action rather than speech, it is not quite a portrait, of either the character or the dancer herself, but some amalgam of the two. Nevertheless, her aplomb and self-possession, whether part of her personal character or of her role, are evident. Two years later, Mapplethorpe photographed the actress Lara Harris, also with a single breast bared, but with less self-confidence.

«1» John Rockwell, New York Times, February 8, 1986.

74 Iggy Pop

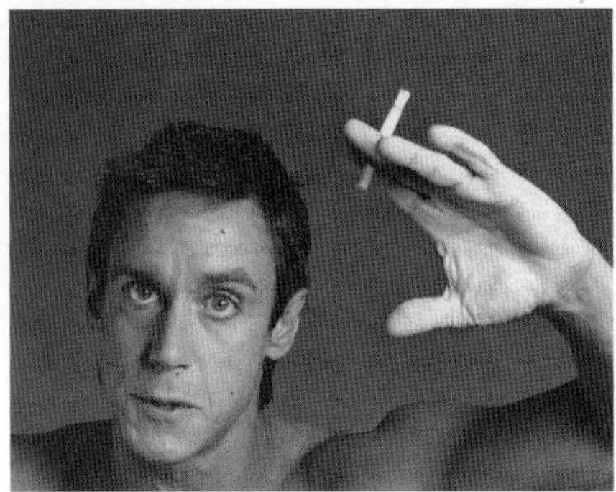

Gelatin silver print, 1985
14 x 17 5/8 in.
MAP 558 / Plate 33

The rock singer and songwriter Iggy Pop (James Osterberg, b. 1947) is nearly invariably shirtless in photographs. As a friend of Patti Smith, he met Mapplethorpe and Sam Wagstaff, by whom he was also photographed. Pop's career, with and without the group he founded, the Stooges, has been notable. His music and on-stage antics have been immensely influential for younger musicians, and he celebrated his sixtieth birthday by once again diving offstage into the crowd below. In Mapplethorpe's portrait, eyes wide open, he seems to be in the middle of making a conversational point as well as smoking. As usual, the photographer's composition is carefully controlled, cool, and elegant.

75 John Pope-Hennessy

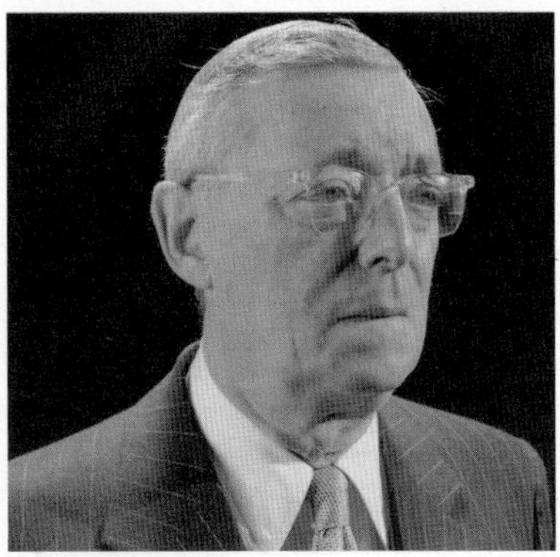

Gelatin silver print, 1986
15 1/4 x 15 1/4 in.
Plate 87

It was Mapplethorpe's first serious artistic mentor, John McKendry (1933–1975), a curator of prints and photographs at the Metropolitan Museum of Art in New York, who introduced him to masterpieces of historic photography by Julia Margaret Cameron, Alfred Stieglitz, and Paul Strand in the Met's collection. McKendry also established important social connections for him. Several other curators at the Met became Mapplethorpe's friends or sitters, among them Henry Geldzahler (see plate 19), Weston Naef and his wife Mary, and the Englishman John Wyndham Pope-Hennessy (1913–1994), the subject of this portrait.«1»

The son of a major general, Pope-Hennessy was knighted in 1971. Often referred to by museum cronies as "The Pope" because of his eminence and austere manner, he had been the director of the Victoria and Albert Museum in London from 1967 to 1973 and of the British Museum from 1974 until 1976, and held a post at the Metropolitan from 1977 until 1986. This scholar of Renaissance sculpture, who is attired in a conservative suit and tie, does not attempt to engage the camera and seems to have deliberately detached himself from his surroundings. His eyes are, apparently, studiously looking at nothing, and his mouth is held in an expression of mild distaste.

«1» Mapplethorpe could also have met Pope-Hennessy through Sam Wagstaff.

76 Robert Rauschenberg

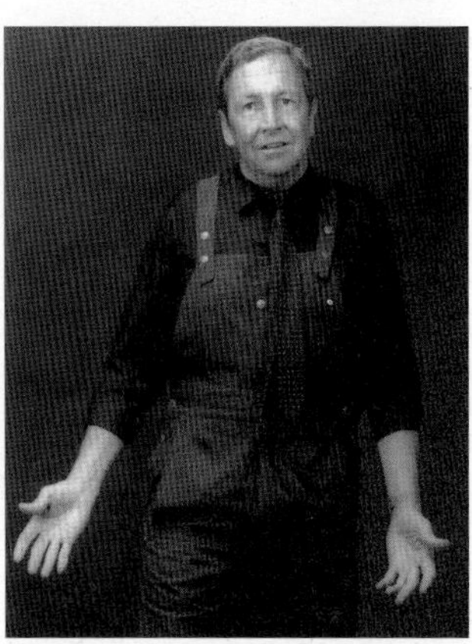

Gelatin silver print, 1983
19 1/8 x 15 1/4 in.
MAP 1159 / Plate 64

Despite his somewhat perturbed look, Robert Rauschenberg (1925–2008) was perhaps only impatient for the shooting to be completed.
In other images, too, from different sittings during the same year, the painter has a similar expression, except when being pictured with friends, such as the choreographer Trisha Brown, who was also in the studio during this sitting. In the shot with her, he looks happy.

Rauschenberg, who was born a Texan, studied painting in Kansas City, in Paris, intermittently at the legendary Black Mountain College in North Carolina, and later at the Art Students League in New York. His early work was entirely abstract, broadly brushed areas of white that were later followed by black canvases, and then by red. His first notoriety came in 1953, when he erased a drawing by de Kooning. At the time, the areas of color in Rauschenberg's paintings were being combined with collage, and he was beginning to incorporate found objects, which would eventually include automobile tires and a stuffed angora goat. These so-called Combines made his reputation, but his work changed in the 1960s. Working in two dimensions, he used found photographs from the media, often of current events or from art history, which he transferred to canvas via a silk-screen process and then painted. Some of those works grew to be of considerable scale. After involvements in stage productions and performance art, he broadened the scope, nature, and means of his printmaking activities, including the use of computer scans and manipulations. Large-scale retrospective exhibitions of his work rewarded his longtime productivity, consistent inventiveness, and startling originality.

Mapplethorpe's portrait of Rauschenberg, who wore tidy overalls and a lopsidedly knotted necktie for the occasion, may have been made for Geo magazine. It is important evidence of Mapplethorpe's connections to artists of the period in other media.

77 Brian Ridley and Lyle Heeter

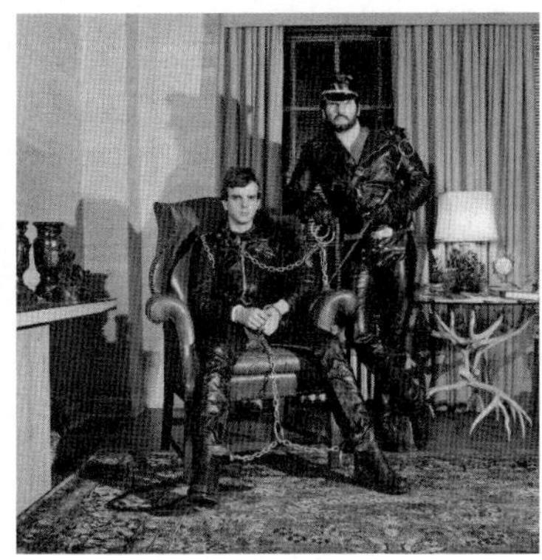

Gelatin silver print, 1979
14 1/8 x 14 in.
MAP 1590 / Plate 22

What seems to be an inherent contradiction between the bourgeois propriety implied by the décor of this living room and the unconventional garb of its leather-clad inhabitants has made this image well known in Mapplethorpe's work. Although he must have relished this disparity, his matter-of-fact approach to this S&M couple did not differ significantly from his procedure when photographing heterosexual couples. He made individual portraits of each of them—in this instance, sitting in the leather wing chair—as well as photographing them together.«1» Theatrically, they are clad in full black leather, and the feet and one wrist of the submissive partner, Brian Ridley, are chained and shackled. The dominant partner, Lyle Heeter, holds a riding crop and a chain connected to Ridley's collar and casts a mildly menacing shadow on the curtain and the grass-cloth–covered wall. Despite the presumed differing nature of their roles in the relationship, they seem equally confident, although not nonchalant, in front of the camera.

Uncommonly for Mapplethorpe, there is an actual context for the sitters and it is more than ample, from the fussy little rococo clock and the copy of Richard Adams's novel The Plague Dogs on the glass-topped table with antler supports to the cameo glass vases on the console table at the left. In showing that the surroundings of sadomasochistic relationships may be reassuringly genteel, the photograph was not intended to be propagandistic but as a direct, even mundane record of how and where some lives are lived. Of all his portraits, this is the closest to those of Diane Arbus, in large part because he has shown his sitters in their environment, as was her practice.

«1» The individual portraits have been published; see Germano Celant, Mapplethorpe, exh. cat. Hayward Gallery, London (Milan: Electa, 1996). The life dates of these sitters are unknown to this writer.

78 Isabella Rossellini

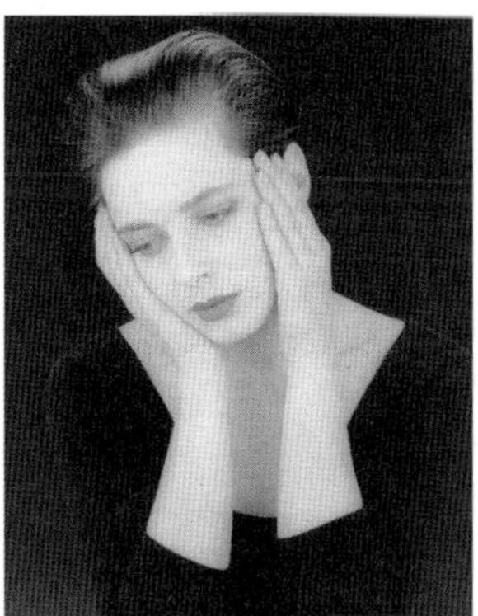

Gelatin silver print, 1988
23 x 19 1/4 in.
MAP 1893 / Plate 100

Although Isabella Rossellini (b. 1952) has starred in many films and frequently appeared in television productions, she is also known as a model, particularly for cosmetics. More recently, she has become known as a writer of memoirs and a spokeswoman for environmental causes. She came to Mapplethorpe's studio to be photographed for Splash magazine. In all three of the exposures of her that Mapplethorpe chose to make into editions of ten prints, he has rendered her very simply—in black and white with nearly no intermediate grays. Here he asked her to place her hands alongside her cheeks, a pose that he had found useful for other sitters, such as Donald Cann (plate 41). As simple as her makeup, the neckline of her black dress dips down from her shoulders in a curve that echoes the line of her jaw. A hair light has been used to differentiate the top of her head from the background black, but basically all attention is concentrated on her lovely face.

79 Edward Ruscha

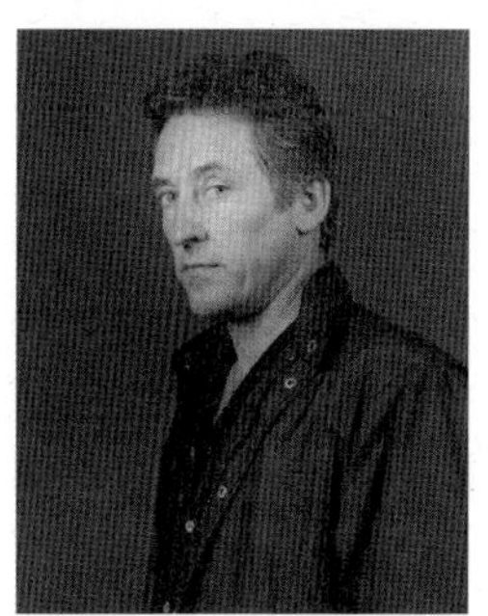

Gelatin silver print, 1984
10 3/4 x 8 1/2 in.
Dagny Corcoran Collection
MAP 1366 / Plate 68

Although the painter, printmaker, and draftsman Ed Ruscha (b. 1937) lives and works in California, he has been represented by Leo Castelli's gallery in New York since the early 1970s. Therefore they may already have met before Mapplethorpe was commissioned as one of a team for a book project that entailed making pictures in Los Angeles within a period of twenty-four hours.«1»

When a helpful friend, Dagny Corcoran, who was exceptionally well-connected to the art world and a vibrant force in it, suggested that he come to her house for dinner that night, as there was to be an interesting group of guests, including several painters, Mapplethorpe accepted. After dinner, he set up his camera and lights outdoors and made portraits of the guests, among them, Ellsworth Kelly, David Hockney (see plates 66 and 4), Christopher Isherwood, and Ruscha. As Mapplethorpe was quick to seize opportunities to expand his roster of sitters engaged in the arts and was pleased with the Ruscha portrait, he later turned it into an edition of ten.

It is perhaps fanciful to suggest that Ruscha's noncommittal expression is a distant echo of the matter-of-fact, quasi-documentary photographs that he himself made and published in the 1960s in small books with blandly descriptive titles such as 34 Parking Lots, 26 Gas Stations, and Every Building on the Sunset Strip. Mapplethorpe liked Ruscha's work well enough to acquire EVIL, one of his screen prints of single words, printed in black ink on a dark maroon ground (1973).

«1» The results of their efforts were published in Klaus Fabricius and Red Saunders, eds., 24 Hours in the Life of Los Angeles, with an introduction by Carol Schwalberg and text by Wanda Coleman and Jeff Spurrier (New York: Alfred Van Der Marck Editions, 1984).

80 Doris Saatchi

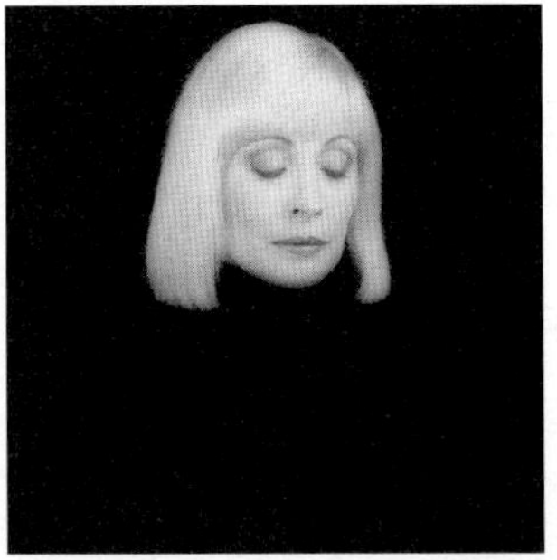

Gelatin silver print, 1983
15 1/8 x 15 1/4 in.
MAP 1500 / Plate 57

The portrait of Doris Lockhart Saatchi (b. 1938) was a commission, either from her then-husband the prolific art collector Charles Saatchi, whose collection she had been instrumental in forming, or from the sitter herself. The stark contrast between the whites of her makeup and platinum hair and the blacks of her turtleneck sweater and the background against which Mapplethorpe photographed her causes her head to float free from her body like a full moon in an inky sky. This disembodiment is heightened by her closed eyes. Her lovely face becomes a sculpted mask that is nearly devoid of expression. Mapplethorpe's contact sheets show that it took eighty-four exposures to achieve this display of icy perfection.

Doris Saatchi, who is a writer on design, contemporary architecture, and art, was one of several sitters whom Mapplethorpe photographed with their eyes closed. Others include the painter Alice Neel (plate 73), the art dealer Barbara Gladstone, the musician Peter Gabriel, and Princess Gloria von Thurn und Taxis. To choose to show a sitter with closed eyes is a kind of minimalism, an experiment to see how much can be subtracted from a conventional portrait and still have it be expressive of personality. This stratagem demonstrates Mapplethorpe's consistent interest in challenging the boundaries of portraiture.

81 David Salle

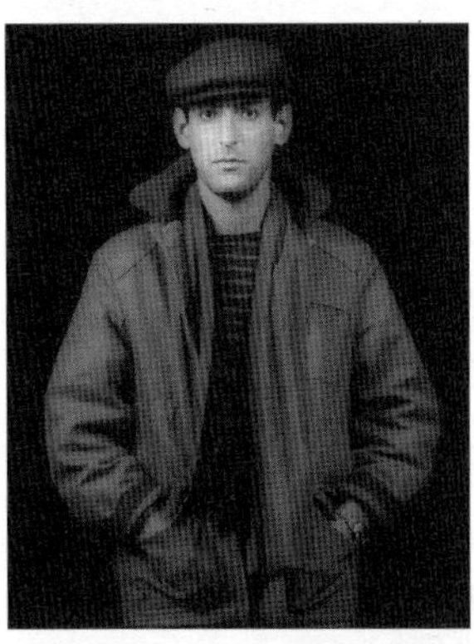

Gelatin silver print, 1983
19 1/8 x 15 1/8 in.
MAP 1038 / Plate 59

In 1983 Mapplethorpe made portraits of several artists. Well-established painters such as Rauschenberg and Warhol sat for him (plates 64 and 60), as did rising art stars, including three American neo-expressionists, Robert Longo, Julian Schnabel, and David Salle, and two of their Italian allies, Sandro Chia and Francesco Clemente (plate 42). Their work had figuration in common, as well as strong coloration and energetic gesture, all of which were distinct stylistic breaks from the then-prevailing minimalism and conceptualism.

Salle (b. 1952) had studied at California Institute of the Arts (Cal Arts) with the painter John Baldessari, whose work often employs the juxtaposition of text with image and of image with dissimilar image. The incongruities inherent in the second of these practices is to be found in Salle's work as well. He gathers the images that he incorporates from a wide variety of sources, ranging from paintings and prints from the past to recent photographs and advertising material. He insists that their sources are less important than the way in which they exist together on the canvas. He also employs digital techniques to manipulate images. As well as painting, Salle has designed stage sets, costumes, and dance productions. His work has often been exhibited, perhaps more often outside the United States than at home.

Mapplethorpe photographed him frontally, using two different light sources that provide even illumination. Salle's parka is weathered and the arc of its turned-up collar frames the lower half of his head and his neck and echoes the curve of the inverted saucer of his cloth cap. The sharp contrast of light and dark between the background and his ears draws attention to their oval shape. As he is wearing a scarf as well as his parka and cap, an impression is given that he has either just arrived or is about to leave, but his resolutely neutral expression masks any idea that he is impatient to be gone. Mapplethorpe photographed Salle in profile in 1986, for publication in 50 New York Artists.«1»

«1» Marshall, 50 New York Artists, 96.

82 Julian Sands

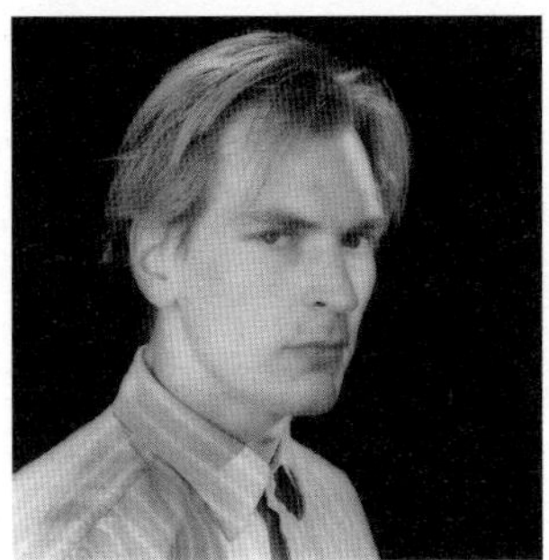

Gelatin silver print, 1986
15 1/8 x 15 1/8 in.
MAP 1684 / Plate 85

Somewhat unusually at this point in Mapplethorpe's career, he used both natural light and studio lights when photographing the British actor Julian Sands (b. 1958). The film that made him a star, Ismail Merchant and James Ivory's Room with a View, opened in New York in March 1986, the year in which this photograph was made, and Sands was about to play the romantic poet Shelley in Ken Russell's film Gothic, which was released the following year.

The slight but distinct shadow that runs the length of his nose seems to be retouching, but is more likely to have been the result of the flash of the strobe.

83 Susan Sarandon

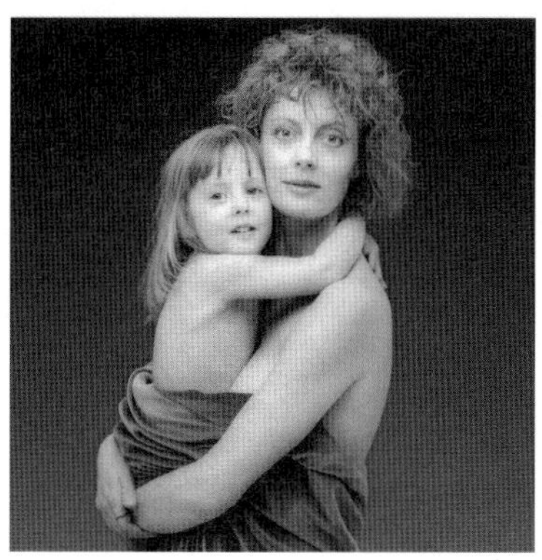

Gelatin silver print, 1988
19 1/4 x 19 1/4 in.
MAP 1954 / Plate 99

The actress Susan Sarandon (b. 1946) was sweetly photographed with her three-year-old, daughter Eva Amurri, who would grow up to become an actress herself. In the course of her long and continuing career, which started in 1970, Sarandon has appeared in at least fifty-eight feature films, and has been nominated for an Academy Award for best actress four times and won once, in 1995 for Dead Man Walking. She has frequently appeared in television movies, in episodes of series, in miniseries, and has narrated numerous documentaries. She has also been actively involved in a variety of liberal social causes. Mapplethorpe and Sarandon were friends. He first photographed her in 1983 and occasionally escorted her to black-tie charity events. As his health deteriorated because of AIDS, she remained actively concerned and recommended doctors and treatments for his condition.«1»

In this image, both mother and daughter seem wholly present in the moment, and the little girl, secure in her mother's arms, seems delighted about being photographed. It appears that they must have required help from him or one of his studio assistants to encircle their two bodies together in one great swath of velvet. As can be deduced from the white rectangles in the upper portion of the irises of the eyes, they are lit from above by a soft box that diffuses the flash of the strobe light. The photograph was originally intended to be part of a portfolio of seven portraits by Mapplethorpe that were to accompany an interview of the photographer by Dominick Dunne for Vanity Fair magazine. Not used then, it was later included in Mapplethorpe's posthumous publication, Some Women,«2» and yet another image from this sitting, of Sarandon alone, was published as the cover of Esquire magazine in March of 1989.

«1» Morrisroe, Mapplethorpe: A Biography, 351, 371.
«2» Mapplethorpe, Some Women.

84 Arnold Schwarzenegger

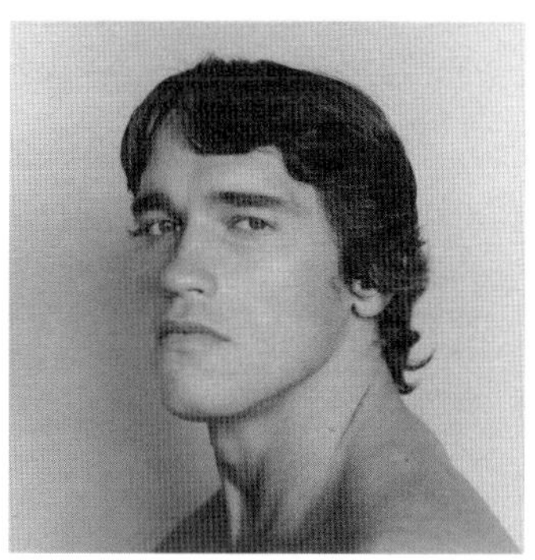

Gelatin silver print, 1976
14 x 14 in.
MAP 72 / Plate 8

Mapplethorpe photographed Arnold Schwarzenegger (b. 1947) toward the middle of the latter's self-propelled transformation from a highly respected bodybuilding champion and relatively recent arrival from Austria into an extremely successful Hollywood actor. By 1976, he had won all the significant bodybuilding awards several times and had appeared in a few films, such as The Long Goodbye and Stay Hungry. His roles as the Terminator and Conan the Barbarian followed in the 1980s, his debut as a comic actor in the 1990s, and his entry into politics at the beginning of the next decade.

Mapplethorpe was commissioned by After Dark magazine to photograph Schwarzenegger and, enjoyed doing so, finding his sitter intelligent, as well as nice. "Arnold's soul," said Mapplethorpe, "is big enough to fill his muscle with his person."«1» He asked Schwarzenegger, who was standing next to a dramatically draped, dark paisley curtain that gave the studio space something of the feel of a stage, to move through at least some of the routine that he performed in bodybuilding competitions. Mapplethorpe later turned four of his exposures of these standard poses into editioned prints of ten. He also made this head shot, in which his subject has turned his head to the camera with a noncommittal but not unfriendly expression. The cover of the February 1977 issue of After Dark bore a photograph of Schwarzenegger and touted an article entitled "Bodybuilding: The New Performance Art," but the cover shot was by another photographer, although some of Mapplethorpe's pictures were included in the magazine.

His images of Schwarzenegger were instantly iconic and sold well. Mapplethorpe thought highly enough of this one that he included it in a briefcase portfolio of the portraits that he took to show people when seeking jobs.

«1» Jack Fritscher, "Pentimento for Robert Mapplethorpe: Fetishes, Faces and Flowers of Evil," Drummer magazine, September 2003.

85 Cindy Sherman

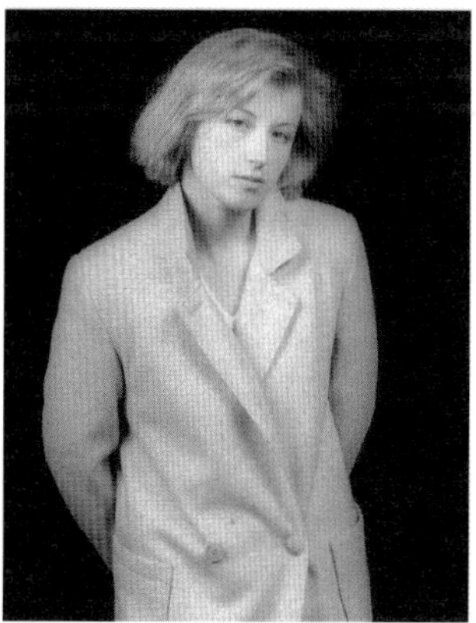

Gelatin silver print, 1983 (?)
19 x 15 1/8 in.
MAP 1018 / Plate 61

For her portrait sitting with Mapplethorpe, the photographer Cindy Sherman (b. 1954), a master of self-disguise in her own work, presented herself very directly. Her hair is brushed but not styled, and she wears next to no makeup and a neutral-colored, loosely tailored blazer over a plain, V-necked T-shirt. Mapplethorpe colluded in simplifying her image by using a strobe to light her straight forwardly and showing her with her hands hidden behind her back. Only the tilt of her head and her questioning eyes animate the image. From her later testimony, the relationship between Sherman and Mapplethorpe was uneasy, marked, she thought, by mutual professional envy.«1»

The sitting was set up to produce an image for inclusion in the publication 50 New York Artists. The photograph that was actually used, however, was another from the same sitting.«2» It is bust-length rather than half-length and, while Sherman's head is no longer cocked, half of her jacket collar is turned up in identical fashion, which lessens the formality of the two portraits. In contrast to her own work, in which Sherman tried to erase herself, here she is wholly, if quietly, present.

«1» Amie Wallach, "Finding Mapplethorpe's Inner Cindy Sherman," New York Times, September 14, 2003; http:query.nytimes.com/gst/fullpage.html?res=9906EEDC153BF9 (accessed August 13, 2008).
«2» Marshall, 50 New York Artists, 108.

86 John Simon

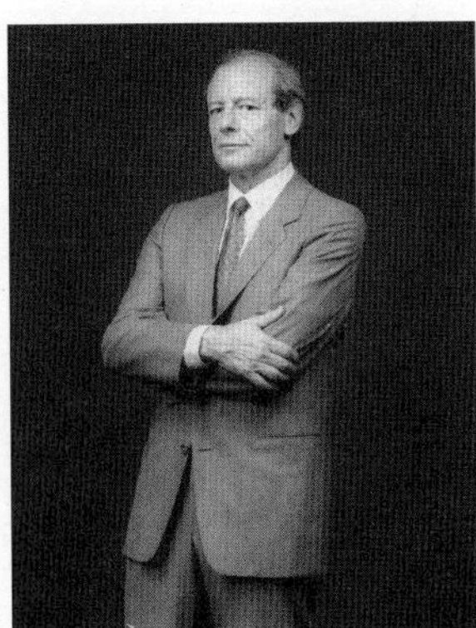

Gelatin silver print, 1983
19 1/8 x 15 1/4 in.
MAP 1154 / Plate 55

The theater and film critic John Simon (b. 1925) seems to be fixing Mapplethorpe with the skeptical eye he brought to bear on the Broadway plays and Hollywood movies that were his principal subject matter. Simon, who was known for the stringency of his finely phrased reviews, also wrote about literature and the proper use of language. As a guess, and to judge from the firmly crossed arms and fixed line of the mouth, this portrait by Mapplethorpe was a commission for publication and Simon a less than enthusiastic sitter. Mapplethorpe once said that, in order to make a successful portrait, he had to summon up the ability to like the sitter—at least for the duration of the shoot.«1»

«1» Anne Horton, Interview, in Robert Mapplethorpe 1986, exh. cat. Raab Galerie, Berlin (Cologne: Kicken-Pausback, 1987).

87 Cynthia Slater

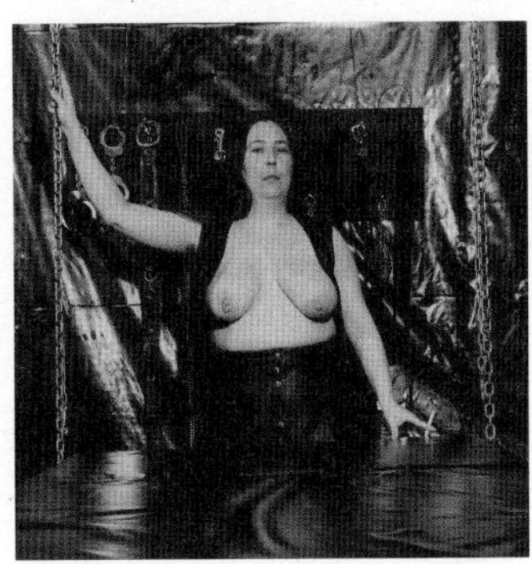

Gelatin silver print, 1980
13 7/8 x 13 7/8 in.
MAP 447 / Plate 29

At the end of the 1970s Mapplethorpe was often in San Francisco, in part because of a romantic liaison, in part because his work was frequently being exhibited there, and in part because of his fascination with the S&M subculture that then flourished in the district south of Market Street. Among his sitters drawn from that milieu was the bisexual dominatrix Cynthia Slater (1949–1989), whom he photographed in a sex club named the Catacombs in a so-called playroom that had less than optimum lighting for photography. An outspoken proponent of extreme sexual behavior, Slater was active in opening traditionally gay male bathhouses, on occasion, to gay women. After the advent of AIDS, she became an advocate for safe sexual practices. She co-founded a still-extant society devoted to "the art of safe, consensual, and non-exploitative power exchange," that is, sado-masochistic sexual encounters.«1»

In the background of this portrait, neatly arranged in rows on a plywood board painted black, are some of the tools that Slater used, including handcuffs, leather restraints with buckles, double spring clips, and other sex toys. A leather-covered platform suspended by hammock chains extends toward the viewer and in her hand is a lit Eve cigarette. The array of paraphernalia, her pierced nipples, and her activities as a proselytizer for radical sexual activities indicate how serious she was about her sexuality.

«1» See http://www.soj.org, the web site of the Society of Janus.

88 Patti Smith

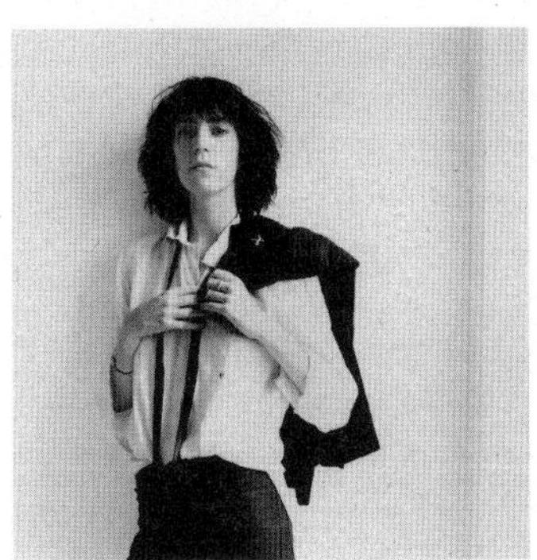

Gelatin silver print, 1975
13 3/4 x 13 3/4 in.
MAP 23 / Plate 3

89 Patti Smith

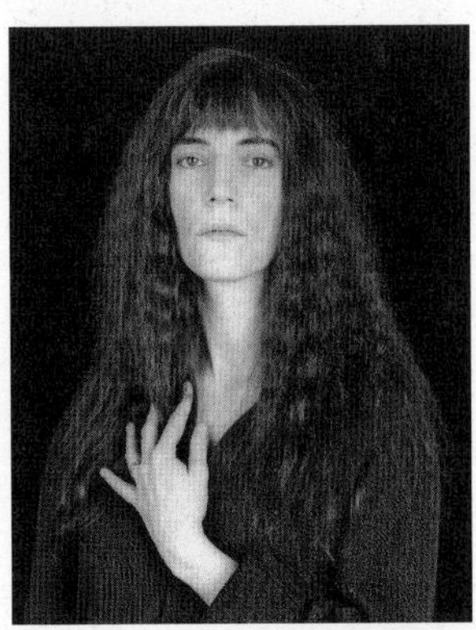

Gelatin silver print, 1986
23 x 19 1/4 in.
MAP 1717 / Plate 91

It is scarcely possible to overstate Patti Smith's importance to Mapplethorpe's life and to his development as a photographer at the very beginning of the 1970s. The poet, who was born in 1946, was in the process of becoming a musician and performance artist. She and the fledgling photographer were nearly inseparable and for a while were romantically involved, living together in the Chelsea Hotel and then in a loft nearby. She was so often a subject for his Polaroid camera that it can be confidently stated that he learned to make portraits of other people by repeatedly photographing her.«1» In one particularly telling sequence, she sits on a draped box and carefully, tentatively, tries one pose after another, with minor variations from one to the next.

Given that he financed the first single that she recorded with a band in 1974, it was inevitable that, when her first album, Horses, was released in 1975, it had a cover photograph made by him. This photograph, which is considered to be one of the best ever made for a record jacket, was shot in Sam Wagstaff's penthouse apartment at 1 Fifth Avenue.«2» With her jacket slung over her shoulder and comfortable in front of Mapplethorpe's camera because he had photographed her so often, Smith projects an image of being simultaneously nonchalant and vulnerable, which contrasts with the overall austerity of the picture. Her boyish clothes bespeak her unconventional nature. The two, photographer and subject, may be deemed to have been, at this point, conspirators in cool.

Mapplethorpe and Smith stopped living together when she became involved with other men and, as their careers developed, their lives diverged, but they remained in contact. During the late 1970s her band, the Patti Smith Group, toured frenetically and continued to make records that received favorable critical attention. Mapplethorpe made a photograph of Smith holding a dove in each hand, which was used as the cover for Wave in 1979 and also for some of the singles extracted from various albums. When Smith abandoned her own career as a musician in 1980 in order to marry the guitarist Fred Smith and move to Detroit, she and Mapplethorpe became further estranged.

It was not until 1986, when she planned to record a comeback album, that they were again in touch. For that album, Dream of Life, this is the photograph (plate 91), with her hair fanned out over her shoulders, that he proposed for the cover, but she thought it too polished an image. Another, less flattering but more realistic image of his was eventually used, but this one survives as an idealization of how he wished to see her. The image can be thought of as a luminous, romanticized extrapolation from the life they once shared.

«1» A variety of these images of her can be found in Wolf, Polaroids 2-5, 30-41.
«2» For Mapplethorpe's portrait of Wagstaff, see plate 17.

90 Smutty Smith

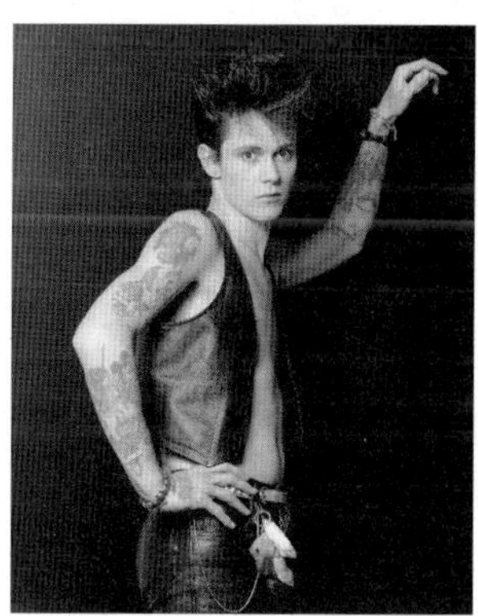

Gelatin silver print, 1982
19 x 15 1/4 in.
MAP 702 / Plate 37

The English rock-and-roller Smutty (b. 1959), a stand-up bassist, was first photographed by Mapplethorpe in 1980, together with the Rockats, the quasi-hillbilly rock band he helped revive. Somewhat more heavily tattooed, he would make his way back, alone, to Mapplethorpe's studio in 1982 to pose seductively for this portrait. The androgyny of his appearance is heightened by his makeup and slender form but belied by his leather vest and trousers, although these are not the kinds of clothes he wore onstage when performing rockabilly music. Bracelets encircle his wrists and a rabbit's foot dangles from his belt. Although his gear and accessories appear to be casual, they are highly calculated. As well as performing onstage, Smith appeared in a fashion show for Stephen Sprouse, which the artificiality of his pose here brings to mind, and he was photographed extensively for Rolling Stone.

91 Susan Sontag

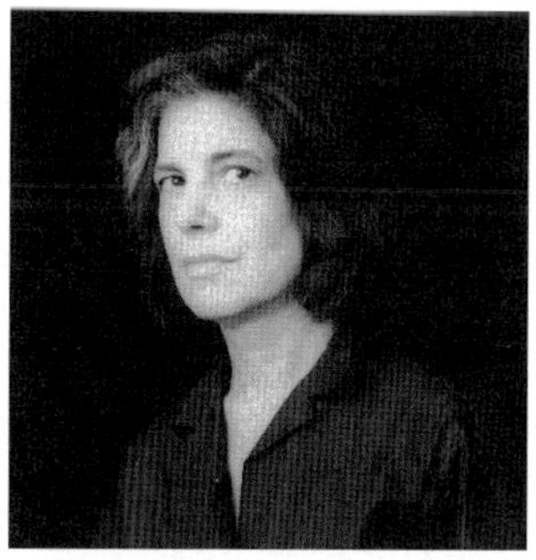

Gelatin silver print, 1984
15 1/8 x 15 1/8 in.
MAP 1417 / Plate 70

Although Mapplethorpe made this portrait of the writer Susan Sontag (1933–2004) on commission from Avenue, a Dutch magazine, he was sufficiently pleased with the result to use the negative later for an edition of ten prints. She, in turn, was interested enough in his work to write a short, insightful essay that served as the introduction to Robert Mapplethorpe: Certain People, a Book of Portraits, which was published in 1985. There, after discussing what it is to sit for a photographer, she describes her reaction to this portrait of herself. "To me, the expression in the photograph Mapplethorpe has taken of me is not really 'my' look. It is a look fabricated for the camera: a frail compromise between trying to be cooperative with a photographer I intensely admire (who is also a friend) while trying to preserve my own dignity, which is hinged to my anxiety. (When I look at my picture I read stubbornness, balked vanity, panic, vulnerability.) I doubt that I've ever looked exactly the way Mapplethorpe has photographed me."«1» Her reading of her own image is, of course, far more perceptive than that of any casual observer, but her intelligence is manifest in the portrait.

Photography was one of Sontag's chosen subjects. On Photography«2» is one of the principal works in a distinguished writing career that started in 1964 with the publication of her essay "Notes on Camp." She was consistently provocative in her challenges to received opinion on a wide range of subjects. Other of her noteworthy nonfiction books include Illness as Metaphor and Regarding the Pain of Others. There were also collections of essays, three novels, and short stories. Beyond being an influential author and a publicly engaged intellectual, she was an ardent champion of human rights.

«1» Susan Sontag, "Certain Mapplethorpes," in Robert Mapplethorpe: Certain People, a Book of Portraits (Pasadena, Calif.: Twelvetrees Press, 1985), n.p.
«2» Sontag, On Photography (New York: Farrar, Straus and Giroux, 1977).

92 Michael Ward Stout

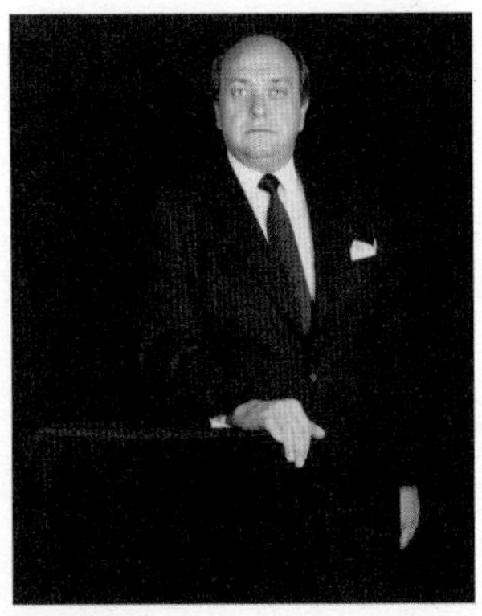

Gelatin silver print, 1986
19 1/8 x 15 1/4 in.
Plate 92

When describing his own appearance in the portrait Mapplethorpe made of him, the attorney Michael Ward Stout (b. 1943) held that it shows a person with power and "just the edge of arrogance."«1» As nearly an aside, Stout supposed that the photographer imagined that power was something that his lawyer must (and perhaps ought to) have. The clear implication is that Mapplethorpe meant to give an impression of strength and, in fact, the image is forceful enough to bring to mind the great portrait that Edward Steichen made, in 1903, of the omnipotent banker J. P. Morgan. Both photographs are dark, with just the sitter's faces, their spotless linen, and one hand fully illuminated, but, where Morgan appears fierce, if not baleful, Stout seems watchful.

Stout was indeed powerful in Mapplethorpe's world. The executor of the artist's estate, Stout has, for twenty years, presided over the Robert Mapplethorpe Foundation. Among the other artists whose lives or estates he has represented are Salvador Dali, Keith Haring (for whom, see plate 75), Jean-Michel Basquiat, and Matthew Barney.

«1» Michael Ward Stout, in an interview broadcast on the television program Arena, produced and directed by Nigel Finch (BBC Television, 1988).

93 Donald Sutherland

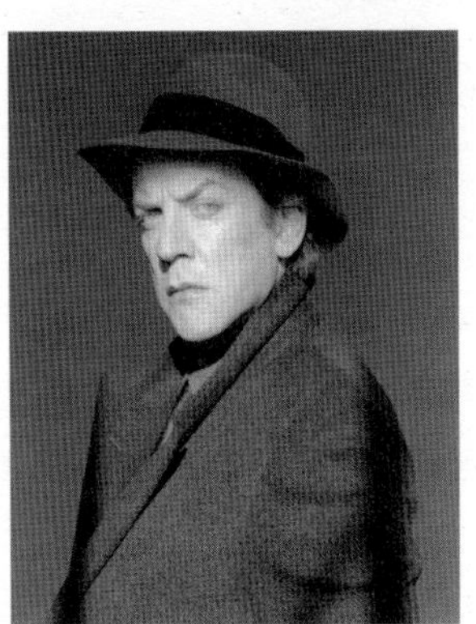

Gelatin silver print, 1983
19 1/4 x 15 1/4 in.
MAP 1050 / Plate 53

The actor Donald Sutherland (b. 1935 in Canada) has played such an astonishing variety of characters during his long career in films that it is hard to know now which role he was reprising for Mapplethorpe's camera, but he certainly seems to be acting. He could be a gangster, a spy, a villain, a character in a horror film, or a suspicious detective, all parts that he has played. His somewhat crushed fedora, his herringbone overcoat with the collar turned up, and his imperiously arched eyebrow suggest any of these possibilities, but not the comedies in which he also excelled. Whatever part it was, apparently he and the photographer had an agreeable time together; a year after the picture was made, Mapplethorpe described Sutherland as being one of the best subjects he had ever photographed.«1» The photograph was commissioned by Interview magazine and was made by natural light in Mapplethorpe's Bond Street studio, close to its south-facing windows, as indicated by the shadow of the exterior fire escape, which can be discerned on the sleeve of Sutherland's coat.

«1» Mapplethorpe, lecture, transcript, p. 13.

94 Tom of Finland

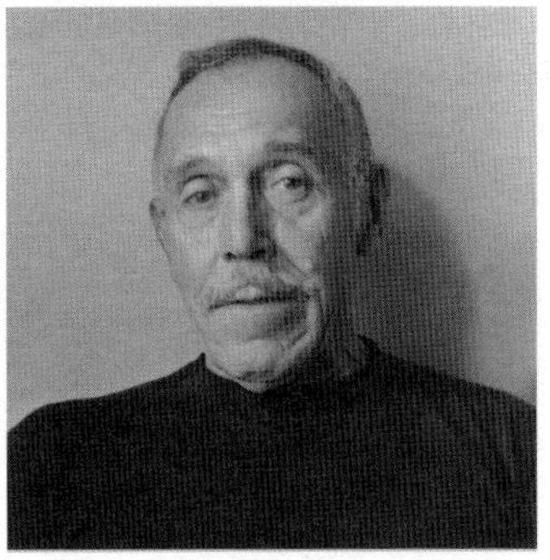

Gelatin silver print, 1978
13 7/8 x 13 7/8 in.
MAP 121 / Plate 12

Particularly during the period in the 1970s when Mapplethorpe was fascinated by the nexus of male homosexual sex and leather accoutrements and was making photographs, including self-portraits, that dealt with S&M, he was an admirer of the erotic drawings made by Tom of Finland (1920–1991; born Touku Laaksonen). In 1978 some of Mapplethorpe's photographs were coupled in an exhibition at the Fey-Way Gallery in San Francisco with Tom of Finland's overtly homoerotic drawings of rugged men with exaggerated anatomical features. His drawings, which Mapplethorpe had collected and would continue to collect, were then considered merely pornographic; they have since been accorded greater recognition and respect and have entered museum collections. The two men first met at the time of the San Francisco exhibition, at supper at the home of Jack Fritscher, the editor of Drummer magazine, for which Mapplethorpe did a cover that year and in which Tom of Finland published drawings.«1» The next year the artist made a strangely dark and stylistically uncharacteristic drawing of the photographer.

This portrait was made at the time of the exhibition in California. The shy but amiable fantasist is simply lit by what seems to be a single overhead artificial light. He regards the photographer with mild amusement, wholly aware of the affinities in their work.

«1» Jack Fritscher, e-mail to author, March 26, 2008.

95 Kathleen Turner

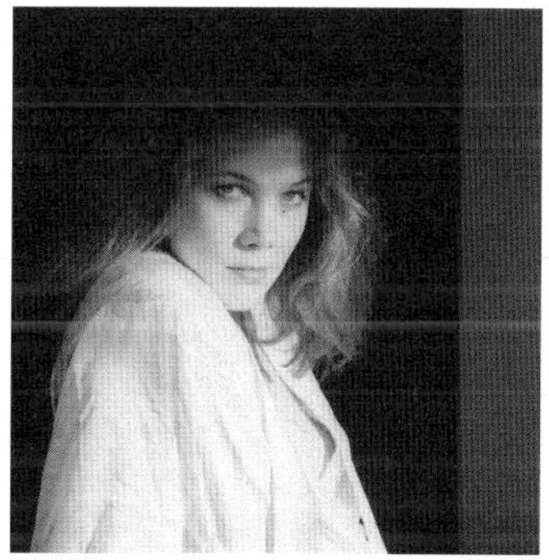

Gelatin silver print, 1982
15 3/8 x 15 3/8 in.
MAP 813 / Plate 40

Mapplethorpe photographed the actress Kathleen Turner (b. 1954) the year after she completed Body Heat, the film that made her famous. As the film included full frontal nudity, at that time a rarity in American movies, Turner became a sex goddess, and she appears appropriately and intentionally sultry in Mapplethorpe's seductive portrait. Because his image of her was made with natural light alone and because she seems so intimately involved with the camera, her portrait is very different from conventional Hollywood movie-star portraiture. The delicacy of the appliqué on her shoulder, the softness of her skin, and the silken torrent of her hair are gently caressed by the light, which seems suggestively to be that of dawn or dusk. Even her makeup is understated.

Mapplethorpe photographed her again in 1986 for American Vogue, but in a pose that was less evidently sexy. Her career as an actress has proved durable and noteworthy, bringing Golden Globe awards for her performances in Romancing the Stone in 1984 and Peggy Sue Got Married in 1986. Recently Turner was acclaimed for her portrayal onstage of the tempestuous, alcoholic faculty wife in Edward Albee's Who's Afraid of Virginia Woolf?

96 Phyllis Tweel

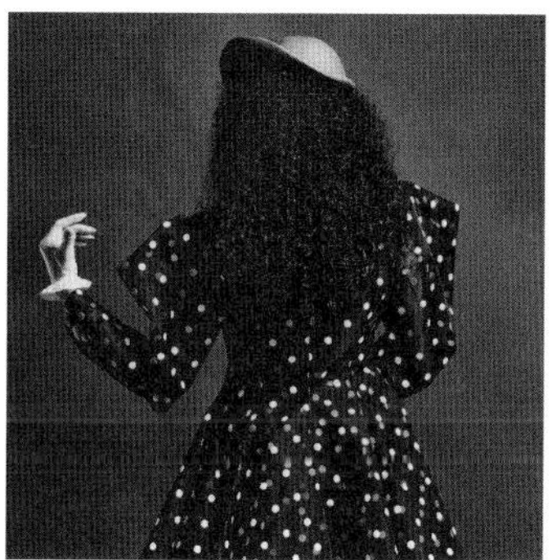

Gelatin silver print, 1979
Collection of David Knaus
14 x 14 in.
MAP 278 / Plate 18

This wholly unconventional portrait of the gossip columnist Phyllis Tweel was made for a two-person exhibition of the work of Mapplethorpe and Lynn Davis at the International Center for Photography. Each photographed the same sixteen sitters as well as each other (see plate 13). The other image that Mapplethorpe made of Tweel is less startling, as it showed her from the front, hands on hips and head cocked to one side. Historical precedents for portraits of the backs of women's heads can be found in the work of Nadar and Onésipe Aguado in the nineteenth century and Cecil Beaton in the twentieth.«1»

About 1856 Nadar photographed the actress Marie Laurent from behind, showing her hair in a chignon, her neck, and her shoulders. A print of that portrait was included in an exhibition of Nadar's work at the Metropolitan Museum in 1977 that was entirely drawn from a cache of images owned by Sam Wagstaff, with whom Mapplethorpe learned about the history of photography and collecting photographs.«2» Mapplethorpe, who also owned a few portraits by Nadar, is likely to have seen that show, Nadar being the photographer whom Mapplethorpe most admired.«3» Much like Nadar's, if more circumscribed and perhaps edgier, Mapplethorpe's career as a photographer brought into being portraits of a pantheon of sitters drawn from the world of the arts.

In Mapplethorpe's image, the cascade of crimped ringlets that springs from under Tweel's fetching hat entirely covers her neck. Save for the sliver of her wrist between the frill of her glove and the cuff of her polka-dotted shirtdress, none of her skin is visible. This is a study of texture and pattern more than of personality, which can only be conjectured from her stylish attire, her ringleted hair, and her jauntily crooked elbow. As her clothes and posture are the principal subjects, this image belongs perhaps less to the category of portraiture and more to that of fashion photography, a world into which Mapplethorpe only occasionally ventured and, save here, without singular success. This is a superlative example of what Mapplethorpe's sometime-studio assistant, the photographer Marcus Leatherdale, referred to as covert portraiture.«4»

«1» Aguado's portrait (see fig. 4, p. 20) is of an unknown woman. It is reproduced in Maria Morris Hambourg et al., The Waking Dream: Photography's First Century, exh. cat. (New York: Metropolitan Museum of Art, 1993), front dust jacket cover and p. 58, and on the cover of Susan Sontag's In America (New York: Farrar, Straus and Giroux, 2000). The subject of Cecil Beaton's portrait is the writer Henry Green.
«2» For Mapplethorpe's portrait of Wagstaff, see plate 17.
«3» Mapplethorpe, lecture, transcript, p. 17.
«4» See cat. 51, page 239, note 2.

97 Frederica von Stade

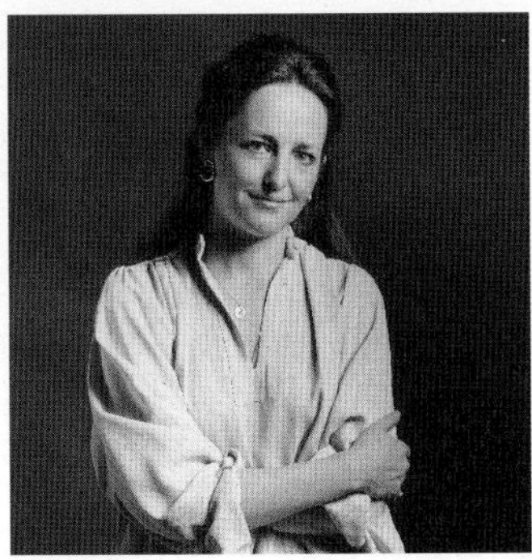

Gelatin silver print, 1979
13 3/4 x 13 3/4 in.
MAP 300 / Plate 21

The illustrious mezzo-soprano Frederica von Stade (b. 1945) dressed casually for her portrait by Mapplethorpe. By 1979 her career as a vivacious interpreter of roles in operas by Mozart, Rossini, and Bellini was in full bloom. Her repertoire would later expand to include works by Richard Strauss and modern parts written specifically for her. Here, her rolled-up shirtsleeves, the simplicity of her jewelry, and the slight tilt of her head give the image an impression of affable informality although the combination of the way her arms are protectively folded across her chest and her expression, which seems to be one of wary amusement, produces an overall air of ambiguity. Was she perhaps charmed but puzzled by the photographer?

98 Sam Wagstaff

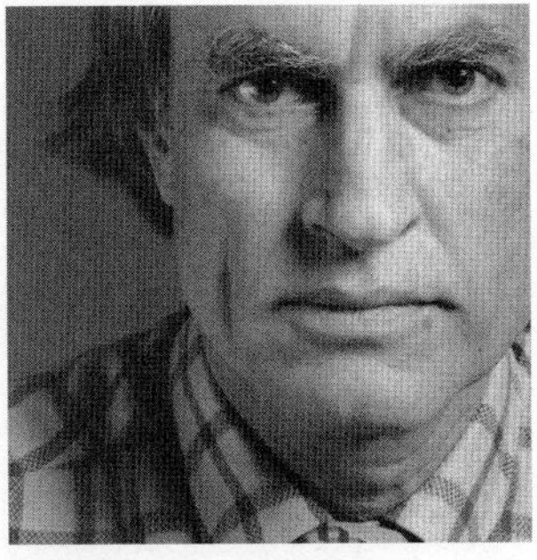

Gelatin silver print, 1979
13 7/8 x 13 7/8 in.
MAP 277 / Plate 17

It was highly unusual for Mapplethorpe to make portraits in extreme close-up but appropriately symbolic for him to have photographed Sam Wagstaff head-on, as the relationship between the two men was intimate from the time they met in 1972.«1» Wagstaff (1921–1987), who had been a curator at the Wadsworth Athenaeum and then at the Detroit Institute of Arts, was for some years Mapplethorpe's lover and patron and had a strong influence on the younger man's career. In 1972 he bought the photographer a loft on Bond Street, New York, in which to live and work; in 1976, a Hasselblad camera; and, in 1985, a larger, better loft on Twenty-third Street. At a time when there were few dedicated collectors of photography, they looked together at work from earlier periods and each formed substantial collections.

This radically composed and striking image, made with a portrait lens attached to the camera he'd given Mapplethorpe, is direct testimony of the force of Wagstaff's personality and his good looks. Save for the calculated negative space in the upper left quadrant, his large head fills the frame. At age fifty-eight he unflinchingly faced the camera with the passionate intensity he brought to bear on life. Wagstaff, whose collection of photographs became a cornerstone of the photography collection in the J. Paul Getty Museum, predeceased Mapplethorpe—as would be expected by the twenty-five-year disparity in their ages—but only by two years. Both died as a result of AIDS.

When part of Wagstaff's photograph collection was first published, in 1978, the sole text in the book, which had still lifes by Mapplethorpe on both its front and back covers, was a droll, typically Wagstaffian understatement: "This book is about pleasure, the pleasure of looking, and the pleasure of seeing, like watching people dancing through an open window. They seem a little mad at first, until you realize they hear the song that you are watching."«2»

«1» A note, dated 1971, from Mapplethorpe, inviting Wagstaff to come to see his work, which would not yet have been primarily photographic, is in the Wagstaff section of the archives of the Detroit Institute of Arts. Evidently the photographer-to-be was aware of the curator and collector before they first met in person.

«2» A Book of Photographs from the Collection of Sam Wagstaff, exh. cat., Corcoran Gallery of Art, Washington, D.C. (New York: Gray Press, 1978), n.p. An image by Mapplethorpe of a crouching, hooded man appeared midway through the book.

99 Jack Walls

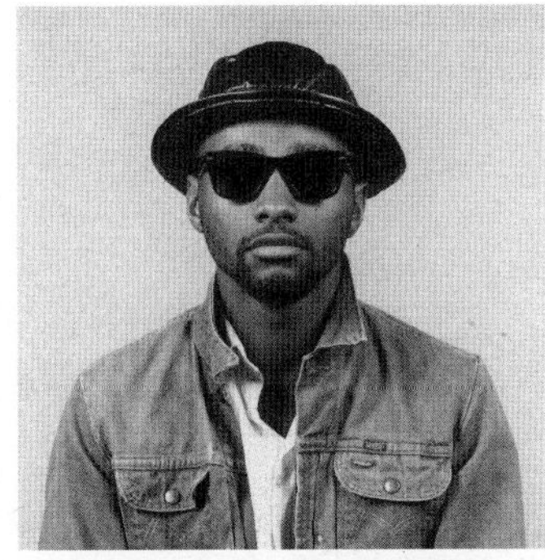

Gelatin silver print, 1982
15 1/4 x 15 1/8 in.
MAP 912 / Plate 48

Because Walls (b. 1957) was photographed wearing dark glasses and has an impassive expression, his face becomes a sort of mask, an example of Mapplethorpe's interest in subverting the conventions of traditional portraiture while remaining within its bounds. Walls, who thought Mapplethorpe had a rock-star look but was sweet and kind, frequently posed for him in the early eighties. The photographer introduced the articulate Walls to the art world during the course of their fitful relationship. Three years later Mapplethorpe again photographed Walls, this time in color and again wearing sunglasses.

There are about thirty other photographs, mostly made in 1983, in which he plays a variety of identifiable roles. Sometimes he wears a sailor's hat or an army uniform; at other times, a turban or a crown of thorns; and in some, he is simply nude. The irrepressible Walls is an artist himself.

100 Andy Warhol

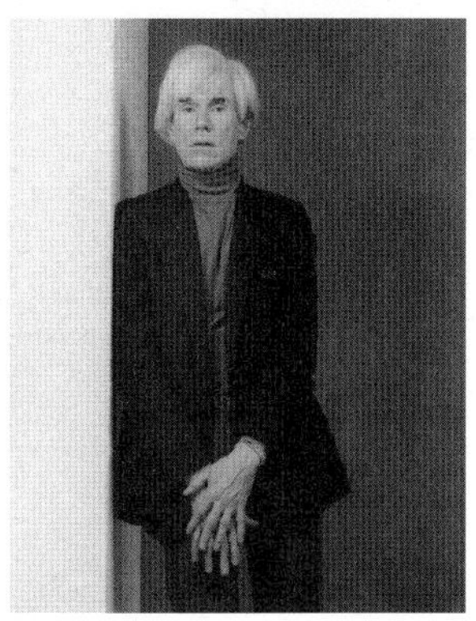

Gelatin silver print, 1983
15 x 14 7/8 in.
MAP 1174 / Plate 60

Mapplethorpe photographed the pop artist Andy Warhol (1928–1997) on a number of occasions, but the relationship between the two men was never comfortable and likely even rivalrous. The older, more established artist was famous for his Brillo box sculptures and paintings of Campbell's soup cans, Marilyn Monroes, and Maos.

The two artists undoubtedly influenced each other, although neither was willing to acknowledge such indebtedness. Perhaps significantly, the self-portraits in drag that Warhol made in conjunction with the photographer Christopher Makos in 1981 date from the year after Mapplethorpe made his own forays into cross-gender self-portraiture. There were also studio practices they seem to have shared. Mapplethorpe's preference, after about 1980, for having the women he pictured made up to be pale may relate to Warhol's practice of having the faces of his female sitters painted white for the Polaroids that he used as a preparatory step in making his silk-screened portraits. As the silk-screen process necessarily simplifies images, Warhol's aim was to intensify the effect of made-up eyes and lips by suppressing the other facial features.

Each photographed the other, and they had many sitters in common, such as Carolina Herrera and Henry Geldzahler, and some mutual friends, such as Mario Amaya and Bob Colacello.«1» This portrait is evidence of at least a nominal tolerance for each other's company and their de facto recognition that each had a place in the relatively small-scale art world in New York during the 1970s and 1980s,«2» and both earned a considerable part of their incomes from portraiture, which may have engendered some competition, although it did not bar Mapplethorpe from being occasionally commissioned by Warhol's Interview magazine to make portraits for publication.

In this picture Warhol has assumed a characteristic pose, leaning against a support with his hands pressed protectively together, one on top of the other, as if to still a tremor. As usual at this period, he is wearing blue jeans without a belt, a turtleneck sweater, a blazer, and an expensive wristwatch. His platinum wig contrasts oddly with his dark eyebrows, but is an essential part of his public persona. He does, however, look less than relaxed.

«1» For Mapplethorpe's images of Herrera, Geldzahler, and Amaya, see plates 16, 19, and 10.
«2» In 1985, New York had 374 galleries; today, more than 1,200.

101 Lawrence Weiner

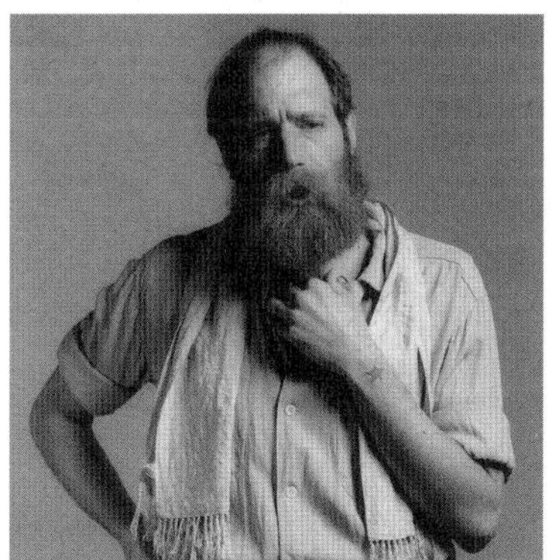

Gelatin silver print, 1982
15 1/8 x 15 1/8 in.
MAP 927 / Plate 38

As the contact sheets for this portrait imply, the conceptual artist Lawrence Weiner (b. 1942) is highly articulate and, in fact, he never stopped talking during the course of the twenty-four successive exposures that Mapplethorpe made of him with his tripod-mounted camera. First he showed Weiner's head turned at a variety of angles away from the camera—starting on one side with the head one-third turned, to halfway, to three-quarters, to seven-eighths, but never quite arriving at a full profile; then similarly ratcheted on the other side; and finally directly facing the lens. His garb is casual but considered: a very narrow belt; dark, slightly pleated trousers; a soft crinkled shirt, the sleeves of which he rolled up; and a short, white, embossed, fringed scarf draped over his shoulders. The star tattoo on his left wrist is appropriately minimalistic for a conceptual artist. Here he has been caught in midsentence.

Weiner was one of the central proponents of postminimalist conceptual art and particularly famous for propounding the theory that an artist can make a piece or have it constructed, but neither is essential: the words describing the work can serve as the work. Except for the inconvenient fact that this photograph actually exists, it is perhaps an extraneous extrapolation or reversal of his ideas. Weiner has been and remains an immensely influential artist.

BIBLIOGRAPHY

Als, Hilton. The Women. New York: Farrar, Straus and Giroux, 1996.

Anderson, Alexandra, and B. J. Archer, Anderson and Archer's Soho: The Essential Guide to Art and Life in Lower Manhattan. New York: Art in America in association with Simon and Schuster, 1979.

Ashbery, John. Mapplethorpe: Pistils. New York: Random House, 1996.

Augur, Julia Childs. American Portraits of the Sixties & Seventies. Exh. cat. Aspen, Colo.: Aspen Center for the Visual Arts, 1979.

Bad Object-Choices, ed. How Do I Look? Queer Film and Video. Seattle: Bay Press, 1991.

Baldwin, Gordon, and Judith Keller. Nadar/Warhol: Paris/New York: Photography and Fame. Los Angeles: J. Paul Getty Museum, 1999.

Barents, Els. Robert Mapplethorpe: 10 x 10. Munich: Schirmer/Mosel, 1988.

Bockris, Victor. Beat Punks. Cambridge, Mass.: Da Capo Press, 2000.

A Book of Photographs from the Collection of Sam Wagstaff. Exh. cat. Corcoran Gallery of Art, Washington, D.C. New York: Gray Press, 1978.

Brilliant, Richard. Portraiture. Cambridge, Mass.: Harvard University Press, 1991.

Burroughs, William. The Seven Deadly Sins. New York: Locodo-Mulder, 1991.

Celant, Germano. Mapplethorpe. Exh. cat. Hayward Gallery, London. Milan: Electa, 1996.

Celant, Germano, and Arkadii Ippolitov. Robert Mapplethorpe and the Classical Tradition: Photographs and Mannerist Prints. With Karole Vail and Jennifer Blessing. Exh. cat. New York: Solomon R. Guggenheim Foundation, 2004.

Clarke, Graham, ed. The Portrait in Photography. London: Reaktion Books, 1992.

Colacello, Bob. Holy Terror: Andy Warhol Close Up. New York: Harper Collins, 1990.

Conrad, Peter. "Twelve Facets of Robert Mapplethorpe." In Robert Mapplethorpe, Mapplethorpe Portraits . . . 1975-1987. London: National Portrait Gallery Publications, 1988.

Cornell, Daniell. "Employing Gender: Narrative and Spectacle in the Photography of Alfred Stieglitz, Imogen Cunningham, Minor White, and Robert Mapplethorpe." PhD diss., City University of New York, 2002.

Cresap, Kelly M. Pop Trickster Fool: Warhol Performs Naivete. Urbana: University of Illinois Press, 2004.

Crump, James. "Art of Acquisition: The Eye of Sam Wagstaff." Archives of American Art Journal 46, no. 3-4 (Fall 2007).

Danto, Arthur. Playing with the Edge: The Photographic Achievement of Robert Mapplethorpe. Berkeley: University of California Press, 1996.

Danto, Arthur. "Instant Gratification: Robert Mapplethorpe's Polaroids, 1970-1976." Aperture, no. 163 (Spring 2001): 41-53.

Davis, Melody D. The Male Nude in Contemporary Art. Philadelphia: Temple University Press, 1991.
Ellenzweig, Allen, The Homoerotic Photograph: Male Images from Durieu/Delacroix to Mapplethorpe. New York: Columbia University Press, 1992.

Fabre, Jan. The Power of Theatrical Madness. Photographs by Robert Mapplethorpe. Introduction by Kathy Acker. Essay by Germano Celant. Catalogue issued in conjunction with performances in various locations, 1984-1986. London: Distribution ICA, 1986.

Fabricius, Klaus, and Red Saunders, eds. 24 Hours in the Life of Los Angeles. Introduction by Carol Schwalberg, text by Wanda Coleman and Jeff Spurrier. New York: Alfred Van Der Marck Editions, 1984.

Fritscher, Jack. Mapplethorpe: Assault with a Deadly Camera. Mamaroneck, N.Y.: Hastings House, 1994.

Golden, Thelma, ed. Black Male. Exh. cat. New York: Whitney Museum of American Art and Harry N. Abrams, 1994.

Hambourg, Maria Morris, et al. The Waking Dream: Photography's First Century. Exh. cat. New York: Metropolitan Museum of Art, 1993.

Hambourg, Maria Morris, Françoise Heilbrun, and Philippe Néagu. Nadar. With contributions by Sylvie Aubenas, André Jammes, Ulrich Keller, Sophie Richard, and André Rouillé. Exh. cat. New York: Metropolitan Museum of Art, 1995.

Hammer, Martin. The Naked Portrait, 1900-2007. Exh. cat. Edinburgh: National Galleries of Scotland, 2007.

Henry, Gerritt. "Robert Mapplethorpe—Collecting Quality: An Interview." Print Collectors Newsletter (New York). September-October 1982.

Hershkovits, David. Robert Mapplethorpe. Exh cat. Tokyo: Parco, 1987.

Hickey, Dave. The Invisible Dragon: Four Essays on Beauty. Los Angeles: Art Issues Press, 1993.

Horton, Anne. Interview. Robert Mapplethorpe 1986. Exh. cat.

Raab Galerie, Berlin. Cologne: Kicken-Pausback, 1987.

Hujar, Peter. Peter Hujar. Essays by Stephen Koch and Thomas Sokolowski. Interviews with Fran Lebowitz and Vince Aletti. Exh. cat. New York: Grey Art Gallery, 1990.

Hujar, Peter. Peter Hujar: Eine Retrospektive. Essays by Max Kozloff and Hripsimé Visser. Exh. cat. Zurich and New York: Scalo, 1994.

Kardon, Janet. Robert Mapplethorpe: The Perfect Moment. With essays by David Joselit and Kay Larson. Dedication by Patti Smith. Exh. cat. Philadelphia: Institute of Contemporary Art, University of Pennsylvania, 1989.

Justim, Estelle. Slave to Beauty: The Eccentric Life and Controversial Career of F. Holland Day. Boston: David R. Godine, 1981.

Levas, Dimitri. Pictures: Robert Mapplethorpe. Santa Fe, N.M.: Arena Editions, 1999.

Mapplethorpe, Robert. The Agency. Exh cat. New York: Hardison Fine Arts Gallery, 1983.

Mapplethorpe, Robert. Lady, Lisa Lyon. Text by Bruce Chatwin. New York: St. Martin's Press, 1983.

Mapplethorpe, Robert. Some Women: By Mapplethorpe. Introduction by Joan Didion. Boston: Bulfinch Press, 1989.

Marra, Claudio. Robert Mapplethorpe: Secret Flowers. Milan: Photology, 1993.

Marshall, Richard D. 50 New York Artists: A Critical Selection of Painters and Sculptors Working in New York. San Francisco: Chronicle Books, 1986.

Marshall, Richard D., ed. Robert Mapplethorpe. With essays by Ingrid Sischy and Richard Howard. Exh. cat. New York and Boston: Whitney Museum of American Art in association with Bulfinch Press, 1988.

Marshall, Richard D., et al. Robert Mapplethorpe. Exh. cat. Tokyo: Mitsukoshi Museum of Art, Shinjuku, 1996.

Marshall, Richard D., Introduction. Robert Mapplethorpe: Autoportrait. Santa Fe, N.M.: Arena Editions 2001.

Meyer, Richard. Outlaw Representation: Censorship and Homosexuality in Twentieth-Century Art. New York: Oxford University Press, 2002.

Moholy-Nagy, László. The New Vision. 1928. 4th rev. ed. Translated by Daphne M. Hoffmann. New York: Wittenborn, Schultz, 1947.

Morgan, Stuart, and Alan Hollinghurst. Robert Mapplethorpe, 1970-1983. Exh. cat. London: Institute of Contemporary Arts, 1983.

Morrisroe, Patricia. Mapplethorpe: A Biography. New York: Random House, 1995.

Muschamp, Herbert. Mapplethorpe: The Complete Flowers. Düsseldorf: teNeues, 2006.

Naef, Weston. Counterparts: Form and Emotion in Photographs. Documentation by Joan Morgan. Exh. cat. New York: Metropolitan Museum of Art, 1982.

Neiman, Roberta. Ever Since Durango. New York: Passenger Press, 1977.

Robert Mapplethorpe: Flowers. Foreword by Patti Smith. Boston: Bulfinch Press, 1990.

Robert Mapplethorpe: Photographs. Introduction by Mario Amaya. Exh. cat. Norfolk, Va.: Chrysler Museum at Norfolk, 1978.
Schultz, Peter. "Robert Mapplethorpe's Flowers." History of Photography 22 (Spring 1988): 84-89.

Sontag, Susan. On Photography. New York: Farrar, Straus and Giroux, 1977.

Sontag, Susan. "Certain Mapplethorpes." In Robert Mapplethorpe: Certain People, a Book of Portraits. Pasadena, Calif.: Twelvetrees Press, 1985.

Sontag, Susan. In America. New York: Farrar, Straus and Giroux, 2000.

Sussman, Elisabeth. Lisette Model. London and New York: Phaidon, 2001.

Wolf, Sylvia. Polaroids: Mapplethorpe. Exh. cat. Whitney Museum of American Art, New York. Munich: Prestel Verlag, 2007.

AUCTION CATALOGUES

Christie, Manson & Woods International. The Collection of Robert Mapplethorpe. Sale catalogue. New York. October 31, 1989.

Sotheby's, Photographs from the Collection of Robert Mapplethorpe. Sale catalogue. New York. May 24, 1982.

VIDEO

Robert Mapplethorpe. Directed by Paul Tschinkel. Art/New York, no. 61. New York: Inner Tube Video, 2006.

INDEX

Note: Illustrations are denoted by underlined page references.

(Fig. 1)
Edward J. Steichen (American, born Belgium, 1879-1973), Greta Garbo. Gelatin silver print, 1928; 13 11/16 x 10 11/16 in. The J. Paul Getty Museum, Los Angeles, 84.XM.848.6. Reprinted with permission of Joanna T. Steichen.

(Fig. 2)
Nadar (Gaspard-Félix Tournachon, French, 1820-1910), Sarah Bernhardt. Negative, c. 1864; gelatin silver print by Paul Nadar (French, 1856-1939), c. 1924; 8 5/16 x 6 3/8 in. The J. Paul Getty Museum, Los Angeles, 84.XM.436.494.

(Fig. 3)
Julia Margaret Cameron (British, born India, 1815-1879), Mary Mother. Albumen print, 1867; 12 11/16 x 10 7/16 in. Courtesy of George Eastman House, Rochester, N.Y., GEH neg. 7766.

(Fig. 4)
Viscount Onésipe Aguado (French, 1827-1894), Woman Seen from the Back. Salted paper print from glass negative, c. 1862; 12 1/8 x 10 3/16 in. The Metropolitan Museum of Art, Gilman Collection, Purchase, Joyce F. Menschel Gift, 2005 (2005.100.1). Copy photograph © The Metropolitan Museum of Art.

(Fig. 5)
Pierre-Louis Pierson (French, 1822-1913), Scherzo di Follia; Game of Madness (Countess de Castiglione Holding Vignette Frame up to Her Eye). Glass negative, 1861-1867; gelatin silver print, c. 1930; 15 11/16 x 11 3/4 in. The Metropolitan Museum of Art, Gilman Collection, Gift of The Howard Gilman Foundation, 2005 (2005.100.198). Copy photograph © The Metropolitan Museum of Art.

(Fig. 6)
© Robert Mapplethorpe Foundation.

(Fig. 7)
Man Ray (American, 1890-1976), Antonin Artaud. Gelatin silver print, 1926; 9 1/4 x 7 in. Museum of Modern Art, New York, Gift of Paul F. Walter, 292.1966. Digital image © The Museum of Modern Art / Licensed by SCALA / Art Resource, N.Y. © 2008 Man Ray Trust / Artists Rights Society (ARS), NY / ADAGP, Paris.

(Fig. 8)
Man Ray (American, 1890-1976), Rrose Sélavy (Marcel Duchamp). Gelatin silver print, 1923; 8 11/16 x 6 15/16 in. The J. Paul Getty Museum, Los Angeles, 84.XM 1000.80. © 2008 Man Ray Trust / Artists Rights Society (ARS), NY / ADAGP, Paris.

(Fig. 9)
László Moholy-Nagy (American, born Hungary, 1895-1946), The Olly and Dolly Sisters. Gelatin silver print, c. 1925; 14 3/4 x 10 13/16 in. The J. Paul Getty Museum, Los Angeles, 84.XM.997.24. © 2008 Artists Rights Society (ARS), New York / VG Bild-Kunst, Bonn.

(Fig. 10)
Horst P. Horst (American, born Germany, 1906-1999), Mainbocher Corset. Gelatin silver print, 1939. © Horst P. Horst / Art + Commerce.

(Fig. 11)
© Robert Mapplethorpe Foundation.

(Fig. 12)
© Robert Mapplethorpe Foundation.

(Fig. 13)
© Robert Mapplethorpe Foundation.